- Go to **awmi.net/sg433** to download PDFs of the following resources for each lesson in this study guide:
  - o Outlines
  - o Discipleship Questions
  - o Scriptures
- Share as many copies as you'd like.
- These documents are not for resale.

CHRISTIAN PHILOSOPHY

- STUDY GUIDE -

ANDREW WOMMACK

Unless otherwise indicated, all Scripture quotations are taken from the *King James Version* of the Bible.

Some Scripture quotations are taken from the *Amplified Bible. Old Testament* copyright © 1965, 1987 by Zondervan Corporation, Grand Rapids, Michigan. *New Testament* Copyright © 1958, 1987 by The Lockman Foundation, La Habra, California. Used by permission.

Some Scripture quotations are taken from the *Holy Bible, New International Version*®, NIV®. Copyright © 1978, 1984 by International Bible Society. Used by permission of Zondervan Publishing House. All rights reserved.

The author has emphasized some words in Scripture quotations with underline.

Christian Philosophy Study Guide
ISBN 13: 978-1-59548-548-9
eBook ISBN 13: 978-1-68031-917-0

Copyright © 2012 by Andrew Wommack Ministries Inc.
PO Box 3333
Colorado Springs CO 80934-3333

awmi.net

All rights reserved under International Copyright Law. Contents and/or cover may not be reproduced in whole or in part in any form without the express written consent of the Publisher.

CONTENTS

1. WHAT IS CHRISTIAN PHILOSOPHY? [5]
   OUTLINE   16
   TEACHER'S GUIDE   25
   DISCIPLESHIP QUESTIONS   33
   SCRIPTURES   33
   ANSWER KEY   39

2. WHY SHOULD I CARE ABOUT PHILOSOPHY? [41]
   OUTLINE   46
   TEACHER'S GUIDE   51
   DISCIPLESHIP QUESTIONS   56
   SCRIPTURES   56
   ANSWER KEY   61

3. IS THE BIBLE TRUE? [63]
   OUTLINE   74
   TEACHER'S GUIDE   87
   DISCIPLESHIP QUESTIONS   99
   SCRIPTURES   99
   ANSWER KEY   108

4. HOW DO WE KNOW THE BIBLE IS INSPIRED? [111]
   OUTLINE   117
   TEACHER'S GUIDE   124
   DISCIPLESHIP QUESTIONS   130
   SCRIPTURES   130
   ANSWER KEY   142

5. HOW DO I FOLLOW GOD? [143]
   OUTLINE   153
   TEACHER'S GUIDE   164
   DISCIPLESHIP QUESTIONS   173
   SCRIPTURES   173
   ANSWER KEY   179

6. CAN I REALLY KNOW GOD? [181]
   OUTLINE   190
   TEACHER'S GUIDE   202
   DISCIPLESHIP QUESTIONS   212
   SCRIPTURES   212
   ANSWER KEY   220

7. IS GOD ANGRY WITH ME? | 223 |
   OUTLINE   233
   TEACHER'S GUIDE   241
   DISCIPLESHIP QUESTIONS   250
   SCRIPTURES   250
   ANSWER KEY   260

8. WHAT ABOUT SUFFERING? | 263 |
   OUTLINE   272
   TEACHER'S GUIDE   282
   DISCIPLESHIP QUESTIONS   291
   SCRIPTURES   291
   ANSWER KEY   298

9. SOCIAL ISSUES: CHRISTIANS MUST SPEAK UP | 301 |
   SCRIPTURES   304

10. CREATION VS. EVOLUTION | 305 |
   SCRIPTURES   324

11. A GODLY PERSPECTIVE ON HOMOSEXUALITY | 327 |
   SCRIPTURES   334

12. FACTS AND STATISTICS REGARDING HOMOSEXUALITY | 337 |
   SCRIPTURES   343

13. ABORTION | 345 |
   SCRIPTURES   356

14. IN THE WORLD, BUT NOT OF IT | 357 |
   SCRIPTURES   362

What Is Christian Philosophy?

Every one of you has a philosophy—whether you realize it or not. Philosophy is simply the basic set of ideas, beliefs, and values that you live by. It's your outlook, or the filter, through which you view life. Every piece of information that comes to you and every situation you face are filtered through your philosophy. In a sense, your philosophy predetermines your response to the things happening around you and the results you see in life. Yet many people are unaware of their philosophies. They have never combined their separate beliefs into a single value system through which they view the world and interpret life.

Pessimism and optimism are two simple examples of opposite philosophies. Pessimists look toward the future and expect the worst, while optimists hope for the best. You could sit a pessimist and an optimist side by side, expose them to identical circumstances, and the optimist would find some positive way to spin what has happened, while the pessimist would focus on the negative. The optimist would look for some opportunity to take advantage of the situation, and the pessimist would focus on the negative and be more likely to get depressed and discouraged.

Philosophy is the reason identical situations can produce completely different responses in different people. Your philosophy filters every experience you have and every piece of information that comes your way. The Apostle Paul emphasized this truth to the Colossians when he warned them to be on the lookout for anyone who would **"spoil"** them through philosophy. A wrong philosophy causes wrong responses to circumstances, and it can cause you to draw wrong conclusions about events and information in life. Christians need a philosophy that is modeled after Christ and not after the traditions of men, vain deceit, or the principles of this world:

> *Beware lest any man spoil you through philosophy and vain deceit, after the tradition of men, after the rudiments of the world, and not after Christ.*
>
> COLOSSIANS 2:8

The believers in Colosse learned about Christ from Epaphras, not from Paul. We know he hadn't preached to the Colossians in person before he wrote to them, because he stated that he hadn't yet seen the Colossians face to face (Col. 2:1). The Colossians were once removed from Paul's teaching, and he wanted to make sure they fully understood the doctrine of Christ. He didn't want them lacking in any area or to be led away by false teaching (Col. 2:4).

Lesson 1 — What Is Christian Philosophy?

Then Paul wrote, **"As ye have therefore received Christ Jesus the Lord, so walk ye in him"** (Col. 2:6). This verse has had a major impact on my life. The way we receive salvation is by putting faith in Jesus, and Paul said this is the same way we receive everything else we need as Christians (healing, deliverance, provision, etc.). It's amazing how people begin their Christian walk by putting faith in what Jesus did for them but then start thinking they are going to be perfected by their own holiness and good works. We can't be saved by the grace of God and then try to earn all of salvation's benefits through our own effort—it won't work.

Paul was writing to Christians, but he had never ministered to the Colossians directly, and he wanted to make sure they had everything they needed to live the abundant lives God intended for them. This has direct application for us today because many people, if not most, who have been born again have not heard the true Gospel. They haven't heard all of the things they need to know in order to prosper and really walk in victory. I don't think there is really any debate about that when the way people in the Bible experienced victory is compared to the average Christian today. The Christian message being proclaimed today is not producing the same degree of victory in the lives of those who hear it as it did during New Testament times. In part, I believe this is because churches aren't teaching the same Gospel that was taught in the first century.

As a whole, the church has left off teaching and making disciples, and is now simply producing converts. Most efforts are aimed at just trying to get people born again so they can go to heaven when they die, but not a lot of energy is aimed at helping converts become true followers of Christ. Yet Jesus commanded us to make disciples, not converts. He said,

> *Go ye therefore, and teach all nations, baptizing them in the name of the Father, and of the Son, and of the Holy Ghost: Teaching them to observe all things whatsoever I have commanded you: and, lo, I am with you alway, even unto the end of the world. Amen.*
> MATTHEW 28:19-20

The Lord told us to teach people to observe **"all things,"** yet the modern church has basically reduced Christianity to confessing Jesus as Lord in order to avoid going to hell, which is only a portion of the Gospel. This is exactly what Paul was warning the Colossians against. He warned them to beware in case they didn't get the full truth, because it would make them susceptible to all of the ways Satan tries to steal the benefits of the Word of God. Paul's advice in Colossians 2:8 is just as applicable to us today as it was 2,000 years ago.

The English word **"beware"** in that verse means "To be on guard (against); be wary (of)" (*The Houghton Mifflin American Heritage Electronic Dictionary* [*HMAHED*]). It comes from two Middle English words "be" and "war" (*HMAHED*), which is signifying to be at war. This reminds me of standing guard duty when I was in the Army. Some people didn't take guard duty seriously and would sleep through their whole shift, but I couldn't do that. We were in a war, and sleeping through guard duty put everyone's lives at risk. In a spiritual sense, many Christians are not heeding Paul's warning to **"beware lest any man spoil you through philosophy."** They don't know they're in a spiritual battle and that Satan is attacking their values every day. He is trying to get them away from the godly way of looking at things that is established in the Word of God.

Lesson 1 — What Is Christian Philosophy?

We are being pressured every hour of every day, and I believe the attack on Christian values is greater now than it has been at any other time in history. Prior to the information age, Christians were able to isolate themselves, in a sense. They didn't have to expose themselves to the things that were going on in the world. But now we live in the information age. Television, radio, printed news, cell phones, and the internet are continuously parading the problems and philosophies of the world in front of us. We are being bombarded with the negative philosophy and thoughts of this world more than any generation of Christians that has ever lived, so it is especially important for us to be on our guard.

During the war in Vietnam, I was stationed on a small fire-support base that was forty-one miles from the nearest U.S. military installation. (A fire-support base is an isolated base that provides artillery support to soldiers patrolling beyond the range of their base camps.) Somebody said that war consists of long periods of boredom sprinkled with a few moments of sheer terror—and that pretty much sums up the experience I had. Nothing would happen for a long time, and then suddenly we would come under attack.

I spent my twenty-first birthday in Vietnam, and it was one of the days we came under attack. We took multiple direct hits on the bunker I was in, and I could see the muzzle fire from our enemies' weapons. On nights like that, I can guarantee you, nobody was sleeping on bunker duty. We took things seriously because we knew that the enemy was out there trying to kill us.

Christians need to get the same sense of vigilance. We need to recognize that we are under attack. Satan is coming against us, and we need to **"beware lest any man spoil"** us. *Spoil* means to carry off the plunder of war, or to carry a person off as a captive and slave.[1] In a battle, the victor strips the enemy of everything valuable, so Paul was using military terms to say, "Beware lest Satan take from you some of the things that God has given you!" God has already given us everything that pertains to life and godliness through knowing and having intimate relationship with Jesus Christ (2 Pet. 1:3-4), but we won't experience those benefits if we allow the world to seduce us into viewing life from an ungodly, unbiblical perspective.

God says that you've already been healed. He has already blessed you. You already have wisdom in abundance. You already have faith. You already have forgiveness. Yet many people aren't experiencing the blessings of God, because they believe the lies society is being bombarded with, and it is robbing them of victory. They aren't experiencing joy, peace, and prosperity. Christians are missing out on what Jesus has purchased for them, because they haven't recognized that they are in a battle. Satan has come into many people's lives and led them away captive, exactly as Paul warned he would: **"through philosophy and vain deceit, after the tradition of men, after the rudiments of the world, and not after Christ."**

The devil doesn't overpower Christians—because he can't. With Adam and Eve, he didn't use the strongest animal in the Garden to force Adam and Eve to submit to him and eat of the fruit of the Tree of the Knowledge of Good and Evil. He didn't use a lion to overcome them and force them to obey. No, what he did was come against them with words and with thoughts, and he corrupted their way of thinking. That's how original sin entered into this earth. This is exactly the point Paul was making to the Colossians. He was telling them to look out lest somebody rob them of what Jesus had provided, seducing them with words and thoughts that corrupt their way of thinking. It's not just changing their individual thoughts but their entire outlook on life, their worldview.

---

[1] Strong's number G4812 as defined at www.blueletterbible.org

Satan comes against us through philosophy and vain deceit, which means lies and deception. Sin wouldn't have entered the world if Adam and Eve had recognized Satan was using the serpent to deceive them.

Paul went on to say that we can be spoiled by **"the tradition of men."** Traditions are tied in with our philosophies; i.e., ways of thinking and behavior that are handed down from generation to generation. It is "the handing down of opinions, doctrines, practices, rites, and customs from…one generation to another."[2] Obviously, secular traditions present an ungodly perspective and are therefore an obvious threat to seduce Christians, but religious traditions can also keep us from experiencing God's best. Not every religious opinion, doctrine, and custom that works its way into the church comes from God—some of them come from people who are mistaken or, worse, self-seeking and deceitful.

During one debate with the Pharisees, Jesus told them they were making the Word of God of none effect through their tradition, which they had handed down, and they did many things like that (Mark 7:13). The Pharisees were the religious leaders of the day. They were trying to serve God, and by all outward appearances, they were. Yet they made their traditions—all of the customs and opinions they had added to the Word of God—equal to God's Word. Jesus said that by elevating their traditions above the Word of God, they neutralized the positive power of His Word.

The world and even the church are full of philosophies, vain deceit, and traditions of men that will carry you away captive if you aren't careful. They will rob you of the blessings that Jesus purchased with His atonement. One of my goals is to expose those philosophies for what they are: deception from the Enemy. Religious and secular traditions have corrupted Christians' way of thinking, and everything in the Christian life revolves around the way they think. Proverbs says,

For as he thinketh in his heart, so is he.

PROVERBS 23:7A

It's as you think at the heart level—not a surface level. Surface-level knowledge is like the information you acquire when you go to school and learn stuff just to pass a test, but it never impacts you in a significant way. You might not even really believe what you learned. Back in school, you might have stored that information in your short-term memory so that you could pass a test, but there's no way you could still pass those tests today. It was information you never meditated on or used, and it didn't go down to the heart level.

Heart-level knowledge is different. Scripture says that as you think in your heart, that's the way you are. In other words, your life is going in the direction of your dominant thoughts, or your dominant philosophy—not individual thoughts, but the pattern, or model, you have combined your opinions and life experiences into, which then shapes how you view the world. This is how your philosophy ends up determining your response to life, and how you will act.

I knew a woman who came out of an abusive marriage, and the experience left her with a chip on her shoulder. She had unresolved hurts and pains that shaped her way of thinking. Her basic philosophy was that all men were out to get her. No doubt, at one time, that attitude helped her avoid abuse from her ex-husband, but her outlook continued to influence her even after she got out of the

2 Century Dictionary

Lesson 1   What Is Christian Philosophy?

abusive relationship. She didn't trust men and was always expecting them to do bad things, so she was sensitive to the slightest provocations. Her philosophy prevented her from having any sort of meaningful relationship with other men, which meant she couldn't keep a job. She had a wrong way of thinking that was robbing her of joy and peace in life. People might not use the term *philosophy* to describe her outlook, but that's exactly what it was.

"Beware!" Paul said, because if you let circumstances in this life affect you and create a response in you that is different from God's outlook, then your wrong perspective is going to rob you of happiness and success. Once you establish a philosophy that causes you to prejudge situations, the same circumstances that caused you to come up with the philosophy in the first place are going to follow you wherever you go. You will filter everything that happens in your life through your philosophy, and it will make you prejudiced to see, hear, and find what you are looking for.

You'll form opinions, make decisions, and base your actions on the things that are happening around you, but if your philosophy is incorrect, then your conclusions are going to be wrong. This is exactly what is happening with so many people today.

A lot of people wish they could be different. They wish they could maintain healthy relationships with other people, for instance, but they just can't seem to get along with others. It doesn't matter how well a relationship starts off, something inside tells them it's going to fall apart. Relationships have always fallen apart for them, so they have come to expect it. In order to get different results, they need to change the way they think. As long as you maintain a way of thinking in your heart, then your philosophy will dictate the results you see—which is exactly what Scripture says: **"For as he thinketh in his heart, so is he."**

Your life is going in the direction of your dominant thoughts. If you can't maintain relationships, then I guarantee you have a wrong philosophy that is causing those results. If you can't succeed in business, even when you have ability and know you should be doing better, it's because you have a wrong philosophy that is defeating you. Philosophies become self-fulfilling prophecies, and if you want to change the results in your life, you have to start by changing the way you think. Philosophy is relevant to your daily life, and establishing a Christian philosophy, or a godly way of thinking, will have tremendous benefit to you. It could literally revolutionize your life.

Many people know separate truths from God's Word, but they don't combine the truths into a way of thinking that impacts their overall outlook on life. That's why I joke that most Christians don't let the Bible get in the way of what they believe. They are just tagging on truth after truth to some sort of hodgepodge system of thought, but there is no organization—no intentional effort to create a godly worldview. In other words, many believers do not have a solid Christian philosophy—they have a jumble of unorganized thoughts.

Simply tacking on more and more separate truths to a wrong philosophy isn't going to create a godly worldview. This is why some people can go to church for decades and memorize half of the Bible but never see any real fruit in their lives. You have to allow God's Word to get down to the foundation of your philosophy, and to do that, you must make a deliberate effort to change the way you think. You have to renew your mind (Rom. 12:1-2).

A while back, we had a woman at Charis Bible College who was in her late sixties and had been raised by parents who struggled through the Great Depression. After living through the Depression, her

Lesson 1 — What Is Christian Philosophy?

parents carried the fear that there might be another total economic collapse, and they instilled the same philosophy in their daughter. When the woman came to our Bible college, she had a lot of money, but she still had a poverty mentality. She would squeeze every nickel and get every last drop of product out of every jar in the house. It's good to be economical, but you can also get out of balance by being too frugal. A poverty mentality like that comes from fear, and it will rob you of peace in your life.

The woman came to me one day and said, "I've heard all of your teachings on prosperity, and intellectually I understand what you're saying. I see that I should be more generous and I shouldn't be afraid, but this is the way I was raised." What she was saying was that she knew her philosophy was wrong, but she felt like she couldn't change the way she looked at life.

Changing the way you think is hard, and it isn't necessarily going to change simply because you get presented with the Truth. Individual truths are not going to change your philosophy unless you make the effort to embrace those truths. The Word says, **"And ye shall know the truth, and the truth shall make you free"** (John 8:32), but it's only the truth you *know* that sets you free. To be set free, you have to have more than a mere mental awareness of truth; you need a heart-level understanding.

Recently I was talking to some friends who told me they know people who have studied every one of my teachings, and they study the Word, but they still aren't operating in faith. They could quote all of the things I say about trusting God, but they don't trust God. The truths they have learned haven't changed their philosophy, and I think that's tragic. You have to get beyond merely possessing individual pieces of information. You need more than facts to set yourself free. You have to combine those facts, connect the dots, and pull them all together so that they change the way you look at life.

We have a tendency to think that our problems are our problem, but they aren't. Often, our problems are just symptoms of deeper heart issues. We're looking for physical or natural reasons to explain why our lives are the way they are, but the condition of our lives is a result of the way we think—not what is going on around us. Outside forces have an impact on us for sure, but they aren't the determining factor. The Apostle Paul said, **"We are troubled on every side, yet not distressed; we are perplexed, but not in despair; Persecuted, but not forsaken; cast down, but not destroyed"** (2 Cor. 4:8-9). It's the way we respond to what happens to us that determines the condition of our lives, and the way we respond is a direct result of our philosophies.

I have seen this very clearly in some of the third world countries I've ministered in. The poverty is so severe; you want to just throw money at the problem. But others have done that, and the people are still struggling. I've come to realize it's because of their philosophy. You can't just give people a fish; you need to teach them to fish. If you just give money to people who have a poverty attitude, they will be poor again. They need a new way of thinking, a new philosophy.

The most important thing you will ever do is renew your mind and form a Christian philosophy, or a Christian worldview. Once you have a Christian way of looking at things, then your philosophy becomes a filter through which you see and experience life. Everything gets filtered through what God has said, and you see the positive instead of the negative. You'll be encouraged when other people are panicking. You'll operate in faith when other people are running scared.

Whether you realize it or not, you have a philosophy, or a way of looking at life. It's an attitude that has been formed by the way you were brought up, by the experiences you've had, and by the things you've

LESSON 1 — WHAT IS CHRISTIAN PHILOSOPHY?

learned. Through all of those things, you have formed a way of seeing life that largely predetermines your responses and even your experience of life.

Right now we're in an economic downturn. Other people, with a less optimistic philosophy, are calling it a worldwide financial crisis. News broadcasts are busy prophesying doom, gloom, and disaster. I don't deny the economic challenges out there, but I'm not a pessimist either. I'm not fearful and preparing for the worst-case scenario. Scripture says that perfect love casts out fear (1 John 4:18). If you are secure in the Lord and you know God is your source—not this world system—then you can prosper while the whole world is falling apart. It doesn't matter what condition the world economy is in, because the world economy isn't your source. God is your source.

My personal finances are prospering, and so is our ministry. While the stock market has been in decline, my portfolio has been increasing. While many organizations are making cutbacks, our ministry is seeing the greatest growth and income we've ever seen. We're reaching more people with the Gospel than ever before, and things are working for us. Our experiences are completely contrary to what the world is saying should be happening.

The reason we are prospering is because I have a philosophy that is based on years and years of walking with God and seeing Him bring me through. My faith and hope are in the Lord—not in the world economy. My Christian philosophy causes me to filter information differently than the world does.

The dominant worldview in modern society is humanistic—which tries to explain life and truth purely from the perspective of what matters to humans. Humanism rejects God totally, but aspects of humanistic philosophy have worked their way into many Christians' belief systems. Instead of filtering life from God's perspective, many Christians are filtering life through mental reasoning. Instead of trusting in God, society is conditioning believers to lean unto their own understanding (Prov. 3:5). Instead of walking by faith, Christians are being encouraged to walk by sight (2 Cor. 5:7). This is exactly what the Apostle Paul warned us against. It is a direct attack from the devil to rob us, as believers of God's promises for us, **"through philosophy and vain deceit, after the tradition of men, after the rudiments of the world, and not after Christ"** (Col. 2:8).

Too many Christians are looking at life from a humanistic standpoint. They aren't factoring in God as their source, and they feel like they are limited to how the world's system is going. When people have a philosophy that doesn't factor in God, they fall into panic when the stock market crashes, jobs are lost, and the media cries about a financial crisis. We've all heard stories about millionaires who committed suicide because they lost money and thought their lives were over. Those kinds of people have their whole identities wrapped up in possessions. People who have a philosophy that God is their source won't fall to pieces in a crisis, because their joy and satisfaction are in God and in relationship with Him.

Putting our hope or trust in the principles and elements of this world is a wrong philosophy. It's a wrong outlook, and the long-term effect is the deterioration of society. A large segment of society doesn't believe in God, and even if they believe in *a* god, they don't believe in heaven or hell. We've taken prayer out of schools and instead teach children to trust in the principles of this world. It's no wonder our society is heading downhill fast.

Several years ago, two boys went into a high school in a Denver, Colorado, suburb and killed thirteen people, and then they killed themselves before they could be captured. They thought they were avoiding prosecution, but, boy, did they miss it. They didn't believe in God and had a wrong philosophy that led them to believe the end of this life was the end of all existence, so they committed suicide to avoid punishment for their crimes. But they didn't escape anything. What they did was eliminate any opportunity for forgiveness and usher themselves straight into an eternity of torment and separation from God.

It's a lot harder to get guns today than it was fifty years ago, but we never had shooting incidents in schools back then. Now we have police officers and metal detectors in schools, but we're seeing terrible violence. It has nothing to do with gun restrictions; it has to do with the removal of moral restrictions as a result of the ungodly worldviews being promoted in society today. It's a philosophy issue.

Everywhere you look, there is a new group trying to pass more laws in an attempt to control the way people behave. Some are even trying to pass laws about fatty foods and what is or isn't acceptable to eat. For the most part, those people don't have a godly worldview, and they think the answer to society's problems is to create more legal restrictions and punishments. In the absence of Christian philosophy, they are trying to come up with controls to limit immorality, but that is the wrong approach. Society doesn't need more laws; the people in society need to embrace morality—specifically, a biblically based way of thinking.

Satan is destroying individuals and societies by leading people captive through ungodly philosophies and traditions. You'd think all Christians would understand the need to have an outlook that conforms to the Word of God, but I'm amazed at how many believers don't seem to get this. Everyone wants to be politically correct. People don't want to tell anybody else that they are wrong or that it is immoral to act in certain ways. The irony is that in a society where everyone is free to act however they want, the government is forced to intrude more and more into civil liberties in order to restrict unwanted behaviors. People without moral restraint have to be controlled by other means.

Unfortunately, you can see this process taking place in the United States and other Western countries. Some people seem to think that being free means being liberal in the way you think, but that's not true. You have to control the way you think. The way people act is a result of how they think, and a thought process that says everything is permissible promotes immoral behavior, which then leads to the deterioration of society.

When the Apostle Paul wrote that we will be spoiled through philosophy, vain deceit, the traditions of men, and the rudiments of this world, he was saying, "Don't think like a lost person. Don't think the way the world thinks." We need a biblical philosophy.

The world is filled with people who have no relationship with God and therefore have a very ungodly philosophy. People who think according to the principles of this world say that God doesn't exist, and they believe that humans evolved by accident over billions of years. They don't acknowledge God, and they don't understand that they were created and designed by Him. So, to think as the world thinks is to think like a lost person.

The world's way of thinking is not a comprehensive and rational philosophy. For instance, how does a society that goes to great lengths to promote the environment and protect even the most obscure animal species arrive at the conclusion that it's okay to abort babies? The world's way of thinking is a wrong

LESSON 1 — WHAT IS CHRISTIAN PHILOSOPHY?

philosophy, and it leads to wrong results. Some of the same people who yell about recycling think that having a baby is a choice, and if having a baby is inconvenient, they think it's okay to kill the baby. Society needs to get its priorities straight. God gave us life. We are not just like the rest of creation, and we are not equal to animals.

I'll be dealing with specific philosophies later on, but right now I just want to show how behavior comes from philosophy and why having a Christian philosophy is important for believers. We can't afford to think like the world thinks; we need to have a philosophy that focuses on God more than all of these secular ideas that are being promoted. The worldly attitudes being pushed on us go against a Christian way of thinking.

Many believers today are establishing a philosophy independent of God and separate from what the Word of God teaches. I read a survey that questioned people about how they established their theology. The survey was only given to people who identified themselves as born-again Christians, and they were asked how they formed their opinions. The majority of people said they are just coming up with their own philosophy based on life experiences and their own way of thinking. One question was if they adhere to the Word of God as being absolute, and only a small percentage answered yes—and these are people who identify themselves as born-again Christians.

Instead of getting their philosophy from the Word of God, they are basing it on how they were raised, what they have been taught in school, books they've read, and the study of principles from other world religions. They have established their philosophy piecemeal. People are taking a buffet-style approach to the assembly of ideas, and that's not a good idea. If you do that, Satan is going to spoil you. He's going to take from you what Jesus has already purchased and what belongs to you by right of inheritance.

A Christian philosophy must be rooted in the Word of God. You can't form a proper Christian worldview without renewing your mind in the Word of God. When Jesus was praying to the Father, He said, **"Sanctify them through thy truth: thy word is truth"** (John 17:17). I just can't overemphasize how important it is for you to conform your mind to the Word of God and not to the philosophies and principles of this world.

Unfortunately, a lot of Christians aren't looking to the Word for their philosophy. They have bought into Satan's deception that the Word of God contains bits and pieces of truth but that it isn't completely accurate. They think it's outdated because it was written 2,000 years ago and that it can't possibly have wisdom for modern society. In fact, some don't believe that the Bible is the inerrant word of God or that Jesus Christ is the only way to salvation—they say He is one of many ways. That's a wrong philosophy, and Satan will use that perspective to come into your life and steal from you.

Psalm 91:4b says, **"His truth shall be thy shield and buckler."** The Word of God and the promises it contains are our armor and protection against the attacks of the Enemy. The Word is 100 percent accurate, it's totally relevant, and it is the only thing Christians should be basing their lives upon. The way you change your core values and obtain a Christian philosophy is by conforming your worldview to the Word of God—instead of just leaning on your own understanding.

If you want to see the results that the Word of God promises, then you have to adopt God's way of thinking. I have conformed my philosophy to the Word and it's working. My health is great, I'm

Lesson 1 — What Is Christian Philosophy?

seeing the miraculous power of God, my stock investments have gained 61 percent in value while the world has been crying about a financial crisis, I'm happy, I'm joyful, my relationships are good, life is good, and God is blessing me in every area of my life. I'm not bragging; I'm just trying to give an example that conforming your way of thinking to the Word of God works. I'm not special—you can have the same results because God doesn't play favorites. All I've done is put God first and recognize that I'm not smart enough to direct my own life. I just do what God tells me to do, instead of doing what makes sense to me or what I feel like doing.

Being a Christian isn't about changing your outward appearance. It isn't about what you do and how you act. If you don't change the wrong concepts and the belief system on the inside, then you're going to have the same results in your life you had before you were saved. That's why God gave you His Word—to change the way you think. The Word of God contains His thoughts, His values, and His way of thinking. It's your ticket to a new life.

I don't care what society says is right or wrong; I follow what God says. Society may say homosexuality is just another lifestyle or that a homosexual union is just as important as a marriage between a man and a woman, but God's Word says differently. If you subscribe to the world's view instead of God's, then the devil is going to steal from you. The world is trying to say that there are many paths to God and that you need to embrace other philosophies. God's Word says you should be on your guard against any philosophy that isn't modeled after Jesus Christ. The world is trying to say that the Bible represents an outdated standard of morality. They want to pretend that the human race has "evolved" beyond the Bible and that now you should just embrace life.

The world's philosophies are simply an attempt by the devil to undermine the Word of God—that same thing Satan did to Adam and Eve. The Enemy wants to strip you of the armor and protection of God's Word so that he can plunder your life and steal what Jesus has already won for you. Jesus said,

> *A good tree cannot bring forth evil fruit, neither can a corrupt tree bring forth good fruit. Every tree that bringeth not forth good fruit is hewn down, and cast into the fire.*
> MATTHEW 7:18-19

The fruit of a tree is directly related to the tree itself. In the same way, you aren't going to get the fruit of God's manifold blessings if your core belief system is conformed to the world's way of thinking. You need a Christian philosophy. If you aren't seeing the fruit in your life that you would like to see, then all you have to do is change the way you think in your heart and adopt God's way of looking at life. Once you do that, the fruit will come.

Conforming your way of thinking to God's Word will bring a harvest of blessings in your life, but they don't all come overnight. The natural law of sowing and reaping means that it takes time for a seed to grow into a fruit-bearing plant, and there is a similar spiritual law of sowing and reaping. God provides miracles when there isn't time to wait for a harvest, like healing sickness, but God's best is for you to walk in His blessings. For instance, it is better to walk in health and never need healing than it is to get sick and need a miracle. Likewise, it is better to have money in the bank to meet all of your needs than it is to need a miracle to pay your rent every month. Even after you renew your mind, it may take time to get to where you don't need a miracle every month, but don't get discouraged. Scripture says,

LESSON 1 — WHAT IS CHRISTIAN PHILOSOPHY?

And let us not be weary in well doing: for in due season we shall reap, if we faint not.
GALATIANS 6:9

This means you have to stay focused on God and meditate on His Word to maintain your Christian perspective and reap the fruit God desires for you. If you are willing to do that and you change the way you think at the heart level, then you will see God's blessings in your life—guaranteed.

I challenge you to prayerfully consider the Christian philosophies I present in the rest of this study guide and embrace them. It will change the way you think, which will change the rest of your life.

LESSON 1

WHAT IS CHRISTIAN PHILOSOPHY?

OUTLINE

I. Every one of you has a philosophy—whether you realize it or not.

   A. Philosophy is simply the basic set of ideas, beliefs, and values that you live by.

   B. It's your outlook, or the filter, through which you view life.

   C. Every piece of information that comes to you and every situation you face are filtered through your philosophy.

   D. In a sense, your philosophy predetermines your response to the things happening around you and the results you see in life.

   E. Yet many people are unaware of their philosophy.

   F. They have never combined their separate beliefs into a single value system through which they view the world and interpret life.

II. Pessimism and optimism are two simple examples of opposite philosophies.

   A. Pessimists look toward the future and expect the worst, while optimists hope for the best.

   B. You could sit a pessimist and an optimist side by side, expose them to identical circumstances, and the optimist would find some positive way to spin what has happened, while the pessimist would focus on the negative.

   C. The optimist would look for some opportunity to take advantage of the situation, and the pessimist would focus on the negative and be more likely to get depressed and discouraged.

   D. Philosophy is the reason identical situations can produce completely different responses in different people.

   E. Your philosophy filters every experience you have and every piece of information that comes your way.

   F. The Apostle Paul emphasized this truth to the Colossians when he warned them to be on the lookout for anyone who would **"spoil"** them through philosophy.

   G. A wrong philosophy causes wrong responses to circumstances, and it can cause you to draw wrong conclusions about events and information in life.

   H. Christians need a philosophy that is modeled after Christ and not after the traditions of men, vain deceit, or the principles of this world:

   Beware lest any man spoil you through philosophy and vain deceit, after the tradition of men, after the rudiments of the world, and not after Christ.

   COLOSSIANS 2:8

   I. Paul was writing to Christians, but he had never ministered to the Colossians directly, and he wanted to make sure they had everything they needed to live the abundant lives God intended for them.

   J. Paul warned them to beware in case they didn't get the full truth, because it would make them susceptible to all of the ways Satan tries to steal the benefits of the Word of God.

   K. His advice is just as applicable to us today as it was 2,000 years ago.

III. The English word **"beware"** in that verse means "To be on guard (against); be wary (of)" (*The Houghton Mifflin American Heritage Electronic Dictionary* [*HMAHED*]).

   A. It comes from two Middle English words "be" and "war" (*HMAHED*), which is signifying to be at war.

Lesson 1 — What Is Christian Philosophy?

B. In a spiritual sense, many Christians are not heeding Paul's warning to **"beware lest any man spoil you through philosophy."**

C. They don't know they're in a spiritual battle and that Satan is attacking their values every day.

D. He is trying to get them away from the godly way of looking at things that is established in the Word of God.

E. I believe the attack on Christian values is greater now than it has been at any other time in history.

F. Television, radio, printed news, cell phones, and the internet are continuously parading the problems and philosophies of the world in front of us.

G. We are being bombarded with the negative philosophy and thoughts of this world more than any generation of Christians that has ever lived, so it is especially important for us to be on our guard.

IV. *Spoil* means to carry off the plunder of war, or to carry a person off as a captive and slave.[1]

A. In a battle, the victor strips the enemy of everything valuable, so Paul was using military terms to say, "Beware lest Satan take from you some of the things that God has given you!"

B. God has already given us everything that pertains to life and godliness through knowing and having intimate relationship with Jesus Christ (2 Pet. 1:3-4), but we won't experience those benefits if we allow the world to seduce us into viewing life from an ungodly, unbiblical perspective.

C. Many people aren't experiencing the blessings of God, because they believe the lies society is being bombarded with, and it is robbing them of victory.

D. Christians are missing out on what Jesus has purchased for them, because they haven't recognized that they are in a battle.

E. Satan has come into many people's lives and led them away captive, exactly as Paul warned he would: **"through philosophy and vain deceit, after the tradition of men, after the rudiments of the world, and not after Christ."**

V. The devil doesn't overpower Christians—because he can't.

A. With Adam and Eve, he didn't use a lion to overcome them and force them to obey.

B. No, what he did was come against them with words and with thoughts, and he corrupted their way of thinking—that's how original sin entered into this earth.

C. This is exactly the point Paul was making to the Colossians, that they should look out lest somebody rob them of what Jesus had provided, seducing them with words and thoughts that corrupt their way of thinking.

D. It's not just changing their individual thoughts but their entire outlook on life, their worldview.

VI. Paul went on to say that we can be spoiled by **"the tradition of men."**

A. Traditions are tied in with our philosophies; i.e., ways of thinking and behavior that are handed down from generation to generation.

B. It is "the handing down of opinions, doctrines, practices, rites, and customs from…one generation to another."[2]

---

[1] Strong's number G4812 as defined at www.blueletterbible.org
[2] Century Dictionary

Lesson 1 — What Is Christian Philosophy?

    C. Obviously, secular traditions present an ungodly perspective and are therefore an obvious threat to seduce Christians, but religious traditions can also keep us from experiencing God's best.

    D. Not every religious opinion, doctrine, and custom that works its way into the church comes from God—some of them come from people who are mistaken or, worse, self-seeking and deceitful.

    E. During one debate with the Pharisees, Jesus told them they were making the Word of God of none effect through their tradition, which they had handed down, and they did many things like that (Mark 7:13).

    F. The Pharisees were the religious leaders of the day.

    G. They were trying to serve God, and by all outward appearances, they were. Yet they made their traditions—all of the customs and opinions they had added to the Word of God—equal to God's Word.

    H. Jesus said that by elevating their traditions above the Word of God, they neutralized the positive power of His Word.

    I. The world, and even the church, are full of philosophies, vain deceit, and traditions of men that will carry you away captive if you aren't careful.

    J. They will rob you of the blessings that Jesus purchased with His atonement.

    K. One of my goals is to expose those philosophies for what they are: deception from the Enemy.

VII. Everything in the Christian life revolves around the way they think.

    A. Proverbs says,

For as he thinketh in his heart, so is he.

                                                                                                     PROVERBS 23:7A

    B. It's as you think at the heart level—not a surface level.

    C. Surface-level knowledge is like the information you acquire when you go to school and learn stuff just to pass a test, but it never impacts you in a significant way—you might not even really believe what you learned.

    D. Back in school, you might have stored that information in your short-term memory so that you could pass a test, but there's no way you could still pass those tests today.

    E. It was information you never meditated on or used, and it didn't go down to the heart level.

    F. Heart-level knowledge is different, because Scripture says that as you think in your heart, that's the way you are.

    G. In other words, your life is going in the direction of your dominant thoughts, or your dominant philosophy—not individual thoughts, but the pattern, or model, you have combined your opinions and life experiences into, which then shapes how you view the world.

    H. This is how your philosophy ends up determining your response to life, and how you will act.

VIII. "Beware!" Paul said, because if you let circumstances in this life affect you and create a response in you that is different from God's outlook, then your wrong perspective is going to rob you of happiness and success.

    A. Once you establish a philosophy that causes you to prejudge situations, the same circumstances that caused you to come up with the philosophy in the first place are going to follow you wherever you go.

    B. You will filter everything that happens in your life through your philosophy, and it will make you prejudiced to see, hear, and find what you are looking for.

Lesson 1 — What Is Christian Philosophy?

    C. You'll form opinions, make decisions, and base your actions on the things that are happening around you, but if your philosophy is incorrect, then your conclusions are going to be wrong.

    D. This is exactly what is happening with so many people today.

        i. If you can't maintain relationships, then I guarantee you have a wrong philosophy that is causing those results.

        ii. If you can't succeed in business, even when you have ability and know you should be doing better, it's because you have a wrong philosophy that is defeating you.

    E. Philosophies become self-fulfilling prophecies, and if you want to change the results in your life, you have to start by changing the way you think.

    F. Philosophy is relevant to your daily life, and establishing a Christian philosophy, or a godly way of thinking, will have tremendous benefit to you.

    G. It could literally revolutionize your life.

IX. Many people know separate truths from God's Word, but they don't combine the truths into a way of thinking that impacts their overall outlook on life.

    A. That's why I joke that most Christians don't let the Bible get in the way of what they believe.

    B. They are just tagging on truth after truth to some sort of hodgepodge system of thought, but there is no organization—no intentional effort to create godly worldview.

    C. In other words, many believers do not have a solid Christian philosophy—they have a jumble of unorganized thoughts.

    D. Simply tacking on more and more separate truths to a wrong philosophy isn't going to create a godly worldview.

    E. This is why some people can go to church for decades and memorize half of the Bible but never see any real fruit in their lives.

    F. You have to allow God's Word to get down to the foundation of your philosophy, and to do that, you must make a deliberate effort to change the way you think.

    G. You have to renew your mind (Rom. 12:1-2).

    H. Individual truths are not going to change your philosophy unless you make the effort to embrace those truths.

    I. The Word says, **"And ye shall know the truth, and the truth shall make you free"** (John 8:32), but it's only the truth you *know* that sets you free.

    J. To be set free, you have to have more than a mere mental awareness of truth; you need a heart-level understanding.

X. Recently I was talking to some friends who told me they know people who have studied every one of my teachings, and they study the Word, but they still aren't operating in faith.

    A. They could quote all of the things I say about trusting God, but they don't trust God.

    B. The truths they have learned haven't changed their philosophy, and I think that's tragic.

    C. You have to get beyond merely possessing individual pieces of information.

Lesson 1 — What Is Christian Philosophy?

- D. You need more than facts to set yourself free. You have to combine those facts, connect the dots, and pull them all together so that they change the way you look at life.

XI. We have a tendency to think that our problems are our problem, but they aren't.

- A. Often, our problems are just symptoms of deeper heart issues.
- B. We're looking for physical or natural reasons to explain why our lives are the way they are, but the condition of our lives is a result of the way we think—not what is going on around us.
- C. Outside forces have an impact on us for sure, but they aren't the determining factor.
- D. The Apostle Paul said, **"We are troubled on every side, yet not distressed; we are perplexed, but not in despair; Persecuted, but not forsaken; cast down, but not destroyed"** (2 Cor. 4:8-9).
- E. It's the way we respond to what happens to us that determines the condition of our lives, and the way we respond is a direct result of our philosophies.
    - i. If we just give money to people who have a poverty attitude, they will be poor again.
    - ii. They need a new way of thinking, a new philosophy.

XII. The most important thing you will ever do is renew your mind and form a Christian philosophy, or a Christian worldview.

- A. Once you have a Christian way of looking at things, then your philosophy becomes a filter through which you see and experience life.
- B. Everything gets filtered through what God has said, and you see the positive instead of the negative.
- C. You'll be encouraged when other people are panicking.
- D. You'll operate in faith when other people are running scared.

XIII. I don't deny the economic challenges out there, but I'm not a pessimist either.

- A. I'm not fearful and preparing for the worst-case scenario.
- B. Scripture says that perfect love casts out fear (1 John 4:18).
- C. If you are secure in the Lord and you know God is your source—not this world system—then you can prosper while the whole world is falling apart.
- D. It doesn't matter what condition the world economy is in, because the world economy isn't your source—God is your source.
- E. My personal finances are prospering, and so is our ministry.
    - i. While the stock market has been in decline, my portfolio has been increasing.
    - ii. While many organizations are making cutbacks, our ministry is seeing the greatest growth and income we've ever seen.
    - iii. We're reaching more people with the Gospel than ever before, and things are working for us.
    - iv. Our experiences are completely contrary to what the world is saying should be happening.
- F. The reason we are prospering is because I have a philosophy that is based on years and years of walking with God and seeing Him bring me through.

Lesson 1 — What Is Christian Philosophy?

- G. My faith and hope are in the Lord—not in the world economy.
- H. My Christian philosophy causes me to filter information differently than the world does.

XIV. The dominant worldview in modern society is humanistic—which tries to explain life and truth purely from the perspective of what matters to humans.

- A. Humanism rejects God totally, but aspects of humanistic philosophy have worked their way into many Christians' belief systems.
- B. Instead of filtering life from God's perspective, many Christians are filtering life through mental reasoning.
- C. Instead of trusting in God, society is conditioning believers to lean unto their own understanding (Prov. 3:5).
- D. Instead of walking by faith, Christians are being encouraged to walk by sight (2 Cor. 5:7).
- E. It is a direct attack from the devil to rob us, as believers of God's promises for us, **"through philosophy and vain deceit, after the tradition of men, after the rudiments of the world, and not after Christ"** (Col. 2:8).

XV. Putting our hope or trust in the principles and elements of this world is a wrong philosophy.

- A. It's a wrong outlook, and the long-term effect is the deterioration of society.
- B. A large segment of society doesn't believe in God, and even if they believe in *a* god, they don't believe in heaven or hell.
- C. We've taken prayer out of schools and instead teach children to trust in the principles of this world.
- D. It's no wonder our society is heading downhill fast.
- E. Now we have police officers and metal detectors in schools, but we're seeing terrible violence.
- F. It has nothing to do with gun restrictions; it has to do with the removal of moral restrictions as a result of the ungodly worldviews being promoted in society today—it's a philosophy issue.
- G. In the absence of Christian philosophy, they are trying to come up with controls to limit immorality, but that is the wrong approach.
- H. Society doesn't need more laws; the people in society need to embrace morality—specifically, a biblically based way of thinking.

XVI. You'd think all Christians would understand the need to have an outlook that conforms to the Word of God, but I'm amazed at how many believers don't seem to get this.

- A. Everyone wants to be politically correct.
- B. People don't want to tell anybody else that they are wrong or that it is immoral to act in certain ways.
- C. The irony is that in a society where everyone is free to act however they want, the government is forced to intrude more and more into civil liberties in order to restrict unwanted behaviors.
- D. People without moral restraint have to be controlled by other means.
- E. Unfortunately, you can see this process taking place in the United States and other Western countries.
- F. Some people seem to think that being free means being liberal in the way you think, but that's not true—you have to control the way you think.
- G. The way people act is a result of how they think, and a thought process that says everything is permissible promotes immoral behavior, which then leads to the deterioration of society.

Lesson 1 — What Is Christian Philosophy?

XVII. When the Apostle Paul wrote that we will be spoiled through philosophy, vain deceit, the traditions of men, and the rudiments of this world, he was saying, "Don't think like a lost person. Don't think the way the world thinks."

    A. The world is filled with people who have no relationship with God and therefore have a very ungodly philosophy.

    B. People who think according to the principles of this world say that God doesn't exist, and they believe that humans evolved by accident over billions of years.

    C. They don't acknowledge God, and they don't understand that they were created and designed by Him. So, to think as the world thinks is to think like a lost person.

    D. The world's way of thinking is not a comprehensive and rational philosophy.

        i. For instance, how does a society that goes to great lengths to promote the environment and protect even the most obscure animal species arrive at the conclusion that it's okay to abort babies?

        ii. Some of the same people who yell about recycling think that having a baby is a choice, and if having a baby is inconvenient, they think it's okay to kill the baby.

        iii. Society needs to get its priorities straight.

        iv. God gave us life.

        v. We are not just like the rest of creation, and we are not equal to animals.

    E. I'll be dealing with specific philosophies later on, but right now I just want to show how behavior comes from philosophy and why having a Christian philosophy is important for believers.

XVIII. Many believers today are establishing a philosophy independent of God and separate from what the Word of God teaches.

    A. I read a survey that was given to people who identified themselves as born-again Christians, and they were asked how they formed their opinions.

    B. The majority of people said they are just coming up with their own philosophy based on life experiences and their own way of thinking.

    C. One question was if they adhere to the Word of God as being absolute, and only a small percentage answered yes.

    D. Instead of getting their philosophy from the Word of God, they are basing it on how they were raised, what they have been taught in school, books they've read, and the study of principles from other world religions.

    E. They have established their philosophy piecemeal.

    F. People are taking a buffet-style approach to the assembly of ideas, and that's not a good idea.

    G. If you do that, Satan is going to spoil you; i.e., take from you what Jesus has already purchased and what belongs to you by right of inheritance.

XIX. A Christian philosophy must be rooted in the Word of God.

    A. You can't form a proper Christian worldview without renewing your mind in the Word of God.

    B. When Jesus was praying to the Father, He said, **"Sanctify them through thy truth: thy word is truth"** (John 17:17).

Lesson 1 — What Is Christian Philosophy?

    C. I just can't overemphasize how important it is for you to conform your mind to the Word of God and not to the philosophies and principles of this world.

    D. Unfortunately, a lot of Christians aren't looking to the Word for their philosophy.

    E. They have bought into Satan's deception that the Word of God contains bits and pieces of truth but that it isn't completely accurate.

    F. They think it's outdated because it was written 2,000 years ago and that it can't possibly have wisdom for modern society.

    G. In fact, some don't believe that the Bible is the inerrant word of God or that Jesus Christ is the only way to salvation—they say He is one of many ways.

    H. That's a wrong philosophy, and Satan will use that perspective to come into your life and steal from you.

XX. Psalm 91:4b says, **"His truth shall be thy shield and buckler."**

    A. The Word of God and the promises it contains are our armor and protection against the attacks of the Enemy.

    B. The Word is 100 percent accurate, it's totally relevant, and it is the only thing Christians should be basing their lives upon.

    C. The way you change your core values and obtain a Christian philosophy is by conforming your worldview to the Word of God—instead of just leaning on your own understanding.

XXI. If you want to see the results that the Word of God promises, then you have to adopt God's way of thinking.

    A. I have conformed my philosophy to the Word and it's working.

    B. My health is great, I'm seeing the miraculous power of God, my stock investments have gained 61 percent in value while the world has been crying about a financial crisis, I'm happy, I'm joyful, my relationships are good, life is good, and God is blessing me in every area of my life.

    C. I'm not bragging; I'm just trying to give an example that conforming your way of thinking to the Word of God works.

    D. I'm not special—you can have the same results because God doesn't play favorites.

    E. All I've done is put God first and recognize that I'm not smart enough to direct my own life.

    F. I just do what God tells me to do, instead of doing what makes sense to me or what I feel like doing.

    G. Being a Christian isn't about changing your outward appearance or what you do and how you act.

    H. If you don't change the wrong concepts and the belief system on the inside, then you're going to have the same results in your life you had before you were saved.

    I. That's why God gave you His Word—to change the way you think.

    J. The Word of God contains His thoughts, His values, and His way of thinking.

    K. It's your ticket to a new life.

XXII. I don't care what society says is right or wrong; I follow what God says.

    A. Society may say homosexuality is just another lifestyle or that a homosexual union is just as important as a marriage between a man and a woman, but God's Word says differently.

Lesson 1 — What Is Christian Philosophy?

    B. If you subscribe to the world's view instead of God's, then the devil is going to steal from you.

    C. The world is trying to say that there are many paths to God and that you need to embrace other philosophies.

    D. God's Word says you should be on your guard against any philosophy that isn't modeled after Jesus Christ.

    E. The world wants to pretend that the human race has "evolved" beyond the Bible and that now you should just embrace life.

    F. The world's philosophies are simply an attempt by the devil to undermine the Word of God—that same thing Satan did to Adam and Eve.

    G. The Enemy wants to strip you of the armor and protection of God's Word so that he can plunder your life and steal what Jesus has already won for you.

XXIII. The fruit of a tree is directly related to the tree itself (Matt. 7:18-19).

    A. In the same way, you aren't going to get the fruit of God's manifold blessings if your core belief system is conformed to the world's way of thinking.

    B. If you aren't seeing the fruit in your life that you would like to see, then all you have to do is change the way you think in your heart and adopt God's way of looking at life.

    C. Once you do that, the fruit will come.

    D. Conforming your way of thinking to God's Word will bring a harvest of blessings in your life, but they don't all come overnight.

    E. The natural law of sowing and reaping means that it takes time for a seed to grow into a fruit-bearing plant, and there is a similar spiritual law of sowing and reaping.

    F. God provides miracles when there isn't time to wait for a harvest, like healing sickness, but God's best is for you to walk in His blessings.

    G. For instance, it is better to walk in health and never need healing than it is to get sick and need a miracle.

    H. Likewise, it is better to have money in the bank to meet all of your needs than it is to need a miracle to pay your rent every month.

    I. Even after you renew your mind, it may take time to get to where you don't need a miracle every month, but don't get discouraged.

    J. Scripture says,

And let us not be weary in well doing: for in due season we shall reap, if we faint not.

GALATIANS 6:9

    K. This means you have to stay focused on God and meditate on His Word to maintain your Christian perspective and reap the fruit God desires for you.

    L. If you are willing to do that and you change the way you think at the heart level, then you will see God's blessings in your life—guaranteed.

    M. I challenge you to prayerfully consider the Christian philosophies I present in the rest of this study guide and embrace them.

    N. It will change the way you think, which will change the rest of your life.

Lesson 1

What Is Christian Philosophy?

TEACHER'S GUIDE

1. Every one of you has a philosophy—whether you realize it or not. Philosophy is simply the basic set of ideas, beliefs, and values that you live by. It's your outlook, or the filter, through which you view life. Every piece of information that comes to you and every situation you face are filtered through your philosophy. In a sense, your philosophy predetermines your response to the things happening around you and the results you see in life. Yet many people are unaware of their philosophy. They have never combined their separate beliefs into a single value system through which they view the world and interpret life.

    1a.   Discussion Question: In your life, how has your philosophy determined your response to the things happening around you and the results you see in life?
(Discussion question)

2. Pessimism and optimism are two simple examples of opposite philosophies. Pessimists look toward the future and expect the worst, while optimists hope for the best. You could sit a pessimist and an optimist side by side, expose them to identical circumstances, and the optimist would find some positive way to spin what has happened, while the pessimist would focus on the negative. The optimist would look for some opportunity to take advantage of the situation, and the pessimist would focus on the negative and be more likely to get depressed and discouraged. Philosophy is the reason identical situations can produce completely different responses in different people. Your philosophy filters every experience you have and every piece of information that comes your way. The Apostle Paul emphasized this truth to the Colossians when he warned them to be on the lookout for anyone who would **"spoil"** them through philosophy. A wrong philosophy causes wrong responses to circumstances, and it can cause you to draw wrong conclusions about events and information in life. Christians need a philosophy that is modeled after Christ and not after the traditions of men, vain deceit, or the principles of this world: **"Beware lest any man spoil you through philosophy and vain deceit, after the tradition of men, after the rudiments of the world, and not after Christ"** (Col. 2:8). Paul was writing to Christians, but he had never ministered to the Colossians directly, and he wanted to make sure they had everything they needed to live the abundant lives God intended for them. Paul warned them to beware in case they didn't get the full truth, because it would make them susceptible to all of the ways Satan tries to steal the benefits of the Word of God. His advice is just as applicable to us today as it was 2,000 years ago.

    2a.   What does your philosophy filter?
(Every experience you have and every piece of information that comes your way)

    2b.   Read Colossians 2:8. Your philosophy needs to modeled after whom?
(Christ)

    2c.   Which two would try to spoil you?
(Man and Satan)

3. The English word **"beware"** in that verse means "To be on guard (against); be wary (of)" (*The Houghton Mifflin American Heritage Dictionary* [*HMAHED*]). It comes from two Middle English words "be" and "war" (*HMAHED*), which is signifying to be at war. In a spiritual sense, many Christians are not heeding Paul's warning to **"beware lest any man spoil you through philosophy."** They don't know they're in a spiritual battle and that Satan is attacking their valueseveryday. He is trying to get them away from the godly way of looking at things that is established in the Word of God. I believe the attack on Christian values is greater now than it has been at any other time in history. Television, radio, printed news, cell phones, and the internet are continuously parading the problems and philosophies of the world in front of us. We are being bombarded with the negative philosophy and thoughts of this world more than any generation of Christians that has ever lived, so it is especially important for us to be on our guard.

    3a.   Discussion Question: What do you think you have to beware of?
(Discussion question)

Lesson 1 — What Is Christian Philosophy?

    3b. A godly way of looking at things is established where?
        A. In your heart
        B. At church
        C. In the Word of God
        D. All of the above
        E. None of the above
        (C. In the Word of God)

4. *Spoil* means to carry off the plunder of war, or to carry a person off as a captive and slave.[1] In a battle, the victor strips the enemy of everything valuable, so Paul was using military terms to say, "Beware lest Satan take from you some of the things that God has given you!" God has already given us everything that pertains to life and godliness through knowing and having intimate relationship with Jesus Christ (2 Pet. 1:3-4), but we won't experience those benefits if we allow the world to seduce us into viewing life from an ungodly, unbiblical perspective. Many people aren't experiencing the blessings of God, because they believe the lies society is being bombarded with, and it is robbing them of victory. Christians are missing out on what Jesus has purchased for them, because they haven't recognized that they are in a battle. Satan has come into many people's lives and led them away captive, exactly as Paul warned he would: **"through philosophy and vain deceit, after the tradition of men, after the rudiments of the world, and not after Christ."**

    4a. Read 2 Peter 1:3-4. How do you have everything that pertains to life and godliness?
        (Through knowing and having intimate relationship with Jesus Christ)

    4b. Discussion Question: What have you missed out on because you haven't recognized you're in a battle?
        (Discussion question)

5. The devil doesn't overpower Christians—because he can't. With Adam and Eve, he didn't use a lion to overcome them and force them to obey. No, what he did was come against them with words and with thoughts, and he corrupted their way of thinking—that's how original sin entered into this earth. This is exactly the point Paul was making to the Colossians, that they should look out lest somebody rob them of what Jesus had provided, seducing them with words and thoughts that corrupt their way of thinking. It's not just changing their individual thoughts but their entire outlook on life, their worldview.

    5a. True or false: Satan can overcome you and force you to obey him.
        (False)

    5b. How does he try to seduce God's people?
        (With words and thoughts that corrupt their way of thinking)

6. Paul went on to say that we can be spoiled by **"the tradition of men."** Traditions are tied in with our philosophies; i.e., ways of thinking and behavior that are handed down from generation to generation. It is "the handing down of opinions, doctrines, practices, rites, and customs from…one generation to another."[2] Obviously, secular traditions present an ungodly perspective and are therefore an obvious threat to seduce Christians, but religious traditions can also keep us from experiencing God's best. Not every religious opinion, doctrine, and custom that works its way into the church comes from God—some of them come from people who are mistaken or, worse, self-seeking and deceitful. During one debate with the Pharisees, Jesus told them they were making the Word of God of none effect through their tradition, which they had handed down, and they did many things like that (Mark 7:13). The Pharisees were the religious leaders of the day. They were trying to serve God, and by all outward appearances, they were. Yet they made their traditions—all of the customs and opinions they had added to the Word of God—equal to God's Word. Jesus said that by elevating their traditions above the Word of God, they neutralized the positive power of His Word. The world, and even the church, are full of philosophies, vain deceit, and traditions of men that will carry you away captive if you aren't careful. They will rob you of the blessings that Jesus purchased with His atonement. One of my goals is to expose those philosophies for what they are: deception from the Enemy.

---

[1] Strong's number G4812 as defined at www.blueletterbible.org
[2] Century Dictionary

Lesson 1 — What Is Christian Philosophy?

6a. Where can religious opinion, doctrine, and custom come from?
(People who are mistaken or, worse, self-seeking and deceitful)

6b. Read Mark 7:13. How was the Word of God made of none effect?
A. Because of the devil
B. Because no one believed it
C. Because of the persecution
D. Because of man's tradition
E. Because no one preached it
(D. Because of man's tradition)

7. Everything in the Christian life revolves around the way they think. Proverbs says, **"For as he thinketh in his heart, so is he"** (Prov. 23:7a). It's as you think at the heart level—not a surface level. Surface-level knowledge is like the information you acquire when you go to school and learn stuff just to pass a test, but it never impacts you in a significant way—you might not even really believe what you learned. Back in school, you might have stored that information in your short-term memory so that you could pass a test, but there's no way you could still pass those tests today. It was information you never meditated on or used, and it didn't go down to the heart level. Heart-level knowledge is different, because Scripture says that as you think in your heart, that's the way you are. In other words, your life is going in the direction of your dominant thoughts, or your dominant philosophy—not individual thoughts, but the pattern, or model, you have combined your opinions and life experiences into, which then shapes how you view the world. This is how your philosophy ends up determining your response to life, and how you will act.

7a. Read Proverbs 23:7. Why does everything in the Christian life revolve around the way you think?
(Because as you think in your heart, so are you)

7b. What is heart-level knowledge?
(Your dominant thoughts, or your dominant philosophy—not individual thoughts, but the pattern, or model, you have combined your opinions and life experiences into, which then shapes how you view the world)

8. "Beware!" Paul said, because if you let circumstances in this life affect you and create a response in you that is different from God's outlook, then your wrong perspective is going to rob you of happiness and success. Once you establish a philosophy that causes you to prejudge situations, the same circumstances that caused you to come up with the philosophy in the first place are going to follow you wherever you go. You will filter everything that happens in your life through your philosophy, and it will make you prejudiced to see, hear, and find what you are looking for. You'll form opinions, make decisions, and base your actions on the things that are happening around you, but if your philosophy is incorrect, then your conclusions are going to be wrong. This is exactly what is happening with so many people today. If you can't maintain relationships, then I guarantee you have a wrong philosophy that is causing those results. If you can't succeed in business, even when you have ability and know you should be doing better, it's because you have a wrong philosophy that is defeating you. Philosophies become self-fulfilling prophecies, and if you want to change the results in your life, you have to start by changing the way you think. Philosophy is relevant to your daily life, and establishing a Christian philosophy, or a godly way of thinking, will have tremendous benefit to you. It could literally revolutionize your life.

8a. Discussion Question: What right philosophy have you had that has produced a good result?
(Discussion question)

9. Many people know separate truths from God's Word, but they don't combine the truths into a way of thinking that impacts their overall outlook on life. That's why I joke that most Christians don't let the Bible get in the way of what they believe. They are just tagging on truth after truth to some sort of hodgepodge system of thought, but there is no organization—no intentional effort to create a godly worldview. In other words, many believers do not have a solid Christian philosophy—they have a jumble of unorganized thoughts. Simply tacking on more and more separate truths to a wrong philosophy isn't going to create a godly worldview. This is why some people can go to church for decades and memorize half of the Bible but never see any real fruit in their lives. You have to allow God's Word to get down to the foundation of your philosophy, and to do that, you must make a deliberate effort to

Lesson 1 — What Is Christian Philosophy?

change the way you think. You have to renew your mind (Rom. 12:1-2). Individual truths are not going to change your philosophy unless you make the effort to embrace those truths. The Word says, **"And ye shall know the truth, and the truth shall make you free"** (John 8:32), but it's only the truth you *know* that sets you free. To be set free, you have to have more than a mere mental awareness of truth; you need a heart-level understanding.

9a. You have to _____ the truths into a way of thinking that impacts your overall outlook on life.
(Combine)

9b. Read Romans 12:1-2. Who has to renew your mind?
(You)

9c. According to John 8:32, what sets you free?
A. Will power
B. The truth
C. The jailer
D. Being bailed out
E. The truth you know
(E. The truth you know)

10. Recently I was talking to some friends who told me they know people who have studied every one of my teachings, and they study the Word, but they still aren't operating in faith. They could quote all of the things I say about trusting God, but they don't trust God. The truths they have learned haven't changed their philosophy, and I think that's tragic. You have to get beyond merely possessing individual pieces of information. You need more than facts to set yourself free. You have to combine those facts, connect the dots, and pull them all together so that they change the way you look at life.

10a. Why isn't it enough to study Andrew's teachings and study the Word?
(Because it's possible to do all those things and yet not operate in faith or let those truths change your philosophy)

10b. How do you change the way you look at life?
(You have to combine facts from the Word, connect the dots, and pull them all together, so that they change the way you look at life)

11. We have a tendency to think that our problems are our problem, but they aren't. Often, our problems are just symptoms of deeper heart issues. We're looking for physical or natural reasons to explain why our lives are the way they are, but the condition of our lives is a result of the way we think—not what is going on around us. Outside forces have an impact on us for sure, but they aren't the determining factor. The Apostle Paul said, **"We are troubled on every side, yet not distressed; we are perplexed, but not in despair; Persecuted, but not forsaken; cast down, but not destroyed"** (2 Cor. 4:8-9). It's the way we respond to what happens to us that determines the condition of our lives, and the way we respond is a direct result of our philosophies. If you just give money to people who have a poverty attitude, they will be poor again. They need a new way of thinking, a new philosophy.

11a. What determines the condition of your life?
(The way you respond to what happens to you)

12. The most important thing you will ever do is renew your mind and form a Christian philosophy, or a Christian worldview. Once you have a Christian way of looking at things, then your philosophy becomes a filter through which you see and experience life. Everything gets filtered through what God has said, and you see the positive instead of the negative. You'll be encouraged when other people are panicking. You'll operate in faith when other people are running scared.

12a. What is the most important thing you will ever do?
(Renew your mind and form a Christian philosophy, or a Christian worldview)

Lesson 1 — What Is Christian Philosophy?

12b. Discussion Question: What do you think this will do for you?
(Discussion question)

13. I don't deny the economic challenges out there, but I'm not a pessimist either. I'm not fearful and preparing for the worst-case scenario. Scripture says that perfect love casts out fear (1 John 4:18). If you are secure in the Lord and you know God is your source—not this world system—then you can prosper while the whole world is falling apart. It doesn't matter what condition the world economy is in, because the world economy isn't your source—God is your source. My personal finances are prospering, and so is our ministry. While the stock market has been in decline, my portfolio has been increasing. While many organizations are making cutbacks, our ministry is seeing the greatest growth and income we've ever seen. We're reaching more people with the Gospel than ever before, and things are working for us. Our experiences are completely contrary to what the world is saying should be happening. The reason we are prospering is because I have a philosophy that is based on years and years of walking with God and seeing Him bring me through. My faith and hope are in the Lord—not in the world economy. My Christian philosophy causes me to filter information differently than the world does.

13a. Discussion Question: What can you learn from Andrew's experience?
(Discussion question)

14. The dominant worldview in modern society is humanistic—which tries to explain life and truth purely from the perspective of what matters to humans. Humanism rejects God totally, but aspects of humanistic philosophy have worked their way into many Christians' belief systems. Instead of filtering life from God's perspective, many Christians are filtering life through mental reasoning. Instead of trusting in God, society is conditioning believers to lean unto their own understanding (Prov. 3:5). Instead of walking by faith, Christians are being encouraged to walk by sight (2 Cor. 5:7). It is a direct attack from the devil to rob us, as believers of God's promises for us, **"through philosophy and vain deceit, after the tradition of men, after the rudiments of the world, and not after Christ"** (Col. 2:8).

14a. What has worked its way into many Christians' belief systems?
(Humanistic philosophy)

14b. Discussion Question: Read Proverbs 3:5. How have you been conditioned to lean on your own understanding?
(Discussion question)

15. Putting our hope or trust in the principles and elements of this world is a wrong philosophy. It's a wrong outlook, and the long-term effect is the deterioration of society. A large segment of society doesn't believe in God, and even if they believe in *a* god, they don't believe in heaven or hell. We've taken prayer out of schools and instead teach children to trust in the principles of this world. It's no wonder our society is heading downhill fast. Now we have police officers and metal detectors in schools, but we're seeing terrible violence. It has nothing to do with gun restrictions; it has to do with the removal of moral restrictions as a result of the ungodly worldviews being promoted in society today—it's a philosophy issue. In the absence of Christian philosophy, they are trying to come up with controls to limit immorality, but that is the wrong approach. Society doesn't need more laws; the people in society need to embrace morality—specifically, a biblically based way of thinking.

15a. True or false: Society doesn't need more laws, but the people need to embrace a biblically based way of thinking.
(True)

16. You'd think all Christians would understand the need to have an outlook that conforms to the Word of God, but I'm amazed at how many believers don't seem to get this. Everyone wants to be politically correct. People don't want to tell anybody else that they are wrong or that it is immoral to act in certain ways. The irony is that in a society where everyone is free to act however they want, the government is forced to intrude more and more

Lesson 1 — What Is Christian Philosophy?

into civil liberties in order to restrict unwanted behaviors. People without moral restraint have to be controlled by other means. Unfortunately, you can see this process taking place in the United States and other Western countries. Some people seem to think that being free means being liberal in the way you think, but that's not true—you have to control the way you think. The way people act is a result of how they think, and a thought process that says everything is permissible promotes immoral behavior, which then leads to the deterioration of society.

    16a. Why is the government forced to intrude more and more into civil liberties?
(To restrict unwanted behaviors, to control people without moral restraint)

    16b. You shouldn't be liberal in the way you think; you should what?
(Control the way you think)

17. When the Apostle Paul wrote that we will be spoiled through philosophy, vain deceit, the traditions of men, and the rudiments of this world, he was saying, "Don't think like a lost person. Don't think the way the world thinks." The world is filled with people who have no relationship with God and therefore have a very ungodly philosophy. People who think according to the principles of this world say that God doesn't exist, and they believe that humans evolved by accident over billions of years. They don't acknowledge God, and they don't understand that they were created and designed by Him. So, to think as the world thinks is to think like a lost person. The world's way of thinking is not a comprehensive and rational philosophy. For instance, how does a society that goes to great lengths to promote the environment and protect even the most obscure animal species arrive at the conclusion that it's okay to abort babies? Some of the same people who yell about recycling think that having a baby is a choice, and if having a baby is inconvenient, they think it's okay to kill the baby. Society needs to get its priorities straight. God gave us life. We are not just like the rest of creation, and we are not equal to animals. I'll be dealing with specific philosophies later on, but right now I just want to show how behavior comes from philosophy and why having a Christian philosophy is important for believers.

    17a. If you have relationship with God, what will you have?
A. A very godly philosophy
B. No time for other things
C. Power others will notice
D. All of the above
E. None of the above
(A. A very godly philosophy)

    17b. Give one reason that societies' priorities aren't straight.
(Because some of the same people who yell about recycling think that having a baby is a choice, and if having a baby is inconvenient, they think it's okay to kill the baby)

18. Many believers today are establishing a philosophy independent of God and separate from what the Word of God teaches. I read a survey that was given to people who identified themselves as born-again Christians, and they were asked how they formed their opinions. The majority of people said they are just coming up with their own philosophy based on life experiences and their own way of thinking. One question was if they adhere to the Word of God as being absolute, and only a small percentage answered yes. Instead of getting their philosophy from the Word of God, they are basing it on how they were raised, what they have been taught in school, books they've read, and the study of principles from other world religions. They have established their philosophy piecemeal. People are taking a buffet-style approach to the assembly of ideas, and that's not a good idea. If you do that, Satan is going to spoil you; i.e., take from you what Jesus has already purchased and what belongs to you by right of inheritance.

    18a. Discussion Question: How do you usually form your opinions?
(Discussion question)

    18b. If you base your philosophy on how you were raised, what you have been taught in school, books you've read, and the study of principles from other world religions, what will happen to you?
(Satan is going to spoil you; i.e., take from you what Jesus has already purchased and what belongs to you by right of inheritance)

Lesson 1 — What Is Christian Philosophy?

19. A Christian philosophy must be rooted in the Word of God. You can't form a proper Christian worldview without renewing your mind in the Word of God. When Jesus was praying to the Father, He said, **"Sanctify them through thy truth: thy word is truth"** (John 17:17). I just can't overemphasize how important it is for you to conform your mind to the Word of God and not to the philosophies and principles of this world. Unfortunately, a lot of Christians aren't looking to the Word for their philosophy. They have bought into Satan's deception that the Word of God contains bits and pieces of truth but that it isn't completely accurate. They think it's outdated because it was written 2,000 years ago and that it can't possibly have wisdom for modern society. In fact, some don't believe that the Bible is the inerrant word of God or that Jesus Christ is the only way to salvation—they say He is one of many ways. That's a wrong philosophy, and Satan will use that perspective to come into your life and steal from you.

   19a. If you don't renew your mind to the Word of God, what will happen?
   (You can't form a proper Christian worldview)

   19b. Read John 17:17. How are you sanctified?
   (Through God's truth)

   19c. What is truth?
   (His Word)

   19d. If you think the Word of God contains bits and pieces of truth but that it isn't completely accurate, you are _____.
   (Deceived)

20. Psalm 91:4b says, **"His truth shall be thy shield and buckler."** The Word of God and the promises it contains are our armor and protection against the attacks of the Enemy. The Word is 100 percent accurate, it's totally relevant, and it is the only thing Christians should be basing their lives upon. The way you change your core values and obtain a Christian philosophy is by conforming your worldview to the Word of God—instead of just leaning on your own understanding.

   20a. The only thing Christians should be basing their lives upon is what?
   (The Word)

21. If you want to see the results that the Word of God promises, then you have to adopt God's way of thinking. I have conformed my philosophy to the Word and it's working. My health is great, I'm seeing the miraculous power of God, my stock investments have gained 61 percent in value while the world has been crying about a financial crisis, I'm happy, I'm joyful, my relationships are good, life is good, and God is blessing me in every area of my life. I'm not bragging; I'm just trying to give an example that conforming your way of thinking to the Word of God works. I'm not special—you can have the same results because God doesn't play favorites. All I've done is put God first and recognize that I'm not smart enough to direct my own life. I just do what God tells me to do, instead of doing what makes sense to me or what I feel like doing. Being a Christian isn't about changing your outward appearance or what you do and how you act. If you don't change the wrong concepts and the belief system on the inside, then you're going to have the same results in your life you had before you were saved. That's why God gave you His Word—to change the way you think. The Word of God contains His thoughts, His values, and His way of thinking. It's your ticket to a new life.

   21a. What do you have to do if you want to see the results that the Word of God promises?
   (Adopt God's way of thinking)

   21b. If you don't, what will you have?
   (The same results in your life you had before you were saved)

Lesson 1 — What Is Christian Philosophy?

22. I don't care what society says is right or wrong; I follow what God says. Society may say homosexuality is just another lifestyle or that a homosexual union is just as important as a marriage between a man and a woman, but God's Word says differently. If you subscribe to the world's view instead of God's, then the devil is going to steal from you. The world is trying to say that there are many paths to God and that you need to embrace other philosophies. God's Word says you should be on your guard against any philosophy that isn't modeled after Jesus Christ. The world wants to pretend that the human race has "evolved" beyond the Bible and that now you should just embrace life. The world's philosophies are simply an attempt by the devil to undermine the Word of God—that same thing Satan did to Adam and Eve. The Enemy wants to strip you of the armor and protection of God's Word so that he can plunder your life and steal what Jesus has already won for you.

    22a. Discussion Question: Why shouldn't you care what society says is right and wrong?
(Discussion question)

    22b. The world's philosophies are simply an attempt by the devil to _____ the Word of God.
(Undermine)

23. The fruit of a tree is directly related to the tree itself (Matt. 7:18-19). In the same way, you aren't going to get the fruit of God's manifold blessings if your core belief system is conformed to the world's way of thinking. If you aren't seeing the fruit in your life that you would like to see, then all you have to do is change the way you think in your heart and adopt God's way of looking at life. Once you do that, the fruit will come. Conforming your way of thinking to God's Word will bring a harvest of blessings in your life, but they don't all come overnight. The natural law of sowing and reaping means that it takes time for a seed to grow into a fruit-bearing plant, and there is a similar spiritual law of sowing and reaping. God provides miracles when there isn't time to wait for a harvest, like healing sickness, but God's best is for you to walk in His blessings. For instance, it is better to walk in health and never need healing than it is to get sick and need a miracle. Likewise, it is better to have money in the bank to meet all of your needs than it is to need a miracle to pay your rent every month. Even after you renew your mind, it may take time to get to where you don't need a miracle every month, but don't get discouraged. Scripture says, **"And let us not be weary in well doing: for in due season we shall reap, if we faint not"** (Gal. 6:9). This means you have to stay focused on God and meditate on His Word to maintain your Christian perspective and reap the fruit God desires for you. If you are willing to do that and you change the way you think at the heart level, then you will see God's blessings in your life—guaranteed. I challenge you to prayerfully consider the Christian philosophies I present in the rest of this study guide and embrace them. It will change the way you think, which will change the rest of your life.

    23a. Read Matthew 7:18-19. You aren't going to get the fruit of God's manifold blessings if your core belief system is conformed to what?
(The world's way of thinking)

    23b. Even though conforming your way of thinking to God's Word will bring a harvest of blessings in your life, why don't they all come overnight?
(Because the natural law of sowing and reaping means that it takes time for a seed to grow into a fruit-bearing plant, and there is a similar spiritual law of sowing and reaping)

    23c. Read Galatians 6:9. What does this mean?
(You have to stay focused on God and meditate on His Word to maintain your Christian perspective and reap the fruit God desires for you)

    23d. Discussion Question: Why is it so important to change the way you think at a heart level?
(Discussion question)

LESSON 1 — WHAT IS CHRISTIAN PHILOSOPHY?

DISCIPLESHIP QUESTIONS

1. Discussion Question: In your life, how has your philosophy determined your response to the things happening around you and the results you see in life?

2. What does your philosophy filter?

3. Read Colossians 2:8. Your philosophy needs to modeled after whom?

4. Which two would try to spoil you?

5. Discussion Question: What do you think you have to beware of?

6. A godly way of looking at things is established where?
    A. In your heart
    B. At church
    C. In the Word of God
    D. All of the above
    E. None of the above

7. Read 2 Peter 1:3-4. How do you have everything that pertains to life and godliness?

8. Discussion Question: What have you missed out on because you haven't recognized you're in a battle?

SCRIPTURES TO USE WITH QUESTIONS

COLOSSIANS 2:8
Beware lest any man spoil you through philosophy and vain deceit, after the tradition of men, after the rudiments of the world, and not after Christ.

COLOSSIANS 2:1
For I would that ye knew what great conflict I have for you, and for them at Laodicea, and for as many as have not seen my face in the flesh.

COLOSSIANS 2:4
And this I say, lest any man should beguile you with enticing words.

COLOSSIANS 2:6
As ye have therefore received Christ Jesus the Lord, so walk ye in him.

MATTHEW 28:19-20
Go ye therefore, and teach all nations, baptizing them in the name of the Father, and of the Son, and of the Holy Ghost: **[20]** *Teaching them to observe all things whatsoever I have commanded you: and, lo, I am with you alway, even unto the end of the world. Amen.*

2 PETER 1:3-4
According as his divine power hath given unto us all things that pertain unto life and godliness, through the knowledge of him that hath called us to glory and virtue: **[4]** *Whereby are given unto us exceeding great and precious promises: that by these ye might be partakers of the divine nature, having escaped the corruption that is in the world through lust.*

Lesson 1 — What Is Christian Philosophy?

DISCIPLESHIP QUESTIONS

9. True or false: Satan can overcome you and force you to obey him.

10. How does he try to seduce God's people?

11. Where can religious opinion, doctrine, and custom come from?

12. Read Mark 7:13. How was the Word of God made of none effect?
    A. Because of the devil
    B. Because no one believed it
    C. Because of the persecution
    D. Because of man's tradition
    E. Because no one preached it

13. Read Proverbs 23:7. Why does everything in the Christian life revolve around the way you think?

14. What is heart-level knowledge?

15. Discussion Question: What right philosophy have you had that has produced a good result?

16. You have to _____ the truths into a way of thinking that impacts your overall outlook on life.

SCRIPTURES TO USE WITH QUESTIONS

MARK 7:13
Making the word of God of none effect through your tradition, which ye have delivered: and many such like things do ye.

PROVERBS 23:7
For as he thinketh in his heart, so is he: Eat and drink, saith he to thee; but his heart is not with thee.

Lesson 1 — What Is Christian Philosophy?

DISCIPLESHIP QUESTIONS

17. Read Romans 12:1-2. Who has to renew your mind?

18. According to John 8:32, what sets you free?
    A. Will power
    B. The truth
    C. The jailer
    D. Being bailed out
    E. The truth you know

19. Why isn't it enough to study Andrew's teachings and study the Word?

20. How do you change the way you look at life?

21. What determines the condition of your life?

22. What is the most important thing you will ever do?

23. Discussion Question: What do you think this will do for you?

24. What can you learn from Andrew's experience?

25. Discussion Question: What has worked its way into many Christians' belief systems?

SCRIPTURES TO USE WITH QUESTIONS

ROMANS 12:1-2
I beseech you therefore, brethren, by the mercies of God, that ye present your bodies a living sacrifice, holy, acceptable unto God, which is your reasonable service. **[2]** *And be not conformed to this world: but be ye transformed by the renewing of your mind, that ye may prove what is that good, and acceptable, and perfect, will of God.*

JOHN 8:32
And ye shall know the truth, and the truth shall make you free.

2 CORINTHIANS 4:8-9
We are troubled on every side, yet not distressed; we are perplexed, but not in despair; **[9]** *Persecuted, but not forsaken; cast down, but not destroyed.*

1 JOHN 4:18
There is no fear in love; but perfect love casteth out fear: because fear hath torment. He that feareth is not made perfect in love.

LESSON 1 — WHAT IS CHRISTIAN PHILOSOPHY?

DISCIPLESHIP QUESTIONS

26. Discussion Question: Read Proverbs 3:5. How have you been conditioned to lean on your own understanding?

27. True or false: Society doesn't need more laws, but the people need to embrace a biblically based way of thinking.

28. Why is the government forced to intrude more and more into civil liberties?

29. You shouldn't be liberal in the way you think; you should what?

30. If you have relationship with God, what will you have?
    A. A very godly philosophy
    B. No time for other things
    C. Power others will notice
    D. All of the above
    E. None of the above

31. Give one reason that societies' priorities aren't straight.

32. Discussion Question: How do you usually form your opinions?

33. If you base your philosophy on how you were raised, what you have been taught in school, books you've read, and the study of principles from other world religions, what will happen to you?

SCRIPTURES TO USE WITH QUESTIONS

PROVERBS 3:5
Trust in the Lord with all thine heart; and lean not unto thine own understanding.

2 CORINTHIANS 5:7
For we walk by faith, not by sight.

Lesson 1 — What Is Christian Philosophy?

DISCIPLESHIP QUESTIONS

34. If you don't renew your mind to the Word of God, what will happen?

35. Read John 17:17. How are you sanctified?

36. What is truth?

37. If you think the Word of God contains bits and pieces of truth but that it isn't completely accurate, you are _____.

38. The only thing Christians should be basing their lives upon is what?

39. What do you have to do if you want to see the results that the Word of God promises?

40. If you don't, what will you have?

41. Discussion Question: Why shouldn't you care what society says is right and wrong?

42. The world's philosophies are simply an attempt by the devil to _____ the Word of God.

SCRIPTURES TO USE WITH QUESTIONS

JOHN 17:17
Sanctify them through thy truth: thy word is truth.

PSALM 91:4
He shall cover thee with his feathers, and under his wings shalt thou trust: his truth shall be thy shield and buckler.

LESSON 1 — WHAT IS CHRISTIAN PHILOSOPHY?

DISCIPLESHIP QUESTIONS

43. Read Matthew 7:18-19. You aren't going to get the fruit of God's manifold blessings if your core belief system is conformed to what?

44. Even though conforming your way of thinking to God's Word will bring a harvest of blessings in your life, why don't they all come overnight?

45. Read Galatians 6:9. What does this mean?

46. Discussion Question: Why is it so important to change the way you think at a heart level?

SCRIPTURES TO USE WITH QUESTIONS

MATTHEW 7:18-19
A good tree cannot bring forth evil fruit, neither can a corrupt tree bring forth good fruit. **[19]** *Every tree that bringeth not forth good fruit is hewn down, and cast into the fire.*

GALATIANS 6:9
And let us not be weary in well doing: for in due season we shall reap, if we faint not.

Lesson 1 — What Is Christian Philosophy?

ANSWER KEY

1. *Discussion question*
2. Every experience you have and every piece of information that comes your way
3. Christ
4. Man and Satan
5. *Discussion question*
6. C. In the Word of God
7. Through knowing and having intimate relationship with Jesus Christ
8. *Discussion question*
9. False
10. With words and thoughts that corrupt their way of thinking
11. People who are mistaken or, worse, self-seeking and deceitful
12. D. Because of man's tradition
13. Because as you think in your heart, so are you
14. Your dominant thoughts, or your dominant philosophy—not individual thoughts, but the pattern, or model, you have combined your opinions and life experiences into, which then shapes how you view the world
15. *Discussion question*
16. Combine
17. You
18. E. The truth you know
19. Because it's possible to do all those things and yet not operate in faith or let those truths change your philosophy
20. You have to combine facts from the Word, connect the dots, and pull them all together, so that they change the way you look at life
21. The way you respond to what happens to you
22. Renew your mind and form a Christian philosophy, or a Christian worldview
23. *Discussion question*
24. *Discussion question*
25. Humanistic philosophy
26. *Discussion question*
27. True
28. To restrict unwanted behaviors, to control people without moral restraint
29. Control the way you think
30. A. A very godly philosophy
31. Because some of the same people who yell about recycling think that having a baby is a choice, and if having a baby is inconvenient, they think it's okay to kill the baby
32. *Discussion question*
33. Satan is going to spoil you; i.e., take from you what Jesus has already purchased and what belongs to you by right of inheritance
34. You can't form a proper Christian worldview
35. Through God's truth
36. His Word
37. Deceived
38. The Word
39. Adopt God's way of thinking
40. The same results in your life you had before you were saved
41. *Discussion question*
42. Undermine

ANSWER KEY

43. The world's way of thinking

44. Because the natural law of sowing and reaping means that it takes time for a seed to grow into a fruit-bearing plant, and there is a similar spiritual law of sowing and reaping

45. You have to stay focused on God and meditate on His Word to maintain your Christian perspective and reap the fruit God desires for you

46. *Discussion question*

Why Should I Care about Philosophy?

I went to Poland a number of times in the 1980s before the Berlin Wall came down, when Poland was still under Communist rule. I stuck out in my cowboy boots, and of course, the moment I opened my mouth, people knew I was an American. Americans were an unusual sight for the Polish people, and they were always gathering around me in curiosity. I wanted to blend in better and get a feel for what life was really like in Poland, so I borrowed some clothes from my interpreter. Then I went out into public wearing his clothes and stayed completely silent so that I could try to pass myself off as Polish.

The interpreter and I started walking down the street, and within five minutes, a crowd of young people had gathered around me, saying, "American! American!" I was wearing Polish clothes and I hadn't said a word, but they could still tell I was an American.

I said to my interpreter, "How do these people know I'm an American?"

"It's your attitude," he said.

"What do you mean my attitude?" I asked. "I haven't said or done anything."

"You don't understand. We've lived under Communist rule for over seventy years," he said. He went on to explain how they had learned to be afraid under the oppression of communism. They never made eye contact with strangers when walking down the street, because they didn't want to draw attention to themselves. They even took on submissive body language. They didn't walk down the street with their heads up and their shoulders square; they stooped and looked at the ground. They didn't start conversations with strangers, because the person might have been KGB. All of their mannerisms were aimed at being as inconspicuous as possible.

I wasn't doing any of those things. I was standing on the street corner looking people in the eye and smiling. I was nodding my head at strangers to say hello. My positive attitude was coming through without speaking a word to anyone, and they could tell I was an American. My philosophy was evident—and so was theirs.

Everyone has a philosophy, whether they acknowledge it or not, and all philosophies produce fruit. A philosophy is a filter that determines how you act. When Proverbs says that you will be as you think in your heart (Prov. 23:7), I believe it's talking about your philosophy. The system of thought that you hold

Lesson 2   Why Should I Care about Philosophy?

in your heart determines the course of your life. As I've said, your life right now is a product of the way you have been thinking.

People don't generally desire divorce, bankruptcy, or sickness, so experiencing those things doesn't mean you desired them. It just means you had a philosophy that made you susceptible to those experiences. For instance, you could have been thinking *Lord, I'm only human. I'm just a man*, instead of thinking about who you are in Christ and conforming your thoughts to the Word, which says, **"Greater is he that is in you, than he that is in the world"** (1 John 4:4). Forgetting that you are a child of God and thinking that you are a nobody makes you susceptible to attacks from the Enemy.

The root word (*philosophos*) for the Greek word translated **"philosophy"** in Paul's admonition to the Colossians (*philosophia*) was used in only one other place in Scripture. It was when Paul was speaking to the Greeks, and it says,

> *Then certain philosophers [philosophos] of the Epicureans, and of the Stoicks, encountered him. And some said, What will this babbler say? other some, He seemeth to be a setter forth of strange gods: because he preached unto them Jesus, and the resurrection.*
>
> ACTS 17:18, BRACKETS MINE

We are still encountering these philosophies today. Epicureans derived their teaching from the philosopher Epicurus who founded a school in Athens, Greece, around 300 B.C. Epicurus taught that "the world is a random combination of atoms and that pleasure is the highest good."[1] His followers soon devolved into a materialistic group, a lot like the materialistic and pleasure-seeking society that the modern philosophy of evolution is giving rise to. Having fun and seeking pleasure pretty much sums up most people's philosophy today. In fact, the theory of evolution is simply a new presentation of the Epicurean belief that life is the result of the random collision of atoms.

A Christian philosophy puts relationship with God above pleasure. I have a philosophy that pleasing God is more important than pleasing myself. If seeking God means doing something that isn't pleasurable, I'll suffer the consequences because I don't make my decisions based on what makes me feel good. The world promotes buying the biggest house you possibly can, owning the biggest car, and indulging every sense you have. The world's philosophy is "Get all you can, can all you get, and sit on your can." But God teaches that it is more blessed to give than to receive (Acts 20:35), and Jesus said that a man's life does not consist in the abundance of possessions (Luke 12:15). People are more important than possessions, and I want to make my life count. That means serving others, not gathering stuff together for myself.

The second part of Epicurus' philosophy was to avoid pain at all costs.[2] Unfortunately, pain is sometimes necessary to accomplish good. Freedom, for example, has a cost. Millions of people have died in battle for freedom. A lot of pain was endured during World War II to provide the freedom that we enjoy today. A self-seeking philosophy doesn't allow for sacrifice like that; it leads people to put their heads in the sand and hope that problems will just go away.

When Hitler began his rise to power and first started implementing his racist policies, a lot of people thought he would just go away. Many governments had come and gone in Germany since they lost the

---

[1]   Definition from Princeton's WordNet, online at http://wordnet.princeton.edu/
[2]   Andrew Wommack, Living Commentary Bible software, note for Acts 17:18.

Lesson 2 — Why Should I Care about Philosophy?

First World War, and people thought Hitler would be another passing fad. Everyone wanted to avoid conflict, so they ignored Hitler and hoped he would fade away. Obviously he didn't, and his plans for a "master race" and the genocide he employed plunged the world into a war in which over fifty million people died.

Today people are hoping their problems will go away just like Europe hoped Hitler would. People are putting their heads in the sand and ignoring attacks upon society—such as abortion and the promotion of the "lesbian, gay, bisexual, and transsexual" agenda—in the hopes that they will all go away. But those attacks aren't going away unless individuals in society make a stand for morality. Ignoring these warning signs is a recipe for disaster. It's a wrong philosophy.

The reference to **"Stoicks"** in the scripture from Acts refers to the Greek philosopher Zeno who founded a competing school of thought at the same time as Epicurus. The Stoics believed that virtue was sufficient for happiness and that the ultimate goal in life was to become free from the fluctuations of emotion—pleasure or pain.[3] They sought to calmly accept all circumstances as the unavoidable result of divine will or the natural order.[4]

A lot of Christians today are stoic in their philosophy. The extreme-sovereignty-of-God doctrine is a perversion of Scripture that falsely teaches that everything that happens in life is preordained by God. It's nothing more than a stoical worldview. People who teach that doctrine think absolutely everything that happens in life is God's will—even evil things such as murder, rape, and sickness. Those people believe that even if God didn't cause the event directly, He must have allowed it to happen because He is all-powerful, and He could have stopped it if it was against His will.

It's true that God is all-powerful, but His Word teaches that He has no part in evil (James 1:13-17). It is the devil who comes into our lives to steal, kill, and destroy. God only comes to give us life, and to give us life abundantly (John 10:10). Everything that happens in life is not the result of God's will. Some things are just attacks from the devil. Thankfully, God has given us the authority to rebuke and resist those attacks. God's Word says,

> *Submit yourselves therefore to God. Resist the devil, and he will flee from you.*
>
> JAMES 4:7

Any teaching that doesn't conform to the Word of God is false, no matter how popular it may be. You have to evaluate your philosophy and make sure it is based on the Word of God, and not on the philosophies of this world or the traditions of men. Everything that God has shown me has helped to form my philosophy. It is all woven together into one dominant way of thinking. The Word of God has dictated my philosophy, and my response to life is in turn dictated by my philosophy. So, the blessings in my life are simply a result of filtering life through God's perspective.

But Stoicism and Epicureanism aren't the only philosophies out there. The philosophy that your parents had when they raised you also has an impact on your belief system—not merely their worldview, but the philosophy they instilled in you by the things they said, by the way they treated you, and through the behavior you witnessed.

---

[3] From the Stanford Encyclopedia of Philosophy, online at http://plato.stanford.edu/entries/stoicism/
[4] The *American Heritage College Dictionary*, 3rd Edition, "stoic."

Lesson 2 — Why Should I Care about Philosophy?

I have a very close friend whose father was a good man in many ways, but he also had a mean streak. When my friend was a boy, his father used to browbeat him constantly. He was always scolding him for doing things incorrectly. Those negative statements became part of the way my friend looked at life. He saw himself as the man his father told him he was.

They lived on a farm, so the father was always fixing cars and other equipment, and my friend would help. One of the things his father used to tell him was that he couldn't put a nut on a bolt without crossing the threads. I remember working on a car with him one time, and I watched him start to shake as he put a nut on a bolt. After he got the nut on, he was afraid it wasn't on right, so he kept taking it off and putting it back on until he actually cross-threaded the bolt. The things his father spoke over him became a curse because my friend took those words to heart and made them a part of his philosophy.

All of us have been influenced by the philosophies that we were raised with or that we picked up through experiences. Racism is an example of a philosophy that is handed down from one generation to the next. It's a kind of tradition. If children raised in a racist environment don't replace those lies with the truth, they will incorporate prejudice into their worldview, and it will affect their experience of life.

America had a tradition of racism that was hard to overcome. Martin Luther King Jr. made a stand for morality and led our country through some difficult times. He didn't stick his head in the sand and hope that the problem of racism would go away. He stood up for a Christian philosophy that says all men are created equal, and he helped to change a nation. Today society often fails to recognize that Martin Luther King Jr. wasn't merely a civil rights leader; he was a Christian leader.

In the same way that society persecuted Martin Luther King Jr. for his stand against racism, I can guarantee that Christians are not going to be universally loved for making a stand against current wrongs in our society. Abortion is a heinous crime, but the majority of society supports it—and there are elements who promote it aggressively. Still, we shouldn't be focused on how other people are going to respond. Our goal should be to do the will of God and to stand for what is right—that's a Christian philosophy. Proverbs says,

> *Righteousness exalteth a nation: but sin is a reproach to any people.*
>
> PROVERBS 14:34

Righteousness is conforming your character and conduct to a right standard. It's conforming to the Word of God, not to philosophies of this world and the traditions of men. What the majority of society says is or is not right is irrelevant. The majority is often wrong. The Word has to be the standard we build our philosophy upon.

Too many of those who call themselves Christians aren't building their philosophy on the Word. Some of them might not truly be born again, but some sincere Christians just haven't become disciples of the Lord Jesus. They haven't learned what the Word says, and they aren't following Him. They haven't made an effort to conform their hearts and actions to a godly standard of righteousness. All they have done is accept Jesus to avoid going to hell. They often have philosophies that are completely contrary to the Word of God, but they don't see any problem with that. Obviously, if you have a philosophy that is contrary to the Word of God, you don't have a Christian philosophy.

Lesson 2 — Why Should I Care about Philosophy?

Some of this is the fault of the church. We have been preaching salvation in order to go to heaven when we die, but we haven't been making disciples as the Lord commanded us. So, some people are truly ignorant of God's values, but others are willfully ignorant. Those people are choosing not to subscribe to God's viewpoint, because it doesn't fit with their lifestyles. Either way, ignorance isn't good for us. God loves us no matter what because He doesn't relate to us based on our performance, but ignorance isn't going to excuse us from the devil's attacks. The world's philosophy says that "what we don't know won't hurt us," but the truth is that ignorance kills (Hos. 4:6).

You can see the influences of Epicurean philosophy in those who aim to please themselves no matter the consequences. The overwhelming majority of abortions are performed on women who aren't married. They are having sexual relations outside of marriage and are using abortion as a form of birth control. God's command restricting sex to a marriage relationship is given to protect you emotionally and to protect children. Sadly, 70 percent of women getting an abortion in the United States identify themselves as Christians at the time of the abortion.[5] This shows the degree to which men and women who have a philosophy putting pleasure first are doing what they want and not worrying about the consequences—even when it means killing an unborn baby.

Christians should not be getting abortions. I'm not saying God is mad at you or that He won't love you anymore if you've ever had an abortion. God dealt with sin when He poured out His wrath on Jesus on the cross, and He isn't dealing with sin anymore. God is a good God who is full of mercy and unfailing love. So, I'm not condemning women who have had an abortion. God's grace is more than enough to cover all of your sins. I'm simply saying that abortion is wrong. Abortion kills innocent children, and there is no room in a Christian philosophy for the tolerance of abortion.

We can't just entertain the information that suits us. A ragbag collection of truths and half-truths will never add up to a unified worldview that is godly and righteous. We need to get our philosophy from the Word of God. Filtering our lives through Scripture and basing our decisions on the philosophy that comes from the Word will keep us on the right path and prevent us from falling into hypocrisy. The reason there is such a wide variance in convictions among Christians is that not everyone is getting their philosophy from the Word.

Your citizenship in heaven can have more influence over you than your upbringing or the worldly ideas that surround you. As the Apostle Paul said, **"Let God be true, and every man a liar"** (Rom. 3:4). Even the religious instruction you received should be tossed aside if it doesn't conform to the Word of God. You might have been taught that God is angry and that He is just waiting to punish you the moment you step out of line or that He uses sickness to correct you. Those are wrong doctrines, and they will allow the Enemy to steal from you. Your beliefs need to be established upon what the Word says, not upon someone else's interpretation of it.

The Bible isn't just another book; it is a supernatural book through which God speaks to you. The Word of God is true. Once you get into the true Word of God and let the Holy Spirit instruct you, you'll see that it is the greatest revelation the world has ever been given. The Bible is a tremendous gift from God that contains the greatest philosophy known, and if you base your life upon the Word, you'll get supernatural results.

---

[5] Alan Guttmacher Institute, Characteristics of U.S. Abortion Patients, 2008 cited on abortionblackout.com

Lesson 2 — Why Should I Care about Philosophy?

OUTLINE

I. Everyone has a philosophy, whether they acknowledge it or not, and all philosophies produce fruit.

   A. A philosophy is a filter that determines how you act.

   B. When Proverbs says that you will be as you think in your heart (Prov. 23:7), I believe it's talking about your philosophy.

   C. The system of thought that you hold in your heart determines the course of your life.

   D. As I've said, your life right now is a product of the way you have been thinking.

II. People don't generally desire divorce, bankruptcy, or sickness, so experiencing those things doesn't mean you desired them.

   A. It just means you had a philosophy that made you susceptible to those experiences.

   B. For instance, you could have been thinking *Lord, I'm only human. I'm just a man*, instead of thinking about who you are in Christ and conforming your thoughts to the Word, which says, **"Greater is he that is in you, than he that is in the world"** (1 John 4:4).

   C. Forgetting that you are a child of God and thinking that you are a nobody makes you susceptible to attacks from the Enemy.

III. The root word (*philosophos*) for the Greek word translated **"philosophy"** in Paul's admonition to the Colossians (*philosophia*) was used in only one other place in Scripture.

   A. It was when Paul was speaking to the Greeks, and it says,

   Then certain philosophers [philosophos] of the Epicureans, and of the Stoicks, encountered him. And some said, What will this babbler say? other some, He seemeth to be a setter forth of strange gods: because he preached unto them Jesus, and the resurrection.
   ACTS 17:18, BRACKETS MINE

   B. We are still encountering these philosophies today.

   C. Epicureans derived their teaching from the philosopher Epicurus who founded a school in Athens, Greece, around 300 B.C.

   D. Epicurus taught that "the world is a random combination of atoms and that pleasure is the highest good."[1]

   E. His followers soon devolved into a materialistic group, a lot like the materialistic and pleasure-seeking society that the modern philosophy of evolution is giving rise to.

   F. Having fun and seeking pleasure pretty much sums up most people's philosophy today.

   G. In fact, the theory of evolution is simply a new presentation of the Epicurean belief that life is the result of the random collision of atoms.

   H. A Christian philosophy puts relationship with God above pleasure.

   I. I have a philosophy that pleasing God is more important than pleasing myself.

   J. If seeking God means doing something that isn't pleasurable, I'll suffer the consequences because I don't make my decisions based on what makes me feel good.

   K. The world promotes buying the biggest house you possibly can, owning the biggest car, and indulging every sense you have.

---

[1] Definition from Princeton's WordNet, online at http://wordnet.princeton.edu/

Lesson 2 — Why Should I Care about Philosophy?

L. The world's philosophy is "Get all you can, can all you get, and sit on your can."

M. But God teaches that it is more blessed to give than to receive (Acts 20:35), and Jesus said that a man's life does not consist in the abundance of possessions (Luke 12:15).

N. People are more important than possessions, and I want to make my life count.

O. That means serving others, not gathering stuff together for myself.

IV. The second part of Epicurus' philosophy was to avoid pain at all costs.[2]

    A. Unfortunately, pain is sometimes necessary to accomplish good.

    B. Freedom, for example, has a cost.

    C. A lot of pain was endured during World War II to provide the freedom that we enjoy today.

    D. A self-seeking philosophy doesn't allow for sacrifice like that; it leads people to put their heads in the sand and hope that problems will just go away.

    E. Today people are hoping their problems will go away just like Europe hoped Hitler would.

    F. People are putting their heads in the sand and ignoring attacks upon society—such as abortion and the promotion of the "lesbian, gay, bisexual, and transsexual" agenda—in the hopes that they will all go away.

    G. But those attacks aren't going away unless individuals in society make a stand for morality.

    H. Ignoring these warning signs is a recipe for disaster.

    I. It's a wrong philosophy.

V. The reference to **"Stoicks"** in the scripture from Acts refers to the Greek philosopher Zeno who founded a competing school of thought at the same time as Epicurus.

    A. The Stoics believed that virtue was sufficient for happiness and that the ultimate goal in life was to become free from the fluctuations of emotion—pleasure or pain.[3]

    B. They sought to calmly accept all circumstances as the unavoidable result of divine will or the natural order.[4]

    C. A lot of Christians today are stoic in their philosophy.

    D. The extreme-sovereignty-of-God doctrine is a perversion of Scripture that falsely teaches that everything that happens in life is preordained by God.

    E. It's nothing more than a stoical worldview.

    F. People who teach that doctrine think absolutely everything that happens in life is God's will—even evil things such as murder, rape, and sickness.

    G. Those people believe that even if God didn't cause the event directly, He must have allowed it to happen because He is all-powerful, and He could have stopped it if it was against His will.

    H. It's true that God is all-powerful, but His Word teaches that He has no part in evil (James 1:13-17).

    I. It is the devil who comes into our lives to steal, kill, and destroy.

    J. God only comes to give us life, and to give us life abundantly (John 10:10).

---

[2] Andrew Wommack, Living Commentary Bible software, note for Acts 17:18.
[3] From the Stanford Encyclopedia of Philosophy, online at http://plato.stanford.edu/entries/stoicism/
[4] The *American Heritage College Dictionary*, 3rd Edition, "stoic."

Lesson 2 — Why Should I Care about Philosophy?

    K. Everything that happens in life is not the result of God's will.

    L. Some things are just attacks from the devil.

    M. Thankfully, God has given us the authority to rebuke and resist those attacks. God's Word says,

Submit yourselves therefore to God. Resist the devil, and he will flee from you.

JAMES 4:7

VI. Any teaching that doesn't conform to the Word of God is false, no matter how popular it may be.

    A. You have to evaluate your philosophy and make sure it is based on the Word of God, and not on the philosophies of this world or the traditions of men.

    B. Everything that God has shown me has helped to form my philosophy.

    C. It is all woven together into one dominant way of thinking.

    D. The Word of God has dictated my philosophy, and my response to life is in turn dictated by my philosophy.

    E. So, the blessings in my life are simply a result of filtering life through God's perspective.

VII. Stoicism and Epicureanism aren't the only philosophies out there.

    A. The philosophy that your parents had when they raised you also has an impact on your belief system—not merely their worldview, but the philosophy they instilled in you by the things they said, by the way they treated you, and through the behavior you witnessed.

    B. All of us have been influenced by the philosophies that we were raised with or that we picked up through experiences.

    C. Racism is an example of a philosophy that is handed down from one generation to the next— it's a kind of tradition.

    D. If children raised in a racist environment don't replace those lies with the truth, they will incorporate prejudice into their worldview, and it will affect their experience of life.

VIII. America had a tradition of racism that was hard to overcome.

    A. Martin Luther King Jr. made a stand for morality and led our country through some difficult times.

    B. He stood up for a Christian philosophy that says all men are created equal, and he helped to change a nation.

    C. Today society often fails to recognize that Martin Luther King Jr. wasn't merely a civil rights leader; he was a Christian leader.

    D. In the same way that society persecuted Martin Luther King Jr. for his stand against racism, I can guarantee that Christians are not going to be universally loved for making a stand against current wrongs in our society.

    E. Abortion is a heinous crime, but the majority of society supports it—and there are elements who promote it aggressively.

    F. Still, we shouldn't be focused on how other people are going to respond.

    G. Our goal should be to do the will of God and to stand for what is right—that's Christian philosophy.

Lesson 2 — Why Should I Care about Philosophy?

H. Proverbs says,

Righteousness exalteth a nation: but sin is a reproach to any people.

PROVERBS 14:34

    I. *Righteousness* is conforming your character and conduct to a right standard.

    J. It's conforming to the Word of God, not to philosophies of this world and the traditions of men.

    K. What the majority of society says is or is not right is irrelevant.

    L. The majority is often wrong. The Word has to be the standard we build our philosophy upon.

IX. Too many of those who call themselves Christians aren't building their philosophy on the Word.

    A. Some of them might not truly be born again, but some sincere Christians just haven't become disciples of the Lord Jesus.

    B. They haven't learned what the Word says, and they aren't following Him.

    C. They haven't made an effort to conform their hearts and actions to a godly standard of righteousness.

    D. All they have done is accept Jesus to avoid going to hell.

    E. They often have philosophies that are completely contrary to the Word of God, but they don't see any problem with that.

    F. Obviously, if you have a philosophy that is contrary to the Word of God, you don't have a Christian philosophy.

    G. Some of this is the fault of the church.

X. We have been preaching salvation in order to go to heaven when we die, but we haven't been making disciples as the Lord commanded us.

    A. So, some people are truly ignorant of God's values, but others are willfully ignorant.

    B. Those people are choosing not to subscribe to God's viewpoint, because it doesn't fit with their lifestyles.

    C. Either way, ignorance isn't good for us.

    D. God loves us no matter what because He doesn't relate to us based on our performance, but ignorance isn't going to excuse us from the devil's attacks.

    E. The world's philosophy says that "what we don't know won't hurt us," but the truth is that ignorance kills (Hos. 4:6).

XI. You can see the influences of Epicurean philosophy in those who aim to please themselves no matter the consequences.

    A. The overwhelming majority of abortions are performed on women who aren't married.

    B. They are having sexual relations outside of marriage and are using abortion as a form of birth control.

    C. God's command restricting sex to a marriage relationship is given to protect you emotionally and to protect children.

    D. Sadly, 70 percent of women getting an abortion in the United States identify themselves as Christians at the time of the abortion.[5]

---

[5] Alan Guttmacher Institute, Characteristics of U.S. Abortion Patients, 2008 cited on abortionblackout.com

Lesson 2 — Why Should I Care about Philosophy?

- E. This shows the degree to which men and women who have a philosophy putting pleasure first are doing what they want and not worrying about the consequences—even when it means killing an unborn baby.

- F. Christians should not be getting abortions.

- G. I'm not saying God is mad at you or that He won't love you anymore if you've ever had an abortion.

- H. God dealt with sin when He poured out His wrath on Jesus on the cross, and He isn't dealing with sin anymore.

- I. God is a good God who is full of mercy and unfailing love.

- J. So, I'm not condemning women who have had an abortion.

- K. God's grace is more than enough to cover all of your sins.

- L. I'm simply saying that abortion is wrong.

- M. Abortion kills innocent children, and there is no room in a Christian philosophy for the tolerance of abortion.

XII. We can't just entertain the information that suits us.

- A. A ragbag collection of truths and half-truths will never add up to a unified worldview that is godly and righteous.

- B. We need to get our philosophy from the Word of God.

- C. Filtering our lives through Scripture and basing our decisions on the philosophy that comes from the Word will keep us on the right path and prevent us from falling into hypocrisy.

- D. The reason there is such a wide variance in convictions among Christians is that not everyone is getting their philosophy from the Word.

XIII. Your citizenship in heaven can have more influence over you than your upbringing or the worldly ideas that surround you.

- A. As the Apostle Paul said, **"Let God be true, and every man a liar"** (Rom. 3:4).

- B. Even the religious instruction you received should be tossed aside if it doesn't conform to the Word of God.

- C. You might have been taught that God is angry and that He is just waiting to punish you the moment you step out of line or that He uses sickness to correct you.

- D. Those are wrong doctrines, and they will allow the Enemy to steal from you.

- E. Your beliefs need to be established upon what the Word says, not upon someone else's interpretation of it.

XIV. The Bible isn't just another book; it is a supernatural book through which God speaks to you.

- A. The Word of God is true.

- B. Once you get into the true Word of God and let the Holy Spirit instruct you, you'll see that it is the greatest revelation the world has ever been given.

- C. The Bible is a tremendous gift from God that contains the greatest philosophy known, and if you base your life upon the Word, you'll get supernatural results.

Lesson 2 — Why Should I Care about Philosophy?

TEACHER'S GUIDE

1. Everyone has a philosophy, whether they acknowledge it or not, and all philosophies produce fruit. A philosophy is a filter that determines how you act. When Proverbs says that you will be as you think in your heart (Prov. 23:7), I believe it's talking about your philosophy. The system of thought that you hold in your heart determines the course of your life. As I've said, your life right now is a product of the way you have been thinking.

   1a. Discussion Question: Why do you think the system of thought that you hold in your heart determines the course of your life?
   (Discussion question)

2. People don't generally desire divorce, bankruptcy, or sickness, so experiencing those things doesn't mean you desired them. It just means you had a philosophy that made you susceptible to those experiences. For instance, you could have been thinking *Lord, I'm only human. I'm just a man*, instead of thinking about who you are in Christ and conforming your thoughts to the Word, which says, **"Greater is he that is in you, than he that is in the world"** (1 John 4:4). Forgetting that you are a child of God and thinking that you are a nobody makes you susceptible to attacks from the Enemy.

   2a. Discussion Question: Why shouldn't you think you're only human?
   (Discussion question)

   2b. Discussion Question: Read 1 John 4:4. Why is it better to conform your thoughts the Word, which says, **"Greater is he that is in you, than he that is in the world"**?
   (Discussion question)

3. The root word (*philosophos*) for the Greek word translated **"philosophy"** in Paul's admonition to the Colossians (*philosophia*) was used in only one other place in Scripture. It was when Paul was speaking to the Greeks, and it says, **"Then certain philosophers [*philosophos*] of the Epicureans, and of the Stoicks, encountered him. And some said, What will this babbler say? other some, He seemeth to be a setter forth of strange gods: because he preached unto them Jesus, and the resurrection"** (Acts 17:18, brackets mine). We are still encountering these philosophies today. Epicureans derived their teaching from the philosopher Epicurus who founded a school in Athens, Greece, around 300 B.C. Epicurus taught that "the world is a random combination of atoms and that pleasure is the highest good."[1] His followers soon devolved into a materialistic group, a lot like the materialistic and pleasure-seeking society that the modern philosophy of evolution is giving rise to. Having fun and seeking pleasure pretty much sums up most people's philosophy today. In fact, the theory of evolution is simply a new presentation of the Epicurean belief that life is the result of the random collision of atoms. A Christian philosophy puts relationship with God above pleasure. I have a philosophy that pleasing God is more important than pleasing myself. If seeking God means doing something that isn't pleasurable, I'll suffer the consequences because I don't make my decisions based on what makes me feel good. The world promotes buying the biggest house you possibly can, owning the biggest car, and indulging every sense you have. The world's philosophy is "Get all you can, can all you get, and sit on your can." But God teaches that it is more blessed to give than to receive (Acts 20:35), and Jesus said that a man's life does not consist in the abundance of possessions (Luke 12:15). People are more important than possessions, and I want to make my life count. That means serving others, not gathering stuff together for myself.

   3a. Discussion Question: Give examples of how what Epicurus taught is still being taught today.
   (Discussion question)

   3b. A Christian philosophy puts relationship with God above _____.
   (Pleasure)

   3c. Discussion Question: What's the problem with making decisions based on what makes you feel good?
   (Discussion question)

   3d. Read Acts 20:35 and Luke 12:15. It is more _____ to give than to receive. A man's _____ does not consist in the abundance of possessions.
   (Blessed/Life)

---

[1] Definition from Princeton's WordNet, online at http://wordnet.princeton.edu/

Lesson 2 Why Should I Care about Philosophy?

4. The second part of Epicurus' philosophy was to avoid pain at all costs.[2] Unfortunately, pain is sometimes necessary to accomplish good. Freedom, for example, has a cost. A lot of pain was endured during World War II to provide the freedom that we enjoy today. A self-seeking philosophy doesn't allow for sacrifice like that; it leads people to put their heads in the sand and hope that problems will just go away. Today people are hoping their problems will go away just like Europe hoped Hitler would. People are putting their heads in the sand and ignoring attacks upon society—such as abortion and the promotion of the "lesbian, gay, bisexual, and transsexual" agenda—in the hopes that they will all go away. But those attacks aren't going away unless individuals in society make a stand for morality. Ignoring these warning signs is a recipe for disaster. It's a wrong philosophy.

    4a.   Discussion Question: Why is it that to accomplish good, pain is sometimes unavoidable?
(Discussion question)

    4b.   Why can't we just put our heads in the sand and hope that the moral problems of the world will go away?
(Because the world's problems aren't going away unless individuals in society make a stand for morality)

5. The reference to **"Stoicks"** in the scripture from Acts refers to the Greek philosopher Zeno who founded a competing school of thought at the same time as Epicurus. The Stoics believed that virtue was sufficient for happiness and that the ultimate goal in life was to become free from the fluctuations of emotion—pleasure or pain.[3] They sought to calmly accept all circumstances as the unavoidable result of divine will or the natural order.[4] A lot of Christians today are stoic in their philosophy. The extreme-sovereignty-of-God doctrine is a perversion of Scripture that falsely teaches that everything that happens in life is preordained by God. It's nothing more than a stoical worldview. People who teach that doctrine think absolutely everything that happens in life is God's will—even evil things such as murder, rape, and sickness. Those people believe that even if God didn't cause the event directly, He must have allowed it to happen because He is all-powerful, and He could have stopped it if it was against His will. It's true that God is all-powerful, but His Word teaches that He has no part in evil (James 1:13-17). It is the devil who comes into our lives to steal, kill, and destroy. God only comes to give us life, and to give us life abundantly (John 10:10). Everything that happens in life is not the result of God's will. Some things are just attacks from the devil. Thankfully, God has given us the authority to rebuke and resist those attacks. God's Word says, **"Submit yourselves therefore to God. Resist the devil, and he will flee from you"** (James 4:7).

    5a.   What did the Stoics believe?
(They believed that virtue was sufficient for happiness and that the ultimate goal in life was to become free from the fluctuations of emotion—pleasure or pain)

    5b.   What group of people tends to be stoic?
A. Philosophers
B. Christians
C. Drill sergeants
D. Pastors
E. Boxers
(B. Christians)

    5c.   Give an example and explain it.
(The extreme-sovereignty-of-God doctrine. Because the people who teach that doctrine think absolutely everything that happens in life is God's will—even evil things such as murder, rape, and sickness)

    5d.   Read James 1:13-17 and John 10:10. Everything that happens in life is _____ the result of God's will.
(Not)

    5e.   Read James 4:7. True or false: We shouldn't submit to everything that happens in life.
(True)

---

[2] Andrew Wommack, Living Commentary Bible software, note for Acts 17:18.
[3] From the Stanford Encyclopedia of Philosophy, online at http://plato.stanford.edu/entries/stoicism/
[4] The *American Heritage College Dictionary*, 3rd Edition, "stoic."

LESSON 2 — WHY SHOULD I CARE ABOUT PHILOSOPHY?

6. Any teaching that doesn't conform to the Word of God is false, no matter how popular it may be. You have to evaluate your philosophy and make sure it is based on the Word of God, and not on the philosophies of this world or the traditions of men. Everything that God has shown me has helped to form my philosophy. It is all woven together into one dominant way of thinking. The Word of God has dictated my philosophy, and my response to life is in turn dictated by my philosophy. So, the blessings in my life are simply a result of filtering life through God's perspective.

    6a.   Popular teaching does not make it what?
           A. Practical
           B. Understandable
           C. True
           D. Comprehensive
           E. Simple
           (C. True)

    6b.   Discussion Question: How has what God has shown you helped form your philosophy?
           (Discussion question)

7. Stoicism and Epicureanism aren't the only philosophies out there. The philosophy that your parents had when they raised you also has an impact on your belief system—not merely their worldview, but the philosophy they instilled in you by the things they said, by the way they treated you, and through the behavior you witnessed. All of us have been influenced by the philosophies that we were raised with or that we picked up through experiences. Racism is an example of a philosophy that is handed down from one generation to the next—it's a kind of tradition. If children raised in a racist environment don't replace those lies with the truth, they will incorporate prejudice into their worldview, and it will affect their experience of life.

    7a.   Besides Stoicism and Epicureanism, what else could have had an impact on your belief system?
           (The philosophy that your parents had—not merely their worldview, but the philosophy they instilled in you by the things they said, by the way they treated you, and through the behavior you witnessed)

    7b.   What would happen to children raised in a racist environment if they don't replace those lies with the truth?
           (They will incorporate prejudice into their worldview, and it will affect their experience of life)

8. America had a tradition of racism that was hard to overcome. Martin Luther King Jr. made a stand for morality and led our country through some difficult times. He stood up for a Christian philosophy that says all men are created equal, and he helped to change a nation. Today society often fails to recognize that Martin Luther King Jr. wasn't merely a civil rights leader; he was a Christian leader. In the same way that society persecuted Martin Luther King Jr. for his stand against racism, I can guarantee that Christians are not going to be universally loved for making a stand against current wrongs in our society. Abortion is a heinous crime, but the majority of society supports it—and there are elements who promote it aggressively. Still, we shouldn't be focused on how other people are going to respond. Our goal should be to do the will of God and to stand for what is right—that's a Christian philosophy. Proverbs says, **"Righteousness exalteth a nation: but sin is a reproach to any people"** (Prov. 14:34). *Righteousness* is conforming your character and conduct to a right standard. It's conforming to the Word of God, not to philosophies of this world and the traditions of men. What the majority of society says is or is not right is irrelevant. The majority is often wrong. The Word has to be the standard we build our philosophy upon.

    8a.   It's a guarantee that you will not be universally _____ for making a stand against current wrongs in our society.
           (Loved)

    8b.   Discussion Question: Why do you think that is?
           (Discussion question)

    8c.   Read Proverbs 13:34. What is righteousness?
           (It is conforming your character and conduct to a right standard. It's conforming to the Word of God, not to philosophies of this world and the traditions of men)

Lesson 2   Why Should I Care about Philosophy?

9. Too many of those who call themselves Christians aren't building their philosophy on the Word. Some of them might not truly be born again, but some sincere Christians just haven't become disciples of the Lord Jesus. They haven't learned what the Word says, and they aren't following Him. They haven't made an effort to conform their hearts and actions to a godly standard of righteousness. All they have done is accept Jesus to avoid going to hell. They often have philosophies that are completely contrary to the Word of God, but they don't see any problem with that. Obviously, if you have a philosophy that is contrary to the Word of God, you don't have a Christian philosophy. Some of this is the fault of the church.

    9a.   What's one reason that too many of those who call themselves Christians aren't building their philosophy on the Word?
(Some of them might not truly be born again)

    9b.   If you have a philosophy that is contrary to the Word of God, then obviously what?
(You don't have a Christian philosophy)

    9c.   True or false: The church is to blame for all this.
(False)

10. We have been preaching salvation in order to go to heaven when we die, but we haven't been making disciples as the Lord commanded us. So, some people are truly ignorant of God's values, but others are willfully ignorant. Those people are choosing not to subscribe to God's viewpoint, because it doesn't fit with their lifestyles. Either way, ignorance isn't good for us. God loves us no matter what because He doesn't relate to us based on our performance, but ignorance isn't going to excuse us from the devil's attacks. The world's philosophy says that "what we don't know won't hurt us," but the truth is that ignorance kills (Hos. 4:6).

    10a.   Discussion Question: Besides abortion and homosexuality, what lifestyles do people hold to instead of subscribing to God's viewpoint?
(Discussion question)

    10b.   Read Hosea 4:6. From this verse, what do you learn about ignorance?
(Ignorance kills)

11. You can see the influences of Epicurean philosophy in those who aim to please themselves no matter the consequences. The overwhelming majority of abortions are performed on women who aren't married. They are having sexual relations outside of marriage and are using abortion as a form of birth control. God's command restricting sex to a marriage relationship is given to protect you emotionally and to protect children. Sadly, 70 percent of women getting an abortion in the United States identify themselves as Christians at the time of the abortion.[5] This shows the degree to which men and women who have a philosophy putting pleasure first are doing what they want and not worrying about the consequences—even when it means killing an unborn baby. Christians should not be getting abortions. I'm not saying God is mad at you or that He won't love you anymore if you've ever had an abortion. God dealt with sin when He poured out His wrath on Jesus on the cross, and He isn't dealing with sin anymore. God is a good God who is full of mercy and unfailing love. So, I'm not condemning women who have had an abortion. God's grace is more than enough to cover all of your sins. I'm simply saying that abortion is wrong. Abortion kills innocent children, and there is no room in a Christian philosophy for the tolerance of abortion.

    11a.   True or false: God is not mad at you if you've had an abortion.
(True)

    11b.   What did God pour out on Jesus on the cross to deal with sin?
A. Wrath
B. Grace
C. Power
D. All of the above
E. None of the above
(A. Wrath)

---

[5] Alan Guttmacher Institute, Characteristics of U.S. Abortion Patients, 2008 cited on abortionblackout.com

Lesson 2 — Why Should I Care about Philosophy?

11c. There is no room in a Christian philosophy for the _____ of abortion.
(Tolerance)

12. We can't just entertain the information that suits us. A ragbag collection of truths and half-truths will never add up to a unified worldview that is godly and righteous. We need to get our philosophy from the Word of God. Filtering our lives through Scripture and basing our decisions on the philosophy that comes from the Word will keep us on the right path and prevent us from falling into hypocrisy. The reason there is such a wide variance in convictions among Christians is that not everyone is getting their philosophy from the Word.

12a. True or false: A ragbag collection of truths and half-truths could add up to a unified worldview that is godly and righteous.
(False)

13. Your citizenship in heaven can have more influence over you than your upbringing or the worldly ideas that surround you. As the Apostle Paul said, **"Let God be true, and every man a liar"** (Rom. 3:4). Even the religious instruction you received should be tossed aside if it doesn't conform to the Word of God. You might have been taught that God is angry and that He is just waiting to punish you the moment you step out of line or that He uses sickness to correct you. Those are wrong doctrines, and they will allow the Enemy to steal from you. Your beliefs need to be established upon what the Word says, not upon someone else's interpretation of it.

13a. Discussion Question: How can your citizenship in heaven have more influence over you than your upbringing or the worldly ideas that surround you?
(Discussion question)

13b. What do your beliefs need to be established upon?
(What the Word says, not upon someone else's interpretation of it)

14. The Bible isn't just another book; it is a supernatural book through which God speaks to you. The Word of God is true. Once you get into the true Word of God and let the Holy Spirit instruct you, you'll see that it is the greatest revelation the world has ever been given. The Bible is a tremendous gift from God that contains the greatest philosophy known, and if you base your life upon the Word, you'll get supernatural results.

14a. What will happen once you get into the true Word of God and let the Holy Spirit instruct you?
(You'll see that it is the greatest revelation the world has ever been given)

14b. You'll get supernatural results if you what?
(If you base your life upon the Word)

Lesson 2 — Why Should I Care about Philosophy?

DISCIPLESHIP QUESTIONS

1. Discussion Question: Why do you think the system of thought that you hold in your heart determines the course of your life?

2. Discussion Question: Why shouldn't you think you're only human?

3. Discussion Question: Read 1 John 4:4. Why is it better to conform your thoughts the Word, which says, **"Greater is he that is in you, than he that is in the world"?**

4. Discussion Question: Give examples of how what Epicurus taught is still being taught today.

5. A Christian philosophy puts relationship with God above _____.

6. Discussion Question: What's the problem with making decisions based on what makes you feel good?

7. Read Acts 20:35 and Luke 12:15. It is more _____ to give than to receive. A man's _____ does not consist in the abundance of possessions.

8. Discussion Question: Why is it that to accomplish good, pain is sometimes unavoidable?

SCRIPTURES TO USE WITH QUESTIONS

PROVERBS 23:7
For as he thinketh in his heart, so is he: Eat and drink, saith he to thee; but his heart is not with thee.

1 JOHN 4:4
Ye are of God, little children, and have overcome them: because greater is he that is in you, than he that is in the world.

ACTS 17:18
Then certain philosophers of the Epicureans, and of the Stoicks, encountered him. And some said, What will this babbler say? other some, He seemeth to be a setter forth of strange gods: because he preached unto them Jesus, and the resurrection.

ACTS 20:35
I have shewed you all things, how that so labouring ye ought to support the weak, and to remember the words of the Lord Jesus, how he said, It is more blessed to give than to receive.

LUKE 12:15
And he said unto them, Take heed, and beware of covetousness: for a man's life consisteth not in the abundance of the things which he possesseth.

Lesson 2 — Why Should I Care about Philosophy?

DISCIPLESHIP QUESTIONS

9. Why can't we just put our heads in the sand and hope that the moral problems of the world will go away?

10. What did the Stoics believe?

11. What group of people tends to be stoic?
    A. Philosophers
    B. Christians
    C. Drill sergeants
    D. Pastors
    E. Boxers

12. Give an example and explain it.

13. Read James 1:13-17 and John 10:10. Everything that happens in life is _____ the result of God's will.

14. Read James 4:7. True or false: We shouldn't submit to everything that happens in life.

15. Popular teaching does not make it what?
    A. Practical
    B. Understandable
    C. True
    D. Comprehensive
    E. Simple

SCRIPTURES TO USE WITH QUESTIONS

JAMES 1:13-17
Let no man say when he is tempted, I am tempted of God: for God cannot be tempted with evil, neither tempteth he any man: **[14]** *But every man is tempted, when he is drawn away of his own lust, and enticed.* **[15]** *Then when lust hath conceived, it bringeth forth sin: and sin, when it is finished, bringeth forth death.* **[16]** *Do not err, my beloved brethren.* **[17]** *Every good gift and every perfect gift is from above, and cometh down from the Father of lights, with whom is no variableness, neither shadow of turning.*

JOHN 10:10
The thief cometh not, but for to steal, and to kill, and to destroy: I am come that they might have life, and that they might have it more abundantly.

JAMES 4:7
Submit yourselves therefore to God. Resist the devil, and he will flee from you.

LESSON 2 — WHY SHOULD I CARE ABOUT PHILOSOPHY?

DISCIPLESHIP QUESTIONS

16. Discussion Question: How has what God has shown you helped form your philosophy?

17. Besides Stoicism and Epicureanism, what else could have had an impact on your belief system?

18. What would happen to children raised in a racist environment if they don't replace those lies with the truth?

19. It's a guarantee that you will not be universally _____ for making a stand against current wrongs in our society.

20. Discussion Question: Why do you think that is?

21. Read Proverbs 14:34. What is righteousness?

22. What's one reason that too many of those who call themselves Christians aren't building their philosophy on the Word?

23. If you have a philosophy that is contrary to the Word of God, then obviously what?

24. True or false: The church is to blame for all this.

SCRIPTURES TO USE WITH QUESTIONS

PROVERBS 14:34
Righteousness exalteth a nation: but sin is a reproach to any people.

Lesson 2 — Why Should I Care about Philosophy?

DISCIPLESHIP QUESTIONS

25. Discussion Question: Besides abortion and homosexuality, what lifestyles do people hold to instead of subscribing to God's viewpoint?

26. Read Hosea 4:6. From this verse, what do you learn about ignorance?

27. True or false: God is not mad at you if you've had an abortion.

28. What did God pour out on Jesus on the cross to deal with sin?
    A. Wrath
    B. Grace
    C. Power
    D. All of the above
    E. None of the above

29. There is no room in a Christian philosophy for the _____ of abortion.

30. True or false: A ragbag collection of truths and half-truths could add up to a unified worldview that is godly and righteous.

31. Discussion Question: How can your citizenship in heaven have more influence over you than your upbringing or the worldly ideas that surround you?

SCRIPTURES TO USE WITH QUESTIONS

HOSEA 4:6
My people are destroyed for lack of knowledge: because thou hast rejected knowledge, I will also reject thee, that thou shalt be no priest to me: seeing thou hast forgotten the law of thy God, I will also forget thy children.

ROMANS 3:4
God forbid: yea, let God be true, but every man a liar; as it is written, That thou mightest be justified in thy sayings, and mightest overcome when thou art judged.

LESSON 2 — WHY SHOULD I CARE ABOUT PHILOSOPHY?

DISCIPLESHIP QUESTIONS

SCRIPTURES TO USE WITH QUESTIONS

32. What do your beliefs need to be established upon?

33. What will happen once you get into the true Word of God and let the Holy Spirit instruct you?

34. You'll get supernatural results if you what?

Lesson 2 — Why Should I Care about Philosophy?

ANSWER KEY

1. *Discussion question*
2. *Discussion question*
3. *Discussion question*
4. *Discussion question*
5. Pleasure
6. *Discussion question*
7. Blessed/Life
8. *Discussion question*
9. Because the world's problems aren't going away unless individuals in society make a stand for morality
10. They believed that virtue was sufficient for happiness and that the ultimate goal in life was to become free from the fluctuations of emotion—pleasure or pain
11. B. Christians
12. The extreme-sovereignty-of-God doctrine. Because the people who teach that doctrine think absolutely everything that happens in life is God's will—even evil things such as murder, rape, and sickness
13. Not
14. True
15. C. True
16. *Discussion question*
17. The philosophy that your parents had—not merely their worldview, but the philosophy they instilled in you by the things they said, by the way they treated you, and through the behavior you witnessed
18. They will incorporate prejudice into their worldview, and it will affect their experience of life
19. Loved
20. *Discussion question*
21. It is conforming your character and conduct to a right standard. It's conforming to the Word of God, not to philosophies of this world and the traditions of men
22. Some of them might not truly be born again
23. You don't have a Christian philosophy
24. False
25. *Discussion question*
26. Ignorance kills
27. True
28. A. Wrath
29. Tolerance
30. False
31. *Discussion question*
32. What the Word says, not upon someone else's interpretation of it
33. You'll see that it is the greatest revelation the world has ever been given
34. If you base your life upon the Word

Is the Bible True?

*For the L*ORD *seeth not as man seeth; for man looketh on the outward appearance, but the L*ORD *looketh on the heart.*

1 SAMUEL 16:7B

Although people focus on behavior and appearance, the Bible approaches change from the heart level. Humans want to deal with external things, but God's way is to deal with the heart. The heart is the source of your external behaviors. It's where your speech and actions come from (Luke 6:45). Man puts emphasis on cleaning up the outward appearance, but God says clean the inside, and the outside will be clean also (Matt. 23:26). If you want your external circumstances to change, you have to go to the heart and change your philosophy. The way you do that is by meditating on the Word. Religion consists of man's thoughts about God, but the Bible isn't a compilation of people's thoughts—it contains God's thoughts, and His philosophy, for you.

Satan has been pretty successful in robbing many Christians of the blessings that God has provided. The reason he has been so successful is that our philosophy is wrong. We have developed philosophies based on our upbringing and the ungodly influences of this world rather than on the Word of God. By challenging the way we think, Satan comes to steal and to deprive us of what God has given. This is evident even from his first dealings with mankind. Concerning the dangers of wrong thinking, the Apostle Paul said,

> *But I fear, lest by any means, as the serpent beguiled Eve through his subtlety, so your minds should be corrupted from the simplicity that is in Christ.*
>
> 2 CORINTHIANS 11:3

And the way Satan came against Adam and Eve is the same way he comes against us today. The devil doesn't have any new tricks; he's still doing the same old thing. It's not like he has a million different ways of tempting people. His only method always boils down to lies and deception.

Temptation falls into just three basic categories: **"the lust of the flesh," "the lust of the eyes,"** and **"the pride of life"** (1 John 2:16). Those are the areas Adam and Eve were tempted in (Gen. 3:6), those are the areas Satan tried to tempt Jesus in (Luke 4:1-13), and they are the same three things the Enemy is trying to tempt us with today. You're being tempted in exactly the same ways that Adam and Eve were tempted. The devil just takes the same old stuff and repackages it, which is helpful in a way because we can avoid making the same mistakes Adam and Eve made by looking at the tactics Satan used against them.

The first thing we notice is that Satan is subtle. Scripture says, **"Now the serpent was more subtil than any beast of the field which the Lord God had made"** (Gen. 3:1). We know that Satan was behind using the serpent to lie, because the Word says that Satan is the father of all lies (John 8:44). The devil created lying, and every time someone lies, they are under the influence of the devil. So, this serpent came and lied to Adam and Eve.

I already pointed out that Satan didn't use some huge animal to intimidate Eve and force her to eat the forbidden fruit. He didn't have any power whatsoever to force Adam and Eve into disobeying God. Instead, what he did was choose the subtlest animal—the most cunning, the craftiest, and the sliest creature. Why? Because it was a battle of wits. The battle against temptation has always been in the mind.

You'll sometimes hear people talk about "spiritual warfare" in the sense of going out and doing battle in the heavens. It's a misunderstanding of a verse that says you are battling evil powers in **"heavenly places"** (Eph. 6:11-12, *New King James Version*). People have actually chartered planes so they could "take their prayers to the sky," or they have gone to the top of skyscrapers to do battle "in heaven." That isn't what this passage of Scripture is talking about. The battle against the Enemy isn't somewhere out in the atmosphere; the battle is right between your ears.

Satan comes at you through your thoughts with lies and deception. It's the same way he has always operated, and that's the reason he chose the serpent to speak to Eve. It was the most cunning, craftiest, and sliest creature. It was able to twist and to deceive better than any other animal, so Satan motivated the snake to go and tempt Adam and Eve.

This is really significant. It shows how deception was Satan's only weapon. It demonstrates that he doesn't have the power to make people do anything. **Satan can't do anything without your consent and cooperation.** You have to reject his lies. Quit consenting to his deception, quit cooperating with him, and you'll leave him powerless. He won't be able to steal your health, your finances, or your peace of mind. When Satan came against Adam and Eve through the serpent, he said,

Yea, hath God said, Ye shall not eat of every tree of the garden?

GENESIS 3:1B

Satan's primary method of attack is to challenge the Word of God: "Did God *really* say that?" Satan asks, "Are you sure He didn't mean something else?" Satan always challenges the Word, asking, "Is the Word really true?" The answer is YES! If Adam and Eve had responded "Yes, God did say that—now, get out of here," that would have been the end of the story. There would have been no Fall, no sin, and suffering wouldn't have entered the world.

This reveals a fundamental principle of establishing a Christian philosophy, or a Christian way of thinking: Never forget that God's Word is always true. If you compromise on this point, Satan is going to rob you blind, and nothing else is going to work. God's Word is the only sure foundation to build a Christian philosophy upon.

LESSON 3 IS THE BIBLE TRUE?

Here's another tip: You can save yourself a lot of trouble by not even getting into conversations with the devil. When he attacks the Word, don't bother arguing with him. Just state the truth and move on. But Eve didn't do that; she decided to have a chat with the serpent and said,

> *We may eat of the fruit of the trees of the garden: But of the fruit of the tree which is in the midst of the garden, God hath said, Ye shall not eat of it, neither shall ye touch it, lest ye die.*
> GENESIS 3:2-3

The problem with what Eve said is that God never said they couldn't *touch* the fruit; He said not to *eat* it. Eve added to what God had said, and she thought that if she even touched the fruit, she would die. When she was enticed by the lust of her eyes and flesh to reach out and touch it and nothing happened, she thought maybe nothing would happen if she ate it too. She discovered that the thoughts she added to what God had said were false—she didn't die when she touched the fruit—and it tempted her to question all of what she believed about God's commands.

This same thing is happening today. Religion has added to the Word of God and nullified it in order to hand down traditions. It's exactly what Jesus accused the scribes and the Pharisees of doing (Mark 7:13). Religion is always adding rules and regulations to the Word of God. It's saying, "Don't even touch it or you'll die!" Religion creates manmade traditions, and when people break the manmade traditions and don't die, they go ahead and break God's Word, too, thinking that everything was just a hoax.

For example, some religious systems today are saying women shouldn't wear makeup or jewelry—which is a misunderstanding of the scripture that says women shouldn't be concerned with outward adorning but rather be concerned with the beauty of their hearts. The scripture says not to be concerned with the **"outward adorning of plaiting the hair, and of wearing of gold, or of putting on of apparel; But let it be the hidden man of the heart"** (1 Pet. 3:3-4). If you interpret this to mean that there should be no plaiting of the hair or wearing of gold, then you have to say there shouldn't be any wearing of apparel either. Obviously, God doesn't want you running around without any clothes on. The intent of this scripture is to encourage people to focus on the condition of their hearts instead of their outward appearance.

Preaching that women should wear their hair in a certain way and dress a certain way or God won't love them anymore isn't true. When a young girl who has grown up hearing those things fails to live up to the supposed dress code but doesn't feel any different (judgment from God)—because God *does* still love her—she calls into question everything she has ever learned about God. This is how religion and the traditions of men can nullify the Word of God.

Satan didn't come right out and say, "Hey, Adam and Eve, eat this forbidden fruit." No, he craftily attacked the Word by asking, "Did God *really* say…?" He cast doubt by criticizing what God had said. Similarly, Satan's biggest triumph in recent centuries has been to make it unfashionable to believe in and trust the Word of God. The world system, inspired by the devil, has come against the Word and put doubt in people's minds about its accuracy and relevance, so the majority of people in society are off doing their own thing. But the doubt and uncertainty Satan has raised are all lies and deception.

Christians have to establish in their hearts that the Bible is the inspired Word of God. As I will show later, the Word is accurate, it is God breathed, and it is God inspired. If you ever start thinking the Bible is merely a book written by men *about* God, Satan is going to eat your lunch and pop the bag. You'll be in serious trouble if you ever adopt the mindset that the Bible has some truth in it but that it also has all kinds of error—leading you to go through and only pull out the parts that *you* think are relevant. If you do that, Satan will have you as surely as he had Adam and Eve.

I think the reason Satan tempted Eve instead of Adam was that Adam heard God's command directly. Genesis says, **"And the L**ORD **God commanded the man, saying, Of every tree of the garden thou mayest freely eat: But of the tree of the knowledge of good and evil, thou shalt not eat of it: for in the day that thou eatest thereof thou shalt surely die"** (Gen. 2:16-17). The next verses describe how God decided Adam shouldn't be alone, and He created Eve to be a companion for Adam and instituted marriage between a man and a woman. So, God gave the command not to eat the forbidden fruit before Eve was even formed, which means she might never have actually heard God give the command.

Any time you have one person repeating what someone else has told them, there is the possibility that they won't repeat it correctly. They might leave something out or add something that the first person never said. I remember playing a game like that as a kid. A bunch of people would line up in a row, and the first person would whisper a phrase to the next person in line. The message was passed down from person to person until you reached the end of the line, but each person only spoke the phrase once. The person couldn't repeat it to make sure it was heard correctly. By the time the last spoke the phrase out loud, it wouldn't even resemble the original statement.

Similarly, Adam heard God in an audible voice tell him not to eat of the Tree of the Knowledge of Good and Evil, but Eve got her information secondhand from Adam. It would have been much harder for the serpent to convince Adam of what God did or didn't say, because Adam heard God directly. So, it was easier for the devil to make Eve doubt that Adam had repeated God's command accurately than it would have been to make Adam doubt what he had heard.

This story shows that you need to get your philosophy from God directly and not depend upon other people to repeat it for you. You need to personalize the Word and make it real to you. It can't be just a book written to people in general but not necessarily to you in particular; you have to believe that the Bible is God's Word to *you*. The majority of people read the Bible like it's an interesting book about God, but they don't read it like it is God speaking to them. The Holy Spirit will use the words in the Bible to speak directly to you, and you have to read the Word with a sense of expectancy that God is going to speak to you through it.

I can't tell you how many people I have dealt with over the years who knew what God's Word says, but they were leaning on their own wisdom. They thought their opinion was better than God's, and they were doing things their own way. Some of those people crashed and burned before they recognized that God was right, but they didn't have to learn by the school of hard knocks; they could've just believed the Word of God. The Bible says,

> *All scripture is given by inspiration of God, and is profitable for doctrine, for reproof, for correction, for instruction in righteousness: That the man of God may be perfect, throughly furnished unto all good works.*
> 2 TIMOTHY 3:16-17

God has spoken to me through thousands of scriptures as I have prayed and asked Him for wisdom. He has used what is written in the Bible to speak directly to me. For instance, God has shown me how

Moses' desire to accomplish God's plan in his own strength cost him forty years in the wilderness, and the nation of Israel spent an extra thirty years in bondage. Those things happened to Moses, but God has taken the scriptures and spoken them to me. He brought the words alive and gave me revelation knowledge that impacted my heart and shaped part of my Christian philosophy. The Bible is a book *from* God, He speaks to me through it, and I believe in the inspiration of Scripture with all of my heart.

God's Word will change you to the degree that you let it dominate your thoughts and life. I certainly haven't renewed my mind perfectly, but I'm also a long way from where I started. God's Word is working in my life. It has changed me, and I see the supernatural power of God as a result of believing what the Word says. God has been speaking to me through His Word for more than forty years—ever since He told me that the way to find His perfect will for my life was to make myself a living sacrifice and to renew my mind by conforming it to the truths in His Word (Rom. 12:1-2).

The easiest way to prove to yourself that the Bible is God's Word and that He will speak to you through it is just to read it. Begin by reading the entire New Testament. You might not understand everything the first time, but the Bible is its own commentary, and the more you read, the more you will understand. Approach it with a sincere heart and say, "God, if this is really inspired by You and it isn't just the thoughts of men about You, then speak to me through it." If you pray in that way and remain open to the possibility that God will speak to you, I guarantee you will be inspired by God. The author of Hebrews wrote,

> *For the word of God is quick, and powerful, and sharper than any twoedged sword, piercing even to the dividing asunder of soul and spirit, and of the joints and marrow, and is a discerner of the thoughts and intents of the heart.*
>
> HEBREWS 4:12

The Word of God is alive, and it will come alive for us if we read it expectantly. Eve was the focus of Satan's temptation because God's command was secondhand to her. But we shouldn't be too hard on Eve for falling into temptation, because she didn't really understand Satan or evil. She didn't know what was at stake. She didn't know what dying was or what the effects of sin would be. In a sense, we can give her a pass because she was innocent and didn't realize what was happening when she succumbed to the lies of the devil.

But we don't get a pass. We live in a fallen world. We have all experienced failure, hurt, pain, and death. We understand the reality of evil. It doesn't make sense for us to bury our heads in the sand and say, "Well, you know, I'm just not sure God speaks to me through the Bible. I'm not sure I can really trust this." We need to come to the resolution that God's Word is alive and that He speaks to us personally through it.

You can't get your knowledge secondhand from me or another preacher. You need to go to the Word and hear God speak to you directly, and then you'll have enough firsthand knowledge to be safe from the deception of false doctrines, traditions of men, and wrong philosophies.

Some Christians are relying on bits and pieces of Scripture that they heard decades ago as children in Sunday school. They are relying on the pastor of their church or another teacher to tell them what the Word says, but they aren't reading it for themselves. Those people are prime targets for the devil. The devil goes about like a roaring lion seeking people to devour, and just like a lion, he looks for the weak (1 Pet. 5:8). He looks for people who don't have the armor and protection of knowing God's Word. This is one reason it is so important to know what God's Word says firsthand.

I'm not saying you can't learn from other people, but it shouldn't be the foundation of your relationship with God. Babies begin by being dependent upon their mothers to feed them, but they don't stay that way. Babies can't grow up to be fully functioning adults if they stay dependent upon other people to feed them. In the same way, all Christians need to learn how to feed themselves from the Word of God. You can't remain dependent upon your pastor to feed you revelation. I know that the cares of this life keep people busy, but if you understand how vital it is to study the Word, you'll find the time to do it.

When the Apostle Peter was getting toward the end of his life, he wrote a letter to believers in which he stressed the inspiration of Scripture and the confidence we can have that God is speaking to us through it. Peter knew that he was going to die shortly, and he was giving final encouragement to the believers. He said,

> *For we have not followed cunningly devised fables, when we made known unto you the power and coming of our Lord Jesus Christ, but were eyewitnesses of his majesty. For he received from God the Father honour and glory, when there came such a voice to him from the excellent glory, This is my beloved Son, in whom I am well pleased. And this voice which came from heaven we heard, when we were with him in the holy mount.*
>
> 2 PETER 1:16-18

Peter was saying, "I'm about to die, but I'm going to write these things down so you can always have this to remember." He was making known that the account he gave of Jesus wasn't something he devised on his own. He wasn't just telling stories. The words he had written down were inspired by God, and they told of Peter's experiences. Peter was with Jesus on the Mount of Transfiguration and heard the audible voice of God say, **"This is my beloved Son, in whom I am well pleased"** (Matt. 17:5). He saw Jesus radiate light that no earthly power could produce. Peter was there! But then Peter wrote,

> *We have also a more sure word of prophecy; whereunto ye do well that ye take heed, as unto a light that shineth in a dark place, until the day dawn, and the day star arise in your hearts: Knowing this first, that no prophecy of the scripture is of any private interpretation. For the prophecy came not in old time by the will of man: but holy men of God spake as they were moved by the Holy Ghost.*
>
> 2 PETER 1:19-21

Peter saw Moses and Elijah talk with Jesus on the Mount of Transfiguration. He saw Jesus radiate light, and he heard God speak with an audible voice from heaven and confirm that Jesus was His Son, but he said we have something even better than that—better than seeing with our eyes or hearing with our ears—we have the written Word of God!

Most people would rather see what Peter saw and hear what he heard than read the Bible. Large crowds will turn out to hear you speak if you advertise that you had a vision and heard the voice of God. People come in droves to hear that sort of thing, but far fewer people show up when you advertise that you're going to be sharing what Scripture says. The reason is that Christian culture puts more emphasis on what they can perceive with their senses than on the Word of God. Peter said you should be doing just the opposite.

LESSON 3   IS THE BIBLE TRUE?

Peter clearly stated that the Word of God was not written by men—it was not of **"any private interpretation."** The Holy Spirit inspired men to write the Scriptures. The Apostle Paul made the same point in his letter to Timothy when he said,

> *All scripture is given by inspiration of God, and is profitable for doctrine, for reproof, for correction, for instruction in righteousness: That the man of God may be perfect, throughly furnished unto all good works.*
> 2 TIMOTHY 3:16-17

The Greek word for **"given by inspiration of God"** is literally translated "divinely breathed."[1] This clearly states that the Word of God didn't come from the thoughts of men. God breathed His thoughts into men, who then put them in writing. The Bible is not a human book; it's God's book written for people.

I believe Scripture, and I've studied it enough to verify for myself that it is the Word of God. I don't need any further proof, but plenty of scholars have also authenticated the Bible from a historical and scientific view. Many books have been written about the accuracy and inspiration of the Bible. I can't cover all of the evidence here, but I want to share a few facts that will give you confidence in the accuracy and inspiration of Scripture.

To begin with, the manuscript evidence supporting the New Testament far outstrips any evidence for secular writings of ancient times. One researcher has said, "The New Testament documents have more manuscripts, earlier manuscripts, and more abundantly supported manuscripts than the best ten pieces of classical literature *combined*."[2]

For example, Caesar's *Gallic War* was written between 58 and 50 B.C. Ten copies of that original work remain, and the earliest was written 900 years after Caesar's day. Livy wrote a 142-volume *History of Rome* sometime between 59 B.C. and A.D. 17, but only 35 volumes survived, in not more than twenty different manuscripts. The text of Tacitus' 14-volume *Histories* and 16-volume *Annals* survives in only two manuscripts written 900 and 1,100 years *after* the original works. The earliest manuscripts of renowned Greek historians Thucydides and Herodotus that are complete enough to be of use to scholars were written more than 1,300 years after the originals.[3]

> THE ABUNDANCE OF ANCIENT MANUSCRIPTS, AND THE NEARNESS OF THEIR COMPOSITION TO THE ACTUAL EVENTS, MAKES THE NEW TESTAMENT THE MOST VERIFIABLE DOCUMENT OF ANTIQUITY.

Homer's *Iliad* is the secular work that has the most supporting evidence, with 643 copies (the earliest being written around 500 years after the original), but it doesn't even compare to the New Testament evidence we have. The number of differences between the copies of the *Iliad* is also greater—even though there are more than twenty times as many New Testament manuscripts being studied and compared.

In contrast to the copies of secular histories given above, *more than 5,600 Greek manuscripts of the New Testament have survived in whole or in part.* Those manuscripts vary in age, the more complete having been written within 150 years, with the earliest manuscript portion written within 30 years of the

---

1   James Strong, *The New Strong's Expanded Exhaustive Concordance of the Bible* (Nashville: Nelson Publishers, 2001), 114. G2315, *theopneustos*.
2   Norman Geisler and Frank Turek, *I Don't Have Enough Faith to Be an Atheist* (Wheaton: Crossway Books, 2004), 225.
3   F.F. Bruce, *The New Testament Documents: Are They Reliable?* 5th ed. rev. (Grand Rapids: The InterVarsity Press, 1988), 16.

original (keep in mind that the New Testament wasn't written as a single book but is composed of many letters written by multiple authors at different times). The fact that so many copies of the New Testament scriptures have survived, combined with the fact that they were written close to the same time as the originals, firmly establishes the historical accuracy of the scriptures we have today.

From a purely human perspective, the chance for error is increased when a document is copied over and over again thousands of times. The more times something is copied, the more errors you should see. This is true in the case of secular works, but not with the Bible. The abundance of ancient New Testament manuscripts have been compared, and there are very few differences—and they contain no differences whatsoever that contradict the Gospel message of Jesus or the historical facts of Christian faith.[4] *Scholars have placed the comparative accuracy between the more than 5,600 manuscripts at 99.5 percent!*[5] This is astounding, and it shows how God has supernaturally preserved the integrity of the Bible through time.

Work	Time Written	Earliest Copies	Time Span between Original and Copy[6]	Number of Copies
Plato	427-347 B.C.	A.D. 900	1,200 years	7
Thucydides	460-400 B.C.	A.D. 900	1,300 years	8
Herodotuc	488-428 B.C.	A.D. 900	1,300 years	8
Caesar	58-50 B.C.	A.D. 900	900 years	10
Livy	59 B.C.- A.D. 17	?	?	20
Tacitus	A.D. 100	A.D. 1100	1,000	20
Aristotle	384-322 B.C.	A.D. 1100	1,400 years	49
Homer (*Iliad*)	900 B.C.	400 B.C.	500 years	643
Greek copies of the New Testament	A.D. 50-100	A.D. 300 and earlier	150[7]	5,686

The nearer in time a copy was made to the original, the more likely, in a purely natural sense, the work is to be correct. Also, the greater number of copies in existence, the easier it is to compare for accuracy. (It should be noted that in addition to the Greek copies of the New Testament, there are thousands more copies of New Testament books produced in other languages during the same timeframe. In fact, researchers have discovered more than 9,000 copies of New Testament manuscripts in other languages—bringing the total number of manuscripts to well over 14,000.) The abundance of ancient manuscripts and the nearness of their composition to the actual events make the New Testament the most verifiable document of antiquity.

Not only do we have copies of the scriptures themselves, but leaders in the early Christian church (often called the Church Fathers) wrote prolifically between A.D. 90 and 160. Their familiarity with the New Testament scriptures we still read today is proven by the fact that *all but eleven verses from the New Testament are quoted in their writings!*[8]

Non-Christians have also given evidence of Jesus as a historical figure in their writings. In A.D. 93, the Jewish historian Flavius Josephus wrote,

---

4   Bruce, *New Testament*, 20.
5   Norman Geisler, *Baker Encyclopedia of Christian Apologetics* (Grand Rapids: Baker Books, 1999), 532.
6   The information in this chart is from Bruce, *New Testament*, 16-20; Geisler, *Baker Encyclopedia*, 527-538; and The Christian Apologetics and Research Ministry online at http://carm.org/manuscript-evidence
7   One small fragment of papyrus that has been discovered, known as the John Rylands papyri, was written only 30 years after the original Gospel of John.
8   Geisler, *Enough Faith*, 229.

Now there was about this time Jesus, a wise man, if it be lawful to call him a man; for he was a doer of wonderful works, a teacher of such men as receive the truth with pleasure. He drew over to him both many of the Jews and many of the Gentiles. He was [the] Christ. And when Pilate, at the suggestion of the principal men amongst us, had condemned him to the cross, those that loved him at the first did not forsake him; for he appeared to them alive again the third day; as the divine prophets had foretold these and ten thousand other wonderful things concerning him. And the tribe of Christians, so named from him, are not extinct at this day.[9]

Josephus also wrote about the persecution and death of James. He said that the Sanhedrin "brought before them the brother of Jesus, who was called Christ, whose name was James, and some others, [or, some of his companions]; and when he had formed an accusation against them as breakers of the law, he delivered them to be stoned."[10]

The Roman historian Tacitus described how the emperor Nero set fire to Rome, and in an effort to deflect the wrath of its citizens, he blamed the fire on the Christians. Tacitus said,

Nero fastened the guilt and inflicted the most exquisite tortures on a class hated for their abominations, called Christians by the populace. Christus, from whom the name had its origin, suffered the extreme penalty during the reign of Tiberius at the hands of one of our procurators, Pontius Pilatus, and a most mischievous superstition, thus checked for the moment, again broke out not only in Judæa, the first source of the evil, but even in Rome, where all things hideous and shameful from every part of the world find their centre and become popular. Accordingly, an arrest was first made of all who pleaded guilty; then, upon their information, an immense multitude was convicted, not so much of the crime of firing the city, as of hatred against mankind. Mockery of every sort was added to their deaths. Covered with the skins of beasts, they were torn by dogs and perished, or were nailed to crosses, or were doomed to the flames and burnt, to serve as a nightly illumination, when daylight had expired.[11]

Without taking into account the evidence contained in the New Testament, we can still show from non-Christian writers that Jesus was a historical figure who lived in Palestine in the early years of the first century, that He gathered followers, and that He was crucified under Pontius Pilate.[12] In fact, within 150 years of Jesus' life, ten non-Christian writers mentioned Jesus. Over that same time span, only nine mentioned the Roman emperor who ruled during Jesus' life—Tiberius Caesar. Not even considering Christian authors, Jesus is more documented than the Roman emperor![13] It is undeniable that Jesus was a man who lived and walked the earth precisely when Scripture says He did.

The discovery of the Dead Sea Scrolls, between 1946 and 1957, in several caves on the shores of the Dead Sea has given us further evidence of the accuracy of the Scriptures that have been handed down to us. Among the Dead Sea Scrolls was an intact copy of the entire book of Isaiah (known as the Great Isaiah Scroll). It is dated at 100 B.C. and is 1,000 years older than the copies that were used to compose the book of Isaiah we read in our Bibles today. After 1,000 years of being copied and recopied by hand, the number of differences between

---

9 Flavius Josephus, *Antiquities of the Jews*, trans. William Whiston (Buffalo: John E. Beardsley, 1895), 18.3.3 online at www.perseus.tufts.edu
10 Josephus, *Antiquities*, 20.9.1.
11 Cornelius Tacitus, *The Annals*. Tacitus, ed. Alfred John Church et. al. (New York: Perseus, Random House, 1942), 15.44 online at www.perseus.tufts.edu
12 Bruce M. Metzger, *The New Testament: Its Background, Growth, and Content*, 15th ed. (Nashville: Abingdon Press, 1980), 78.
13 Geisler, *Enough Faith*, 222.

the Great Isaiah Scroll and our book of Isaiah are miniscule—the variations consisting mostly of spelling mistakes and simple copying errors.[14] The discovery of the Dead Sea Scrolls also proves that the Messianic prophecies we read in Isaiah were definitely written prior to the birth of Jesus, which reinforces the case that Scripture makes for Jesus as the Messiah.

The bottom line is that the Bible has been handed down through the ages with such accuracy that it can't be just a human book. The different copies we have of ancient secular writings have significant differences in them because they were simply copied by men—they weren't inspired and preserved by God. The Bible, on the other hand, has been supernaturally preserved by God, and all of the evidence we have supports that it was written by the inspiration of God. The last words of David, king of Israel and author of the Messianic prophecies in Psalm 22, reveal how the Holy Spirit inspired the men who wrote Scripture:

The Spirit of the Lord spake by me, and his word was in my tongue.

2 SAMUEL 23:2

"We still can't trust the Bible," some will argue, "because it's only a translation, and translations aren't inspired." Well, Jesus didn't share that opinion. He quoted from the Septuagint, which was a Greek translation of the Hebrew Old Testament, and He equated Scripture with words proceeding from the mouth of God (Matt. 4:4). Jesus' use of Scripture throughout the Gospels also shows that He believed it was the final authority, particularly when the devil was challenging God's commands.

Additionally, the Apostle Paul hinged the thrust of his letter to the Galatians on the fact that God made His promise to the seed (singular) of Abraham, instead of to his seed*s* (plural) (Gal. 3:16). Paul made an argument for Jesus as the promised seed of Abraham based on the singular form of one word from a translation of the original scripture—which shows that God is well able to preserve the truth in His Word for us, even through translations.

I spend nearly all of my time studying the Word. Scripture says, **"Thy word have I hid in mine heart, that I might not sin against thee"** (Ps. 119:11). It doesn't tell us to hide historical information about New Testament manuscripts. Nevertheless, scholarship and historical inquiry *do* support the claims of Christianity. Ancient manuscript discoveries show that the scriptures we read today are the same as the original inspired writings, and further research shows that the New Testament is completely unique among the books of antiquity. No other book in history is as verifiable as the Bible—which is exactly what is expected from a book given to us by God.

But even if there was no evidence outside the Bible that the Word of God is inspired, I would still be fully convinced. I don't have enough space to tell you every way that the Word of God has been proven true in my life. It has shown me how to deal with sickness, problems, and rejection. The Word showed me how to find a wife and how to stay married after I found her! I couldn't tell you how many times I have applied the truths from God's Word in my life and watched God's promises come to pass. I have verified for myself beyond all doubt that Scripture is the inspired Word of God, and it is accurate in all of its detail.

People sometimes don't understand how the Bible can say things in different books that seem to be in opposition to one another. Atheists love to pick out scriptures meant to balance one another and pretend that the statements are mutually exclusive, and therefore—they say—the Bible is flawed and

---

14   Geisler, Baker Encyclopedia, 187-189.

Lesson 3 — Is the Bible True?

can't be from God. But that isn't true. Certain passages in the Bible might appear to be contradictions, but opposite statements are sometimes intentional. The Bible is its own commentary, and separate—apparently opposing—scriptures can hold a single truth in balance by presenting it in different ways.

For example, one scripture says, **"For by grace are ye saved through faith; and that not of yourselves: it is the gift of God: Not of works, lest any man should boast"** (Eph. 2:8-9). Another says, **"But wilt thou know, O vain man, that faith without works is dead?"** (James 2:20). Both statements are true, and each is a commentary on the other—they describe the balance of grace and faith.

Every Christian needs to come to the conclusion that the Word of God is accurate and inspired. The Word has to be the foundation of your worldview, or Satan is going to steal from you. The devil is roaming about looking to devour people who doubt God's Word—just as he was able to spoil Eve because she wasn't absolutely convinced that God's command was true. The Word of God is 100 percent trustworthy. Personally, I doubt my little peanut brain before I question the accuracy of the Word. I haven't figured everything out, but I know the problem isn't with the Word—it's with my inability to interpret and comprehend the depths of God.

Accepting God's Word as being absolute truth and authority goes against cultural norms today. In most Western nations, the majority of people who say they believe the Bible is God's Word do not seem to believe that it is accurate and trustworthy enough to base their lives upon it. The majority of believers are getting their philosophy elsewhere, and that's why their worldview doesn't line up with God's perspective.

You will not prosper in the Lord unless you accept the Bible as God's Word. You may have periods in your life when it looks like you are doing fine, but deviating from the Word of God leads to wrong ways of thinking, and eventually, those wrong thought patterns are going to cause you trouble. Eve was fine for a while too—until she began to question God's Word, and then Satan gained a foothold into her life and plunged the entire human race into the destruction we see today.

The best thing you can do for yourself and for your relationship with God is trust that His Word is inspired and accurate in all of its detail. If the Word of God says something is okay, then it's okay—and when His Word says something is wrong, then it's wrong. Basing your worldview on the Bible will lead you to respond to life in a positive way and put you on the path to prosperity. It will also prevent the devil from gaining access to you through wrong philosophies, the traditions of men, or the wisdom and principles of this world. The Word of God is the only sure foundation to build your philosophy on, and it is your ticket to the blessed life.

LESSON 3 — IS THE BIBLE TRUE?

OUTLINE

I. **"For the LORD seeth not as man seeth; for man looketh on the outward appearance, but the LORD looketh on the heart"** (1 Sam. 16:7b).

   A. Although people focus on behavior and appearance, the Bible approaches change from the heart level.

   B. Humans want to deal with external things, but God's way is to deal with the heart.

   C. The heart is the source of your external behaviors.

   D. It's where your speech and actions come from (Luke 6:45).

   E. Man puts emphasis on cleaning up the outward appearance, but God says clean the inside, and the outside will be clean also (Matt. 23:26).

   F. If you want your external circumstances to change, you have to go to the heart and change your philosophy.

   G. The way you do that is by meditating on the Word.

   H. Religion consists of man's thoughts about God, but the Bible isn't a compilation of people's thoughts—it contains God's thoughts, and His philosophy, for you.

II. Satan has been pretty successful in robbing many Christians of the blessings that God has provided.

   A. The reason he has been so successful is that our philosophy is wrong.

   B. We have developed philosophies based on our upbringing and the ungodly influences of this world rather than on the Word of God.

   C. By challenging the way we think, Satan comes to steal and to deprive us of what God has given.

   D. This is evident even from his first dealings with mankind.

   E. Concerning the dangers of wrong thinking, the Apostle Paul said,

   But I fear, lest by any means, as the serpent beguiled Eve through his subtlety, so your minds should be corrupted from the simplicity that is in Christ.

   2 CORINTHIANS 11:3

   F. The devil doesn't have any new tricks; he's still doing the same old thing.

   G. It's not like he has a million different ways of tempting people.

   H. His only method always boils down to lies and deception.

III. Temptation falls into just three basic categories: **"the lust of the flesh," "the lust of the eyes,"** and **"the pride of life"** (1 John 2:16).

   A. Those are the areas Adam and Eve were tempted in (Gen. 3:6), those are the areas Satan tried to tempt Jesus in (Luke 4:1-13), and they are the same three things the Enemy is trying to tempt us with today.

   B. We're being tempted in exactly the same ways that Adam and Eve were tempted.

   C. The devil just takes the same old stuff and repackages it, which is helpful in a way because we can avoid making the same mistakes Adam and Eve made by looking at the tactics Satan used against them.

Lesson 3 — Is the Bible True?

IV. The first thing we notice is that Satan is subtle.

    A. Scripture says, **"Now the serpent was more subtil than any beast of the field which the Lord God had made"** (Gen. 3:1).

    B. We know that Satan was behind using the serpent to lie, because the Word says that Satan is the father of all lies (John 8:44).

    C. The devil created lying, and every time someone lies, they are under the influence of the devil.

    D. Satan didn't have any power whatsoever to force Adam and Eve into disobeying God.

    E. Instead, what he did was choose the subtlest animal—the most cunning, the craftiest, and the sliest creature—because it was a battle of wits.

    F. The battle against temptation has always been in the mind.

    G. We'll sometimes hear people talk about "spiritual warfare" in the sense of going out and doing battle in the heavens.

    H. It's a misunderstanding of a verse that says we are battling evil powers in **"heavenly places"** (Eph. 6:11-12, *New King James Version*).

    I. People have actually chartered planes so they could "take their prayers to the sky," or they have gone to the top of skyscrapers to do battle "in heaven."

    J. That isn't what this passage of Scripture is talking about.

    K. The battle against the Enemy isn't somewhere out in the atmosphere; the battle is right between our ears.

    L. Satan comes at us through our thoughts with lies and deception.

    M. It's the same way he has always operated, and that's the reason he chose the serpent to speak to Eve.

    N. It was able to twist and to deceive better than any other animal, so Satan motivated the snake to go and tempt Adam and Eve.

    O. This is really significant. It shows how deception was Satan's only weapon.

    P. It demonstrates that he doesn't have the power to make people do anything.

    Q. **Satan can't do anything without our consent and cooperation.**

    R. We have to reject his lies.

    S. We need to quit consenting to his deception, quit cooperating with him, and we'll leave him powerless.

    T. He won't be able to steal our health, our finances, or our peace of mind.

V. When Satan came against Adam and Eve through the serpent, he said,

> *Yea, hath God said, Ye shall not eat of every tree of the garden?*
>
> GENESIS 3:1B

    A. Satan's primary method of attack is to challenge the Word of God: "Did God *really* say that?"

    B. Satan asks, "Are you sure He didn't mean something else?" Satan always challenges the Word, asking, "Is the Word really true?"

    C. The answer is YES!

Lesson 3 — Is the Bible True?

- D. If Adam and Eve had responded "Yes, God did say that—now, get out of here," that would have been the end of the story.
- E. There would have been no Fall, no sin, and suffering wouldn't have entered the world.
- F. This reveals a fundamental principle of establishing a Christian philosophy, or a Christian way of thinking: Never forget that God's Word is always true.
- G. If you compromise on this point, Satan is going to rob you blind, and nothing else is going to work.
- H. God's Word is the only sure foundation to build a Christian philosophy upon.

VI. Here's another tip: You can save yourself a lot of trouble by not even getting into conversations with the devil.

- A. When he attacks the Word, don't bother arguing with him. Just state the truth and move on.
- B. But Eve didn't do that; she decided to have a chat with the serpent and said,

We may eat of the fruit of the trees of the garden: But of the fruit of the tree which is in the midst of the garden, God hath said, Ye shall not eat of it, neither shall ye touch it, lest ye die.
GENESIS 3:2-3

- C. The problem with what Eve said is that God never said they couldn't *touch* the fruit; He said not to *eat* it.
- D. Eve added to what God had said, and she thought that if she even touched the fruit, she would die.
- E. When she was enticed by the lust of her eyes and flesh to reach out and touch it and nothing happened, she thought maybe nothing would happen if she ate it too.
- F. She discovered that the thoughts she added to what God had said were false—she didn't die when she touched the fruit—and it tempted her to question all of what she believed about God's commands.
- G. This same thing is happening today.

VII. Religion has added to the Word of God and nullified it in order to hand down traditions.

- A. It's exactly what Jesus accused the scribes and the Pharisees of doing (Mark 7:13).
- B. Religion is always adding rules and regulations to the Word of God.
- C. It's saying, "Don't even touch it or you'll die!"
- D. Religion creates manmade traditions, and when people break the manmade traditions and don't die, they go ahead and break God's Word, too, thinking that everything was just a hoax.
- E. For example, some religious systems today are saying women shouldn't wear makeup or jewelry—which is a misunderstanding of the scripture that says women shouldn't be concerned with outward adorning but rather be concerned with the beauty of their hearts.
- F. The scripture says not to be concerned with the **"outward adorning of plaiting the hair, and of wearing of gold, or of putting on of apparel; But let it be the hidden man of the heart"** (1 Pet. 3:3-4).
- G. If you interpret this to mean that there should be no plaiting of the hair or wearing of gold, then you have to say there shouldn't be any wearing of apparel either.
- H. Obviously, God doesn't want you running around without any clothes on.
- I. The intent of this scripture is to encourage people to focus on the condition of their hearts instead of their outward appearance.

	J.	Preaching that women should wear their hair in a certain way and dress a certain way or God won't love them anymore isn't true.
	K.	When a young girl who has grown up hearing those things fails to live up to the supposed dress code but doesn't feel any different (judgment from God)—because God *does* still love her—she calls into question everything she has ever learned about God.
	L.	This is how religion and the traditions of men can nullify the Word of God.
VIII.		Satan didn't come right out and say, "Hey, Adam and Eve, eat this forbidden fruit."
	A.	No, he cast doubt by criticizing what God had said.
	B.	Similarly, Satan's biggest triumph in recent centuries has been to make it unfashionable to believe in and trust the Word of God.
	C.	The world system, inspired by the devil, has come against the Word and put doubt in people's minds about its accuracy and relevance, so the majority of people in society are off doing their own thing.
	D.	But the doubt and uncertainty Satan has raised are all lies and deception.
	E.	Christians have to establish in their hearts that the Bible is the inspired Word of God.
	F.	As I will show later, the Word is accurate, it is God breathed, and it is God inspired.
	G.	If you ever start thinking the Bible is merely a book written by men *about* God, Satan is going to eat your lunch and pop the bag.
	H.	You'll be in serious trouble if you ever adopt the mindset that the Bible has some truth in it but that it also has all kinds of error—leading you to go through and only pull out the parts that *you* think are relevant.
	I.	If you do that, Satan will have you as surely as he had Adam and Eve.
IX.		I think the reason Satan tempted Eve instead of Adam was that Adam heard God's command directly.
	A.	Genesis says, **"And the LORD God commanded the man, saying, Of every tree of the garden thou mayest freely eat: But of the tree of the knowledge of good and evil, thou shalt not eat of it: for in the day that thou eatest thereof thou shalt surely die"** (Gen. 2:16-17).
	B.	The next verses describe how God decided Adam shouldn't be alone, and He created Eve to be a companion for Adam and instituted marriage between a man and a woman.
	C.	So, God gave the command not to eat the forbidden fruit before Eve was even formed, which means she might never have actually heard God give the command.
	D.	Any time you have one person repeating what someone else has told them, there is the possibility that they won't repeat it correctly.
	E.	They might leave something out or add something that the first person never said.
	F.	Adam heard God in an audible voice tell him not to eat of the Tree of the Knowledge of Good and Evil, but Eve got her information secondhand from Adam.
	G.	It would have been much harder for the serpent to convince Adam of what God did or didn't say, because Adam heard God directly.
	H.	So, it was easier for the devil to make Eve doubt that Adam had repeated God's command accurately than it would have been to make Adam doubt what he had heard.

Lesson 3 — Is the Bible True?

X. This story shows that you need to get your philosophy from God directly and not depend upon other people to repeat it for you.

    A. You need to personalize the Word and make it real to you.

    B. It can't be just a book written to people in general but not necessarily to you in particular; you have to believe that the Bible is God's Word to *you*.

    C. The majority of people read the Bible like it's an interesting book about God, but they don't read it like it is God speaking to them.

    D. The Holy Spirit will use the words in the Bible to speak directly to you, and you have to read the Word with a sense of expectancy that God is going to speak to you through it.

    E. I can't tell you how many people I have dealt with over the years who knew what God's Word says, but they were leaning on their own wisdom.

    F. They thought their opinion was better than God's, and they were doing things their own way.

    G. Some of those people crashed and burned before they recognized that God was right, but they didn't have to learn by the school of hard knocks; they could've just believed the Word of God.

    H. The Bible says,

All scripture is given by inspiration of God, and is profitable for doctrine, for reproof, for correction, for instruction in righteousness: That the man of God may be perfect, throughly furnished unto all good works.
                                          2 TIMOTHY 3:16-17

    I. God has spoken to me through thousands of scriptures as I have prayed and asked Him for wisdom.

    J. He has used what is written in the Bible to speak directly to me.

    K. For instance, God has shown me how Moses' desire to accomplish God's plan in his own strength cost him forty years in the wilderness, and the nation of Israel spent an extra thirty years in bondage.

    L. Those things happened to Moses, but God has taken the scriptures and spoken them to me.

    M. He brought the words alive and gave me revelation knowledge that impacted my heart and shaped part of my Christian philosophy.

    N. The Bible is a book *from* God, He speaks to me through it, and I believe in the inspiration of Scripture with all of my heart.

XI. God's Word will change you to the degree that you let it dominate your thoughts and life.

    A. I certainly haven't renewed my mind perfectly, but I'm also a long way from where I started.

    B. God's Word is working in my life.

    C. It has changed me, and I see the supernatural power of God as a result of believing what the Word says.

    D. God has been speaking to me through His Word for more than forty years—ever since He told me that the way to find His perfect will for my life was to make myself a living sacrifice and to renew my mind by conforming it to the truths in His Word (Rom. 12:1-2).

    E. The easiest way to prove to yourself that the Bible is God's Word and that He will speak to you through it is just to read it.

    F. Begin by reading the entire New Testament.

- G. You might not understand everything the first time, but the Bible is its own commentary, and the more you read, the more you will understand.

- H. Approach it with a sincere heart and say, "God, if this is really inspired by You and it isn't just the thoughts of men about You, then speak to me through it."

- I. If you pray in that way and remain open to the possibility that God will speak to you, I guarantee you will be inspired by God.

XII. The author of Hebrews wrote,

For the word of God is quick, and powerful, and sharper than any twoedged sword, piercing even to the dividing asunder of soul and spirit, and of the joints and marrow, and is a discerner of the thoughts and intents of the heart.

HEBREWS 4:12

- A. The Word of God is alive, and it will come alive for us if we read it expectantly.

- B. Eve was the focus of Satan's temptation because God's command was secondhand to her.

- C. But we shouldn't be too hard on Eve for falling into temptation, because she didn't really understand Satan or evil.

- D. She didn't know what was at stake.

- E. She didn't know what dying was or what the effects of sin would be.

- F. In a sense, we can give her a pass because she was innocent and didn't realize what was happening when she succumbed to the lies of the devil.

- G. But we don't get a pass.

- H. We understand the reality of evil.

- I. It doesn't make sense for us to bury our heads in the sand and say, "Well, you know, I'm just not sure God speaks to me through the Bible. I'm not sure I can really trust this."

- J. We need to come to the resolution that God's Word is alive and that He speaks to us personally through it.

XIII. You can't get your knowledge secondhand from me or another preacher.

- A. You need to go to the Word and hear God speak to you directly, and then you'll have enough firsthand knowledge to be safe from the deception of false doctrines, traditions of men, and wrong philosophies.

- B. Some Christians are relying on bits and pieces of Scripture that they heard decades ago as children in Sunday school.

- C. They are relying on the pastor of their church or another teacher to tell them what the Word says, but they aren't reading it for themselves.

- D. Those people are prime targets for the devil.

- E. The devil goes about like a roaring lion seeking people to devour, and just like a lion, he looks for the weak (1 Pet. 5:8).

- F. He looks for people who don't have the armor and protection of knowing God's Word.

- G. This is one reason it is so important to know what God's Word says firsthand.

H. I'm not saying you can't learn from other people, but it shouldn't be the foundation of your relationship with God.

I. Babies begin by being dependent upon their mothers to feed them, but they don't stay that way.

J. Babies can't grow up to be fully functioning adults if they stay dependent upon other people to feed them.

K. In the same way, all Christians need to learn how to feed themselves from the Word of God.

L. You can't remain dependent upon your pastor to feed you revelation.

M. I know that the cares of this life keep people busy, but if you understand how vital it is to study the Word, you'll find the time to do it.

XIV. When the Apostle Peter was getting toward the end of his life, he wrote a letter to believers in which he stressed the inspiration of Scripture and the confidence we can have that God is speaking to us through it.

A. Peter knew that he was going to die shortly, and he was giving final encouragement to the believers.

B. He said,

For we have not followed cunningly devised fables, when we made known unto you the power and coming of our Lord Jesus Christ, but were eyewitnesses of his majesty. For he received from God the Father honour and glory, when there came such a voice to him from the excellent glory, This is my beloved Son, in whom I am well pleased. And this voice which came from heaven we heard, when we were with him in the holy mount.
2 PETER 1:16-18

C. Peter was saying, "I'm about to die, but I'm going to write these things down so you can always have this to remember."

D. He was making known that the account he gave of Jesus wasn't something he devised on his own.

E. He wasn't just telling stories.

F. The words he had written down were inspired by God, and they told of Peter's experiences.

G. Peter was with Jesus on the Mount of Transfiguration and heard the audible voice of God say, **"This is my beloved Son, in whom I am well pleased"** (Matt. 17:5).

H. He saw Jesus radiate light that no earthly power could produce.

I. But then Peter wrote,

We have also a more sure word of prophecy; whereunto ye do well that ye take heed, as unto a light that shineth in a dark place, until the day dawn, and the day star arise in your hearts: Knowing this first, that no prophecy of the scripture is of any private interpretation. For the prophecy came not in old time by the will of man: but holy men of God spake as they were moved by the Holy Ghost.
2 PETER 1:19-21

J. Peter said we have something even better than seeing with our eyes or hearing with our ears—we have the written Word of God!

K. Most people would rather see what Peter saw and hear what he heard than read the Bible.

L. Large crowds will turn out to hear a person speak if he or she advertises that they had a vision and heard the voice of God.

M. But far fewer people show up when a person advertises that he or she is going to be sharing what Scripture says.

LESSON 3   IS THE BIBLE TRUE?

N. The reason is that Christian culture puts more emphasis on what they can perceive with their senses than on the Word of God.

O. Peter said you should be doing just the opposite.

P. Peter clearly stated that the Word of God was not written by men—it was not of **"any private interpretation."**

Q. The Holy Spirit inspired men to write the Scriptures.

R. The Apostle Paul made the same point in his letter to Timothy when he said,

All scripture is given by inspiration of God, and is profitable for doctrine, for reproof, for correction, for instruction in righteousness: That the man of God may be perfect, throughly furnished unto all good works.
2 TIMOTHY 3:16-17

S. The Greek word for **"given by inspiration of God"** is literally translated "divinely breathed."[1]

T. This clearly states that the Word of God didn't come from the thoughts of men. God breathed His thoughts into men, who then put them in writing.

U. The Bible is not a human book; it's God's book written for people.

XV. I believe Scripture, and I've studied it enough to verify for myself that it is the Word of God.

    A. I don't need any further proof, but plenty of scholars have also authenticated the Bible from a historical and scientific view.

    B. Many books have been written about the accuracy and inspiration of the Bible.

    C. I can't cover all of the evidence here, but I want to share a few facts that will give you confidence in the accuracy and inspiration of Scripture.

    D. To begin with, the manuscript evidence supporting the New Testament far outstrips any evidence for secular writings of ancient times.

    E. One researcher has said, "The New Testament documents have more manuscripts, earlier manuscripts, and more abundantly supported manuscripts than the best ten pieces of classical literature *combined*."[2]

    F. For example, Caesar's *Gallic War* was written between 58 and 50 B.C.

    G. Ten copies of that original work remain, and the earliest was written 900 years after Caesar's day.

    H. Livy wrote a 142-volume *History of Rome* sometime between 59 B.C. and A.D. 17, but only 35 volumes survived, in not more than twenty different manuscripts.

    I. The text of Tacitus' 14-volume *Histories* and 16-volume *Annals* survives in only two manuscripts written 900 and 1,100 years *after* the original works.

    J. The earliest manuscripts of renowned Greek historians Thucydides and Herodotus that are complete enough to be of use to scholars were written more than 1,300 years after the originals.[3]

    K. Homer's *Iliad* is the secular work that has the most supporting evidence, with 643 copies (the earliest being written around 500 years after the original), but it doesn't even compare to the New Testament evidence we have.

    L. The number of differences between the copies of the *Iliad* is also greater—even though there are more than twenty times as many New Testament manuscripts being studied and compared.

---

[1] James Strong, *The New Strong's Expanded Exhaustive Concordance of the Bible* (Nashville: Nelson Publishers, 2001), 114. G2315, *theopneustos*.
[2] Norman Geisler and Frank Turek, *I Don't Have Enough Faith to Be an Atheist* (Wheaton: Crossway Books, 2004), 225.
[3] F.F. Bruce, *The New Testament Documents: Are They Reliable?* 5th ed. rev. (Grand Rapids: The InterVarsity Press, 1988), 16.

LESSON 3 — IS THE BIBLE TRUE?

M. In contrast to the copies of secular histories given above, *more than 5,600 Greek manuscripts of the New Testament have survived in whole or in part.*

N. Those manuscripts vary in age, the more complete having been written within 150 years, with the earliest manuscript portion written within 30 years of the original (keep in mind that the New Testament wasn't written as a single book but is composed of many letters written by multiple authors at different times).

O. The fact that so many copies of the New Testament scriptures have survived, combined with the fact that they were written close to the same time as the originals, firmly establishes the historical accuracy of the scriptures we have today.

XVI. From a purely human perspective, the chance for error is increased when a document is copied over and over again thousands of times.

A. The more times something is copied, the more errors you should see.

B. This is true in the case of secular works, but not with the Bible.

C. The abundance of ancient New Testament manuscripts have been compared, and there are very few differences—and they contain no differences whatsoever that contradict the Gospel message of Jesus or the historical facts of Christian faith.[4]

D. *Scholars have placed the comparative accuracy between the more than 5,600 manuscripts at 99.5 percent!*[5]

E. This is astounding, and it shows how God has supernaturally preserved the integrity of the Bible through time.

Work	Time Written	Earliest Copies	Time Span between Original and Copy[6]	Number of Copies
Plato	427-347 B.C.	A.D. 900	1,200 years	7
Thucydides	460-400 B.C.	A.D. 900	1,300 years	8
Herodotuc	488-428 B.C.	A.D. 900	1,300 years	8
Caesar	58-50 B.C.	A.D. 900	900 years	10
Livy	59 B.C.- A.D. 17	?	?	20
Tacitus	A.D. 100	A.D. 1100	1,000	20
Aristotle	384-322 B.C.	A.D. 1100	1,400 years	49
Homer (*Iliad*)	900 B.C.	400 B.C.	500 years	643
Greek copies of the New Testament	A.D. 50-100	A.D. 300 and earlier	150[7]	5,686

F. The nearer in time a copy was made to the original, the more likely, in a purely natural sense, the work is to be correct.

G. Also, the greater number of copies in existence, the easier it is to compare for accuracy.

H. (It should be noted that in addition to the Greek copies of the New Testament, there are thousands more copies of New Testament books produced in other languages during the same timeframe. In fact, researchers have discovered more than 9,000 copies of New Testament manuscripts in other languages—bringing the total number of manuscripts to well over 14,000.)

I. The abundance of ancient manuscripts and the nearness of their composition to the actual events make the New Testament the most verifiable document of antiquity.

---

4   Bruce, *New Testament*, 20.
5   Norman Geisler, *Baker Encyclopedia of Christian Apologetics* (Grand Rapids: Baker Books, 1999), 532.
6   The information in this chart is from Bruce, *New Testament*, 16-20; Geisler, *Baker Encyclopedia*, 527-538; and The Christian Apologetics and Research Ministry online at http://carm.org/manuscript-evidence
7   One small fragment of papyrus that has been discovered, known as the John Rylands papyri, was written only 30 years after the original Gospel of John.

J. Not only do we have copies of the scriptures themselves, but leaders in the early Christian church (often called the Church Fathers) wrote prolifically between A.D. 90 and 160.

K. Their familiarity with the New Testament scriptures we still read today is proven by the fact that *all but eleven verses from the New Testament are quoted in their writings*![8]

XVII. Non-Christians have also given evidence of Jesus as a historical figure in their writings.

A. In A.D. 93, the Jewish historian Flavius Josephus wrote,

> Now there was about this time Jesus, a wise man, if it be lawful to call him a man; for he was a doer of wonderful works, a teacher of such men as receive the truth with pleasure. He drew over to him both many of the Jews and many of the Gentiles. He was [the] Christ. And when Pilate, at the suggestion of the principal men amongst us, had condemned him to the cross, those that loved him at the first did not forsake him; for he appeared to them alive again the third day; as the divine prophets had foretold these and ten thousand other wonderful things concerning him. And the tribe of Christians, so named from him, are not extinct at this day.[9]

B. Josephus also wrote about the persecution and death of James when he said that the Sanhedrin…

> …brought before them the brother of Jesus, who was called Christ, whose name was James, and some others, [or, some of his companions]; and when he had formed an accusation against them as breakers of the law, he delivered them to be stoned.[10]

C. The Roman historian Tacitus described how the emperor Nero set fire to Rome, and in an effort to deflect the wrath of its citizens, he blamed the fire on the Christians.

D. Tacitus said,

> Nero fastened the guilt and inflicted the most exquisite tortures on a class hated for their abominations, called Christians by the populace. Christus, from whom the name had its origin, suffered the extreme penalty during the reign of Tiberius at the hands of one of our procurators, Pontius Pilatus, and a most mischievous superstition, thus checked for the moment, again broke out not only in Judæa, the first source of the evil, but even in Rome, where all things hideous and shameful from every part of the world find their centre and become popular. Accordingly, an arrest was first made of all who pleaded guilty; then, upon their information, an immense multitude was convicted, not so much of the crime of firing the city, as of hatred against mankind. Mockery of every sort was added to their deaths. Covered with the skins of beasts, they were torn by dogs and perished, or were nailed to crosses, or were doomed to the flames and burnt, to serve as a nightly illumination, when daylight had expired.[11]

XVIII. Without taking into account the evidence contained in the New Testament, we can still show from non-Christian writers that Jesus was a historical figure who lived in Palestine in the early years of the first century, that He gathered followers, and that He was crucified under Pontius Pilate.[12]

A. In fact, within 150 years of Jesus' life, ten non-Christian writers mentioned Jesus.

B. Over that same time span, only nine mentioned the Roman emperor who ruled during Jesus' life—Tiberius Caesar.

---

8   Geisler, *Enough Faith*, 229.
9   Flavius Josephus, *Antiquities of the Jews*, trans. William Whiston (Buffalo: John E. Beardsley, 1895), 18.3.3 online at www.perseus.tufts.edu
10 Josephus, *Antiquities*, 20.9.1.
11 Cornelius Tacitus, *The Annals*. Tacitus, ed. Alfred John Church et. al. (New York: Perseus, Random House, 1942), 15.44 online at www.perseus.tufts.edu
12 Bruce M. Metzger, *The New Testament: Its Background, Growth, and Content*, 15th ed. (Nashville: Abingdon Press, 1980), 78.

LESSON 3   IS THE BIBLE TRUE?

        C. Not even considering Christian authors, Jesus is more documented than the Roman emperor![13]

        D. It is undeniable that Jesus was a man who lived and walked the earth precisely when Scripture says He did.

XIX. The discovery of the Dead Sea Scrolls, between 1946 and 1957, in several caves on the shores of the Dead Sea has given us further evidence of the accuracy of the Scriptures that have been handed down to us.

        A. Among the Dead Sea Scrolls was an intact copy of the entire book of Isaiah (known as the Great Isaiah Scroll).

        B. It is dated at 100 B.C. and is 1,000 years older than the copies that were used to compose the book of Isaiah we read in our Bibles today.

        C. After 1,000 years of being copied and recopied by hand, the number of differences between the Great Isaiah Scroll and our book of Isaiah are miniscule—the variations consisting mostly of spelling mistakes and simple copying errors.[14]

        D. The discovery of the Dead Sea Scrolls also proves that the Messianic prophecies we read in Isaiah were definitely written prior to the birth of Jesus, which reinforces the case that Scripture makes for Jesus as the Messiah.

XX. The bottom line is that the Bible has been handed down through the ages with such accuracy that it can't be just a human book.

        A. The different copies we have of ancient secular writings have significant differences in them because they were simply copied by men—they weren't inspired and preserved by God.

        B. The Bible, on the other hand, has been supernaturally preserved by God, and all of the evidence we have supports that it was written by the inspiration of God.

XXI. "We still can't trust the Bible," some will argue, "because it's only a translation, and translations aren't inspired."

        A. Well, Jesus didn't share that opinion, as He quoted from the Septuagint, which was a Greek translation of the Hebrew Old Testament, and He equated Scripture with words proceeding from the mouth of God (Matt. 4:4).

        B. Jesus' use of Scripture throughout the Gospels also shows that He believed it was the final authority, particularly when the devil was challenging God's commands.

        C. Additionally, the Apostle Paul hinged the thrust of his letter to the Galatians on the fact that God made His promise to the seed (singular) of Abraham, instead of to his seeds (plural) (Gal. 3:16).

        D. Paul made an argument for Jesus as the promised seed of Abraham based on the singular form of one word from a translation of the original scripture—which shows that God is well able to preserve the truth in His Word for us, even through translations.

        E. I spend nearly all of my time studying the Word.

        F. Scripture says, **"Thy word have I hid in mine heart, that I might not sin against thee"** (Ps. 119:11).

        G. It doesn't tell us to hide historical information about New Testament manuscripts.

        H. Nevertheless, scholarship and historical inquiry *do* support the claims of Christianity.

        I. Ancient manuscript discoveries show that the scriptures we read today are the same as the original inspired writings, and further research shows that the New Testament is completely unique among the books of antiquity.

---

[13] Geisler, *Enough Faith*, 222.
[14] Geisler, Baker Encyclopedia, 187-189.

LESSON 3 — IS THE BIBLE TRUE?

J. No other book in history is as verifiable as the Bible—which is exactly what is expected from a book given to us by God.

XXII. But even if there was no evidence outside the Bible that the Word of God is inspired, I would still be fully convinced.

　A. I don't have enough space to tell you every way that the Word of God has been proven true in my life.

　B. It has shown me how to deal with sickness, problems, and rejection.

　C. The Word showed me how to find a wife and how to stay married after I found her!

　D. I couldn't tell you how many times I have applied the truths from God's Word in my life and watched God's promises come to pass.

　E. I have verified for myself beyond all doubt that Scripture is the inspired Word of God, and it is accurate in all of its detail.

XXIII. People sometimes don't understand how the Bible can say things in different books that seem to be in opposition to one another.

　A. Atheists love to pick out scriptures meant to balance one another and pretend that the statements are mutually exclusive, and therefore—they say—the Bible is flawed and can't be from God.

　B. But that isn't true—certain passages in the Bible might appear to be contradictions, but opposite statements are sometimes intentional.

　C. The Bible is its own commentary, and separate—apparently opposing—scriptures can hold a single truth in balance by presenting it in different ways.

　D. For example, one scripture says, **"For by grace are ye saved through faith; and that not of yourselves: it is the gift of God: Not of works, lest any man should boast"** (Eph. 2:8-9).

　E. Another says, **"But wilt thou know, O vain man, that faith without works is dead?"** (James 2:20).

　F. Both statements are true, and each is a commentary on the other—they describe the balance of grace and faith.

XXIV. Every Christian needs to come to the conclusion that the Word of God is accurate and inspired.

　A. The Word has to be the foundation of your worldview, or Satan is going to steal from you.

　B. The devil is roaming about looking to devour people who doubt God's Word—just as he was able to spoil Eve because she wasn't absolutely convinced that God's command was true.

　C. The Word of God is 100 percent trustworthy.

　D. Personally, I doubt my little peanut brain before I question the accuracy of the Word.

　E. I haven't figured everything out, but I know the problem isn't with the Word—it's with my inability to interpret and comprehend the depths of God.

XXV. Accepting God's Word as being absolute truth and authority goes against cultural norms today.

　A. In most Western nations, the majority of people who say they believe the Bible is God's Word do not seem to believe that it is accurate and trustworthy enough to base their lives upon it.

　B. The majority of believers are getting their philosophy elsewhere, and that's why their worldview doesn't line up with God's perspective.

Lesson 3 — Is the Bible True?

    C. You will not prosper in the Lord unless you accept the Bible as God's Word.

    D. You may have periods in your life when it looks like you are doing fine, but deviating from the Word of God leads to wrong ways of thinking, and eventually, those wrong thought patterns are going to cause you trouble.

    E. Eve was fine for a while too—until she began to question God's Word, and then Satan gained a foothold into her life and plunged the entire human race into the destruction we see today.

XXVI. The best thing you can do for yourself and for your relationship with God is trust that His Word is inspired and accurate in all of its detail.

    A. If the Word of God says something is okay, then it's okay—and when His Word says something is wrong, then it's wrong.

    B. Basing your worldview on the Bible will lead you to respond to life in a positive way and put you on the path to prosperity.

    C. It will also prevent the devil from gaining access to you through wrong philosophies, the traditions of men, or the wisdom and principles of this world.

    D. The Word of God is the only sure foundation to build your philosophy on, and it is your ticket to the blessed life.

LESSON 3 — IS THE BIBLE TRUE?

TEACHER'S GUIDE

1. **"For the LORD seeth not as man seeth; for man looketh on the outward appearance, but the LORD looketh on the heart"** (1 Sam. 16:7b). Although people focus on behavior and appearance, the Bible approaches change from the heart level. Humans want to deal with external things, but God's way is to deal with the heart. The heart is the source of your external behaviors. It's where your speech and actions come from (Luke 6:45). Man puts emphasis on cleaning up the outward appearance, but God says clean the inside, and the outside will be clean also (Matt. 23:26). If you want your external circumstances to change, you have to go to the heart and change your philosophy. The way you do that is by meditating on the Word. Religion consists of man's thoughts about God, but the Bible isn't a compilation of people's thoughts—it contains God's thoughts, and His philosophy, for you.

    1a. Discussion Question: What are some ways God has dealt with you on a heart level?
    (Discussion question)

    1b. Read Matthew 23:26. What happens when the inside of something gets clean?
    A. The outside is ready to be cleaned
    B. The outside will be clean as well
    C. The inside is ready to be inspected
    D. All of the above
    E. None of the above
    (B. The outside will be clean as well)

2. Satan has been pretty successful in robbing many Christians of the blessings that God has provided. The reason he has been so successful is that their philosophy is wrong. They have developed philosophies based on their upbringing and the ungodly influences of this world rather than on the Word of God. By challenging the way they think, Satan comes to steal and to deprive them of what God has given. This is evident even from his first dealings with mankind. Concerning the dangers of wrong thinking, the Apostle Paul said, **"But I fear, lest by any means, as the serpent beguiled Eve through his subtlety, so your minds should be corrupted from the simplicity that is in Christ"** (2 Cor. 11:3). The devil doesn't have any new tricks; he's still doing the same old thing. It's not like he has a million different ways of tempting people. His only method always boils down to lies and deception.

    2a. Read 2 Corinthians 11:3. Satan tries to corrupt you from what?
    (The simplicity that is in Christ)

3. Temptation falls into just three basic categories: **"the lust of the flesh," "the lust of the eyes,"** and **"the pride of life"** (1 John 2:16). Those are the areas Adam and Eve were tempted in (Gen. 3:6), those are the areas Satan tried to tempt Jesus in (Luke 4:1-13), and they are the same three things the Enemy is trying to tempt us with today. We're being tempted in exactly the same ways that Adam and Eve were tempted. The devil just takes the same old stuff and repackages it, which is helpful in a way because we can avoid making the same mistakes Adam and Eve made by looking at the tactics Satan used against them.

    3a. Read 1 John 2:16. What three categories does temptation fall into?
    ("The lust of the flesh," "the lust of the eyes," and "the pride of life")

    3b. Read Genesis 3:6 and Luke 4:1-13. What do you learn about how Satan tempts man?
    (You're being tempted in exactly the same ways)

    3c. How is this helpful?
    (It's helpful because we can avoid making the same mistakes Adam and Eve made by looking at the tactics Satan used against them)

4. The first thing we notice is that Satan is subtle. Scripture says, **"Now the serpent was more subtil than any beast of the field which the LORD God had made"** (Gen. 3:1). We know that Satan was behind using the serpent to lie, because the Word says that Satan is the father of all lies (John 8:44). The devil created lying, and every time someone lies, they

Lesson 3 — Is the Bible True?

are under the influence of the devil. Satan didn't have any power whatsoever to force Adam and Eve into disobeying God. Instead, what he did was choose the subtlest animal—the most cunning, the craftiest, and the sliest creature—because it was a battle of wits. The battle against temptation has always been in the mind. We'll sometimes hear people talk about "spiritual warfare" in the sense of going out and doing battle in the heavens. It's a misunderstanding of a verse that says we are battling evil powers in **"heavenly places"** (Eph. 6:11-12, *New King James Version*). People have actually chartered planes so they could "take their prayers to the sky," or they have gone to the top of skyscrapers to do battle "in heaven." That isn't what this passage of Scripture is talking about. The battle against the Enemy isn't somewhere out in the atmosphere; the battle is right between our ears. Satan comes at us through our thoughts with lies and deception. It's the same way he has always operated, and that's the reason he chose the serpent to speak to Eve. It was able to twist and to deceive better than any other animal, so Satan motivated the snake to go and tempt Adam and Eve. This is really significant. It shows how deception was Satan's only weapon. It demonstrates that he doesn't have the power to make people do anything. **Satan can't do anything without our consent and cooperation.** We have to reject his lies. We need to quit consenting to his deception, quit cooperating with him, and we'll leave him powerless. He won't be able to steal our health, our finances, or our peace of mind.

    4a.   Where has the battle against temptation always been?
            (In the mind)

    4b.   Why is it significant that Satan motivated a snake—a creature that was able to twist and deceive better than any other animal—to tempt Adam and Eve?
            (Because it shows that deception is his only weapon and that he doesn't have the power to make people do anything)

5. When Satan came against Adam and Eve through the serpent, he said, **"Yea, hath God said, Ye shall not eat of every tree of the garden?"** (Gen. 3:1b). Satan's primary method of attack is to challenge the Word of God: "Did God *really* say that? Satan asks, "Are you sure He didn't mean something else?" Satan always challenges the Word, asking, "Is the Word really true?" The answer is YES! If Adam and Eve had responded "Yes, God did say that—now, get out of here," that would have been the end of the story. There would have been no Fall, no sin, and suffering wouldn't have entered the world. This reveals a fundamental principle of establishing a Christian philosophy, or a Christian way of thinking: Never forget that God's Word is always true. If you compromise on this point, Satan is going to rob you blind, and nothing else is going to work. God's Word is the only sure foundation to build a Christian philosophy upon.

    5a.   Discussion Question: Give some examples of how knowing God's Word is true is fundamental to establishing a Christian philosophy.
            (Discussion question)

6. Here's another tip: You can save yourself a lot of trouble by not even getting into conversations with the devil. When he attacks the Word, don't bother arguing with him. Just state the truth and move on. But Eve didn't do that; she decided to have a chat with the serpent and said, **"We may eat of the fruit of the trees of the garden: But of the fruit of the tree which is in the midst of the garden, God hath said, Ye shall not eat of it, neither shall ye touch it, lest ye die"** (Gen. 3:2-3). The problem with what Eve said is that God never said they couldn't *touch* the fruit; He said not to *eat* it. Eve added to what God had said, and she thought that if she even touched the fruit, she would die. When she was enticed by the lust of her eyes and flesh to reach out and touch it and nothing happened, she thought maybe nothing would happen if she ate it too. She discovered that the thoughts she added to what God had said were false—she didn't die when she touched the fruit—and it tempted her to question all of what she believed about God's commands. This same thing is happening today.

    6a.   You can save yourself a lot of trouble by not even getting into _____ with the devil.
            (Conversations)

    6b.   True or false: God only said don't eat the fruit.
            (True)

    6c.   Discussion Question: What happens when you add to what God has said?
            (Discussion question)

| LESSON 3 | IS THE BIBLE TRUE? |

7. Religion has added to the Word of God and nullified it in order to hand down traditions. It's exactly what Jesus accused the scribes and the Pharisees of doing (Mark 7:13). Religion is always adding rules and regulations to the Word of God. It's saying, "Don't even touch it or you'll die!" Religion creates manmade traditions, and when people break the manmade traditions and don't die, they go ahead and break God's Word, too, thinking that everything was just a hoax. For example, some religious systems today are saying women shouldn't wear makeup or jewelry—which is a misunderstanding of the scripture that says women shouldn't be concerned with outward adorning but rather be concerned with the beauty of their hearts. The scripture says not to be concerned with the **"outward adorning of plaiting the hair, and of wearing of gold, or of putting on of apparel; But let it be the hidden man of the heart"** (1 Pet. 3:3-4). If you interpret this to mean that there should be no plaiting of the hair or wearing of gold, then you have to say there shouldn't be any wearing of apparel either. Obviously, God doesn't want you running around without any clothes on. The intent of this scripture is to encourage people to focus on the condition of their hearts instead of their outward appearance. Preaching that women should wear their hair in a certain way and dress a certain way or God won't love them anymore isn't true. When a young girl who has grown up hearing those things fails to live up to the supposed dress code but doesn't feel any different (judgment from God)—because God *does* still love her—she calls into question everything she has ever learned about God. This is how religion and the traditions of men can nullify the Word of God.

    7a.   What does religion always do?
           (Add rules and regulations to the Word of God)

    7b.   Read 1 Peter 3:3-4. What is the intent of this scripture?
           (It is to encourage people to focus on the condition of their hearts instead of their outward appearance)

    7c.   What do people tend to do if they don't experience God's wrath for violating man's rules?
           A. They tend to never break the rule again
           B. They tend to keep the violation to themselves
           C. They tend to repent in sackcloth and ashes
           D. They tend to question everything else they learned about God
           E. They tend to ridicule the person who taught them about the rule
           (D. They tend to question everything else they learned about God)

8. Satan didn't come right out and say, "Hey, Adam and Eve, eat this forbidden fruit." No, he cast doubt by criticizing what God had said. Similarly, Satan's biggest triumph in recent centuries has been to make it unfashionable to believe in and trust the Word of God. The world system, inspired by the devil, has come against the Word and put doubt in people's minds about its accuracy and relevance, so the majority of people in society are off doing their own thing. But the doubt and uncertainty Satan has raised are all lies and deception. Christians have to establish in their hearts that the Bible is the inspired Word of God. As I will show later, the Word is accurate, it is God breathed, and it is God inspired. If you ever start thinking the Bible is merely a book written by men *about* God, Satan is going to eat your lunch and pop the bag. You'll be in serious trouble if you ever adopt the mindset that the Bible has some truth in it but that it also has all kinds of error—leading you to go through and only pull out the parts that you think are relevant. If *you* do that, Satan will have you as surely as he had Adam and Eve.

    8a.   Discussion Question: How has your life been countercultural because of God's Word?
           (Discussion question)

9. I think the reason Satan tempted Eve instead of Adam was that Adam heard God's command directly. Genesis says, **"And the Lord God commanded the man, saying, Of every tree of the garden thou mayest freely eat: But of the tree of the knowledge of good and evil, thou shalt not eat of it: for in the day that thou eatest thereof thou shalt surely die"** (Gen. 2:16-17). The next verses describe how God decided Adam shouldn't be alone, and He created Eve to be a companion for Adam and instituted marriage between a man and a woman. So, God gave the command not to eat the forbidden fruit before Eve was even formed, which means she might never have actually heard God give the command. Any time you have one person repeating what someone else has told them, there is the possibility that they won't repeat it correctly. They might leave something out or add something that the first person never said. Adam heard God in an audible voice tell him not to eat of the Tree of the Knowledge of Good and Evil, but Eve got her information secondhand from Adam. It would have been much harder for the serpent to

convince Adam of what God did or didn't say, because Adam heard God directly. So, it was easier for the devil to make Eve doubt that Adam had repeated God's command accurately than it would have been to make Adam doubt what he had heard.

    9a.   It's easier to be deceived if what you've heard is what?
(Secondhand information)

10. This story shows that you need to get your philosophy from God directly and not depend upon other people to repeat it for you. You need to personalize the Word and make it real to you. It can't be just a book written to people in general but not necessarily to you in particular; you have to believe that the Bible is God's Word to *you*. The majority of people read the Bible like it's an interesting book about God, but they don't read it like it is God speaking to them. The Holy Spirit will use the words in the Bible to speak directly to you, and you have to read the Word with a sense of expectancy that God is going to speak to you through it. I can't tell you how many people I have dealt with over the years who knew what God's Word says, but they were leaning on their own wisdom. They thought their opinion was better than God's, and they were doing things their own way. Some of those people crashed and burned before they recognized that God was right, but they didn't have to learn by the school of hard knocks; they could've just believed the Word of God. The Bible says, **"All scripture is given by inspiration of God, and is profitable for doctrine, for reproof, for correction, for instruction in righteousness: That the man of God may be perfect, throughly furnished unto all good works"** (2 Tim. 3:16-17). God has spoken to me through thousands of scriptures as I have prayed and asked Him for wisdom. He has used what is written in the Bible to speak directly to me. For instance, God has shown me how Moses' desire to accomplish God's plan in his own strength cost him forty years in the wilderness, and the nation of Israel spent an extra thirty years in bondage. Those things happened to Moses, but God has taken the scriptures and spoken them to me. He brought the words alive and gave me revelation knowledge that impacted my heart and shaped part of my Christian philosophy. The Bible is a book *from* God, He speaks to me through it, and I believe in the inspiration of Scripture with all of my heart.

    10a.   You have to read the Bible like it is God speaking what?
A. Hebrew
B. At you
C. To you
D. Greek
E. Latin
(C. To you)

    10b.   True or false: Whenever you read the Word, you shouldn't always have a sense of expectancy that God is going to speak to you through it.
(False)

    10c.   Discussion Question: Share how God has spoken to you as you've read the Word.
(Discussion question)

11. God's Word will change you to the degree that you let it dominate your thoughts and life. I certainly haven't renewed my mind perfectly, but I'm also a long way from where I started. God's Word is working in my life. It has changed me, and I see the supernatural power of God as a result of believing what the Word says. God has been speaking to me through His Word for more than forty years—ever since He told me that the way to find His perfect will for my life was to make myself a living sacrifice and to renew my mind by conforming it to the truths in His Word (Rom. 12:1-2). The easiest way to prove to yourself that the Bible is God's Word and that He will speak to you through it is just to read it. Begin by reading the entire New Testament. You might not understand everything the first time, but the Bible is its own commentary, and the more you read, the more you will understand. Approach it with a sincere heart and say, "God, if this is really inspired by You and it isn't just the thoughts of men about You, then speak to me through it." If you pray in that way and remain open to the possibility that God will speak to you, I guarantee you will be inspired by God.

11a. God's Word won't change you if you don't let it what?
   A. Dominate your thoughts and life
   B. Sow and reap in your life
   C. Replace your personality
   D. All of the above
   E. None of the above
   (A. Dominate your thoughts and life)

11b. What's the easiest way to prove that the Bible is God's Word and that He will speak to you through it?
   A. Compare it with other religions
   B. Leave it to your pastor to interpret it
   C. Read it with a sincere heart
   D. All of the above
   E. None of the above
   (C. Read it with a sincere heart)

12. The author of Hebrews wrote, **"For the word of God is quick, and powerful, and sharper than any twoedged sword, piercing even to the dividing asunder of soul and spirit, and of the joints and marrow, and is a discerner of the thoughts and intents of the heart"** (Heb. 4:12). The Word of God is alive, and it will come alive for us if we read it expectantly. Eve was the focus of Satan's temptation because God's command was secondhand to her. But we shouldn't be too hard on Eve for falling into temptation, because she didn't really understand Satan or evil. She didn't know what was at stake. She didn't know what dying was or what the effects of sin would be. In a sense, we can give her a pass because she was innocent and didn't realize what was happening when she succumbed to the lies of the devil. But we don't get a pass. We understand the reality of evil. It doesn't make sense for us to bury our heads in the sand and say, "Well, you know, I'm just not sure God speaks to me through the Bible. I'm not sure I can really trust this." We need to come to the resolution that God's Word is alive and that He speaks to us personally through it.

   12a. Discussion Question: Read Hebrews 4:12. How have you experienced the Word being alive?
   (Discussion question)

   12b. Discussion Question: Why doesn't it make sense for you to bury your head in the sand and say, "Well, you know, I'm just not sure God speaks to me through the Bible. I'm not sure I can really trust this"?
   (Discussion question)

13. You can't get your knowledge secondhand from me or another preacher. You need to go to the Word and hear God speak to you directly, and then you'll have enough firsthand knowledge to be safe from the deception of false doctrines, traditions of men, and wrong philosophies. Some Christians are relying on bits and pieces of Scripture that they heard decades ago as children in Sunday school. They are relying on the pastor of their church or another teacher to tell them what the Word says, but they aren't reading it for themselves. Those people are prime targets for the devil. The devil goes about like a roaring lion seeking people to devour, and just like a lion, he looks for the weak (1 Pet. 5:8). He looks for people who don't have the armor and protection of knowing God's Word. This is one reason it is so important to know what God's Word says firsthand. I'm not saying you can't learn from other people, but it shouldn't be the foundation of your relationship with God. Babies begin by being dependent upon their mothers to feed them, but they don't stay that way. Babies can't grow up to be fully functioning adults if they stay dependent upon other people to feed them. In the same way, all Christians need to learn how to feed themselves from the Word of God. You can't remain dependent upon your pastor to feed you revelation. I know that the cares of this life keep people busy, but if you understand how vital it is to study the Word, you'll find the time to do it.

   13a. When you go to the Word and hear God speak to you directly, you'll have enough firsthand knowledge to be what?
   (Safe from the deception of false doctrines, traditions of men, and wrong philosophies)

   13b. Read 1 Peter 5:8. True or false: The devil can devour all.
   (False)

Lesson 3 — Is the Bible True?

13c. Learning from other people shouldn't be the foundation of your relationship with _____.
   A. Them
   B. Churches
   C. God
   D. All of the above
   E. None of the above
   (C. God)

13d. You'll find time to study the Word if you understand what?
   (How vital it is)

14. When the Apostle Peter was getting toward the end of his life, he wrote a letter to believers in which he stressed the inspiration of Scripture and the confidence we can have that God is speaking to us through it. Peter knew that he was going to die shortly, and he was giving final encouragement to the believers. He said, **"For we have not followed cunningly devised fables, when we made known unto you the power and coming of our Lord Jesus Christ, but were eyewitnesses of his majesty. For he received from God the Father honour and glory, when there came such a voice to him from the excellent glory, This is my beloved Son, in whom I am well pleased. And this voice which came from heaven we heard, when we were with him in the holy mount"** (2 Pet. 1:16-18). Peter was saying, "I'm about to die, but I'm going to write these things down so you can always have this to remember." He was making known that the account he gave of Jesus wasn't something he devised on his own. He wasn't just telling stories. The words he had written down were inspired by God, and they told of Peter's experiences. Peter was with Jesus on the Mount of Transfiguration and heard the audible voice of God say, **"This is my beloved Son, in whom I am well pleased"** (Matt. 17:5). He saw Jesus radiate light that no earthly power could produce. But then Peter wrote, **"We have also a more sure word of prophecy; whereunto ye do well that ye take heed, as unto a light that shineth in a dark place, until the day dawn, and the day star arise in your hearts: Knowing this first, that no prophecy of the scripture is of any private interpretation. For the prophecy came not in old time by the will of man: but holy men of God spake as they were moved by the Holy Ghost"** (2 Pet. 1:19-21). Peter said we have something even better than seeing with our eyes or hearing with our ears—we have the written Word of God! Most people would rather see what Peter saw and hear what he heard than read the Bible. Large crowds will turn out to hear a person speak if he or she advertises that they had a vision and heard the voice of God. But far fewer people show up when a person advertises that he or she is going to be sharing what Scripture says. The reason is that Christian culture puts more emphasis on what they can perceive with their senses than on the Word of God. Peter said you should be doing just the opposite. Peter clearly stated that the Word of God was not written by men—it was not of **"any private interpretation."** The Holy Spirit inspired men to write the Scriptures. The Apostle Paul made the same point in his letter to Timothy when he said, **"All scripture is given by inspiration of God, and is profitable for doctrine, for reproof, for correction, for instruction in righteousness: That the man of God may be perfect, throughly furnished unto all good works"** (2 Tim. 3:16-17). The Greek word for "given by inspiration of God" is literally translated "divinely breathed."[1] This clearly states that the Word of God didn't come from the thoughts of men. God breathed His thoughts into men, who then put them in writing. The Bible is not a human book; it's God's book written for people.

14a. Discussion Question: Why is it more important to put more emphasis on the Word of God than on what your senses tell you?
   (Discussion question)

14b. Discussion Question: Read 2 Peter 1:19-21 and 2 Timothy 3:16-17. Discuss what these passages mean to you.
   (Discussion question)

15. I believe Scripture, and I've studied it enough to verify for myself that it is the Word of God. I don't need any further proof, but plenty of scholars have also authenticated the Bible from a historical and scientific view. Many books have been written about the accuracy and inspiration of the Bible. I can't cover all of the evidence here, but I want to share a few facts that will give you confidence in the accuracy and inspiration of Scripture. To begin with, the manuscript evidence supporting the New Testament far outstrips any evidence for secular writings of ancient times. One researcher has said, "The New Testament documents have more manuscripts, earlier manuscripts, and

---

[1] James Strong, *The New Strong's Expanded Exhaustive Concordance of the Bible* (Nashville: Nelson Publishers, 2001), 114. G2315, *theopneustos*.

Lesson 3 — Is the Bible True?

more abundantly supported manuscripts than the best ten pieces of classical literature *combined*."[2] For example, Caesar's *Gallic War* was written between 58 and 50 B.C. Ten copies of that original work remain, and the earliest was written 900 years after Caesar's day. Livy wrote a 142-volume *History of Rome* sometime between 59 B.C. and A.D. 17, but only 35 volumes survived, in not more than twenty different manuscripts. The text of Tacitus' 14-volume *Histories* and 16-volume *Annals* survives in only two manuscripts written 900 and 1,100 years *after* the original works. The earliest manuscripts of renowned Greek historians Thucydides and Herodotus that are complete enough to be of use to scholars were written more than 1,300 years after the originals.[3] Homer's *Iliad* is the secular work that has the most supporting evidence, with 643 copies (the earliest being written around 500 years after the original), but it doesn't even compare to the New Testament evidence we have. The number of differences between the copies of the *Iliad* is also greater—even though there are more than twenty times as many New Testament manuscripts being studied and compared. In contrast to the copies of secular histories given above, *more than 5,600 Greek manuscripts of the New Testament have survived in whole or in part*. Those manuscripts vary in age, the more complete having been written within 150 years, with the earliest manuscript portion written within 30 years of the original (keep in mind that the New Testament wasn't written as a single book but is composed of many letters written by multiple authors at different times). The fact that so many copies of the New Testament scriptures have survived, combined with the fact that they were written close to the same time as the originals, firmly establishes the historical accuracy of the scriptures we have today.

15a. "The New Testament documents have more manuscripts, earlier manuscripts, and more abundantly supported manuscripts than the best ten pieces of classical literature _____."
(Combined)

15b. How many Greek manuscripts of the New Testament have survived in whole or in part?
(More than 5,600)

15c. True or false: The New Testament was written as a single book.
(False)

15d. Why is it important that the New Testament scriptures were written close to the same time as the originals?
(Because it helps to firmly establish the historical accuracy of the scriptures today)

16. From a purely human perspective, the chance for error is increased when a document is copied over and over again thousands of times. The more times something is copied, the more errors you should see. This is true in the case of secular works, but not with the Bible. The abundance of ancient New Testament manuscripts have been compared, and there are very few differences—and they contain no differences whatsoever that contradict the Gospel message of Jesus or the historical facts of Christian faith.[4] *Scholars have placed the comparative accuracy between the more than 5,600 manuscripts at 99.5 percent!*[5] This is astounding, and it shows how God has supernaturally preserved the integrity of the Bible through time.

Work	Time Written	Earliest Copies	Time Span between Original and Copy[6]	Number of Copies
Plato	427-347 B.C.	A.D. 900	1,200 years	7
Thucydides	460-400 B.C.	A.D. 900	1,300 years	8
Herodotuc	488-428 B.C.	A.D. 900	1,300 years	8
Caesar	58-50 B.C.	A.D. 900	900 years	10
Livy	59 B.C.- A.D. 17	?	?	20
Tacitus	A.D. 100	A.D. 1100	1,000	20
Aristotle	384-322 B.C.	A.D. 1100	1,400 years	49
Homer (Iliad)	900 B.C.	400 B.C.	500 years	643
Greek copies of the New Testament	A.D. 50-100	A.D. 300 and earlier	150[7]	5,686

---

2 Norman Geisler and Frank Turek, *I Don't Have Enough Faith to Be an Atheist* (Wheaton: Crossway Books, 2004), 225.
3 F.F. Bruce, *The New Testament Documents: Are They Reliable?* 5th ed. rev. (Grand Rapids: The InterVarsity Press, 1988), 16.
4 Bruce, *New Testament*, 20.
5 Norman Geisler, *Baker Encyclopedia of Christian Apologetics* (Grand Rapids: Baker Books, 1999), 532.
6 The information in this chart is from Bruce, *New Testament*, 16-20; Geisler, *Baker Encyclopedia*, 527-538; and The Christian Apologetics and Research Ministry online at http://carm.org/manuscript-evidence
7 One small fragment of papyrus that has been discovered, known as the John Rylands papyri, was written only 30 years after the original Gospel of John.

The nearer in time a copy was made to the original, the more likely, in a purely natural sense, the work is to be correct. Also, the greater number of copies in existence, the easier it is to compare for accuracy. (It should be noted that in addition to the Greek copies of the New Testament, there are thousands more copies of New Testament books produced in other languages during the same timeframe. In fact, researchers have discovered more than 9,000 copies of New Testament manuscripts in other languages—bringing the total number of manuscripts to well over 14,000.) The abundance of ancient manuscripts and the nearness of their composition to the actual events make the New Testament the most verifiable document of antiquity. Not only do we have copies of the scriptures themselves, but leaders in the early Christian church (often called the Church Fathers) wrote prolifically between A.D. 90 and 160. Their familiarity with the New Testament scriptures we still read today is proven by the fact that *all but eleven verses from the New Testament are quoted in their writings!*[8]

    16a. True or false: When a document is copied over and over again thousands of times, the chance for error is likely decreased.
(False)

    16b. Why isn't it true that error has crept into the Bible, since it's been copied thousands of times?
(Because the abundance of ancient New Testament manuscripts have been compared, and they contain no differences whatsoever that contradict the Gospel message of Jesus or the historical facts of Christian faith—the greater number of copies in existence, the easier it is to compare for accuracy)

    16c. The Church Fathers quoted all but _____ verses from the Scriptures still read today.
(Eleven)

17. Non-Christians have also given evidence of Jesus as a historical figure in their writings. In A.D. 93, the Jewish historian Flavius Josephus wrote,

> Now there was about this time Jesus, a wise man, if it be lawful to call him a man; for he was a doer of wonderful works, a teacher of such men as receive the truth with pleasure. He drew over to him both many of the Jews and many of the Gentiles. He was [the] Christ. And when Pilate, at the suggestion of the principal men amongst us, had condemned him to the cross, those that loved him at the first did not forsake him; for he appeared to them alive again the third day; as the divine prophets had foretold these and ten thousand other wonderful things concerning him. And the tribe of Christians, so named from him, are not extinct at this day.[9]

Josephus also wrote about the persecution and death of James when he said that the Sanhedrin…

> …brought before them the brother of Jesus, who was called Christ, whose name was James, and some others, [or, some of his companions]; and when he had formed an accusation against them as breakers of the law, he delivered them to be stoned.[10]

The Roman historian Tacitus described how the emperor Nero set fire to Rome, and in an effort to deflect the wrath of its citizens, he blamed the fire on the Christians. Tacitus said,

> Nero fastened the guilt and inflicted the most exquisite tortures on a class hated for their abominations, called Christians by the populace. Christus, from whom the name had its origin, suffered the extreme penalty during the reign of Tiberius at the hands of one of our procurators, Pontius Pilatus, and a most mischievous superstition, thus checked for the moment, again broke out not only in Judæa, the first source of the evil, but even in Rome, where all things hideous and shameful from every part of the world find their centre and become popular. Accordingly, an arrest was first made of all who pleaded guilty; then, upon their information, an immense multitude was convicted, not so much of the crime of firing the city, as of hatred against mankind. Mockery of every sort was added to their deaths. Covered with the skins of beasts, they were torn by dogs and perished, or were nailed to crosses, or were doomed to the flames and burnt, to serve as a nightly illumination, when daylight had expired.[11]

---

8   Geisler, *Enough Faith*, 229.
9   Flavius Josephus, *Antiquities of the Jews*, trans. William Whiston (Buffalo: John E. Beardsley, 1895), 18.3.3 online at www.perseus.tufts.edu
10 Josephus, *Antiquities*, 20.9.1.
11 Cornelius Tacitus, *The Annals*. Tacitus, ed. Alfred John Church et. al. (New York: Perseus, Random House, 1942), 15.44 online at www.perseus.tufts.edu

17a. True or false: A non-Christian gave evidence of Jesus as a historical figure.
(True)

17b. What things did he give evidence of?
A. Jesus' wonderful works
B. That Jesus was the Christ
C. Jesus' persecution and death
D. All of the above
E. None of the above
(D. All of the above)

17c. Tacitus' account verifies not only the existence of Jesus and His death but also the multiplication and persecution of whom?
(Jesus' followers)

18. Without taking into account the evidence contained in the New Testament, we can still show from non-Christian writers that Jesus was a historical figure who lived in Palestine in the early years of the first century, that He gathered followers, and that He was crucified under Pontius Pilate.[12] In fact, within 150 years of Jesus' life, ten non-Christian writers mentioned Jesus. Over that same time span, only nine mentioned the Roman emperor who ruled during Jesus' life—Tiberius Caesar. Not even considering Christian authors, Jesus is more documented than the Roman emperor![13] It is undeniable that Jesus was a man who lived and walked the earth precisely when Scripture says He did.

18a. Not even considering Christian authors, Jesus is more documented than whom?
(The Roman Emperor Tiberius Caesar)

18b. Discussion Question: The fact that Jesus is so well documented in history means what for today?
(Discussion question)

19. The discovery of the Dead Sea Scrolls, between 1946 and 1957, in several caves on the shores of the Dead Sea has given us further evidence of the accuracy of the Scriptures that have been handed down to us. Among the Dead Sea Scrolls was an intact copy of the entire book of Isaiah (known as the Great Isaiah Scroll). It is dated at 100 B.C. and is 1,000 years older than the copies that were used to compose the book of Isaiah we read in our Bibles today. After 1,000 years of being copied and recopied by hand, the number of differences between the Great Isaiah Scroll and our book of Isaiah are miniscule—the variations consisting mostly of spelling mistakes and simple copying errors.[14] The discovery of the Dead Sea Scrolls also proves that the Messianic prophecies we read in Isaiah were definitely written prior to the birth of Jesus, which reinforces the case that Scripture makes for Jesus as the Messiah.

19a. What was found with the Dead Sea Scrolls when they were discovered?
(An intact copy of the entire book of Isaiah)

19b. How many years older was it than the book of Isaiah read in Bibles today?
(1,000 years)

19c. Comparing the two, how many errors were found?
(The errors were miniscule—the variations consisting mostly of spelling mistakes and simple copying errors)

19d. What else does finding the Dead Sea Scrolls prove?
(That the Messianic prophecies read in Isaiah were definitely written prior to the birth of Jesus, which reinforces the case that Scripture makes for Jesus as the Messiah)

---

12 Bruce M. Metzger, *The New Testament: Its Background, Growth, and Content*, 15th ed. (Nashville: Abingdon Press, 1980), 78.
13 Geisler, *Enough Faith*, 222.
14 Geisler, *Baker Encyclopedia*, 187-189.

LESSON 3　　　　　　　　　　　　　　　　　　　　　　　　IS THE BIBLE TRUE?

20. The bottom line is that the Bible has been handed down through the ages with such accuracy that it can't be just a human book. The different copies we have of ancient secular writings have significant differences in them because they were simply copied by men—they weren't inspired and preserved by God. The Bible, on the other hand, has been supernaturally preserved by God, and all of the evidence we have supports that it was written by the inspiration of God.

    20a.   Why isn't the Bible just a human book?
           (Because it has been handed down through the ages with such accuracy)

    20b.   This shows that it was _____ preserved by God.
           (Supernaturally)

21. "We still can't trust the Bible," some will argue, "because it's only a translation, and translations aren't inspired." Well, Jesus didn't share that opinion, as He quoted from the Septuagint, which was a Greek translation of the Hebrew Old Testament, and He equated Scripture with words proceeding from the mouth of God (Matt. 4:4). Jesus' use of Scripture throughout the Gospels also shows that He believed it was the final authority, particularly when the devil was challenging God's commands. Additionally, the Apostle Paul hinged the thrust of his letter to the Galatians on the fact that God made His promise to the seed (singular) of Abraham, instead of to his seed*s* (plural) (Gal. 3:16). Paul made an argument for Jesus as the promised seed of Abraham based on the singular form of one word from a translation of the original scripture—which shows that God is well able to preserve the truth in His Word for us, even through translations. I spend nearly all of my time studying the Word. Scripture says, **"Thy word have I hid in mine heart, that I might not sin against thee"** (Ps. 119:11). It doesn't tell us to hide historical information about New Testament manuscripts. Nevertheless, scholarship and historical inquiry *do* support the claims of Christianity. Ancient manuscript discoveries show that the scriptures we read today are the same as the original inspired writings, and further research shows that the New Testament is completely unique among the books of antiquity. No other book in history is as verifiable as the Bible—which is exactly what is expected from a book given to us by God.

    21a.   Even though the Scriptures have been translated, why can we still trust the Bible?
           (Because Jesus quoted from the Septuagint, which was a Greek translation of the Hebrew Old Testament, and He equated Scripture with words proceeding from the mouth of God)

    21b.   Read Galatians 3:16. What did Paul say to further validate translations?
           (Paul made an argument for Jesus as the promised seed of Abraham based on the singular form of one word from a translation of the original scripture)

22. But even if there was no evidence outside the Bible that the Word of God is inspired, I would still be fully convinced. I don't have enough space to tell you every way that the Word of God has been proven true in my life. It has shown me how to deal with sickness, problems, and rejection. The Word showed me how to find a wife and how to stay married after I found her! I couldn't tell you how many times I have applied the truths from God's Word in my life and watched God's promises come to pass. I have verified for myself beyond all doubt that Scripture is the inspired Word of God, and it is accurate in all of its detail.

    22a.   Even if there was no evidence outside of the Bible that the Word of God is inspired, why would Andrew still be fully convinced that it is?
           (Because of his personal experience)

    22b.   Discussion Question: What personal experiences have you had to verify that the Word of God is inspired?
           (Discussion question)

23. People sometimes don't understand how the Bible can say things in different books that seem to be in opposition to one another. Atheists love to pick out scriptures meant to balance one another and pretend that the statements are mutually exclusive, and therefore—they say—the Bible is flawed and can't be from God. But that isn't true—certain passages in the Bible might appear to be contradictions, but opposite statements are sometimes

LESSON 3 — IS THE BIBLE TRUE?

intentional. The Bible is its own commentary, and separate—apparently opposing—scriptures can hold a single truth in balance by presenting it in different ways. For example, one scripture says, **"For by grace are ye saved through faith; and that not of yourselves: it is the gift of God: Not of works, lest any man should boast"** (Eph. 2:8-9). Another says, **"But wilt thou know, O vain man, that faith without works is dead?"** (James 2:20). Both statements are true, and each is a commentary on the other—they describe the balance of grace and faith.

23a. Read Ephesians 2:8-9 and James 2:20. Even though certain passages in the Bible might appear to be contradictions, why are opposite statements sometimes intentional?
(Because the Bible is its own commentary, and separate—apparently opposing—scriptures can hold a single truth in balance by presenting it in different ways)

24. Every Christian needs to come to the conclusion that the Word of God is accurate and inspired. The Word has to be the foundation of your worldview, or Satan is going to steal from you. The devil is roaming about looking to devour people who doubt God's Word—just as he was able to spoil Eve because she wasn't absolutely convinced that God's command was true. The Word of God is 100 percent trustworthy. Personally, I doubt my little peanut brain before I question the accuracy of the Word. I haven't figured everything out, but I know the problem isn't with the Word—it's with my inability to interpret and comprehend the depths of God.

24a. Who does the devil look to devour?
(Those who doubt God's Word)

24b. What does Andrew doubt before he questions the accuracy of the Word?
(His brain)

25. Accepting God's Word as being absolute truth and authority goes against cultural norms today. In most Western nations, the majority of people who say they believe the Bible is God's Word do not seem to believe that it is accurate and trustworthy enough to base their lives upon it. The majority of believers are getting their philosophy elsewhere, and that's why their worldview doesn't line up with God's perspective. You will not prosper in the Lord unless you accept the Bible as God's Word. You may have periods in your life when it looks like you are doing fine, but deviating from the Word of God leads to wrong ways of thinking, and eventually, those wrong thought patterns are going to cause you trouble. Eve was fine for a while too—until she began to question God's Word, and then Satan gained a foothold into her life and plunged the entire human race into the destruction we see today.

25a. Discussion Question: Why is it that the majority of people who say they believe the Bible is God's Word do not seem to believe that it is accurate and trustworthy enough to base their lives upon it?
(Discussion question)

25b. Deviating from the Word of God leads to wrong ways of _____, and eventually, those wrong thought patterns are going to cause you _____.
A. Studying/Damage
B. Giving/Pain
C. Motivation/Grief
D. Listening/Problems
E. Thinking/Trouble
(E. Thinking/Trouble)

26. The best thing you can do for yourself and for your relationship with God is trust that His Word is inspired and accurate in all of its detail. If the Word of God says something is okay, then it's okay—and when His Word says something is wrong, then it's wrong. Basing your worldview on the Bible will lead you to respond to life in a positive way and put you on the path to prosperity. It will also prevent the devil from gaining access to you through wrong philosophies, the traditions of men, or the wisdom and principles of this world. The Word of God is the only sure foundation to build your philosophy on, and it is your ticket to the blessed life.

Lesson 3 — Is the Bible True?

26a. Discussion Question: If the Word of God says something is okay, then it's okay—and when His Word says something is wrong, then it's wrong. Give an example from your life how this is true.
(Discussion question)

26b. Basing your worldview on the Bible will prevent the devil from what?
(Gaining access to you through wrong philosophies, the traditions of men, or the wisdom and principles of this world)

26c. The Word of God is the only sure foundation to build your philosophy on, and it is your what to the blessed kind of life?
A. Responsibility
B. Ticket
C. Gift
D. All of the above
E. None of the above
(B. Ticket)

LESSON 3 — Is the Bible True?

DISCIPLESHIP QUESTIONS

1. Discussion Question: What are some ways God has dealt with you on a heart level?

2. Read Matthew 23:26. What happens when the inside of something gets clean?
   A. The outside is ready to be cleaned
   B. The outside will be clean as well
   C. The inside is ready to be inspected
   D. All of the above
   E. None of the above

3. Read 2 Corinthians 11:3. Satan tries to corrupt you from what?

4. Read 1 John 2:16. What three categories does temptation fall into?

SCRIPTURES TO USE WITH QUESTIONS

1 SAMUEL 16:7
But the Lord said unto Samuel, Look not on his countenance, or on the height of his stature; because I have refused him: for the Lord seeth not as man seeth; for man looketh on the outward appearance, but the Lord looketh on the heart.

LUKE 6:45
A good man out of the good treasure of his heart bringeth forth that which is good; and an evil man out of the evil treasure of his heart bringeth forth that which is evil: for of the abundance of the heart his mouth speaketh.

MATTHEW 23:26
Thou blind Pharisee, cleanse first that which is within the cup and platter, that the outside of them may be clean also.

2 CORINTHIANS 11:3
But I fear, lest by any means, as the serpent beguiled Eve through his subtilty, so your minds should be corrupted from the simplicity that is in Christ.

1 JOHN 2:16
For all that is in the world, the lust of the flesh, and the lust of the eyes, and the pride of life, is not of the Father, but is of the world.

LESSON 3 — IS THE BIBLE TRUE?

DISCIPLESHIP QUESTIONS

5. Read Genesis 3:6 and Luke 4:1-13. What do you learn about how Satan tempts man?

6. How is this helpful?

7. Where has the battle against temptation always been?

8. Why is it significant that Satan motivated a snake—a creature that was able to twist and deceive better than any other animal—to tempt Adam and Eve?

9. Discussion Question: Give some examples of how knowing God's Word is true is fundamental to establishing a Christian philosophy.

10. You can save yourself a lot of trouble by not even getting into _____ with the devil.

11. True or false: God only said don't eat the fruit.

12. Discussion Question: What happens when you add to what God has said?

13. What does religion always do?

SCRIPTURES TO USE WITH QUESTIONS

GENESIS 3:6
And when the woman saw that the tree was good for food, and that it was pleasant to the eyes, and a tree to be desired to make one wise, she took of the fruit thereof, and did eat, and gave also unto her husband with her; and he did eat.

LUKE 4:1-13
And Jesus being full of the Holy Ghost returned from Jordan, and was led by the Spirit into the wilderness, **[2]** *Being forty days tempted of the devil. And in those days he did eat nothing: and when they were ended, he afterward hungered.* **[3]** *And the devil said unto him, If thou be the Son of God, command this stone that it be made bread.* **[4]** *And Jesus answered him, saying, It is written, That man shall not live by bread alone, but by every word of God.* **[5]** *And the devil, taking him up into an high mountain, shewed unto him all the kingdoms of the world in a moment of time.* **[6]** *And the devil said unto him, All this power will I give thee, and the glory of them: for that is delivered unto me; and to whomsoever I will I give it.* **[7]** *If thou therefore wilt worship me, all shall be thine.* **[8]** *And Jesus answered and said unto him, Get thee behind me, Satan: for it is written, Thou shalt worship the Lord thy God, and him only shalt thou serve.* **[9]** *And he brought him to Jerusalem, and set him on a pinnacle of the temple, and said unto him, If thou be the Son of God, cast thyself down from hence:* **[10]** *For it is written, He shall give his angels charge over thee, to keep thee:* **[11]** *And in their hands they shall bear thee up, lest at any time thou dash thy foot against a stone.* **[12]** *And Jesus answering said unto him, It is said, Thou shalt not tempt the Lord thy God.* **[13]** *And when the devil had ended all the temptation, he departed from him for a season.*

LESSON 3 — IS THE BIBLE TRUE?

DISCIPLESHIP QUESTIONS

14. Read 1 Peter 3:3-4. What is the intent of this scripture?

15. What do people tend to do if they don't experience God's wrath for violating man's rules?
    A. They tend to never break the rule again
    B. They tend to keep the violation to themselves
    C. They tend to repent in sackcloth and ashes
    D. They tend to question everything else they learned about God
    E. They tend to ridicule the person who taught them about the rule

16. Discussion Question: How has your life been countercultural because of God's Word?

17. It's easier to be deceived if what you've heard is what?

18. You have to read the Bible like it is God speaking what?
    A. Hebrew
    B. At you
    C. To you
    D. Greek
    E. Latin

19. True or false: Whenever you read the Word, you shouldn't always have a sense of expectancy that God is going to speak to you through it.

20. Discussion Question: Share how God has spoken to you as you've read the Word.

SCRIPTURES TO USE WITH QUESTIONS

GENESIS 3:1-3
Now the serpent was more subtil than any beast of the field which the Lord God had made. And he said unto the woman, Yea, hath God said, Ye shall not eat of every tree of the garden? [2] *And the woman said unto the serpent, We may eat of the fruit of the trees of the garden:* [3] *But of the fruit of the tree which is in the midst of the garden, God hath said, Ye shall not eat of it, neither shall ye touch it, lest ye die.*

JOHN 8:44
Ye are of your father the devil, and the lusts of your father ye will do. He was a murderer from the beginning, and abode not in the truth, because there is no truth in him. When he speaketh a lie, he speaketh of his own: for he is a liar, and the father of it.

EPHESIANS 6:11-12 (NEW KING JAMES VERSION)
Put on the whole armor of God, that you may be able to stand against the wiles of the devil. [12] *For we do not wrestle against flesh and blood, but against principalities, against powers, against the rulers of the darkness of this age, against spiritual hosts of wickedness in the heavenly places.*

MARK 7:13
Making the word of God of none effect through your tradition, which ye have delivered: and many such like things do ye.

1 PETER 3:3-4
Whose adorning let it not be that outward adorning of plaiting the hair, and of wearing of gold, or of putting on of apparel; [4] *But let it be the hidden man of the heart, in that which is not corruptible, even the ornament of a meek and quiet spirit, which is in the sight of God of great price.*

LESSON 3 — IS THE BIBLE TRUE?

DISCIPLESHIP QUESTIONS

21. God's Word won't change you if you don't let it what?
    - A. Dominate your thoughts and life
    - B. Sow and reap in your life
    - C. Replace your personality
    - D. All of the above
    - E. None of the above

22. What's the easiest way to prove that the Bible is God's Word and that He will speak to you through it?
    - A. Compare it with other religions
    - B. Leave it to your pastor to interpret it
    - C. Read it with a sincere heart
    - D. All of the above
    - E. None of the above

23. Discussion Question: Read Hebrews 4:12. How have you experienced the Word being alive?

24. Discussion Question: Why doesn't it make sense for you to bury your head in the sand and say, "Well, you know, I'm just not sure God speaks to me through the Bible. I'm not sure I can really trust this"?

25. When you go to the Word and hear God speak to you directly, you'll have enough firsthand knowledge to be what?

SCRIPTURES TO USE WITH QUESTIONS

GENESIS 2:16-17
And the Lord God commanded the man, saying, Of every tree of the garden thou mayest freely eat: **[17]** *But of the tree of the knowledge of good and evil, thou shalt not eat of it: for in the day that thou eatest thereof thou shalt surely die.*

ROMANS 12:1-2
I beseech you therefore, brethren, by the mercies of God, that ye present your bodies a living sacrifice, holy, acceptable unto God, which is your reasonable service. **[2]** *And be not conformed to this world: but be ye transformed by the renewing of your mind, that ye may prove what is that good, and acceptable, and perfect, will of God.*

HEBREWS 4:12
For the word of God is quick, and powerful, and sharper than any twoedged sword, piercing even to the dividing asunder of soul and spirit, and of the joints and marrow, and is a discerner of the thoughts and intents of the heart.

Lesson 3 — Is the Bible True?

DISCIPLESHIP QUESTIONS

26. Read 1 Peter 5:8. True or false: The devil can devour all.

27. Learning from other people shouldn't be the foundation of your relationship with _____.
    A. Them
    B. Churches
    C. God
    D. All of the above
    E. None of the above

28. You'll find time to study the Word if you understand what?

29. Discussion Question: Why is it more important to put more emphasis on the Word of God than on what your senses tell you?

30. Discussion Question: Read 2 Peter 1:19-21 and 2 Timothy 3:16-17. Discuss what these passages mean to you.

31. "The New Testament documents have more manuscripts, earlier manuscripts, and more abundantly supported manuscripts than the best ten pieces of classical literature _____."

32. How many Greek manuscripts of the New Testament have survived in whole or in part?

33. True or false: The New Testament was written as a single book.

SCRIPTURES TO USE WITH QUESTIONS

1 PETER 5:8
Be sober, be vigilant; because your adversary the devil, as a roaring lion, walketh about, seeking whom he may devour.

2 PETER 1:16-21
For we have not followed cunningly devised fables, when we made known unto you the power and coming of our Lord Jesus Christ, but were eyewitnesses of his majesty. **[17]** *For he received from God the Father honour and glory, when there came such a voice to him from the excellent glory, This is my beloved Son, in whom I am well pleased.* **[18]** *And this voice which came from heaven we heard, when we were with him in the holy mount.* **[19]** *We have also a more sure word of prophecy; whereunto ye do well that ye take heed, as unto a light that shineth in a dark place, until the day dawn, and the day star arise in your hearts:* **[20]** *Knowing this first, that no prophecy of the scripture is of any private interpretation.* **[21]** *For the prophecy came not in old time by the will of man: but holy men of God spake as they were moved by the Holy Ghost.*

2 TIMOTHY 3:16-17
All scripture is given by inspiration of God, and is profitable for doctrine, for reproof, for correction, for instruction in righteousness: **[17]** *That the man of God may be perfect, throughly furnished unto all good works.*

MATTHEW 17:5
While he yet spake, behold, a bright cloud overshadowed them: and behold a voice out of the cloud, which said, This is my beloved Son, in whom I am well pleased; hear ye him.

LESSON 3 — IS THE BIBLE TRUE?

DISCIPLESHIP QUESTIONS

SCRIPTURES TO USE WITH QUESTIONS

2 SAMUEL 23:2
The Spirit of the Lord spake by me, and his word was in my tongue.

MATTHEW 4:4
But he answered and said, It is written, Man shall not live by bread alone, but by every word that proceedeth out of the mouth of God.

34. Why is it important that the New Testament scriptures were written close to the same time as the originals?

35. True or false: When a document is copied over and over again thousands of times, the chance for error is likely decreased.

36. Why isn't it true that error has crept into the Bible, since it's been copied thousands of times?

37. The Church Fathers quoted all but _____ verses from the Scriptures still read today.

38. True or false: A non-Christian gave evidence of Jesus as a historical figure.

39. What things did he give evidence of?
    A. Jesus' wonderful works
    B. That Jesus was the Christ
    C. Jesus' persecution and death
    D. All of the above
    E. None of the above

40. Tacitus' account verifies not only the existence of Jesus and His death but also the multiplication and persecution of whom?

41. Not even considering Christian authors, Jesus is more documented than whom?

LESSON 3 — IS THE BIBLE TRUE?

DISCIPLESHIP QUESTIONS

42. Discussion Question: The fact that Jesus is so well documented in history means what for today?

43. What was found with the Dead Sea Scrolls when they were discovered?

44. How many years older was it than the book of Isaiah read in Bibles today?

45. Comparing the two, how many errors were found?

46. What else does finding the Dead Sea Scrolls prove?

47. Why isn't the Bible just a human book?

48. This shows that it was _____ preserved by God.

49. Even though the Scriptures have been translated, why can we still trust the Bible?

50. Read Galatians 3:16. What did Paul say to further validate translations?

SCRIPTURES TO USE WITH QUESTIONS

GALATIANS 3:16
Now to Abraham and his seed were the promises made. He saith not, And to seeds, as of many; but as of one, And to thy seed, which is Christ.

PSALM 119:11
Thy word have I hid in mine heart, that I might not sin against thee.

LESSON 3 — IS THE BIBLE TRUE?

DISCIPLESHIP QUESTIONS

51. Even if there was no evidence outside of the Bible that the Word of God is inspired, why would Andrew still be fully convinced that it is?

52. Discussion Question: What personal experiences have you had to verify that the Word of God is inspired?

53. Read Ephesians 2:8-9 and James 2:20. Even though certain passages in the Bible might appear to be contradictions, why are opposite statements sometimes intentional?

54. Who does the devil look to devour?

55. What does Andrew doubt before he questions the accuracy of the Word?

56. Discussion Question: Why is it that the majority of people who say they believe the Bible is God's Word do not seem to believe that it is accurate and trustworthy enough to base their lives upon it?

57. Deviating from the Word of God leads to wrong ways of _____, and eventually, those wrong thought patterns are going to cause you _____.
    A. Studying/Damage
    B. Giving/Pain
    C. Motivation/Grief
    D. Listening/Problems
    E. Thinking/Trouble

SCRIPTURES TO USE WITH QUESTIONS

EPHESIANS 2:8-9
For by grace are ye saved through faith; and that not of yourselves: it is the gift of God: **[9]** *Not of works, lest any man should boast.*

JAMES 2:20
But wilt thou know, O vain man, that faith without works is dead?

Lesson 3 — Is the Bible True?

DISCIPLESHIP QUESTIONS

SCRIPTURES TO USE WITH QUESTIONS

58. Discussion Question: If the Word of God says something is okay, then it's okay—and when His Word says something is wrong, then it's wrong. Give an example from your life how this is true.

59. Basing your worldview on the Bible will prevent the devil from what?

60. The Word of God is the only sure foundation to build your philosophy on, and it is your what to the blessed kind of life?
    A. Responsibility
    B. Ticket
    C. Gift
    D. All of the above
    E. None of the above

LESSON 3 — IS THE BIBLE TRUE?

ANSWER KEY

1. *Discussion question*
2. B. The outside will be clean as well
3. The simplicity that is in Christ
4. **"The lust of the flesh," "the lust of the eyes," and "the pride of life"**
5. You're being tempted in exactly the same ways
6. It's helpful because we can avoid making the same mistakes Adam and Eve made by looking at the tactics Satan used against them
7. In the mind
8. Because it shows that deception is his only weapon and that he doesn't have the power to make people do anything
9. *Discussion question*
10. Conversations
11. True
12. *Discussion question*
13. Add rules and regulations to the Word of God
14. It is to encourage people to focus on the condition of their hearts instead of their outward appearance
15. D. They tend to question everything else they learned about God
16. *Discussion question*
17. Secondhand information
18. C. To you
19. False
20. *Discussion question*
21. A. Dominate your thoughts and life
22. C. Read it with a sincere heart
23. *Discussion question*
24. *Discussion question*
25. Safe from the deception of false doctrines, traditions of men, and wrong philosophies
26. False
27. C. God
28. How vital it is
29. *Discussion question*
30. *Discussion question*
31. Combined
32. More than 5,600
33. False
34. Because it helps to firmly establish the historical accuracy of the scriptures today
35. False
36. Because the abundance of ancient New Testament manuscripts have been compared, and they contain no differences whatsoever that contradict the Gospel message of Jesus or the historical facts of Christian faith—the greater number of copies in existence, the easier it is to compare for accuracy
37. Eleven
38. True
39. D. All of the above
40. Jesus' followers
41. The Roman Emperor Tiberius Caesar
42. *Discussion question*
43. An intact copy of the entire book of Isaiah
44. 1,000 years

LESSON 3 — IS THE BIBLE TRUE?

ANSWER KEY

45. The errors were miniscule—the variations consisting mostly of spelling mistakes and simple copying errors

46. That the Messianic prophecies read in Isaiah were definitely written prior to the birth of Jesus, which reinforces the case that Scripture makes for Jesus as the Messiah

47. Because it has been handed down through the ages with such accuracy

48. Supernaturally

49. Because Jesus quoted from the Septuagint, which was a Greek translation of the Hebrew Old Testament, and He equated Scripture with words proceeding from the mouth of God

50. Paul made an argument for Jesus as the promised seed of Abraham based on the singular form of one word from a translation of the original scripture

51. Because of his personal experience

52. *Discussion question*

53. Because the Bible is its own commentary, and separate—apparently opposing—scriptures can hold a single truth in balance by presenting it in different ways

54. Those who doubt God's Word

55. His brain

56. *Discussion question*

57. E. Thinking/Trouble

58. *Discussion question*

59. Gaining access to you through wrong philosophies, the traditions of men, or the wisdom and principles of this world

60. B. Ticket

How Do We Know the Bible Is Inspired?

Instead of looking to God for guidance, many Christians today are turning to science or the principles of this world to answer their questions—but that is exactly what the Apostle Paul warned not to do (Col. 2:8). The Word of God is a far more reliable place to look for answers and a much surer foundation for our worldview. Jesus didn't go around citing the traditions of the Pharisees or the laws of the scribes; He quoted the Word of God as the final authority.

Science itself is not bad; it is merely the observation and interpretation of data. The problem lies in the interpretation, which is sometimes based on the assumption that God doesn't exist—an obvious problem for Christians. Unfortunately, many people today have chosen to put their faith in science, which really means they are putting their faith in the interpretations and opinions of man rather than God. However, despite efforts by atheists to disprove the existence of God, not a single scrap of scientific evidence has ever been produced that invalidates Scripture.

The word *science* is used by many to imply "incontrovertible laws," but nothing could be further from the truth. Throughout history, what was promoted as being unassailably true by science one day has often been disproven the next. Scientific theories are in a constant state of revision. The principles of this world are here today and gone tomorrow, but the Bible has stood the test of time. The Word of God remains unchanged. Jesus said,

> *Heaven and earth shall pass away, but my words shall not pass away.*
>
> MATTHEW 24:35

The Bible is not a science textbook, nor does it attempt to answer questions of mathematics and natural science, but the Bible has always proven accurate in all of its prophecies and details. This is remarkable when you consider that Scripture was written during a time when the world was steeped in superstition and ignorance, and it once again underscores the fact that the Bible was written by God through men.

For instance, the Bible teaches that the universe had a beginning (Gen. 1:1), when the common ancient view was that the universe was eternal. Isaiah wrote in 800 B.C. that the earth was round (Is. 40:22), but Western society didn't embrace that truth for another 2,000 years. The Word teaches that no new matter is being created in the universe (Gen. 2:2), and the first law of thermodynamics states the same thing. Also, the second law of thermodynamics claims that the amount of energy in the universe is decreasing, and that is what the Psalmist declared:

LESSON 4   HOW DO WE KNOW THE BIBLE IS INSPIRED?

> *Of old hast thou laid the foundation of the earth: and the heavens are the work of thy hands. They shall perish, but thou shalt endure: yea, all of them shall wax old like a garment; as a vesture shalt thou change them, and they shall be changed: But thou art the same, and thy years shall have no end.*
> PSALM 102:25-27

I don't base my faith in God on the ability of scholars to reconcile the Word of God to current scientific theories, and I don't believe we should, because the Bible is more trustworthy than the fashionable ideas of any time period. God is unchanging and His Word has proven true over and over again. However, the scientific accuracy contained in the Bible—which was written well ahead of any contemporary discovery—is another indication of its supernatural origins.

But more than any external evidence, I think Scripture itself is the greatest proof that the Word of God is accurate and inspired. Back when I first started walking with God, before I had proven the Word true in my life, the one thing that really convinced me about the inspiration of the Bible was the amount of prophecy fulfilled in Scripture—and the accuracy of those prophecies. Merely human predictions are usually so vague that they can be fulfilled in a hundred different ways. A horoscope in the newspaper, or a fortune cookie from a restaurant, can do that. The prophecies of the Bible are on a whole different level. The Bible is in a category all by itself.

The Old Testament prophecies about the Messiah were written 400 years or more before New Testament times, and Jesus fulfilled them down to every last detail. The total number of prophecies Jesus fulfilled is in the hundreds, but I'll just mention a few of them here.[1]

It was prophesied in Scripture that the Messiah would not see corruption (meaning that His body wouldn't decay [Ps. 16:9-10]), which was fulfilled when Jesus rose from the dead (Acts 2:27, 31; and 13:35). Scripture says that Christ would feel forsaken (Ps. 22:1), and when Jesus was on the cross, He called out, **"My God, my God, why hast thou forsaken me?"** (Matt. 27:46 and Mark 15:34). It says that the Messiah would be mocked and ridiculed (Ps. 22:7-8), and that came to pass exactly (Luke 23:35).

It says they would pierce His hands and His feet (Ps. 22:16). You can't get any more specific than that—and at the time this prophecy was written, the Romans hadn't even invented the punishment of crucifixion yet! Yet Scripture describes Jesus' crucifixion perfectly (Mark 15:25; Luke 23:33; John 19:37, and 20:25).

Scripture prophesies that people would divide Jesus' garments and cast lots for them (Ps. 22:18). The soldiers at the cross did precisely that (Luke 23:34 and John 19:23-24). They divided His clothes among themselves, and when they got to His robe, they discovered it was an expensive robe woven as one piece without a single seam. Rather than tear it apart, they cast lots for it.

Scripture prophesies that not one of Jesus' bones would be broken (Ps. 34:20). The Romans often broke the leg bones of those being crucified to hasten death, but when they came to Jesus, they saw that He was already dead, so they didn't break His bones (John 19:33 and 36).

Scripture prophesies that Jesus would be hated without cause (Ps. 35:19) and be betrayed by a close friend (Ps. 41:9). The Word says that He would be despised and rejected by people (Is. 53:3), people

---

[1]   Andrew Wommack, Living Commentary Bible Software, note for Matthew 26:24 (many of these prophecies).

passing by would wag their heads at Him (Ps. 109:25), He would be given vinegar mixed with gall to drink (Ps. 69:21), He would die but rise from the dead, and He would ascend to the right hand of God. All of those prophecies were fulfilled (Matt. 27:34, 39; Luke 22:47-48; John 1:10-11, and 15:24-25).

It says the Messiah would bear our sicknesses and carry our diseases (Is. 53:4-5). Jesus' life demonstrated God's desire to heal us, and many scriptures confirm that Jesus purchased health for us in His atonement (Matt. 8:16-17 and 1 Pet. 2:24). The Word prophesies that Christ would cause the deaf to hear, the blind to see, the dumb to talk, and the lame to leap (Is. 35:4-6). The entire New Testament is a record of **"how God anointed Jesus of Nazareth with the Holy Ghost and with power: who went about doing good, and healing all that were oppressed of the devil; for God was with him"** (Acts 10:38). And He's still doing it. The Holy Spirit is continuing Jesus' earthly ministry by giving sight to the blind, health to the sick, and liberty to captives (Luke 4:17-18).

Scripture says Jesus was wounded for our transgressions (Is. 53:5). It says He would stay silent before His accusers (Is. 53:7), which is completely contrary to human nature. An innocent person facing a severely painful and cruel death would try to make some kind of a defense to get out of it, but Jesus didn't say a word (Matt. 27:12, 14; Mark 14:61, 15:5; and 1 Pet. 2:23).

Scripture prophesies that the Messiah would be killed with sinners and buried with the rich (Is. 53:9 and 12). Jesus was crucified between two thieves (Mark 15:27-28) and buried in a rich man's tomb (Matt. 27:57-60). Like the virgin birth, being born in Bethlehem, or the manner of His death, these are prophecies that no man can control through his own effort.

Lesson 4 — How Do We Know the Bible Is Inspired?

Old Testament Scripture	Some Prophecies Regarding the Messiah that Were Fulfilled in Jesus	New Testament Fulfillment
Ps. 16:10	He would not see corruption	Acts 2:27-31
Ps. 22:1	He would feel forsaken	Matt. 27:46, Mark 15:34
Ps. 22:7-8	He would be mocked and ridiculed	Matt. 27:29, Mark 15:19-20, Luke 23:35
Ps. 22:16	His hands and feet would be pierced	Mark 15:25, Luke 23:33
Ps. 22:18	They would cast lots for His clothing	Matt. 27:35, Mark 15:24, Luke 23:34, John 19:24
Ps. 34:20	None of the Messiah's bones would be broken	John 19:31-36
Ps. 35:11	He would be falsely accused	Mark 14:57-58
Ps. 35:19	He would be hated without cause	John 15:24-25
Ps. 41:9	He would be betrayed by a close friend	Luke 22:47-48
Ps. 69:21	He would be given vinegar mixed with gall to drink	Matt. 27:34, 48; Mark 15:36; John 19:29
Ps. 109:25	Those who looked upon Him would wag their heads	Matt. 27:39
Ps. 49:15, 16:10	He would conquer death by ressurrection	Acts 2:24-36, Mark 16:6-7
Ps. 68:18	His ascension to the right hand of God	Mark 16:19, Acts 1:9-10, Eph. 4:8
Mic. 5:2-5	Be born in the town of Bethlehem in Judea	Matt. 2:1-6
Is. 7:14	He would be born of a virgin	Matt. 1:18-23, Luke 1:26-35
Is. 35:4-6, 29:18	He would cause the deaf to hear, the blind to see, the dumb to talk, and the lame to leap	Matt. 11:5, 15:30, 21:14; John 5:8-9; Acts 3:2-8
Is. 52:14	Others would mar His appearance, and He would be so disfigured that He hardly looked human	Matt. 26:67, 27:26, 29-30; Mark 15:15-19; John 19:34
Is. 53:3	He would be despised and rejected of men	John 1:10-11
Is. 53:4-5	He would bear our sickness and carry our diseases	Matt. 8:16-17, 1 Pet. 2:24
Is. 53:5-6	He was wounded for our transgressions (**"offences"**)	Rom. 4:25, 1 Pet. 3:18
Is. 53:7	He would be silent before His accusers, as a lamb led to the slaughter	Matt. 27:12-14; Mark 14:61, 15:5; 1 Pet. 2:23
Is. 53:9	He would be buried with the rich	Matt. 27:57-60
Is. 53:11	His death would justify many	Rom. 5:18-19, 1 John 2:1-2
Is. 53:12	He would be numbered with transgressors in His death	Matt. 27:38, Mark 15:28, Luke 22:37
Zech. 9:9	He would come to Jerusalem riding on a donkey	Mark 11:1-10, Matt. 21:1-5, Luke 19:28-38, John 12:12-15
Zech. 11:12-13	He would be betrayed for thirty pieces of silver, and it would be used to buy a potter's field	Matt. 27:3-10

One mathematician famously calculated the probability of just eight of these Old Testament prophecies

Lesson 4 — How Do We Know the Bible Is Inspired?

being fulfilled accidentally as 1 in 100 quadrillion, or 10^{17}—a number beyond comprehension.[2] In other words, the odds that the following could have happened by chance to one man is 1 in 100 quadrillion: Jesus was born in Bethlehem; had a prophet go before Him and prepare His way; was a ruler who entered Jerusalem on a donkey; was betrayed by a friend and had that betrayal result in wounding His hands; was betrayed for exactly thirty pieces of silver; His cost of betrayal (thirty pieces of silver) was thrown on the temple floor and used to buy a potter's field; He made no defense when on trial for His life, though He was innocent; and was one of the few men in all of history who was killed by crucifixion.

To give you a sense of how large a number 100 quadrillion is, consider this: if you had $100 quadrillion and you spent $1 million every *second* of every day, it would take you 3,168 years to spend all of that money.

Or, if you stacked $1 bills on top of each other, $100 quadrillion would make seventy-three separate stacks of bills stretching the 93 million miles from earth to the sun (pretending that the heat of the sun didn't incinerate the paper bills). Let's say that somewhere in those seventy-three stacks is a single dollar bill marked with a black "X." Imagine a ladder that leans up against those stacks of bills and stretches all the way to the sun. Now, get on that ladder and start climbing. Stop anywhere you want along the *93 million miles* and pull a single bill from any one of the seventy-three stacks. The chances that you will pick the one-dollar bill with a black X on it are the same chances that any man could have accidentally fulfilled eight of the prophecies that Jesus fulfilled as the Messiah.

One hundred quadrillion is an *absurdly* large number. Then consider that Jesus fulfilled hundreds of prophecies—not a mere eight—and you begin to understand what a testimony to the inspiration of Scripture Jesus' life truly was (in addition to certain proof that He is the Messiah).

Other prophecies in the Bible predicted events unrelated to the Messiah that were also fulfilled historically. For instance, about 200 years before Cyrus, king of Persia, was born, the prophet Isaiah said that God would raise up a Gentile king named Cyrus who would facilitate the rebuilding of the temple (Is. 44:28)—and that is exactly what happened (2 Chr. 36:22-23).

Another prophecy arose when Jeroboam, king of Israel, was offering sacrifices to a demon god, and a prophet stood before the altar and cried, **"O altar, altar, thus saith the LORD; Behold, a child shall be born unto the house of David, Josiah by name; and upon thee shall he offer the priests of the high places that burn incense upon thee, and men's bones shall be burnt upon thee"** (1 Kin. 13:2). About three hundred years later, the prophecy was fulfilled by the righteous King Josiah (2 Kin. 23:15-20).

By the time Josiah was born, the nation of Israel had fallen far from God. The ten northern tribes in Israel had already been led into captivity by Gentiles, but the southern tribes of Judah and Benjamin were still in existence. Josiah was king over both tribes, but he only learned how far they had strayed from God after a copy of the book of the Law was found in the temple—most likely a copy of the Pentateuch; i.e., the first five books of the Bible, written by Moses (2 Kin. 22:8). After reading the Old Testament scriptures, Josiah became convicted about the condition of the kingdom and set out to restore righteousness. He put a stop to pagan worship, and then he dug up the graves of the false prophets and burned their bones on the very altar that Jeroboam had sacrificed to idols on. You can't get any more specific than that.

---

[2] Peter Stoner, *Science Speaks* (Chicago: Moody Press, 1976) online at sciencespeaks.dstoner.net/Christ_of_Prophecy.html#c9

Lesson 4 — How Do We Know the Bible Is Inspired?

No book written by a human has prophesied events hundreds of years in advance down to every last detail. The supposed prophecies of people like Nostradamus are so vague that they can be fulfilled in a multitude of ways. In contrast, the Word of God describes in precise detail events that are fulfilled hundreds of years later. The difference is that the Bible is inspired by God. It wasn't created by the minds of mere humans.

Christians who aren't basing their philosophy on the Word of God need to "rediscover" Scripture much like Josiah did. The Bible was written by men but inspired by God, and it contains God's thoughts for us. It shows us how God looks at the world, and everything we need to know about current social issues is in the Bible. It tells us God's perspective on murder, lying, stealing, homosexuality, divorce, integrity, abortion, and every other issue. The Bible is God's philosophy written out for us to understand.

Many Christians today are basically ignoring God's way of thinking and coming up with their own way of looking at things. They are trying a little of this and a little of that, doing whatever works for them. That is a recipe for disaster. Satan comes against us through the way we think. We give the Enemy free access to our lives when we base our philosophy on the world's viewpoint. The Word of God needs to become the standard we use to judge everything. God said to Joshua,

> *This book of the law shall not depart out of thy mouth; but thou shalt meditate therein day and night, that thou mayest observe to do according to all that is written therein: for then thou shalt make thy way prosperous, and then thou shalt have good success.*
>
> JOSHUA 1:8

You aren't going to prosper and succeed until you take the Word of God and put it in your heart and meditate on it. Some people in the world appear to be prospering—they have power and possessions—but those things don't last. You can prosper momentarily outside of pursuing God, but that kind of prosperity isn't going to fulfill you. Tabloids are filled with stories of the rich and famous trying to commit suicide. Many wealthy and powerful people who don't know God are more miserable and bitter than the poorest of the poor. Jesus said, **"For what is a man profited, if he shall gain the whole world, and lose his own soul? or what shall a man give in exchange for his soul?"** (Matt. 16:26).

There is a right and a wrong way to prosper. If you want to prosper God's way—in a way that doesn't take away your life—then you're going to have to base your prosperity on the Word of God. You have to take God's values and do it His way.

When you do things God's way, life isn't all about acquiring possessions—it's about relationship with God and experiencing His love. Scripture says that if you seek God's kingdom first, then He will give you everything you need (Matt. 6:33). God will take care of you when you are seeking Him first. The Word contains God's instructions to you on how to prosper. It gives His revelation on how to make your marriage work, how to walk in health, and how to have joy and peace.

The evidence we have examined leaves no doubt that the Bible is the inspired Word of God. The Bible contains God's instructions for our success, and it is accurate in every detail. We have to put our faith in the Word of God, above all other information or ideas. If we compromise on this point or begin to doubt that the Bible is the inspired Word of God, then we start down a slippery slope that will undermine our faith in God. The Bible is not a book about God; it is a book *from* God, and it has to be the foundation of all Christian philosophy.

LESSON 4 — HOW DO WE KNOW THE BIBLE IS INSPIRED?

OUTLINE

I. Instead of looking to God for guidance, many Christians today are turning to science or the principles of this world to answer their questions—but that is exactly what the Apostle Paul warned not to do (Col. 2:8).

   A. The Word of God is a far more reliable place to look for answers and a much surer foundation for our worldview.

   B. Jesus didn't go around citing the traditions of the Pharisees or the laws of the scribes; He quoted the Word of God as the final authority.

   C. Science itself is not bad; it is merely the observation and interpretation of data.

   D. The problem lies in the interpretation, which is sometimes based on the assumption that God doesn't exist—an obvious problem for Christians.

   E. Unfortunately, many people today have chosen to put their faith in science, which really means they are putting their faith in the interpretations and opinions of man rather than God.

   F. However, despite efforts by atheists to disprove the existence of God, not a single scrap of scientific evidence has ever been produced that invalidates Scripture.

   G. The word science is used by many to imply "incontrovertible laws," but nothing could be further from the truth.

   H. Throughout history, what was promoted as being unassailably true by science one day has often been disproven the next.

   I. Scientific theories are in a constant state of revision.

   J. The principles of this world are here today and gone tomorrow, but the Bible has stood the test of time.

   K. The Word of God remains unchanged.

   L. Jesus said,

   Heaven and earth shall pass away, but my words shall not pass away.

   MATTHEW 24:35

II. The Bible is not a science textbook, nor does it attempt to answer questions of mathematics and natural science, but the Bible has always proven accurate in all of its prophecies and details.

   A. This is remarkable when you consider that Scripture was written during a time when the world was steeped in superstition and ignorance, and it once again underscores the fact that the Bible was written by God through men.

   B. For instance, the Bible teaches that the universe had a beginning (Gen. 1:1), when the common ancient view was that the universe was eternal.

   C. Isaiah wrote in 800 B.C. that the earth was round (Is. 40:22), but Western society didn't embrace that truth for another 2,000 years.

   D. The Word teaches that no new matter is being created in the universe (Gen. 2:2), and the first law of thermodynamics states the same thing.

Lesson 4 — How Do We Know the Bible Is Inspired?

    E. Also, the second law of thermodynamics claims that the amount of energy in the universe is decreasing, and that is what the Psalmist declared:

Of old hast thou laid the foundation of the earth: and the heavens are the work of thy hands. They shall perish, but thou shalt endure: yea, all of them shall wax old like a garment; as a vesture shalt thou change them, and they shall be changed: But thou art the same, and thy years shall have no end.
                                                  PSALM 102:25-27

    F. I don't base my faith in God on the ability of scholars to reconcile the Word of God to current scientific theories, and I don't believe we should, because the Bible is more trustworthy than the fashionable ideas of any time period.

    G. God is unchanging and His Word has proven true over and over again.

    H. However, the scientific accuracy contained in the Bible—which was written well ahead of any contemporary discovery—is another indication of its supernatural origins.

III. Even more than any external evidence, I think Scripture itself is the greatest proof that the Word of God is accurate and inspired.

    A. Back when I first started walking with God, before I had proven the Word true in my life, the one thing that really convinced me about the inspiration of the Bible was the amount of prophecy fulfilled in Scripture—and the accuracy of those prophecies.

    B. Merely human predictions are usually so vague that they can be fulfilled in a hundred different ways.

    C. A horoscope in the newspaper, or a fortune cookie from a restaurant, can do that.

    D. The prophecies of the Bible are on a whole different level.

    E. The Bible is in a category all by itself.

    F. The Old Testament prophecies about the Messiah were written 400 years or more before New Testament times, and Jesus fulfilled them down to every last detail.

    G. The total number of prophecies Jesus fulfilled is in the hundreds, but I'll just mention a few of them here.

        i. It was prophesied in Scripture that the Messiah would not see corruption (meaning that His body wouldn't decay [Ps. 16:9-10]), which was fulfilled when Jesus rose from the dead (Acts 2:27, 31; and 13:35).

        ii. Scripture says that Christ would feel forsaken (Ps. 22:1), and when Jesus was on the cross, He called out, "My God, my God, why hast thou forsaken me?" (Matt. 27:46 and Mark 15:34).

        iii. It says that the Messiah would be mocked and ridiculed (Ps. 22:7-8), and that came to pass exactly (Luke 23:35).

        iv. It says they would pierce His hands and His feet (Ps. 22:16). You can't get any more specific than that—and at the time this prophecy was written, the Romans hadn't even invented the punishment of crucifixion yet! Yet Scripture describes Jesus' crucifixion perfectly (Mark 15:25; Luke 23:33; John 19:37, and 20:25).

        v. Scripture prophesies that people would divide Jesus' garments and cast lots for them (Ps. 22:18). The soldiers at the cross did precisely that (Luke 23:34 and John 19:23-24). They divided His clothes among themselves, and when they got to His robe, they discovered it was an expensive robe woven as one piece without a single seam. Rather than tear it apart, they cast lots for it.

        vi. Scripture prophesies that not one of Jesus' bones would be broken (Ps. 34:20). The Romans often broke the leg bones of those being crucified to hasten death, but when they came to Jesus, they saw that He was already dead, so they didn't break His bones (John 19:33 and 36).

vii. Scripture prophesies that Jesus would be hated without cause (Ps. 35:19) and be betrayed by a close friend (Ps. 41:9). The Word says that He would be despised and rejected by people (Is. 53:3), people passing by would wag their heads at Him (Ps. 109:25), He would be given vinegar mixed with gall to drink (Ps. 69:21), He would die but rise from the dead, and He would ascend to the right hand of God. All of those prophecies were fulfilled (Matt. 27:34, 39; Luke 22:47-48; John 1:10-11, and 15:24-25).

viii. It says the Messiah would bear our sicknesses and carry our diseases (Is. 53:4-5). Jesus' life demonstrated God's desire to heal us, and many scriptures confirm that Jesus purchased health for us in His atonement (Matt. 8:16-17 and 1 Pet. 2:24).

ix. The Word prophesies that Christ would cause the deaf to hear, the blind to see, the dumb to talk, and the lame to leap (Is. 35:4-6). The entire New Testament is a record of **"how God anointed Jesus of Nazareth with the Holy Ghost and with power: who went about doing good, and healing all that were oppressed of the devil; for God was with him"** (Acts 10:38). And He's still doing it. The Holy Spirit is continuing Jesus' earthly ministry by giving sight to the blind, health to the sick, and liberty to captives (Luke 4:17-18).

x. Scripture says Jesus was wounded for our transgressions (Is. 53:5).

xi. It says He would stay silent before His accusers (Is. 53:7), which is completely contrary to human nature. An innocent person facing a severely painful and cruel death would try to make some kind of a defense to get out of it, but Jesus didn't say a word (Matt. 27:12, 14; Mark 14:61, 15:5; and 1 Pet. 2:23).

xii. Scripture prophesies that the Messiah would be killed with sinners and buried with the rich (Is. 53:9 and 12). Jesus was crucified between two thieves (Mark 15:27-28) and buried in a rich man's tomb (Matt. 27:57-60).

xiii. Like the virgin birth, being born in Bethlehem, or the manner of His death, these are prophecies that no man can control through his own effort.

Lesson 4 — How Do We Know the Bible Is Inspired?

Old Testament Scripture	Some Prophecies Regarding the Messiah that Were Fulfilled in Jesus	New Testament Fulfillment
Ps. 16:10	He would not see corruption	Acts 2:27-31
Ps. 22:1	He would feel forsaken	Matt. 27:46, Mark 15:34
Ps. 22:7-8	He would be mocked and ridiculed	Matt. 27:29, Mark 15:19-20, Luke 23:35
Ps. 22:16	His hands and feet would be pierced	Mark 15:25, Luke 23:33
Ps. 22:18	They would cast lots for His clothing	Matt. 27:35, Mark 15:24, Luke 23:34, John 19:24
Ps. 34:20	None of the Messiah's bones would be broken	John 19:31-36
Ps. 35:11	He would be falsely accused	Mark 14:57-58
Ps. 35:19	He would be hated without cause	John 15:24-25
Ps. 41:9	He would be betrayed by a close friend	Luke 22:47-48
Ps. 69:21	He would be given vinegar mixed with gall to drink	Matt. 27:34, 48; Mark 15:36; John 19:29
Ps. 109:25	Those who looked upon Him would wag their heads	Matt. 27:39
Ps. 49:15, 16:10	He would conquer death by ressurrection	Acts 2:24-36, Mark 16:6-7
Ps. 68:18	His ascension to the right hand of God	Mark 16:19, Acts 1:9-10, Eph. 4:8
Mic. 5:2-5	Be born in the town of Bethlehem in Judea	Matt. 2:1-6
Is. 7:14	He would be born of a virgin	Matt. 1:18-23, Luke 1:26-35
Is. 35:4-6, 29:18	He would cause the deaf to hear, the blind to see, the dumb to talk, and the lame to leap	Matt. 11:5, 15:30, 21:14; John 5:8-9; Acts 3:2-8
Is. 52:14	Others would mar His appearance, and He would be so disfigured that He hardly looked human	Matt. 26:67, 27:26, 29-30; Mark 15:15-19; John 19:34
Is. 53:3	He would be despised and rejected of men	John 1:10-11
Is. 53:4-5	He would bear our sickness and carry our diseases	Matt. 8:16-17, 1 Pet. 2:24
Is. 53:5-6	He was wounded for our transgressions ("**offences**")	Rom. 4:25, 1 Pet. 3:18
Is. 53:7	He would be silent before His accusers, as a lamb led to the slaughter	Matt. 27:12-14; Mark 14:61, 15:5; 1 Pet. 2:23
Is. 53:9	He would be buried with the rich	Matt. 27:57-60
Is. 53:11	His death would justify many	Rom. 5:18-19, 1 John 2:1-2
Is. 53:12	He would be numbered with transgressors in His death	Matt. 27:38, Mark 15:28, Luke 22:37
Zech. 9:9	He would come to Jerusalem riding on a donkey	Mark 11:1-10, Matt. 21:1-5, Luke 19:28-38, John 12:12-15
Zech. 11:12-13	He would be betrayed for thirty pieces of silver, and it would be used to buy a potter's field	Matt. 27:3-10

| LESSON 4 | HOW DO WE KNOW THE BIBLE IS INSPIRED? |

IV. One mathematician famously calculated the probability of just eight of these Old Testament prophecies being fulfilled accidentally as 1 in 100 quadrillion, or 10^{17}—a number beyond comprehension.[1]

    A. In other words, the odds that the following could have happened by chance to one man is 1 in 100 quadrillion: Jesus was born in Bethlehem; had a prophet go before Him and prepare His way; was a ruler who entered Jerusalem on a donkey; was betrayed by a friend and had that betrayal result in wounding His hands; was betrayed for exactly thirty pieces of silver; His cost of betrayal (thirty pieces of silver) was thrown on the temple floor and used to buy a potter's field; He made no defense when on trial for His life, though He was innocent; and was one of the few men in all of history who was killed by crucifixion.

    B. One hundred quadrillion is an *absurdly* large number.

    C. Then consider that Jesus fulfilled hundreds of prophecies—not a mere eight—and you begin to understand what a testimony to the inspiration of Scripture Jesus' life truly was (in addition to certain proof that He is the Messiah).

V. Other prophecies in the Bible predicted events unrelated to the Messiah that were also fulfilled historically.

    A. For instance, about 200 years before Cyrus, king of Persia, was born, the prophet Isaiah said that God would raise up a Gentile king named Cyrus who would facilitate the rebuilding of the temple (Is. 44:28)—and that is exactly what happened (2 Chr. 36:22-23).

    B. Another prophecy arose when Jeroboam, king of Israel, was offering sacrifices to a demon god, and a prophet stood before the altar and cried, **"O altar, altar, thus saith the Lord; Behold, a child shall be born unto the house of David, Josiah by name; and upon thee shall he offer the priests of the high places that burn incense upon thee, and men's bones shall be burnt upon thee"** (1 Kin. 13:2)—about three hundred years later, the prophecy was fulfilled by the righteous King Josiah (2 Kin. 23:15-20).

        i. By the time Josiah was born, the nation of Israel had fallen far from God.

        ii. The ten northern tribes in Israel had already been led into captivity by Gentiles, but the southern tribes of Judah and Benjamin were still in existence.

        iii. Josiah was king over both tribes, but he only learned how far they had strayed from God after a copy of the book of the Law was found in the temple—most likely a copy of the Pentateuch; i.e., the first five books of the Bible, written by Moses (2 Kin. 22:8).

        iv. After reading the Old Testament scriptures, Josiah became convicted about the condition of the kingdom and set out to restore righteousness.

        v. He put a stop to pagan worship, and then he dug up the graves of the false prophets and burned their bones on the very altar that Jeroboam had sacrificed to idols on.

        vi. You can't get any more specific than that.

    C. No book written by a human has prophesied events hundreds of years in advance down to every last detail.

    D. The supposed prophecies of people like Nostradamus are so vague that they can be fulfilled in a multitude of ways.

    E. In contrast, the Word of God describes in precise detail events that are fulfilled hundreds of years later.

    F. The difference is that the Bible is inspired by God.

    G. It wasn't created by the minds of mere humans.

VI. Christians who aren't basing their philosophy on the Word of God need to "rediscover" Scripture much like Josiah did.

---

[1] Peter Stoner, *Science Speaks* (Chicago: Moody Press, 1976) online at sciencespeaks.dstoner.net/Christ_of_Prophecy.html#c9

Lesson 4   How Do We Know the Bible Is Inspired?

    A. The Bible was written by men but inspired by God, and it contains God's thoughts for us.

    B. It shows us how God looks at the world, and everything we need to know about current social issues is in the Bible.

    C. It tells us God's perspective on murder, lying, stealing, homosexuality, divorce, integrity, abortion, and every other issue.

    D. The Bible is God's philosophy written out for us to understand.

    E. Many Christians today are basically ignoring God's way of thinking and coming up with their own way of looking at things.

    F. They are trying a little of this and a little of that, doing whatever works for them.

    G. That is a recipe for disaster.

    H. Satan comes against us through the way we think.

    I. We give the Enemy free access to our lives when we base our philosophy on the world's viewpoint.

    J. The Word of God needs to become the standard we use to judge everything.

VII. God said to Joshua,

This book of the law shall not depart out of thy mouth; but thou shalt meditate therein day and night, that thou mayest observe to do according to all that is written therein: for then thou shalt make thy way prosperous, and then thou shalt have good success.

                                                                                                    JOSHUA 1:8

    A. You aren't going to prosper and succeed until you take the Word of God and put it in your heart and meditate on it.

    B. Some people in the world appear to be prospering—they have power and possessions—but those things don't last.

    C. You can prosper momentarily outside of pursuing God, but that kind of prosperity isn't going to fulfill you.

    D. Tabloids are filled with stories of the rich and famous trying to commit suicide.

    E. Many wealthy and powerful people who don't know God are more miserable and bitter than the poorest of the poor.

    F. Jesus said, **"For what is a man profited, if he shall gain the whole world, and lose his own soul? or what shall a man give in exchange for his soul?"** (Matt. 16:26).

    G. There is a right and a wrong way to prosper.

    H. If you want to prosper God's way—in a way that doesn't take away your life—then you're going to have to base your prosperity on the Word of God.

    I. You have to take God's values and do it His way.

    J. When you do things God's way, life isn't all about acquiring possessions—it's about relationship with God and experiencing His love.

    K. Scripture says that if you seek God's kingdom first, then He will give you everything you need (Matt. 6:33).

    L. God will take care of you when you are seeking Him first.

LESSON 4 — HOW DO WE KNOW THE BIBLE IS INSPIRED?

    M. The Word contains God's instructions to you on how to prosper.

    N. It gives His revelation on how to make your marriage work, how to walk in health, and how to have joy and peace.

VIII. The evidence we have examined leaves no doubt that the Bible is the inspired Word of God.

    A. The Bible contains God's instructions for our success, and it is accurate in every detail.

    B. We have to put our faith in the Word of God, above all other information or ideas.

    C. If we compromise on this point or begin to doubt that the Bible is the inspired Word of God, then we start down a slippery slope that will undermine our faith in God.

    D. The Bible is not a book about God; it is a book *from* God, and it has to be the foundation of all Christian philosophy.

LESSON 4   HOW DO WE KNOW THE BIBLE IS INSPIRED?

TEACHER'S GUIDE

1. Instead of looking to God for guidance, many Christians today are turning to science or the principles of this world to answer their questions—but that is exactly what the Apostle Paul warned not to do (Col. 2:8). The Word of God is a far more reliable place to look for answers and a much surer foundation for our worldview. Jesus didn't go around citing the traditions of the Pharisees or the laws of the scribes; He quoted the Word of God as the final authority. Science itself is not bad; it is merely the observation and interpretation of data. The problem lies in the interpretation, which is sometimes based on the assumption that God doesn't exist—an obvious problem for Christians. Unfortunately, many people today have chosen to put their faith in science, which really means they are putting their faith in the interpretations and opinions of man rather than God. However, despite efforts by atheists to disprove the existence of God, not a single scrap of scientific evidence has ever been produced that invalidates Scripture. The word *science* is used by many to imply "incontrovertible laws," but nothing could be further from the truth. Throughout history, what was promoted as being unassailably true by science one day has often been disproven the next. Scientific theories are in a constant state of revision. The principles of this world are here today and gone tomorrow, but the Bible has stood the test of time. The Word of God remains unchanged. Jesus said, **"Heaven and earth shall pass away, but my words shall not pass away"** (Matt. 24:35).

    1a.   When you choose to put faith in science rather than God, you are really putting your faith in the interpretations and opinions of _____.
            A. Evolution
            B. Clergy
            C. Man
            D. All of the above
            E. None of the above
            (C. Man)

    1b.   Discussion Question: If scientific theories are in a constant state of revision, what does that tell you about science?
            (Discussion question)

2. The Bible is not a science textbook, nor does it attempt to answer questions of mathematics and natural science, but the Bible has always proven accurate in all of its prophecies and details. This is remarkable when you consider that Scripture was written during a time when the world was steeped in superstition and ignorance, and it once again underscores the fact that the Bible was written by God through men. For instance, the Bible teaches that the universe had a beginning (Gen. 1:1), when the common ancient view was that the universe was eternal. Isaiah wrote in 800 B.C. that the earth was round (Is. 40:22), but Western society didn't embrace that truth for another 2,000 years. The Word teaches that no new matter is being created in the universe (Gen. 2:2), and the first law of thermodynamics states the same thing. Also, the second law of thermodynamics claims that the amount of energy in the universe is decreasing, and that is what the Psalmist declared: **"Of old hast thou laid the foundation of the earth: and the heavens are the work of thy hands. They shall perish, but thou shalt endure: yea, all of them shall wax old like a garment; as a vesture shalt thou change them, and they shall be changed: But thou art the same, and thy years shall have no end"** (Ps. 102:25-27). I don't base my faith in God on the ability of scholars to reconcile the Word of God to current scientific theories, and I don't believe we should, because the Bible is more trustworthy than the fashionable ideas of any time period. God is unchanging and His Word has proven true over and over again. However, the scientific accuracy contained in the Bible—which was written well ahead of any contemporary discovery—is another indication of its supernatural origins.

    2a.   Even though the Bible does not attempt to answer questions of mathematics and natural science, it has always proven accurate in all of its _____ and _____.
            (Prophecies and details)

    2b.   Read Genesis 1:1, Isaiah 40:22, Genesis 2:2, and Psalm 102:25-27. Give some examples of where the Bible is accurate and science was either proven false or supportive of Scripture.
            (The universe having a beginning, the earth being round, no new matter is being created, the amount of energy in the universe is decreasing)

    2c.   True or false: The Bible is more trustworthy than the fashionable ideas of certain time periods.
            (False)

Lesson 4   How Do We Know the Bible Is Inspired?

3. Even more than any external evidence, I think Scripture itself is the greatest proof that the Word of God is accurate and inspired. Back when I first started walking with God, before I had proven the Word true in my life, the one thing that really convinced me about the inspiration of the Bible was the amount of prophecy fulfilled in Scripture—and the accuracy of those prophecies. Merely human predictions are usually so vague that they can be fulfilled in a hundred different ways. A horoscope in the newspaper, or a fortune cookie from a restaurant, can do that. The prophecies of the Bible are on a whole different level. The Bible is in a category all by itself. The Old Testament prophecies about the Messiah were written 400 years or more before New Testament times, and Jesus fulfilled them down to every last detail. The total number of prophecies Jesus fulfilled is in the hundreds, but I'll just mention a few of them here.[1] It was prophesied in Scripture that the Messiah would not see corruption (meaning that His body wouldn't decay [Ps. 16:9-10]), which was fulfilled when Jesus rose from the dead (Acts 2:27, 31; and 13:35). Scripture says that Christ would feel forsaken (Ps. 22:1), and when Jesus was on the cross, He called out, **"My God, my God, why hast thou forsaken me?"** (Matt. 27:46 and Mark 15:34). It says that the Messiah would be mocked and ridiculed (Ps. 22:7-8), and that came to pass exactly (Luke 23:35). It says they would pierce His hands and His feet (Ps. 22:16). You can't get any more specific than that—and at the time this prophecy was written, the Romans hadn't even invented the punishment of crucifixion yet! Yet Scripture describes Jesus' crucifixion perfectly (Mark 15:25; Luke 23:33; John 19:37, and 20:25). Scripture prophesies that people would divide Jesus' garments and cast lots for them (Ps. 22:18). The soldiers at the cross did precisely that (Luke 23:34 and John 19:23-24). They divided His clothes among themselves, and when they got to His robe, they discovered it was an expensive robe woven as one piece without a single seam. Rather than tear it apart, they cast lots for it. Scripture prophesies that not one of Jesus' bones would be broken (Ps. 34:20). The Romans often broke the leg bones of those being crucified to hasten death, but when they came to Jesus, they saw that He was already dead, so they didn't break His bones (John 19:33 and 36). Scripture prophesies that Jesus would be hated without cause (Ps. 35:19) and be betrayed by a close friend (Ps. 41:9). The Word says that He would be despised and rejected by people (Is. 53:3), people passing by would wag their heads at Him (Ps. 109:25), He would be given vinegar mixed with gall to drink (Ps. 69:21), He would die but rise from the dead, and He would ascend to the right hand of God. All of those prophecies were fulfilled (Matt. 27:34, 39; Luke 22:47-48; John 1:10-11, and 15:24-25). It says the Messiah would bear our sicknesses and carry our diseases (Is. 53:4-5). Jesus' life demonstrated God's desire to heal us, and many scriptures confirm that Jesus purchased health for us in His atonement (Matt. 8:16-17 and 1 Pet. 2:24). The Word prophesies that Christ would cause the deaf to hear, the blind to see, the dumb to talk, and the lame to leap (Is. 35:4-6). The entire New Testament is a record of **"how God anointed Jesus of Nazareth with the Holy Ghost and with power: who went about doing good, and healing all that were oppressed of the devil; for God was with him"** (Acts 10:38). And He's still doing it. The Holy Spirit is continuing Jesus' earthly ministry by giving sight to the blind, health to the sick, and liberty to captives (Luke 4:17-18). Scripture says Jesus was wounded for our transgressions (Is. 53:5). It says He would stay silent before His accusers (Is. 53:7), which is completely contrary to human nature. An innocent person facing a severely painful and cruel death would try to make some kind of a defense to get out of it, but Jesus didn't say a word (Matt. 27:12, 14; Mark 14:61, 15:5; and 1 Pet. 2:23). Scripture prophesies that the Messiah would be killed with sinners and buried with the rich (Is. 53:9 and 12). Jesus was crucified between two thieves (Mark 15:27-28) and buried in a rich man's tomb (Matt. 27:57-60). Like the virgin birth, being born in Bethlehem, or the manner of His death, these are prophecies that no man can control through his own effort.

    3a.   Jesus fulfilled prophecies that were made when?
            (Four hundred years or more before New Testament times)

    3b.   Discussion Question: List some of the prophecies that are important to you and explain why they are.
            (Discussion question)

---

[1] Andrew Wommack, Living Commentary Bible Software, note for Matthew 26:24 (many of these prophecies).

Lesson 4 — How Do We Know the Bible Is Inspired?

Old Testament Scripture	Some Prophecies Regarding the Messiah that Were Fulfilled in Jesus	New Testament Fulfillment
Ps. 16:10	He would not see corruption	Acts 2:27-31
Ps. 22:1	He would feel forsaken	Matt. 27:46, Mark 15:34
Ps. 22:7-8	He would be mocked and ridiculed	Matt. 27:29, Mark 15:19-20 Luke 23:35
Ps. 22:16	His hands and feet would be pierced	Mark 15:25, Luke 23:33
Ps. 22:18	They would cast lots for His clothing	Matt. 27:35, Mark 15:24, Luke 23:34, John 19:24
Ps. 34:20	None of the Messiah's bones would be broken	John 19:31-36
Ps. 35:11	He would be falsely accused	Mark 14:57-58
Ps. 35:19	He would be hated without cause	John 15:24-25
Ps. 41:9	He would be betrayed by a close friend	Luke 22:47-48
Ps. 69:21	He would be given vinegar mixed with gall to drink	Matt. 27:34, 48; Mark 15:36; John 19:29
Ps. 109:25	Those who looked upon Him would wag their heads	Matt. 27:39
Ps. 49:15, 16:10	He would conquer death by ressurrection	Acts 2:24-36, Mark 16:6-7
Ps. 68:18	His ascension to the right hand of God	Mark 16:19, Acts 1:9-10, Eph. 4:8
Mic. 5:2-5	Be born in the town of Bethlehem in Judea	Matt. 2:1-6
Is. 7:14	He would be born of a virgin	Matt. 1:18-23, Luke 1:26-35
Is. 35:4-6, 29:18	He would cause the deaf to hear, the blind to see, the dumb to talk, and the lame to leap	Matt. 11:5, 15:30, 21:14; John 5:8-9; Acts 3:2-8
Is. 52:14	Others would mar His appearance, and He would be so disfigured that He hardly looked human	Matt. 26:67, 27:26, 29-30; Mark 15:15-19; John 19:34
Is. 53:3	He would be despised and rejected of men	John 1:10-11
Is. 53:4-5	He would bear our sickness and carry our diseases	Matt. 8:16-17, 1 Pet. 2:24
Is. 53:5-6	He was wounded for our transgressions (**"offences"**)	Rom. 4:25, 1 Pet. 3:18
Is. 53:7	He would be silent before His accusers, as a lamb led to the slaughter	Matt. 27:12-14; Mark 14:61, 15:5; 1 Pet. 2:23
Is. 53:9	He would be buried with the rich	Matt. 27:57-60
Is. 53:11	His death would justify many	Rom. 5:18-19, 1 John 2:1-2
Is. 53:12	He would be numbered with transgressors in His death	Matt. 27:38, Mark 15:28, Luke 22:37
Zech. 9:9	He would come to Jerusalem riding on a donkey	Mark 11:1-10, Matt. 21:1-5, Luke 19:28-38, John 12:12-15
Zech. 11:12-13	He would be betrayed for thirty pieces of silver, and it would be used to buy a potter's field	Matt. 27:3-10

LESSON 4 — HOW DO WE KNOW THE BIBLE IS INSPIRED?

4. One mathematician famously calculated the probability of just eight of these Old Testament prophecies being fulfilled accidentally as 1 in 100 quadrillion, or 10^{17}—a number beyond comprehension.[2] In other words, the odds that the following could have happened by chance to one man is 1 in 100 quadrillion: Jesus was born in Bethlehem; had a prophet go before Him and prepare His way; was a ruler who entered Jerusalem on a donkey; was betrayed by a friend and had that betrayal result in wounding His hands; was betrayed for exactly thirty pieces of silver; His cost of betrayal (thirty pieces of silver) was thrown on the temple floor and used to buy a potter's field; He made no defense when on trial for His life, though He was innocent; and was one of the few men in all of history who was killed by crucifixion. One hundred quadrillion is an *absurdly* large number. Then consider that Jesus fulfilled hundreds of prophecies—not a mere eight—and you begin to understand what a testimony to the inspiration of Scripture Jesus' life truly was (in addition to certain proof that He is the Messiah).

    4a.   The odds of just eight of the prophecies happening to one person are what?
            (1 in 10^{17}, or 1 in 100 quadrillion)

    4b.   But Jesus fulfilled _____ of prophecies.
            (Hundreds)

5. Other prophecies in the Bible predicted events unrelated to the Messiah that were also fulfilled historically. For instance, about 200 years before Cyrus, king of Persia, was born, the prophet Isaiah said that God would raise up a Gentile king named Cyrus who would facilitate the rebuilding of the temple (Is. 44:28)—and that is exactly what happened (2 Chr. 36:22-23). Another prophecy arose when Jeroboam, king of Israel, was offering sacrifices to a demon god, and a prophet stood before the altar and cried, **"O altar, altar, thus saith the LORD; Behold, a child shall be born unto the house of David, Josiah by name; and upon thee shall he offer the priests of the high places that burn incense upon thee, and men's bones shall be burnt upon thee"** (1 Kin. 13:2). About three hundred years later, the prophecy was fulfilled by the righteous King Josiah (2 Kin. 23:15-20). By the time Josiah was born, the nation of Israel had fallen far from God. The ten northern tribes in Israel had already been led into captivity by Gentiles, but the southern tribes of Judah and Benjamin were still in existence. Josiah was king over both tribes, but he only learned how far they had strayed from God after a copy of the book of the Law was found in the temple—most likely a copy of the Pentateuch; i.e., the first five books of the Bible, written by Moses (2 Kin. 22:8). After reading the Old Testament scriptures, Josiah became convicted about the condition of the kingdom and set out to restore righteousness. He put a stop to pagan worship, and then he dug up the graves of the false prophets and burned their bones on the very altar that Jeroboam had sacrificed to idols on. You can't get any more specific than that. No book written by a human has prophesied events hundreds of years in advance down to every last detail. The supposed prophecies of people like Nostradamus are so vague that they can be fulfilled in a multitude of ways. In contrast, the Word of God describes in precise detail events that are fulfilled hundreds of years later. The difference is that the Bible is inspired by God. It wasn't created by the minds of mere humans.

    5a.   How are prophecies in the Word of God different from other prophecies?
            (Prophecies in the Word of God describe in precise detail events that are fulfilled hundreds of years later)

6. Christians who aren't basing their philosophy on the Word of God need to "rediscover" Scripture much like Josiah did. The Bible was written by men but inspired by God, and it contains God's thoughts for us. It shows us how God looks at the world, and everything we need to know about current social issues is in the Bible. It tells us God's perspective on murder, lying, stealing, homosexuality, divorce, integrity, abortion, and every other issue. The Bible is God's philosophy written out for us to understand. Many Christians today are basically ignoring God's way of thinking and coming up with their own way of looking at things. They are trying a little of this and a little of that, doing whatever works for them. That is a recipe for disaster. Satan comes against us through the way we think. We give the Enemy free access to our lives when we base our philosophy on the world's viewpoint. The Word of God needs to become the standard we use to judge everything.

---

[2] Peter Stoner, *Science Speaks* (Chicago: Moody Press, 1976) online at sciencespeaks.dstoner.net/Christ_of_Prophecy.html#c9

Lesson 4 — How Do We Know the Bible Is Inspired?

- 6a. Everything you need to know about current social issues is where?
  A. In school
  B. In the news
  C. In church
  D. In heavenly places
  E. In the Bible
  (E. In the Bible)

- 6b. What happens when we base our philosophy on the world's viewpoint?
  (We give the Enemy free access to our lives)

7. God said to Joshua, **"This book of the law shall not depart out of thy mouth; but thou shalt meditate therein day and night, that thou mayest observe to do according to all that is written therein: for then thou shalt make thy way prosperous, and then thou shalt have good success"** (Josh. 1:8). You aren't going to prosper and succeed until you take the Word of God and put it in your heart and meditate on it. Some people in the world appear to be prospering—they have power and possessions—but those things don't last. You can prosper momentarily outside of pursuing God, but that kind of prosperity isn't going to fulfill you. Tabloids are filled with stories of the rich and famous trying to commit suicide. Many wealthy and powerful people who don't know God are more miserable and bitter than the poorest of the poor. Jesus said, **"For what is a man profited, if he shall gain the whole world, and lose his own soul? or what shall a man give in exchange for his soul?"** (Matt. 16:26). There is a right and a wrong way to prosper. If you want to prosper God's way—in a way that doesn't take away your life—then you're going to have to base your prosperity on the Word of God. You have to take God's values and do it His way. When you do things God's way, life isn't all about acquiring possessions—it's about relationship with God and experiencing His love. Scripture says that if you seek God's kingdom first, then He will give you everything you need (Matt. 6:33). God will take care of you when you are seeking Him first. The Word contains God's instructions to you on how to prosper. It gives His revelation on how to make your marriage work, how to walk in health, and how to have joy and peace.

- 7a. Read Joshua 1:8. What do you have to do to prosper and succeed?
  (You have to take the Word of God and put it in your heart and meditate on it)

- 7b. True or false: You can prosper momentarily outside of pursuing God.
  (True)

- 7c. Discussion Question: Why wouldn't you be fulfilled by prospering that way?
  (Discussion question)

- 7d. Read Matthew 16:26. If you want to prosper God's way, in a way that doesn't take away your _____, then you're going to have to base your prosperity on the Word of God.
  A. Time
  B. Money
  C. Energy
  D. Life
  E. Job
  (D. Life)

8. The evidence we have examined leaves no doubt that the Bible is the inspired Word of God. The Bible contains God's instructions for our success, and it is accurate in every detail. We have to put our faith in the Word of God, above all other information or ideas. If we compromise on this point or begin to doubt that the Bible is the inspired Word of God, then we start down a slippery slope that will undermine our faith in God. The Bible is not a book about God; it is a book *from* God, and it has to be the foundation of all Christian philosophy.

- 8a. What leaves no doubt that the Bible is the inspired Word of God?
  (The evidence you've examined)

- 8b. Discussion Question: Why should you put your faith in the Word of God, above all other information or ideas?
  (Discussion question)

Lesson 4 — How Do We Know the Bible Is Inspired?

8c. If you compromise on this point or begin to doubt that the Bible is the inspired Word of God, then you start down a slippery slope that will what?
(Undermine your faith in God)

8d. Discussion Question: Why is it important to know that the Bible is a book *from* God?
(Discussion question)

Lesson 4 — How Do We Know the Bible Is Inspired?

DISCIPLESHIP QUESTIONS

1. When you choose to put faith in science rather than God, you are really putting your faith in the interpretations and opinions of _____.
   - A. Evolution
   - B. Clergy
   - C. Man
   - D. All of the above
   - E. None of the above

2. Discussion Question: If scientific theories are in a constant state of revision, what does that tell you about science?

3. Even though the Bible does not attempt to answer questions of mathematics and natural science, it has always proven accurate in all of its _____ and _____.

4. Read Genesis 1:1, Isaiah 40:22, Genesis 2:2, and Psalm 102:25-27. Give some examples of where the Bible is accurate and science was either proven false or supportive of Scripture.

5. True or false: The Bible is more trustworthy than the fashionable ideas of certain time periods.

6. Jesus fulfilled prophecies that were made when?

7. Discussion Question: List some of the prophecies that are important to you and explain why they are.

SCRIPTURES TO USE WITH QUESTIONS

COLOSSIANS 2:8
Beware lest any man spoil you through philosophy and vain deceit, after the tradition of men, after the rudiments of the world, and not after Christ.

MATTHEW 24:35
Heaven and earth shall pass away, but my words shall not pass away.

GENESIS 1:1
In the beginning God created the heaven and the earth.

ISAIAH 40:22
It is he that sitteth upon the circle of the earth, and the inhabitants thereof are as grasshoppers; that stretcheth out the heavens as a curtain, and spreadeth them out as a tent to dwell in.

GENESIS 2:2
And on the seventh day God ended his work which he had made; and he rested on the seventh day from all his work which he had made.

PSALM 102:25-27
Of old hast thou laid the foundation of the earth: and the heavens are the work of thy hands. **[26]** *They shall perish, but thou shalt endure: yea, all of them shall wax old like a garment; as a vesture shalt thou change them, and they shall be changed:* **[27]** *But thou art the same, and thy years shall have no end.*

LESSON 4 — How Do We Know the Bible Is Inspired?

DISCIPLESHIP QUESTIONS

8. The odds of just eight of the prophecies happening to one person are what?

9. But Jesus fulfilled _____ of prophecies.

10. How are prophecies in the Word of God different from other prophecies?

11. Everything you need to know about current social issues is where?
    A. In school
    B. In the news
    C. In church
    D. In heavenly places
    E. In the Bible

12. What happens when we base our philosophy on the world's viewpoint?

13. Read Joshua 1:8. What do you have to do to prosper and succeed?

14. True or false: You can prosper momentarily outside of pursuing God.

15. Discussion Question: Why wouldn't you be fulfilled by prospering that way?

SCRIPTURES TO USE WITH QUESTIONS

JOSHUA 1:8
This book of the law shall not depart out of thy mouth; but thou shalt meditate therein day and night, that thou mayest observe to do according to all that is written therein: for then thou shalt make thy way prosperous, and then thou shalt have good success.

LESSON 4 — HOW DO WE KNOW THE BIBLE IS INSPIRED?

DISCIPLESHIP QUESTIONS

16. Read Matthew 16:26. If you want to prosper God's way—in a way that doesn't take away your _____—then you're going to have to base your prosperity on the Word of God.
    - A. Time
    - B. Money
    - C. Energy
    - D. Life
    - E. Job

17. What leaves no doubt that the Bible is the inspired Word of God?

18. Discussion Question: Why should you put your faith in the Word of God, above all other information or ideas?

19. If you compromise on this point or begin to doubt that the Bible is the inspired Word of God, then you start down a slippery slope that will what?

20. Discussion Question: Why is it important to know that the Bible is a book from God?

SCRIPTURES TO USE WITH QUESTIONS

MATTHEW 16:26
For what is a man profited, if he shall gain the whole world, and lose his own soul? or what shall a man give in exchange for his soul?

LESSON 4 — HOW DO WE KNOW THE BIBLE IS INSPIRED?

ADDITIONAL SCRIPTURES

PSALM 16:9-10
Therefore my heart is glad, and my glory rejoiceth: my flesh also shall rest in hope. [10] For thou wilt not leave my soul in hell; neither wilt thou suffer thine Holy One to see corruption.

ACTS 2:24-36
Whom God hath raised up, having loosed the pains of death: because it was not possible that he should be holden of it. [25] For David speaketh concerning him, I foresaw the Lord always before my face, for he is on my right hand, that I should not be moved: [26] Therefore did my heart rejoice, and my tongue was glad; moreover also my flesh shall rest in hope: [27] Because thou wilt not leave my soul in hell, neither wilt thou suffer thine Holy One to see corruption. [28] Thou hast made known to me the ways of life; thou shalt make me full of joy with thy countenance. [29] Men and brethren, let me freely speak unto you of the patriarch David, that he is both dead and buried, and his sepulchre is with us unto this day. [30] Therefore being a prophet, and knowing that God had sworn with an oath to him, that of the fruit of his loins, according to the flesh, he would raise up Christ to sit on his throne; [31] He seeing this before spake of the resurrection of Christ, that his soul was not left in hell, neither his flesh did see corruption. [32] This Jesus hath God raised up, whereof we all are witnesses. [33] Therefore being by the right hand of God exalted, and having received of the Father the promise of the Holy Ghost, he hath shed forth this, which ye now see and hear. [34] For David is not ascended into the heavens: but he saith himself, The Lord said unto my Lord, Sit thou on my right hand, [35] Until I make thy foes thy footstool. [36] Therefore let all the house of Israel know assuredly, that God hath made that same Jesus, whom ye have crucified, both Lord and Christ.

ACTS 13:35
Wherefore he saith also in another psalm, Thou shalt not suffer thine Holy One to see corruption.

PSALM 22:1
My God, my God, why hast thou forsaken me? why art thou so far from helping me, and from the words of my roaring?

MATTHEW 27:46
And about the ninth hour Jesus cried with a loud voice, saying, Eli, Eli, lama sabachthani? that is to say, My God, my God, why hast thou forsaken me?

MARK 15:34
And at the ninth hour Jesus cried with a loud voice, saying, Eloi, Eloi, lama sabachthani? which is, being interpreted, My God, my God, why hast thou forsaken me?

PSALM 22:7-8
All they that see me laugh me to scorn: they shoot out the lip, they shake the head, saying, [8] He trusted on the Lord that he would deliver him: let him deliver him, seeing he delighted in him.

LUKE 23:33-35
And when they were come to the place, which is called Calvary, there they crucified him, and the malefactors, one on the right hand, and the other on the left. [34] Then said Jesus, Father, forgive them; for they know not what they do. And they parted his raiment, and cast lots. [35] And the people stood beholding. And the rulers also with them derided him, saying, He saved others; let him save himself, if he be Christ, the chosen of God.

PSALM 22:16
For dogs have compassed me: the assembly of the wicked have inclosed me: they pierced my hands and my feet.

MARK 15:24-25
And when they had crucified him, they parted his garments, casting lots upon them, what every man should take. [25] And it was the third hour, and they crucified him.

LESSON 4   HOW DO WE KNOW THE BIBLE IS INSPIRED?

ADDITIONAL SCRIPTURES

JOHN 19:31-37
The Jews therefore, because it was the preparation, that the bodies should not remain upon the cross on the sabbath day, (for that sabbath day was an high day,) besought Pilate that their legs might be broken, and that they might be taken away. [32] Then came the soldiers, and brake the legs of the first, and of the other which was crucified with him. [33] But when they came to Jesus, and saw that he was dead already, they brake not his legs: [34] But one of the soldiers with a spear pierced his side, and forthwith came there out blood and water. [35] And he that saw it bare record, and his record is true: and he knoweth that he saith true, that ye might believe. [36] For these things were done, that the scripture should be fulfilled, A bone of him shall not be broken. [37] And again another scripture saith, They shall look on him whom they pierced.

JOHN 20:25
The other disciples therefore said unto him, We have seen the Lord. But he said unto them, Except I shall see in his hands the print of the nails, and put my finger into the print of the nails, and thrust my hand into his side, I will not believe.

PSALM 22:18
They part my garments among them, and cast lots upon my vesture.

JOHN 19:23-24
Then the soldiers, when they had crucified Jesus, took his garments, and made four parts, to every soldier a part; and also his coat: now the coat was without seam, woven from the top throughout. [24] They said therefore among themselves, Let us not rend it, but cast lots for it, whose it shall be: that the scripture might be fulfilled, which saith, They parted my raiment among them, and for my vesture they did cast lots. These things therefore the soldiers did.

PSALM 34:20
He keepeth all his bones: not one of them is broken.

PSALM 35:19
Let not them that are mine enemies wrongfully rejoice over me: neither let them wink with the eye that hate me without a cause.

PSALM 41:9
Yea, mine own familiar friend, in whom I trusted, which did eat of my bread, hath lifted up his heel against me.

ISAIAH 53:3-7
He is despised and rejected of men; a man of sorrows, and acquainted with grief: and we hid as it were our faces from him; he was despised, and we esteemed him not. [4] Surely he hath borne our griefs, and carried our sorrows: yet we did esteem him stricken, smitten of God, and afflicted. [5] But he was wounded for our transgressions, he was bruised for our iniquities: the chastisement of our peace was upon him; and with his stripes we are healed. [6] All we like sheep have gone astray; we have turned every one to his own way; and the Lord hath laid on him the iniquity of us all. [7] He was oppressed, and he was afflicted, yet he opened not his mouth: he is brought as a lamb to the slaughter, and as a sheep before her shearers is dumb, so he openeth not his mouth.

PSALM 109:25
I became also a reproach unto them: when they looked upon me they shaked their heads.

PSALM 69:21
They gave me also gall for my meat; and in my thirst they gave me vinegar to drink.

MATTHEW 26:24
The Son of man goeth as it is written of him: but woe unto that man by whom the Son of man is betrayed! it had been good for that man if he had not been born.

LESSON 4 — HOW DO WE KNOW THE BIBLE IS INSPIRED?

ADDITIONAL SCRIPTURES

MATTHEW 27:34-35
They gave him vinegar to drink mingled with gall: and when he had tasted thereof, he would not drink. **[35]** *And they crucified him, and parted his garments, casting lots: that it might be fulfilled which was spoken by the prophet, They parted my garments among them, and upon my vesture did they cast lots.*

MATTHEW 27:38-39
Then were there two thieves crucified with him, one on the right hand, and another on the left. **[39]** *And they that passed by reviled him, wagging their heads.*

LUKE 22:47-48
And while he yet spake, behold a multitude, and he that was called Judas, one of the twelve, went before them, and drew near unto Jesus to kiss him. **[48]** *But Jesus said unto him, Judas, betrayest thou the Son of man with a kiss?*

JOHN 1:10-11
He was in the world, and the world was made by him, and the world knew him not. **[11]** *He came unto his own, and his own received him not.*

JOHN 15:24-25
If I had not done among them the works which none other man did, they had not had sin: but now have they both seen and hated both me and my Father. **[25]** *But this cometh to pass, that the word might be fulfilled that is written in their law, They hated me without a cause.*

MATTHEW 8:16-17
When the even was come, they brought unto him many that were possessed with devils: and he cast out the spirits with his word, and healed all that were sick: **[17]** *That it might be fulfilled which was spoken by Esaias the prophet, saying, Himself took our infirmities, and bare our sicknesses.*

1 PETER 2:23-24
Who, when he was reviled, reviled not again; when he suffered, he threatened not; but committed himself to him that judgeth righteously: **[24]** *Who his own self bare our sins in his own body on the tree, that we, being dead to sins, should live unto righteousness: by whose stripes ye were healed.*

ISAIAH 35:4-6
Say to them that are of a fearful heart, Be strong, fear not: behold, your God will come with vengeance, even God with a recompence; he will come and save you. **[5]** *Then the eyes of the blind shall be opened, and the ears of the deaf shall be unstopped.* **[6]** *Then shall the lame man leap as an hart, and the tongue of the dumb sing: for in the wilderness shall waters break out, and streams in the desert.*

ACTS 10:38
How God anointed Jesus of Nazareth with the Holy Ghost and with power: who went about doing good, and healing all that were oppressed of the devil; for God was with him.

LUKE 4:17-18
And there was delivered unto him the book of the prophet Esaias. And when he had opened the book, he found the place where it was written, **[18]** *The Spirit of the Lord is upon me, because he hath anointed me to preach the gospel to the poor; he hath sent me to heal the brokenhearted, to preach deliverance to the captives, and recovering of sight to the blind, to set at liberty them that are bruised.*

MATTHEW 27:12-14
And when he was accused of the chief priests and elders, he answered nothing. **[13]** *Then said Pilate unto him, Hearest thou not how many things they witness against thee?* **[14]** *And he answered him to never a word; insomuch that the governor marvelled greatly.*

LESSON 4   How Do We Know the Bible Is Inspired?

ADDITIONAL SCRIPTURES

MARK 14:61
But he held his peace, and answered nothing. Again the high priest asked him, and said unto him, Art thou the Christ, the Son of the Blessed?

MARK 15:5
But Jesus yet answered nothing; so that Pilate marvelled.

ISAIAH 53:9
And he made his grave with the wicked, and with the rich in his death; because he had done no violence, neither was any deceit in his mouth.

ISAIAH 53:11-12
He shall see of the travail of his soul, and shall be satisfied: by his knowledge shall my righteous servant justify many; for he shall bear their iniquities. **[12]** *Therefore will I divide him a portion with the great, and he shall divide the spoil with the strong; because he hath poured out his soul unto death: and he was numbered with the transgressors; and he bare the sin of many, and made intercession for the transgressors.*

MARK 15:27-28
And with him they crucify two thieves; the one on his right hand, and the other on his left. **[28]** *And the scripture was fulfilled, which saith, And he was numbered with the transgressors.*

MATTHEW 27:57-60
When the even was come, there came a rich man of Arimathaea, named Joseph, who also himself was Jesus' disciple: **[58]** *He went to Pilate, and begged the body of Jesus. Then Pilate commanded the body to be delivered.* **[59]** *And when Joseph had taken the body, he wrapped it in a clean linen cloth,* **[60]** *And laid it in his own new tomb, which he had hewn out in the rock: and he rolled a great stone to the door of the sepulchre, and departed.*

MATTHEW 27:29-30
And when they had platted a crown of thorns, they put it upon his head, and a reed in his right hand: and they bowed the knee before him, and mocked him, saying, Hail, King of the Jews! **[30]** *And they spit upon him, and took the reed, and smote him on the head.*

MARK 15:15-20
And so Pilate, willing to content the people, released Barabbas unto them, and delivered Jesus, when he had scourged him, to be crucified. **[16]** *And the soldiers led him away into the hall, called Praetorium; and they call together the whole band.* **[17]** *And they clothed him with purple, and platted a crown of thorns, and put it about his head,* **[18]** *And began to salute him, Hail, King of the Jews!* **[19]** *And they smote him on the head with a reed, and did spit upon him, and bowing their knees worshipped him.* **[20]** *And when they had mocked him, they took off the purple from him, and put his own clothes on him, and led him out to crucify him.*

PSALM 35:11
False witnesses did rise up; they laid to my charge things that I knew not.

MARK 14:57-58
And there arose certain, and bare false witness against him, saying, **[58]** *We heard him say, I will destroy this temple that is made with hands, and within three days I will build another made without hands.*

MATTHEW 27:48
And straightway one of them ran, and took a spunge, and filled it with vinegar, and put it on a reed, and gave him to drink.

LESSON 4 — How Do We Know the Bible Is Inspired?

ADDITIONAL SCRIPTURES

MARK 15:36
And one ran and filled a spunge full of vinegar, and put it on a reed, and gave him to drink, saying, Let alone; let us see whether Elias will come to take him down.

JOHN 19:29
Now there was set a vessel full of vinegar: and they filled a spunge with vinegar, and put it upon hyssop, and put it to his mouth.

PSALM 49:15
But God will redeem my soul from the power of the grave: for he shall receive me. Selah.

MARK 16:6-7
And he saith unto them, Be not affrighted: Ye seek Jesus of Nazareth, which was crucified: he is risen; he is not here: behold the place where they laid him. [7] But go your way, tell his disciples and Peter that he goeth before you into Galilee: there shall ye see him, as he said unto you.

PSALM 68:18
Thou hast ascended on high, thou hast led captivity captive: thou hast received gifts for men; yea, for the rebellious also, that the Lord God might dwell among them.

MARK 16:19
So then after the Lord had spoken unto them, he was received up into heaven, and sat on the right hand of God.

ACTS 1:9-10
And when he had spoken these things, while they beheld, he was taken up; and a cloud received him out of their sight. [10] And while they looked stedfastly toward heaven as he went up, behold, two men stood by them in white apparel.

EPHESIANS 4:8
Wherefore he saith, When he ascended up on high, he led captivity captive, and gave gifts unto men.

MICAH 5:2-5
But thou, Bethlehem Ephratah, though thou be little among the thousands of Judah, yet out of thee shall he come forth unto me that is to be ruler in Israel; whose goings forth have been from of old, from everlasting. [3] Therefore will he give them up, until the time that she which travaileth hath brought forth: then the remnant of his brethren shall return unto the children of Israel. [4] And he shall stand and feed in the strength of the Lord, in the majesty of the name of the Lord his God; and they shall abide: for now shall he be great unto the ends of the earth. [5] And this man shall be the peace, when the Assyrian shall come into our land: and when he shall tread in our palaces, then shall we raise against him seven shepherds, and eight principal men.

MATTHEW 2:1-6
Now when Jesus was born in Bethlehem of Judaea in the days of Herod the king, behold, there came wise men from the east to Jerusalem, [2] Saying, Where is he that is born King of the Jews? for we have seen his star in the east, and are come to worship him. [3] When Herod the king had heard these things, he was troubled, and all Jerusalem with him. [4] And when he had gathered all the chief priests and scribes of the people together, he demanded of them where Christ should be born. [5] And they said unto him, In Bethlehem of Judaea: for thus it is written by the prophet, [6] And thou Bethlehem, in the land of Juda, art not the least among the princes of Juda: for out of thee shall come a Governor, that shall rule my people Israel.

ISAIAH 7:14
Therefore the Lord himself shall give you a sign; Behold, a virgin shall conceive, and bear a son, and shall call his name Immanuel.

LESSON 4 — How Do We Know the Bible Is Inspired?

ADDITIONAL SCRIPTURES

MATTHEW 1:18-23
Now the birth of Jesus Christ was on this wise: When as his mother Mary was espoused to Joseph, before they came together, she was found with child of the Holy Ghost. **[19]** *Then Joseph her husband, being a just man, and not willing to make her a publick example, was minded to put her away privily.* **[20]** *But while he thought on these things, behold, the angel of the Lord appeared unto him in a dream, saying, Joseph, thou son of David, fear not to take unto thee Mary thy wife: for that which is conceived in her is of the Holy Ghost.* **[21]** *And she shall bring forth a son, and thou shalt call his name Jesus: for he shall save his people from their sins.* **[22]** *Now all this was done, that it might be fulfilled which was spoken of the Lord by the prophet, saying,* **[23]** *Behold, a virgin shall be with child, and shall bring forth a son, and they shall call his name Emmanuel, which being interpreted is, God with us.*

LUKE 1:26-35
And in the sixth month the angel Gabriel was sent from God unto a city of Galilee, named Nazareth, **[27]** *To a virgin espoused to a man whose name was Joseph, of the house of David; and the virgin's name was Mary.* **[28]** *And the angel came in unto her, and said, Hail, thou that art highly favoured, the Lord is with thee: blessed art thou among women.* **[29]** *And when she saw him, she was troubled at his saying, and cast in her mind what manner of salutation this should be.* **[30]** *And the angel said unto her, Fear not, Mary: for thou hast found favour with God.* **[31]** *And, behold, thou shalt conceive in thy womb, and bring forth a son, and shalt call his name Jesus.* **[32]** *He shall be great, and shall be called the Son of the Highest: and the Lord God shall give unto him the throne of his father David:* **[33]** *And he shall reign over the house of Jacob for ever; and of his kingdom there shall be no end.* **[34]** *Then said Mary unto the angel, How shall this be, seeing I know not a man?* **[35]** *And the angel answered and said unto her, The Holy Ghost shall come upon thee, and the power of the Highest shall overshadow thee: therefore also that holy thing which shall be born of thee shall be called the Son of God.*

ISAIAH 29:18
And in that day shall the deaf hear the words of the book, and the eyes of the blind shall see out of obscurity, and out of darkness.

MATTHEW 11:5
The blind receive their sight, and the lame walk, the lepers are cleansed, and the deaf hear, the dead are raised up, and the poor have the gospel preached to them.

MATTHEW 15:30
And great multitudes came unto him, having with them those that were lame, blind, dumb, maimed, and many others, and cast them down at Jesus' feet; and he healed them.

MATTHEW 21:14
And the blind and the lame came to him in the temple; and he healed them.

JOHN 5:8-9
Jesus saith unto him, Rise, take up thy bed, and walk. **[9]** *And immediately the man was made whole, and took up his bed, and walked: and on the same day was the sabbath.*

ACTS 3:2-8
And a certain man lame from his mother's womb was carried, whom they laid daily at the gate of the temple which is called Beautiful, to ask alms of them that entered into the temple; **[3]** *Who seeing Peter and John about to go into the temple asked an alms.* **[4]** *And Peter, fastening his eyes upon him with John, said, Look on us.* **[5]** *And he gave heed unto them, expecting to receive something of them.* **[6]** *Then Peter said, Silver and gold have I none; but such as I have give I thee: In the name of Jesus Christ of Nazareth rise up and walk.* **[7]** *And he took him by the right hand, and lifted him up: and immediately his feet and ankle bones received strength.* **[8]** *And he leaping up stood, and walked, and entered with them into the temple, walking, and leaping, and praising God.*

LESSON 4 — HOW DO WE KNOW THE BIBLE IS INSPIRED?

ADDITIONAL SCRIPTURES

ISAIAH 52:14
As many were astonied at thee; his visage was so marred more than any man, and his form more than the sons of men.

MATTHEW 26:67
Then did they spit in his face, and buffeted him; and others smote him with the palms of their hands.

MATTHEW 27:26
Then released he Barabbas unto them: and when he had scourged Jesus, he delivered him to be crucified.

JOHN 1:10-11
He was in the world, and the world was made by him, and the world knew him not. [11] He came unto his own, and his own received him not.

ROMANS 4:25
Who was delivered for our offences, and was raised again for our justification.

1 PETER 3:18
For Christ also hath once suffered for sins, the just for the unjust, that he might bring us to God, being put to death in the flesh, but quickened by the Spirit.

ROMANS 5:18-19
Therefore as by the offence of one judgment came upon all men to condemnation; even so by the righteousness of one the free gift came upon all men unto justification of life. [19] For as by one man's disobedience many were made sinners, so by the obedience of one shall many be made righteous.

1 JOHN 2:1-2
My little children, these things write I unto you, that ye sin not. And if any man sin, we have an advocate with the Father, Jesus Christ the righteous: [2] And he is the propitiation for our sins: and not for ours only, but also for the sins of the whole world.

LUKE 22:37
For I say unto you, that this that is written must yet be accomplished in me, And he was reckoned among the transgressors: for the things concerning me have an end.

ZECHARIAH 9:9
Rejoice greatly, O daughter of Zion; shout, O daughter of Jerusalem: behold, thy King cometh unto thee: he is just, and having salvation; lowly, and riding upon an ass, and upon a colt the foal of an ass.

MARK 11:1-10
And when they came nigh to Jerusalem, unto Bethphage and Bethany, at the mount of Olives, he sendeth forth two of his disciples, [2] And saith unto them, Go your way into the village over against you: and as soon as ye be entered into it, ye shall find a colt tied, whereon never man sat; loose him, and bring him. [3] And if any man say unto you, Why do ye this? say ye that the Lord hath need of him; and straightway he will send him hither. [4] And they went their way, and found the colt tied by the door without in a place where two ways met; and they loose him. [5] And certain of them that stood there said unto them, What do ye, loosing the colt? [6] And they said unto them even as Jesus had commanded: and they let them go. [7] And they brought the colt to Jesus, and cast their garments on him; and he sat upon him. [8] And many spread their garments in the way: and others cut down branches off the trees, and strawed them in the way. [9] And they that went before, and they that followed, cried, saying, Hosanna; Blessed is he that cometh in the name of the Lord: [10] Blessed be the kingdom of our father David, that cometh in the name of the Lord: Hosanna in the highest.

LESSON 4 — How Do We Know the Bible Is Inspired?

ADDITIONAL SCRIPTURES

MATTHEW 21:1-5
And when they drew nigh unto Jerusalem, and were come to Bethphage, unto the mount of Olives, then sent Jesus two disciples, **[2]** *Saying unto them, Go into the village over against you, and straightway ye shall find an ass tied, and a colt with her: loose them, and bring them unto me.* **[3]** *And if any man say ought unto you, ye shall say, The Lord hath need of them; and straightway he will send them.* **[4]** *All this was done, that it might be fulfilled which was spoken by the prophet, saying,* **[5]** *Tell ye the daughter of Sion, Behold, thy King cometh unto thee, meek, and sitting upon an ass, and a colt the foal of an ass.*

LUKE 19:28-38
And when he had thus spoken, he went before, ascending up to Jerusalem. **[29]** *And it came to pass, when he was come nigh to Bethphage and Bethany, at the mount called the mount of Olives, he sent two of his disciples,* **[30]** *Saying, Go ye into the village over against you; in the which at your entering ye shall find a colt tied, whereon yet never man sat: loose him, and bring him hither.* **[31]** *And if any man ask you, Why do ye loose him? thus shall ye say unto him, Because the Lord hath need of him.* **[32]** *And they that were sent went their way, and found even as he had said unto them.* **[33]** *And as they were loosing the colt, the owners thereof said unto them, Why loose ye the colt?* **[34]** *And they said, The Lord hath need of him.* **[35]** *And they brought him to Jesus: and they cast their garments upon the colt, and they set Jesus thereon.* **[36]** *And as he went, they spread their clothes in the way.* **[37]** *And when he was come nigh, even now at the descent of the mount of Olives, the whole multitude of the disciples began to rejoice and praise God with a loud voice for all the mighty works that they had seen;* **[38]** *Saying, Blessed be the King that cometh in the name of the Lord: peace in heaven, and glory in the highest.*

JOHN 12:12-15
On the next day much people that were come to the feast, when they heard that Jesus was coming to Jerusalem, **[13]** *Took branches of palm trees, and went forth to meet him, and cried, Hosanna: Blessed is the King of Israel that cometh in the name of the Lord.* **[14]** *And Jesus, when he had found a young ass, sat thereon; as it is written,* **[15]** *Fear not, daughter of Sion: behold, thy King cometh, sitting on an ass's colt.*

ZECHARIAH 11:12-13
And I said unto them, If ye think good, give me my price; and if not, forbear. So they weighed for my price thirty pieces of silver. **[13]** *And the Lord said unto me, Cast it unto the potter: a goodly price that I was prised at of them. And I took the thirty pieces of silver, and cast them to the potter in the house of the Lord.*

MATTHEW 27:3-10
Then Judas, which had betrayed him, when he saw that he was condemned, repented himself, and brought again the thirty pieces of silver to the chief priests and elders, **[4]** *Saying, I have sinned in that I have betrayed the innocent blood. And they said, What is that to us? see thou to that.* **[5]** *And he cast down the pieces of silver in the temple, and departed, and went and hanged himself.* **[6]** *And the chief priests took the silver pieces, and said, It is not lawful for to put them into the treasury, because it is the price of blood.* **[7]** *And they took counsel, and bought with them the potter's field, to bury strangers in.* **[8]** *Wherefore that field was called, The field of blood, unto this day.* **[9]** *Then was fulfilled that which was spoken by Jeremy the prophet, saying, And they took the thirty pieces of silver, the price of him that was valued, whom they of the children of Israel did value;* **[10]** *And gave them for the potter's field, as the Lord appointed me.*

ISAIAH 44:28
That saith of Cyrus, He is my shepherd, and shall perform all my pleasure: even saying to Jerusalem, Thou shalt be built; and to the temple, Thy foundation shall be laid.

2 CHRONICLES 36:22-23
Now in the first year of Cyrus king of Persia, that the word of the Lord spoken by the mouth of Jeremiah might be accomplished, the Lord stirred up the spirit of Cyrus king of Persia, that he made a proclamation throughout all his kingdom, and put it also in writing, saying, **[23]** *Thus saith Cyrus king of Persia, All the kingdoms of the earth hath the Lord God of heaven given me; and he hath charged me to build him an house in Jerusalem, which is in Judah. Who is there among you of all his people? The Lord his God be with him, and let him go up.*

LESSON 4 — How Do We Know the Bible Is Inspired?

ADDITIONAL SCRIPTURES

1 KINGS 13:2
And he cried against the altar in the word of the Lord, and said, O altar, altar, thus saith the Lord; Behold, a child shall be born unto the house of David, Josiah by name; and upon thee shall he offer the priests of the high places that burn incense upon thee, and men's bones shall be burnt upon thee.

2 KINGS 23:15-20
Moreover the altar that was at Bethel, and the high place which Jeroboam the son of Nebat, who made Israel to sin, had made, both that altar and the high place he brake down, and burned the high place, and stamped it small to powder, and burned the grove. **[16]** *And as Josiah turned himself, he spied the sepulchres that were there in the mount, and sent, and took the bones out of the sepulchres, and burned them upon the altar, and polluted it, according to the word of the Lord which the man of God proclaimed, who proclaimed these words.* **[17]** *Then he said, What title is that that I see? And the men of the city told him, It is the sepulchre of the man of God, which came from Judah, and proclaimed these things that thou hast done against the altar of Bethel.* **[18]** *And he said, Let him alone; let no man move his bones. So they let his bones alone, with the bones of the prophet that came out of Samaria.* **[19]** *And all the houses also of the high places that were in the cities of Samaria, which the kings of Israel had made to provoke the Lord to anger, Josiah took away, and did to them according to all the acts that he had done in Bethel.* **[20]** *And he slew all the priests of the high places that were there upon the altars, and burned men's bones upon them, and returned to Jerusalem.*

2 KINGS 22:8
And Hilkiah the high priest said unto Shaphan the scribe, I have found the book of the law in the house of the Lord. And Hilkiah gave the book to Shaphan, and he read it.

MATTHEW 6:33
But seek ye first the kingdom of God, and his righteousness; and all these things shall be added unto you.

LESSON 4 — How Do We Know the Bible Is Inspired?

ANSWER KEY

1. C. Man
2. *Discussion question*
3. Prophecies and details
4. The universe having a beginning, the earth being round, no new matter is being created, the amount of energy in the universe is decreasing
5. False
6. Four hundred years or more before New Testament times
7. *Discussion question*
8. 1 in 10^{17}, or 1 in 100 quadrillion
9. Hundreds
10. Prophecies in the Word of God describe in precise detail events that are fulfilled hundreds of years later
11. E. In the Bible
12. We give the Enemy free access to our lives
13. You have to take the Word of God and put it in your heart and meditate on it
14. True
15. *Discussion question*
16. D. Life
17. The evidence you've examined
18. *Discussion question*
19. Undermine your faith in God
20. *Discussion question*

How Do I Follow God?

I remember a young man who came to me for counsel one time about going to Charis Bible College. He said that he knew God was telling him to go, but everyone in his life was telling him not to. He went into a long story detailing all of the reasons the pastor of his church, his parents, and his girlfriend thought he shouldn't go.

After about ten minutes, he finally asked me, "So, what do you think?"

I said, "You lost me the moment you said that you know God is telling you to go."

If God tells you to do something, then you just do what God tells you to do. Why would you even debate it? God is the Creator of the universe, He knows all things, and He knows what is best for you. Why would you care what anybody else thinks or what people might say about you? In comparison with God, no one else's opinion should matter.

Your relationship with God should soak all the way down to the very core of your being. When that happens, your actions will be determined by your philosophy instead of by your environment or emotions. It really simplifies life to realize Jesus is Lord and you aren't. Then, when God tells you to do something, you just do it. This attitude is one part of a Christian philosophy that will really simplify your life.

I couldn't tell you how many people have told me over the years that they felt God was calling them to come to Charis Bible College, but they didn't think it was wise to go. They would say, for instance, that it was only ten years until they retired. They were focused on securing their financial futures, and they were leaning unto their own understanding. My opinion is that when God wants you to do something ten years from now, He'll tell you ten years from now. If God is telling you now, He either wants you to do it now, or He wants you to start taking the necessary steps to get the ball rolling. Some things take a while to come to pass, so God will give you instruction in advance, but when God tells you to do something, you just do it. That's all there is to it.

The first time I drove through the tiny town of Pritchett on the eastern edge of Colorado, I was not impressed. The landscape was a flat, treeless plain as barren as any desert. The only shrubbery I could see was planted in people's yards, which didn't exactly provide lush green scenery, considering only 140 people lived in the entire town. It looked like the end of the earth to me. I started joking with a friend who was in the car with me about how God was going to send him to this small village on the edge of nowhere.

Lesson 5 — How Do I Follow God?

"Thus saith the Lord," I told him, "you're being called to Pritchett, Colorado." We had a good time laughing about that. If it wasn't the edge of the world, you could see it from there—it was that close.

I stopped in Pritchett to preach at a church of 10 people. We saw a man raised from the dead, and church attendance jumped up to around 100 people. They wanted me to stay and continue teaching them the full Gospel.

"You can't just come in here, challenge everything we thought we knew about God, and then leave town," they said.

I just laughed and said, "No way—I am not moving to Pritchett!"

No part of me wanted to live in Pritchett, but as we were driving out of town, I began to sense in my heart that God was telling me to stay there and teach those people the Word. By the time I got back to my house in Childress, Texas, I knew I was supposed to move. From a purely logical standpoint, there was no reason for me to go. The church only had ten members, they had no money, the church building was too small, and the town had nothing going for it. I could have given you a thousand reasons as to why it didn't seem like a good idea.

How could I fulfill my big vision in such a small place? Pritchett wasn't on the way to anywhere. It wasn't a steppingstone to something better. It was a dead end. The only way to leave Pritchett was feet first, in a coffin. That's exactly the way I felt.

On the other hand, I was prospering in Childress, Texas. For the first time since I started in ministry, it looked like I might succeed. We had food and money on a regular basis, and things were going well for us. Our church had fifty or sixty people in regular attendance, I had a broadcast on the local radio station, and our church was making a difference. Everything was going great.

But once I knew that God wanted me to move to Pritchett, Colorado, the debate was over. Jesus is Lord of my life, and my attitude was that if God wanted me to do something, then I was going to do it—and enjoy doing it. Once I was convinced of God's will for me to move to Pritchett, I began to praise Him for leading and guiding me. Within days, my entire attitude had changed, and I was excited about going. There were some hardships associated with living in such a remote area, but I loved living in Pritchett as much as any place I've ever lived. It was wonderful.

I made Jesus Lord of my life on March 23, 1968, and I haven't tried to direct my own life since. God is Lord, I'm not, and He knows what's best for me. I have feelings and opinions like everybody else, but the discussion ends once I'm sure God is telling me to do something. I trust God's judgment more than I trust my own, and I just do what He leads me to do. I couldn't even tell you how many decisions I've made in my life based purely on the fact that I was sure God was leading me.

It would really simplify your life to run up a white flag and surrender to Jesus as Lord. One of my favorite passages of Scripture is from Jeremiah. He was wondering out loud how a people whom God rescued from Egypt and preserved through many miracles could forget the Lord who delivered them and turn to vain idols. In the middle of his grieving, Jeremiah answered his own question by saying,

Lesson 5   How Do I Follow God?

O LORD, I know that the way of man is not in himself: it is not in man that walketh to direct his steps.
JEREMIAH 10:23

The Jews had fallen from a position of favor because they started doing things their own way. Jeremiah recognized that God didn't create us to rule our own lives. He gave us the free will to make our own choices, but God never intended for us to direct our own steps. We have the freedom to decide for ourselves, because God doesn't force His will upon us, but the correct choice is to recognize our complete dependency on God. We aren't smart enough to run our own lives. God said,

I call heaven and earth to record this day against you, that I have set before you life and death, blessing and cursing: therefore choose life, that both thou and thy seed may live.
DEUTERONOMY 30:19

God gives us a choice, but He also tells us which option is best: He says, "Choose life!" We need to trust in the Lord with all our hearts and not try to figure things out on our own. We need to seek His will in everything we do, and He'll show us the path to take—that's the smart choice (Prov. 3:5-6). That's how we're supposed to live. We're meant to make Jesus our Lord and follow His guidance.

The world would be a different place if Adam and Eve had followed this philosophy. It was very clear that the serpent was enticing them to do something contrary to what God had told them, but they didn't follow God's guidance. They knew God as their Creator and recognized His provision for them, but they didn't submit to God as Lord of their lives. They knew He was kind to them and that He met with them and talked with them, but they didn't bow to Him and determine that they wouldn't lean unto their own understanding. They failed to surrender to God's sovereignty, and Satan went right through that open door to lead them into sin.

A solid Christian philosophy requires believing in the Word of God as our supreme authority and making Jesus Lord of our lives—not merely in the sense of recognizing His authority and attributes, but by submitting to His leadership.

A rich man once kneeled down before Jesus and asked, "Good Master, what must I do to inherit eternal life?"

"Why do you call Me good?" Jesus replied. "None is good except God alone." In other words, Jesus was saying, "Either call Me God and make Me Lord, or quit calling Me good!"

The rich man responded by calling Jesus "Master" again. He wasn't willing to go all the way and make Jesus his Lord and Savior. He wanted the salvation Jesus provides, but he didn't want to completely commit himself to following Jesus as Lord. Jesus knew the man wasn't totally sincere, but He still loved him. Jesus told him, "Go, sell everything you have, and give the proceeds to the poor. It will give you treasure in heaven. Then come, take up your cross, and follow Me." The rich man couldn't do it, and he walked away grieved (Mark 10:17-22).

Jesus presented salvation as making Him Lord and Master over your life—not just acknowledging His greatness. Scripture says that in order to be saved, you have to confess with your mouth that Jesus is Lord and believe in your heart that God raised Him from the dead (Rom. 10:9-10). I believe that salvation should be presented as turning your life over to Jesus—lock, stock, and barrel—but that's not how salvation is usually presented. The message many people are hearing is that they should be saved just so they can go to heaven when they die. Obviously, that is an important part of salvation, but it isn't the whole message. As a result, a lot of born-again believers will go to heaven when they die, but they haven't submitted to Jesus as Director and Leader of their everyday lives.

In my own case, I was born again when I was eight years old, but I didn't submit to Jesus as Lord until I was eighteen. During that ten-year interval, I believe I was born again. I loved God and I had a relationship with Him to the degree that I would have gone to heaven if I had died, but I wasn't allowing Jesus to direct my life. I didn't submit to Jesus as Lord until March 23, 1968. I haven't lived perfectly since that time—obviously—but whenever I know God is telling me to do something, I do it. I yield to Jesus as my Lord, and my submission has led to a blessed life. Everything I set my hand unto prospers. God is a good God, and He leads me along good paths.

I believe this philosophy is absolutely essential. You need to adopt this way of thinking: You are going to do whatever God tells you to do, regardless of any other factors. Whether it is through the Word of God or by special instruction from the Holy Spirit, decide ahead of time that you are going to follow God's leading—no discussion, no debate.

Over the years, I have discovered that God will tell me to do things, but if I don't do them right away, He doesn't argue with me. He just tells me what He wants me to do, and then I have the choice of whether or not to follow Him. To the best of my ability, I do what God tells me to do, but if I miss His leadership, He won't debate the issue with me. So, if you're waiting for God to convince you to do the thing you already know He wants you to do, you'll be waiting a long time because it isn't going to happen. God doesn't get into debates with you over His will for your life. He will lead and He will direct, but He isn't going to argue with you about what you already know.

Doing whatever you want and asking God to bless it as an afterthought is not the same thing as following God. God tells you to do things for your own good. Really, being a Christian is simple: All you have to do is make Jesus Lord of your life, follow the leading of the Holy Spirit, and do what God's Word tells you to do. You'll solve a lot of problems in your life by following those few simple steps.

In order to remain sensitive to God's leading, you have to guard your heart against the negative philosophies that are being promoted in the world. Every time you watch a television program, read a book, listen to the radio, browse the internet, or watch a movie, you encounter ideas that are contrary to God's philosophy. Satan uses words to attack you through the way you think, and the modern media is the ideal way to push the world's philosophy. Every time you encounter those lies, you need to reject them. Isaiah says,

> *No weapon that is formed against thee shall prosper; and every tongue that shall rise against thee in judgment thou shalt condemn. This is the heritage of the servants of the LORD, and their righteousness is of me, saith the LORD.*
>
> ISAIAH 54:17

The promise here is that attacks against us won't succeed. Notice that Isaiah then mentioned the words spoken against us. The number one weapon Satan uses against us is deceitful words. He steals from people through vain philosophies and lies. This scripture says we are to **"condemn"** the lies that rise against us. The word *condemn* is defined by *The Houghton Mifflin American Heritage Electronic Dictionary* (*HMAHED*) as "1. To express disapproval of; denounce. 2. a. To convict. b. To sentence to a punishment. 3. To declare unfit for use."

We have to take the authority God has given us and condemn those negative words, philosophies, and thoughts. Anything that is contrary to God's Word must be rejected.

This is more important than most of us realize. Most people go through the day hardly paying attention to all of the garbage, unbelief, doubt, and complaining that come at them through the media and that wander through their minds. All of those words and thoughts will corrupt us. Scripture says,

> *Be not deceived: evil communications corrupt good manners.*
> 1 CORINTHIANS 15:33

The truth of this scripture is demonstrated in the life of Lot and the infamous city of Sodom. Lot was a godly man and the evil of the society he lived in was a continual grief to him, but his association with the city of Sodom cost him dearly. He never participated in their sins, but he ended up losing his wife and daughters in the judgment that came against Sodom (2 Pet. 2:7-8). Lot is an example of the danger of trying to blend in and also of the mistake in thinking that the evil in society around you won't affect you. You have to condemn the negative things around you.

Christians don't just wake up one morning and discover that they have a worldly philosophy; it happens slowly over time. You can see the process reflected in Satan's temptation of Eve. Satan didn't immediately call God a liar; he started out by questioning whether God had really told her not to eat of every tree in the Garden (Gen. 3:1). From there, he led Eve down a path of deceit until she was looking at things from his perspective and finally disobeyed God's command. It's like the story of putting a frog into a pot of boiling water: It will jump out of the hot water immediately, but if you put that same frog in lukewarm water and turn the heat up very slowly, you can boil it alive, and it will never try to escape—because it won't notice the gradual temperature change. This is how the devil works. He doesn't come at you all at once; instead, he drops little doubts here and there and attacks the integrity of God's Word piece by piece.

I heard a story one time about a father who was trying to protect his kids from the influence of the world by monitoring the movies and television they watched. One day, his daughter asked to go see a movie with her friends.

"What's it rated?" he asked.

"R," she mumbled in response.

"Well, then, you can't go see it."

"But, Dad," she argued, "Everyone says it's a great movie. All the other kids at church have seen it."

"What's in the movie that makes it rated R?" he asked.

"I'm not sure," she said. "I've heard there is a little nudity and some swearing, but not much. And it's supposed to be a great movie."

"I'm sorry, honey, but I can't let you go see it," the father said.

The daughter was angry, but her dad wouldn't budge, so she had her friends come over to the house that night instead. While she was hanging out with her friends and playing games, her father made everyone brownies. After everything was set, they all lined up to get dessert.

"Now, before you eat," he said over the excitement, "I just want to let you know that I put a little bit of dog poop in the recipe this time. It's not much. You probably won't taste it, and it won't make you sick or anything—but it is in there. Don't worry about it, though—for the most part—these are really tasty brownies." I seriously doubt those kids ate any brownies. No matter how little dog poop ends up in the dessert, it's still spoiled. Why should we be any more tolerant of ungodliness in our entertainment?

The world we live in is fallen and corrupt, but many of us have accepted the condition of the world and have grown tolerant of the ungodliness that surrounds us. We watch the same movies and television programs, read the same books, and listen to the same music—even though we know they aren't exactly right. We know they don't meet God's standard, but it's just a little bit of ungodliness—it's just a little nudity or profanity. Repeated exposure to that stuff leads to an increased tolerance for worldly viewpoints until, eventually, we are indulging attitudes and beliefs that are totally contrary to a godly perspective.

Our great-grandparents would be shocked to see the things that are on television and in magazines today. My wife and I have had a subscription to *Reader's Digest* magazine for years, and traditionally, it has been a very wholesome, family-oriented publication. Recently they have begun including racy advertisements like those that feature the backs of nude women. It isn't nudity exactly, but it shows how the magazine is taking a step in the direction of more relaxed moral standards. Today many popular magazines feature ads that would have been considered pornography a few generations ago.

I don't watch a lot of television, but I have an hour drive from my house into the office, and I listen to the news on the radio. I don't listen to it for long, though, because most of it is false prophecy. They take a small event and blow it up by focusing on all of the negative things that *could* happen—usually with an emphasis on how it *will* happen, and maybe it will happen *to you*. You can ask anybody who rides in the car with me: I condemn the negative words that I hear over the radio.

When the news broadcast comes on and says "It's flu season out there…Have you had your flu shot?" I say, "Oh, no, it isn't. In the name of Jesus, it's not flu season for me." To the commercial that asks "Are you having such-and-such medical problem? We can help," I say, "No. Thank You, Jesus, I'm not having that problem."

I talk back to the radio and defend my belief system. I believe that when you hear a philosophy that is contrary to God's Word, you have to stand against it—that's what Eve should have done. When Satan asked "Did God really say…?" Eve should have said, "Yes, God did say, and He is not a liar—so go away."

This might all sound a little weird, but it's just a component of guarding your heart. Scripture says you should guard your heart above everything else in life because it determines the course of your life

(Prov. 4:23). Satan tries to come against you through the way you think, so when I hear a lie, I condemn it. *Condemn* means "to express disapproval of; denounce" (*HMAHED*). And that's what I do—I speak the truth from God's Word to counter the lie. It's a part of guarding my heart.

When the media says sickness is rampant, I confess that by Jesus' stripes, I'm healed (Is. 53:5 and 1 Pet. 2:24). When the newspaper says the economy is in the toilet, I flush that thought and confess that God supplies all my needs according to His riches in glory (Phil. 4:19). When I fall short and thoughts of condemnation rise up, I confess that there is no longer condemnation for those who are in Christ Jesus and walk after the spirit (Rom. 8:1). Wherever and whenever the Enemy attacks God's Word with a lie, I counter the lie by speaking the truth (John 17:17).

This is just a practical application of two philosophies I have been discussing. First, we have to believe that the Word of God is inspired and without error. Second, Jesus is Lord, and we shouldn't question His instructions. Those two philosophies will prevent Satan from having any access to us. Whenever we hear something that is contrary to God's Word, we should just reject it.

The philosophy of making Jesus Lord means that when God tells you to do something, you just do it. Unfortunately, many Christians debate with God about whether or not they are going to do what He asks. For instance, Scripture says we're supposed to give, and the tithe (or 10 percent of your income) is just a starting place. Ten percent was the requirement under the Old Covenant. Nothing is required under the New Covenant of grace, but we should *desire* to give even more. God has promised that if we seek His kingdom first, He will freely give us the food, clothing, and shelter we need (Matt. 6:33). Most Christians give a little from the abundance of their wealth, but they don't give joyfully. Scripture says,

> *Every man according as he purposeth in his heart, so let him give; not grudgingly, or of necessity: for God loveth a cheerful giver. And God is able to make all grace abound toward you; that ye, always having all sufficiency in all things, may abound to every good work.*
> 2 CORINTHIANS 9:7-8

A lot of people don't trust God to supply their needs, so they cling to money and material possessions as their safety net. They don't give joyfully, because they are afraid God won't come through on His promise to give back. We have to trust God that His Word is a sure promise. No marriage or friendship can thrive unless the partners trust one another, and relationship with God is no different in that respect. Following Jesus means trusting Him to do what He says He will do.

But many people who say Jesus is Lord prove by their actions that they don't really trust Him. The Bible tells us to love our enemies, to bless those who curse us, to do good to those who hate us, and to pray for those who persecute us and despitefully use us (Matt. 5:44). We know we're supposed to turn the other cheek and we teach that principle to our children, but how many of us instantly slide into gossip and anger when someone comes against us? When we do that, we aren't submitting to Jesus as Lord of our lives. Our actions prove who is really sitting on the throne.

I'm not saying that we can be perfect after we submit to Jesus as Lord or that any failure in our lives means we haven't submitted to Jesus. It isn't possible for us to live perfectly. We're still going to make mistakes. Even though our spirits are perfect, our bodies and souls won't be perfected until the Lord comes back and gives us glorified bodies and new souls. But our desire should be to follow Jesus' commands perfectly. Whenever we recognize that we are doing something contrary to the Word, we need to humble ourselves and turn back to God.

I certainly haven't lived perfectly. I've gossiped about people and said things in anger after someone has done something to hurt me. I've sinned plenty, but the moment I realize I am behaving contrary to God's instructions, I humble myself and turn away from whatever it was I was doing. My desire is that Jesus reigns as Lord of my life, and I follow His commands.

We are in a battle. We win eternal life when we are born again, but in this world, we still have to fight the lies that come against us (Eph. 6:12-13). We win those battles by making the determination that Jesus will reign as Lord in our lives and by submitting to His leadership. When God leads us to do something, then we need to do it. The debate should end once God's will is clear in any area of our lives. No matter what the circumstances look like, we should follow God. The only way the Enemy can win is for us to consider and submit to his lies instead of following God's leading. God didn't create us to run our own lives. He gave us the freedom to make our own choices in life, but He also told us that the right option is to choose life. The correct choice is to use our free will to make Jesus Lord and to follow His leading.

The great heroes of the Bible were people who followed God's way of thinking even when it meant putting their lives on the line. Shadrach, Meshach, and Abednego come immediately to mind. They were three young men who had been taken to Babylon during the captivity. After Daniel correctly interpreted one of King Nebuchadnezzar's dreams, they were elevated to positions of leadership within the king's government. After some time, the king made an idol of gold and instructed everyone to bow down and worship it. When Shadrach, Meshach, and Abednego refused, they were brought before the king to be punished. The king told them that if they bowed down and worshiped the image, he would let them live, but if they refused, he would throw them into a burning furnace. Then he challenged them by saying, "Who is the God who will deliver you from my hands then?"

They replied,

> *O Nebuchadnezzar, we are not careful to answer thee in this matter. If it be so, our God whom we serve is able to deliver us from the burning fiery furnace, and he will deliver us out of thine hand, O king. But if not, be it known unto thee, O king, that we will not serve thy gods, nor worship the golden image which thou hast set up.*
>
> DANIEL 3:16-18

Shadrach, Meshach, and Abednego knew God was capable of saving them, but they didn't have a specific promise that He *would*. Still, they were not afraid of the king's threats, so they told him that they were going to follow God, and they didn't care what he said or did about it. It didn't matter to them that the king was planning to roast them alive. They demonstrated that their commitment to God went beyond all other considerations, even the desire to live.

Most Christians have not made such a strong commitment to God. Many will serve God and talk about the Gospel as long as they aren't persecuted, but as soon as someone starts making fun of them, they shrink back. When friends start deserting them and family members call them fanatics, they back off preaching the Gospel. As long as your philosophy allows for you to back down from your commitment to God, then the devil is going to have an inroad into your life. The Enemy will use your concern over other people's opinions to manipulate you into conforming to his worldview. All he will have to do to stop you from following God's will for your life is bring people along to make fun of you. That's why the Bible says,

> *The fear of man bringeth a snare: but whoso putteth his trust in the LORD shall be safe.*
> PROVERBS 29:25

Shadrach, Meshach, and Abednego maintained a philosophy that God is absolute Lord. He was the only one they would serve, and they would bow to no one else. Of course, their reply infuriated King Nebuchadnezzar. He was so angry that he ordered the furnace to be heated seven times hotter than usual. The king ordered the strongest men in his army to tie up Shadrach, Meshach, and Abednego and throw them into the fire—and it was so hot that the king's men were killed by the flames as they tossed the three Hebrews into the furnace.

The king gazed into the flames, watching to see the three Israelites consumed by the fire, but he soon stood up in amazement and said, "Didn't we cast three men into the fire?" And his advisors said, "Certainly we did, sir." And the king said,

> *Lo, I see four men loose, walking in the midst of the fire, and they have no hurt; and the form of the fourth is like the Son of God.*
> DANIEL 3:25

In astonishment, the king went near to the fiery furnace, calling the names of Shadrach, Meshach, and Abednego and ordering them to come out of the fire. They walked out from the middle of the flames, and Scripture says, **"The princes, governors, and captains, and the king's counsellors, being gathered together, saw these men, upon whose bodies the fire had no power, nor was an hair of their head singed, neither were their coats changed, nor the smell of fire had passed on them"** (Dan. 3:27). The flames that consumed the king's strongest men had zero effect upon the three Hebrews who were totally committed to God.

Shadrach, Meshach, and Abednego refused to compromise and God preserved them. Daniel was preserved in the same way when he was thrown into a den of lions after refusing to follow a law that forbade praying to God (Dan. 6). These biblical stories illustrate that commitment to God can't be a negotiable issue. Whatever you have to compromise to keep or obtain, you will eventually lose. Compromise is the language of the devil. You need to make the decision that Jesus is Lord and that you are going to remain absolutely committed to Him no matter what anyone else says or does—it's a necessary step in becoming grounded in a Christian worldview.

God should be our number one priority every day, but with many of us, He gets pushed to the end of our agenda. We should be seeking God about how to plan our days instead of planning our days and then seeing if we can squeeze in time for relationship with God. We should spend some time asking God, "What do *You* want me to do today?" We should present our calendars to God and say, "Here's my schedule, God. What would *You* like me to do?" This is how God intended for us to live when He created us. We should be allowing the Lord to direct our steps, not trying to figure out life with our limited understanding.

Lesson 5 — How Do I Follow God?

A common misconception in the church today is that only really devout Christians need to make a total commitment to God. You might think that what I'm suggesting is just for the minority of "super saints" whom God has given a special grace to excel in the Lord's work, but that isn't true. There are no super saints. All believers have received an abundance of grace to reign in this life as kings and queens (Rom. 5:17). Making Jesus Lord of your life and believing that the Word of God is the absolute authority are simply basic steps in establishing a godly perspective. These are simple ideas that are foundational components of a Christian philosophy, and adopting this philosophy will radically change your life.

This may come as a surprise, but God's plans for your life are better than your plans for your life. You can trust Him. He desires good things for you (Jer. 29:11). The commands the Bible gives you about how to approach life are for your own good. It really simplifies life once you submit to Jesus as Lord and follow His commands regardless of what you think, feel, or see going on around you. Just make the decision that you are going to do what the Word says and follow the leadership of the Holy Spirit no matter what, and you will experience a drastic improvement in your quality of life.

LESSON 5 — HOW DO I FOLLOW GOD?

OUTLINE

I. I remember a young man who came to me for counsel one time about going to Charis Bible College.

    A. He said that he knew God was telling him to go, but everyone in his life was telling him not to.

    B. He asked me "So, what do you think?" and I said, "You lost me the moment you said that you know God is telling you to go."

    C. If God tells you to do something, then you just do what God tells you to do.

    D. God is the Creator of the universe, He knows all things, and He knows what is best for you.

    E. Why would you care what anybody else thinks or what people might say about you?

    F. In comparison with God, no one else's opinion should matter.

    G. Your relationship with God should soak all the way down to the very core of your being.

    H. When that happens, your actions will be determined by your philosophy instead of by your environment or emotions.

    I. It really simplifies life to realize Jesus is Lord and you aren't.

    J. Then, when God tells you to do something, you just do it.

    K. This attitude is one part of a Christian philosophy that will really simplify your life.

II. I couldn't tell you how many people have told me over the years that they felt God was calling them to come to Charis Bible College, but they didn't think it was wise to go.

    A. They would say, for instance, that it was only ten years until they retired.

    B. They were focused on securing their financial futures, and they were leaning unto their own understanding.

    C. My opinion is that when God wants you to do something ten years from now, He'll tell you ten years from now.

    D. If God is telling you now, He either wants you to do it now, or He wants you to start taking the necessary steps to get the ball rolling.

    E. Some things take a while to come to pass, so God will give you instruction in advance, but when God tells you to do something, you just do it.

    F. That's all there is to it.

    G. I stopped in Pritchett, Colorado, to preach at a church of 10 people.

    H. We saw a man raised from the dead, and church attendance jumped up to around 100 people.

    I. They wanted me to stay and continue teaching them the full Gospel.

    J. No part of me wanted to live in Pritchett, but as we were driving out of town, I began to sense in my heart that God was telling me to stay there and teach those people the Word.

    K. By the time I got back to my house in Childress, Texas, I knew I was supposed to move.

    L. From a purely logical standpoint, there was no reason for me to go.

Lesson 5 — How Do I Follow God?

    M. The church only had ten members, they had no money, the church building was too small, and the town had nothing going for it.

    N. I could have given you a thousand reasons as to why it didn't seem like a good idea.

    O. How could I fulfill my big vision in such a small place?

    P. On the other hand, I was prospering in Childress, Texas.

    Q. But once I knew that God wanted me to move to Pritchett, Colorado, the debate was over.

    R. Jesus is Lord of my life, and my attitude was that if God wanted me to do something, then I was going to do it—and enjoy doing it.

    S. Once I was convinced of God's will for me to move to Pritchett, I began to praise Him for leading and guiding me.

    T. Within days, my entire attitude had changed, and I was excited about going.

    U. There were some hardships associated with living in such a remote area, but I loved living in Pritchett as much as any place I've ever lived. It was wonderful.

III. I made Jesus Lord of my life on March 23, 1968, and I haven't tried to direct my own life since.

    A. God is Lord, I'm not, and He knows what's best for me.

    B. I have feelings and opinions like everybody else, but the discussion ends once I'm sure God is telling me to do something.

    C. I trust God's judgment more than I trust my own, and I just do what He leads me to do.

    D. I couldn't even tell you how many decisions I've made in my life based purely on the fact that I was sure God was leading me.

    E. It would really simplify your life to run up a white flag and surrender to Jesus as Lord.

IV. One of my favorite passages of Scripture is from Jeremiah.

    A. He was wondering out loud how a people whom God rescued from Egypt and preserved through many miracles could forget the Lord who delivered them and turn to vain idols.

    B. In the middle of his grieving, Jeremiah answered his own question by saying,

> *O LORD, I know that the way of man is not in himself: it is not in man that walketh to direct his steps.*
> JEREMIAH 10:23

    C. The Jews had fallen from a position of favor because they started doing things their own way.

    D. Jeremiah recognized that God didn't create us to rule our own lives.

    E. He gave us the free will to make our own choices, but God never intended for us to direct our own steps.

    F. We have the freedom to decide for ourselves, because God doesn't force His will upon us, but the correct choice is to recognize our complete dependency on God.

    G. We aren't smart enough to run our own lives. God said,

> *I call heaven and earth to record this day against you, that I have set before you life and death, blessing and cursing: therefore choose life, that both thou and thy seed may live.*
> DEUTERONOMY 30:19

Lesson 5 — How Do I Follow God?

- H. God gives us a choice, but He also tells us which option is best: He says, "Choose life!"
- I. We need to trust in the Lord with all our hearts and not try to figure things out on our own.
- J. We need to seek His will in everything we do, and He'll show us the path to take—that's the smart choice (Prov. 3:5-6).
- K. That's how we're supposed to live.
- L. We're meant to make Jesus our Lord and follow His guidance.

V. The world would be a different place if Adam and Eve had followed this philosophy.

- A. It was very clear that the serpent was enticing them to do something contrary to what God had told them, but they didn't follow God's guidance.
- B. They knew God as their Creator and recognized His provision for them, but they didn't submit to God as Lord of their lives.
- C. They knew He was kind to them and that He met with them and talked with them, but they didn't bow to Him and determine that they wouldn't lean unto their own understanding.
- D. They failed to surrender to God's sovereignty, and Satan went right through that open door to lead them into sin.
- E. A solid Christian philosophy requires believing in the Word of God as our supreme authority and making Jesus Lord of our lives—not merely in the sense of recognizing His authority and attributes, but by submitting to His leadership.

VI. A rich man once kneeled down before Jesus and asked, "Good Master, what must I do to inherit eternal life?"

- A. "Why do you call Me good?" Jesus replied. "None is good except God alone."
- B. In other words, Jesus was saying, "Either call Me God and make Me Lord, or quit calling Me good!"
- C. The rich man responded by calling Jesus "Master" again—he wasn't willing to go all the way and make Jesus his Lord and Savior.
- D. He wanted the salvation Jesus provides, but he didn't want to completely commit himself to following Jesus as Lord.
- E. Jesus knew the man wasn't totally sincere, but He still loved him.
- F. Jesus told him, "Go, sell everything you have, and give the proceeds to the poor. It will give you treasure in heaven. Then come, take up your cross, and follow Me."
- G. The rich man couldn't do it, and he walked away grieved (Mark 10:17-22).
- H. Jesus presented salvation as making Him Lord and Master over your life—not just acknowledging His greatness.
- I. Scripture says that in order to be saved, you have to confess with your mouth that Jesus is Lord and believe in your heart that God raised Him from the dead (Rom. 10:9-10).
- J. I believe that salvation should be presented as turning your life over to Jesus—lock, stock, and barrel—but that's not how salvation is usually presented.
- K. The message many people are hearing is that they should be saved just so they can go to heaven when they die.

Lesson 5 — How Do I Follow God?

    L. Obviously, that is an important part of salvation, but it isn't the whole message.

    M. As a result, a lot of born-again believers will go to heaven when they die, but they haven't submitted to Jesus as Director and Leader of their everyday lives.

VII. In my own case, I was born again when I was eight years old, but I didn't submit to Jesus as Lord until I was eighteen.

    A. During that ten-year interval, I loved God and I had a relationship with Him to the degree that I would have gone to heaven if I had died, but I wasn't allowing Jesus to direct my life.

    B. Though I submitted to Jesus as Lord on March 23, 1968, I haven't lived perfectly, but whenever I know that God is telling me to do something, I do it.

    C. I yield to Jesus as my Lord, and my submission has led to a blessed life.

    D. Everything I set my hand unto prospers.

    E. God is a good God, and He leads me along good paths.

    F. I believe this philosophy is absolutely essential.

    G. You need to adopt this way of thinking: You are going to do whatever God tells you to do, regardless of any other factors.

    H. Whether it is through the Word of God or by special instruction from the Holy Spirit, decide ahead of time that you are going to follow God's leading—no discussion, no debate.

VIII. Over the years, I have discovered that God will tell me to do things, but if I don't do them right away, He doesn't argue with me.

    A. He just tells me what He wants me to do, and then I have the choice of whether or not to follow Him.

    B. To the best of my ability, I do what God tells me to do, but if I miss His leadership, He won't debate the issue with me.

    C. So, if you're waiting for God to convince you to do the thing you already know He wants you to do, you'll be waiting a long time because it isn't going to happen.

    D. God doesn't get into debates with you over His will for your life.

    E. He will lead and He will direct, but He isn't going to argue with you about what you already know.

    F. Doing whatever you want and asking God to bless it as an afterthought is not the same thing as following God.

    G. God tells you to do things for your own good.

    H. Really, being a Christian is simple: All you have to do is make Jesus Lord of your life, follow the leading of the Holy Spirit, and do what God's Word tells you to do.

    I. You'll solve a lot of problems in your life by following those few simple steps.

IX. In order to remain sensitive to God's leading, you have to guard your heart against the negative philosophies that are being promoted in the world.

    A. Every time you watch a television program, read a book, listen to the radio, browse the internet, or watch a movie, you encounter ideas that are contrary to God's philosophy.

Lesson 5 — How Do I Follow God?

B. Satan uses words to attack you through the way you think, and the modern media is the ideal way to push the world's philosophy.

C. Every time you encounter those lies, you need to reject them.

D. Isaiah says,

No weapon that is formed against thee shall prosper; and every tongue that shall rise against thee in judgment thou shalt condemn. This is the heritage of the servants of the Lord, and their righteousness is of me, saith the Lord.

ISAIAH 54:17

E. The promise here is that attacks against you won't succeed.

F. Notice that Isaiah then mentioned the words spoken against you.

G. The number one weapon Satan uses against you is deceitful words.

H. He steals from people through vain philosophies and lies.

I. This scripture says you are to **"condemn"** the lies that rise against you.

J. The word *condemn* is defined by *The Houghton Mifflin American Heritage Electronic Dictionary* (*HMAHED*) as "1. To express disapproval of; denounce. 2. a. To convict. b. To sentence to a punishment. 3. To declare unfit for use."

K. You have to take the authority God has given you and condemn those negative words, philosophies, and thoughts.

L. Anything that is contrary to God's Word must be rejected.

M. This is more important than most Christians realize.

N. Most people go through the day hardly paying attention to all of the garbage, unbelief, doubt, and complaining that come at them through the media and that wander through their minds.

O. All of those words and thoughts will corrupt you.

P. Scripture says,

Be not deceived: evil communications corrupt good manners.

1 CORINTHIANS 15:33

Q. The truth of this scripture is demonstrated in the life of Lot and the infamous city of Sodom.

R. Lot was a godly man and the evil of the society he lived in was a continual grief to him, but his association with the city of Sodom cost him dearly.

S. He never participated in their sins, but he ended up losing his wife and daughters in the judgment that came against Sodom (2 Pet. 2:7-8).

T. Lot is an example of the danger of trying to blend in and also of the mistake in thinking that the evil in society around you won't affect you.

U. You have to condemn the negative things around you.

X. Christians don't just wake up one morning and discover that they have a worldly philosophy; it happens slowly over time.

    A. You can see the process reflected in Satan's temptation of Eve.

Lesson 5 — How Do I Follow God?

    B. Satan didn't immediately call God a liar; he started out by questioning whether God had really told her not to eat of every tree in the Garden (Gen. 3:1).

    C. From there, he led Eve down a path of deceit until she was looking at things from his perspective and finally disobeyed God's command.

    D. It's like the story of putting a frog into a pot of boiling water: It will jump out of the hot water immediately, but if you put that same frog in lukewarm water and turn the heat up very slowly, you can boil it alive, and it will never try to escape—because it won't notice the gradual temperature change.

    E. This is how the devil works.

    F. He doesn't come at you all at once; instead, he drops little doubts here and there and attacks the integrity of God's Word piece by piece.

XI. I heard a story one time about a father who was trying to protect his kids from the influence of the world by monitoring the movies and television they watched.

    A. One day, his daughter asked to go see an R-rated movie with her friends. "What's in the movie that makes it rated R?" he asked. She said, "I've heard there is a little nudity and some swearing, but not much. And it's supposed to be a great movie." "I'm sorry, honey, but I can't let you go see it," the father said. The daughter was angry, but her dad wouldn't budge, so she had her friends come over to the house that night instead. While she was hanging out with her friends and playing games, her father made everyone brownies. "Now, before you eat," he said, "I just want to let you know that I put a little bit of dog in the recipe this time. It's not much. You probably won't taste it, and it won't make you sick or anything—but it is in there. Don't worry about it, though—for the most part—these are really tasty brownies." I seriously doubt those kids ate any brownies.

    B. Why should we be any more tolerant of ungodliness in our entertainment?

    C. The world we live in is fallen and corrupt, but many of us have accepted the condition of the world and have grown tolerant of the ungodliness that surrounds us.

    D. We watch the same movies and television programs, read the same books, and listen to the same music—even though we know they aren't exactly right.

    E. We know they don't meet God's standard, but it's just a little bit of ungodliness—it's just a little nudity or profanity.

    F. Repeated exposure to that stuff leads to an increased tolerance for worldly viewpoints until, eventually, we are indulging attitudes and beliefs that are totally contrary to a godly perspective.

    G. Our great-grandparents would be shocked to see the things that are on television and in magazines today.

    H. My wife and I have had a subscription to *Reader's Digest* magazine for years, and traditionally, it has been a very wholesome, family-oriented publication.

    I. Recently they have begun including racy advertisements like those that feature the backs of nude women.

    J. It isn't nudity exactly, but it shows how the magazine is taking a step in the direction of more relaxed moral standards.

    K. Today many popular magazines feature ads that would have been considered pornography a few generations ago.

XII. I don't watch a lot of television, but I have an hour drive from my house into the office, and I listen to the news on the radio.

    A. I don't listen to it for long, though, because most of it is false prophecy.

Lesson 5 — How Do I Follow God?

B. They take a small event and blow it up by focusing on all of the negative things that *could* happen—usually with an emphasis on how it *will* happen, and maybe it will happen *to you*.

C. You can ask anybody who rides in the car with me: I condemn the negative words that I hear over the radio.

D. When the news broadcast comes on and says "It's flu season out there…Have you had your flu shot?" I say, "Oh, no, it isn't. In the name of Jesus, it's not flu season for me."

E. To the commercial that asks "Are you having such-and-such medical problem? We can help," I say, "No. Thank You, Jesus, I'm not having that problem."

F. I talk back to the radio and defend my belief system.

G. I believe that when you hear a philosophy that is contrary to God's Word, you have to stand against it—that's what Eve should have done.

H. When Satan asked "Did God really say…?" Eve should have said, "Yes, God did say, and He is not a liar—so go away."

I. This might all sound a little weird, but it's just a component of guarding your heart.

J. Scripture says you should guard your heart above everything else in life because it determines the course of your life (Prov. 4:23).

K. Satan tries to come against you through the way you think, so when I hear a lie, I condemn it.

L. *Condemn* means "to express disapproval of; denounce" (*HMAHED*).

M. And that's what I do—I speak the truth from God's Word to counter the lie.

N. It's a part of guarding my heart.

O. When the media says sickness is rampant, I confess that by Jesus' stripes, I'm healed (Is. 53:5 and 1 Pet. 2:24).

P. When the newspaper says the economy is in the toilet, I flush that thought and confess that God supplies all my needs according to His riches in glory (Phil. 4:19).

Q. When I fall short and thoughts of condemnation rise up, I confess that there is no longer condemnation for those who are in Christ Jesus and walk after the spirit (Rom. 8:1).

R. Wherever and whenever the Enemy attacks God's Word with a lie, I counter the lie by speaking the truth (John 17:17).

XIII. This is just a practical application of two philosophies I have been discussing.

A. First, we have to believe that the Word of God is inspired and without error.

B. Second, Jesus is Lord, and we shouldn't question His instructions.

C. Those two philosophies will prevent Satan from having any access to us.

D. Whenever we hear something that is contrary to God's Word, we should just reject it.

E. The philosophy of making Jesus Lord means that when God tells you to do something, you just do it.

F. Unfortunately, many Christians debate with God about whether or not they are going to do what He asks.

G. For instance, Scripture says we're supposed to give, and the tithe (or 10 percent of your income) is just a starting place.

Lesson 5 — How Do I Follow God?

    H. Ten percent was the requirement under the Old Covenant.

    I. Nothing is required under the New Covenant of grace, but we should *desire* to give even more.

    J. God has promised that if we seek His kingdom first, He will freely give us the food, clothing, and shelter we need (Matt. 6:33).

    K. Most Christians give a little from the abundance of their wealth, but they don't give joyfully.

    L. Scripture says,

> *Every man according as he purposeth in his heart, so let him give; not grudgingly, or of necessity: for God loveth a cheerful giver. And God is able to make all grace abound toward you; that ye, always having all sufficiency in all things, may abound to every good work.*
>
> 2 CORINTHIANS 9:7-8

    M. A lot of people don't trust God to supply their needs, so they cling to money and material possessions as their safety net.

    N. They don't give joyfully, because they are afraid God won't come through on His promise to give back.

    O. We have to trust God that His Word is a sure promise.

    P. No marriage or friendship can thrive unless the partners trust one another, and relationship with God is no different in that respect.

    Q. Following Jesus means trusting Him to do what He says He will do.

    R. But many people who say Jesus is Lord prove by their actions that they don't really trust Him.

    S. The Bible tells us to love our enemies, to bless those who curse us, to do good to those who hate us, and to pray for those who persecute us and despitefully use us (Matt. 5:44).

    T. We know we're supposed to turn the other cheek and we teach that principle to our children, but how many of us instantly slide into gossip and anger when someone comes against us?

    U. When we do that, we aren't submitting to Jesus as Lord of our lives.

    V. Our actions prove who is really sitting on the throne.

XIV. I'm not saying that we can be perfect after we submit to Jesus as Lord or that any failure in our lives means we haven't submitted to Jesus.

    A. It isn't possible for us to live perfectly—we're still going to make mistakes.

    B. Even though our spirits are perfect, our bodies and souls won't be perfected until the Lord comes back and gives us glorified bodies and new souls.

    C. But our desire should be to follow Jesus' commands perfectly.

    D. Whenever we recognize that we are doing something contrary to the Word, we need to humble ourselves and turn back to God.

    E. I certainly haven't lived perfectly—I've gossiped about people and said things in anger after someone has done something to hurt me.

    F. I've sinned plenty, but the moment I realize I am behaving contrary to God's instructions, I humble myself and turn away from whatever it was I was doing.

    G. My desire is that Jesus reigns as Lord of my life, and I follow His commands.

Lesson 5 — How Do I Follow God?

XV. We are in a battle.

  A. We win eternal life when we are born again, but in this world, we still have to fight the lies that come against us (Eph. 6:12-13).

  B. We win those battles by making the determination that Jesus will reign as Lord in our lives and by submitting to His leadership.

  C. When God leads us to do something, then we need to do it.

  D. The debate should end once God's will is clear in any area of our lives.

  E. No matter what the circumstances look like, we should follow God.

  F. The only way the Enemy can win is for us to consider and submit to his lies instead of following God's leading.

  G. God didn't create us to run our own lives.

  H. He gave us the freedom to make our own choices in life, but He also told us that the right option is to choose life.

  I. The correct choice is to use our free will to make Jesus Lord and to follow His leading.

XVI. The great heroes of the Bible were people who followed God's way of thinking even when it meant putting their lives on the line.

  A. Shadrach, Meshach, and Abednego come immediately to mind.

  B. They were three young men who had been taken to Babylon during the captivity.

  C. After Daniel correctly interpreted one of King Nebuchadnezzar's dreams, they were elevated to positions of leadership within the king's government.

  D. After some time, the king made an idol of gold and instructed everyone to bow down and worship it.

  E. When Shadrach, Meshach, and Abednego refused, they were brought before the king to be punished.

  F. The king told them that if they bowed down and worshiped the image, he would let them live, but if they refused, he would throw them into a burning furnace.

  G. Then he challenged them by saying, "Who is the God who will deliver you from my hands then?" They replied,

  O Nebuchadnezzar, we are not careful to answer thee in this matter. If it be so, our God whom we serve is able to deliver us from the burning fiery furnace, and he will deliver us out of thine hand, O king. But if not, be it known unto thee, O king, that we will not serve thy gods, nor worship the golden image which thou hast set up.

  DANIEL 3:16-18

  H. Shadrach, Meshach, and Abednego knew God was capable of saving them, but they didn't have a specific promise that He *would*.

  I. Still, they were not afraid of the king's threats, so they told him that they were going to follow God, and they didn't care what he said or did about it.

  J. It didn't matter to them that the king was planning to roast them alive.

  K. They demonstrated that their commitment to God went beyond all other considerations, even the desire to live.

Lesson 5 — How Do I Follow God?

XVII. Most Christians have not made such a strong commitment to God. Many will serve God and talk about the Gospel as long as they aren't persecuted, but as soon as someone starts making fun of them, they shrink back.

   A. When friends start deserting them and family members call them fanatics, they back off preaching the Gospel.

   B. As long as your philosophy allows for you to back down from your commitment to God, then the devil is going to have an inroad into your life.

   C. The Enemy will use your concern over other people's opinions to manipulate you into conforming to his worldview.

   D. All he will have to do to stop you from following God's will for your life is bring people along to make fun of you.

   E. That's why the Bible says,

   The fear of man bringeth a snare: but whoso putteth his trust in the L<small>ORD</small> shall be safe.
   PROVERBS 29:25

XVIII. Shadrach, Meshach, and Abednego maintained a philosophy that God is absolute Lord.

   A. He was the only one they would serve, and they would bow to no one else.

   B. Of course, their reply infuriated King Nebuchadnezzar.

   C. He was so angry that he ordered the furnace to be heated seven times hotter than usual.

   D. The king ordered the strongest men in his army to tie up Shadrach, Meshach, and Abednego and throw them into the fire—and it was so hot that the king's men were killed by the flames as they tossed the three Hebrews into the furnace.

   E. The king gazed into the flames, watching to see the three Israelites consumed by the fire, but he soon stood up in amazement and said, "Didn't we cast three men into the fire?" And his advisors said, "Certainly we did, sir." And the king said,

   Lo, I see four men loose, walking in the midst of the fire, and they have no hurt; and the form of the fourth is like the Son of God.
   DANIEL 3:25

   F. In astonishment, the king went near to the fiery furnace, calling the names of Shadrach, Meshach, and Abednego and ordering them to come out of the fire.

   G. They walked out from the middle of the flames, and Scripture says, **"The princes, governors, and captains, and the king's counsellors, being gathered together, saw these men, upon whose bodies the fire had no power, nor was an hair of their head singed, neither were their coats changed, nor the smell of fire had passed on them"** (Dan. 3:27).

   H. The flames that consumed the king's strongest men had zero effect upon the three Hebrews who were totally committed to God.

   I. Shadrach, Meshach, and Abednego refused to compromise and God preserved them.

   J. Daniel was preserved in the same way when he was thrown into a den of lions after refusing to follow a law that forbade praying to God (Dan. 6).

   K. These biblical stories illustrate that commitment to God can't be a negotiable issue.

   L. Whatever you have to compromise to keep or obtain, you will eventually lose.

Lesson 5 — How Do I Follow God?

M. Compromise is the language of the devil.

N. You need to make the decision that Jesus is Lord and that you are going to remain absolutely committed to Him no matter what anyone else says or does—it's a necessary step in becoming grounded in a Christian worldview.

XIX. God should be our number one priority every day, but with many of us, He gets pushed to the end of our agenda.

    A. We should be seeking God about how to plan our days instead of planning our days and then seeing if we can squeeze in time for relationship with God.

    B. We should spend some time asking God, "What do *You* want me to do today?"

    C. We should present our calendars to God and say, "Here's my schedule, God. What would *You* like me to do?"

    D. This is how God intended for us to live when He created us.

    E. We should be allowing the Lord to direct our steps, not trying to figure out life with our limited understanding.

XX. A common misconception in the church today is that only really devout Christians need to make a total commitment to God.

    A. You might think that what I'm suggesting is just for the minority of "super saints" whom God has given a special grace to excel in the Lord's work, but that isn't true.

    B. There are no super saints. All believers have received an abundance of grace to reign in this life as kings and queens (Rom. 5:17).

    C. Making Jesus Lord of your life and believing that the Word of God is the absolute authority are simply basic steps in establishing a godly perspective.

    D. These are simple ideas that are foundational components of a Christian philosophy, and adopting this philosophy will radically change your life.

XXI. This may come as a surprise, but God's plans for your life are better than your plans for your life.

    A. You can trust Him. He desires good things for you (Jer. 29:11).

    B. The commands the Bible gives you about how to approach life are for your own good.

    C. It really simplifies life once you submit to Jesus as Lord and follow His commands regardless of what you think, feel, or see going on around you.

    D. Just make the decision that you are going to do what the Word says and follow the leadership of the Holy Spirit no matter what, and you will experience a drastic improvement in your quality of life.

| LESSON 5 | HOW DO I FOLLOW GOD? |

TEACHER'S GUIDE

1. I remember a young man who came to me for counsel one time about going to Charis Bible College. He said that he knew God was telling him to go, but everyone in his life was telling him not to. He asked me "So, what do you think?" and I said, "You lost me the moment you said that you know God is telling you to go." If God tells you to do something, then you just do what God tells you to do. God is the Creator of the universe, He knows all things, and He knows what is best for you. Why would you care what anybody else thinks or what people might say about you? In comparison with God, no one else's opinion should matter. Your relationship with God should soak all the way down to the very core of your being. When that happens, your actions will be determined by your philosophy instead of by your environment or emotions. It really simplifies life to realize Jesus is Lord and you aren't. Then, when God tells you to do something, you just do it. This attitude is one part of a Christian philosophy that will really simplify your life.

    1a.   Discussion Question: What should you do if God tells you to do something that involves more people than just you?
(Discussion question)

    1b.   Your actions will be determined by your philosophy instead of by your environment or emotions, when what?
(Your relationship with God should soak all the way down to the very core of your being)

2. I couldn't tell you how many people have told me over the years that they felt God was calling them to come to Charis Bible College, but they didn't think it was wise to go. They would say, for instance, that it was only ten years until they retired. They were focused on securing their financial futures, and they were leaning unto their own understanding. My opinion is that when God wants you to do something ten years from now, He'll tell you ten years from now. If God is telling you now, He either wants you to do it now, or He wants you to start taking the necessary steps to get the ball rolling. Some things take a while to come to pass, so God will give you instruction in advance, but when God tells you to do something, you just do it. That's all there is to it. I stopped in Pritchett, Colorado, to preach at a church of 10 people. We saw a man raised from the dead, and church attendance jumped up to around 100 people. They wanted me to stay and continue teaching them the full Gospel. No part of me wanted to live in Pritchett, but as we were driving out of town, I began to sense in my heart that God was telling me to stay there and teach those people the Word. By the time I got back to my house in Childress, Texas, I knew I was supposed to move. From a purely logical standpoint, there was no reason for me to go. The church only had ten members, they had no money, the church building was too small, and the town had nothing going for it. I could have given you a thousand reasons as to why it didn't seem like a good idea. How could I fulfill my big vision in such a small place? On the other hand, I was prospering in Childress, Texas. But once I knew that God wanted me to move to Pritchett, Colorado, the debate was over. Jesus is Lord of my life, and my attitude was that if God wanted me to do something, then I was going to do it—and enjoy doing it. Once I was convinced of God's will for me to move to Pritchett, I began to praise Him for leading and guiding me. Within days, my entire attitude had changed, and I was excited about going. There were some hardships associated with living in such a remote area, but I loved living in Pritchett as much as any place I've ever lived. It was wonderful.

    2a.   If God is telling you to do something, what could be the reasons?
(Either He wants you to do it now, or He wants you to start taking the necessary steps to get the ball rolling)

    2b.   Since some things can take a while to come to pass, what will God do?
(He will give you instruction in advance)

3. I made Jesus Lord of my life on March 23, 1968, and I haven't tried to direct my own life since. God is Lord, I'm not, and He knows what's best for me. I have feelings and opinions like everybody else, but the discussion ends once I'm sure God is telling me to do something. I trust God's judgment more than I trust my own, and I just do what He leads me to do. I couldn't even tell you how many decisions I've made in my life based purely on the fact that I was sure God was leading me. It would really simplify your life to run up a white flag and surrender to Jesus as Lord.

    3a.   What does it mean to surrender to Jesus as Lord?
(Discussion question)

LESSON 5 — HOW DO I FOLLOW GOD?

4. One of my favorite passages of Scripture is from Jeremiah. He was wondering out loud how a people whom God rescued from Egypt and preserved through many miracles could forget the Lord who delivered them and turn to vain idols. In the middle of his grieving, Jeremiah answered his own question by saying, **"O Lord, I know that the way of man is not in himself: it is not in man that walketh to direct his steps"** (Jer. 10:23). The Jews had fallen from a position of favor because they started doing things their own way. Jeremiah recognized that God didn't create us to rule our own lives. He gave us the free will to make our own choices, but God never intended for us to direct our own steps. We have the freedom to decide for ourselves, because God doesn't force His will upon us, but the correct choice is to recognize our complete dependency on God. We aren't smart enough to run our own lives. God said, **"I call heaven and earth to record this day against you, that I have set before you life and death, blessing and cursing: therefore choose life, that both thou and thy seed may live"** (Deut. 30:19). God gives us a choice, but He also tells us which option is best: He says, "Choose life!" We need to trust in the Lord with all our hearts and not try to figure things out on our own. We need to seek His will in everything we do, and He'll show us the path to take—that's the smart choice (Prov. 3:5-6). That's how we're supposed to live. We're meant to make Jesus our Lord and follow His guidance.

    4a.   True or false: Having free will means you have to direct your own steps.
(False)

    4b.   Discussion Question: Read Deuteronomy 30:19. Why does God tell you which option is best?
(Discussion question)

    4c.   You're _____ to make Jesus your Lord and follow His guidance.
(Meant)

5. The world would be a different place if Adam and Eve had followed this philosophy. It was very clear that the serpent was enticing them to do something contrary to what God had told them, but they didn't follow God's guidance. They knew God as their Creator and recognized His provision for them, but they didn't submit to God as Lord of their lives. They knew He was kind to them and that He met with them and talked with them, but they didn't bow to Him and determine that they wouldn't lean unto their own understanding. They failed to surrender to God's sovereignty, and Satan went right through that open door to lead them into sin. A solid Christian philosophy requires believing in the Word of God as our supreme authority and making Jesus Lord of our lives—not merely in the sense of recognizing His authority and attributes, but by submitting to His leadership.

    5a.   What didn't Adam and Eve determine?
(That they wouldn't lean to their own understanding)

    5b.   What does a solid Christian philosophy require?
A. It requires making Jesus Lord of your life
B. It requires knowing what the Bible says
C. It requires believing in the Word of God as your supreme authority
D. A and C
E. A and B
(D. A and C)

6. A rich man once kneeled down before Jesus and asked, "Good Master, what must I do to inherit eternal life?" "Why do you call Me good?" Jesus replied. "None is good except God alone." In other words, Jesus was saying, "Either call Me God and make Me Lord, or quit calling Me good!" The rich man responded by calling Jesus "Master" again. He wasn't willing to go all the way and make Jesus his Lord and Savior. He wanted the salvation Jesus provides, but he didn't want to completely commit himself to following Jesus as Lord. Jesus knew the man wasn't totally sincere, but He still loved him. Jesus told him, "Go, sell everything you have, and give the proceeds to the poor. It will give you treasure in heaven. Then come, take up your cross, and follow Me." The rich man couldn't do it, and he walked away grieved (Mark 10:17-22). Jesus presented salvation as making Him Lord and Master over your life—not just acknowledging His greatness. Scripture says that in order to be saved, you have to confess with your mouth that Jesus is Lord and believe in your heart that God raised Him from the dead (Rom. 10:9-10). I believe that salvation should be presented as turning your life over to Jesus—lock, stock, and barrel—but that's not how salvation is usually presented. The message many people are hearing is that they should be saved just so they can go to heaven when they die. Obviously, that is an important part of salvation, but it isn't the whole message.

LESSON 5 — HOW DO I FOLLOW GOD?

As a result, a lot of born-again believers will go to heaven when they die, but they haven't submitted to Jesus as Director and Leader of their everyday lives.

    6a.   Discussion Question: Why should you accept Jesus as Lord and not just Savior?
(Discussion question)

7. In my own case, I was born again when I was eight years old, but I didn't submit to Jesus as Lord until I was eighteen. During that ten-year interval, I loved God and I had a relationship with Him to the degree that I would have gone to heaven if I had died, but I wasn't allowing Jesus to direct my life. Though I submitted to Jesus as Lord on March 23, 1968, I haven't lived perfectly, but whenever I know that God is telling me to do something, I do it. I yield to Jesus as my Lord, and my submission has led to a blessed life. Everything I set my hand unto prospers. God is a good God, and He leads me along good paths. I believe this philosophy is absolutely essential. You need to adopt this way of thinking: You are going to do whatever God tells you to do, regardless of any other factors. Whether it is through the Word of God or by special instruction from the Holy Spirit, decide ahead of time that you are going to follow God's leading—no discussion, no debate.

    7a.   You have to _____ Jesus to direct your life.
(Allow)

    7b.   Discussion Question: Why do you think submission to the Lord leads to a blessed life?
(Discussion question)

    7c.   When should you decide to follow God's leading?
(Ahead of time)

8. Over the years, I have discovered that God will tell me to do things, but if I don't do them right away, He doesn't argue with me. He just tells me what He wants me to do, and then I have the choice of whether or not to follow Him. To the best of my ability, I do what God tells me to do, but if I miss His leadership, He won't debate the issue with me. So, if you're waiting for God to convince you to do the thing you already know He wants you to do, you'll be waiting a long time because it isn't going to happen. God doesn't get into debates with you over His will for your life. He will lead and He will direct, but He isn't going to argue with you about what you already know. Doing whatever you want and asking God to bless it as an afterthought is not the same thing as following God. God tells you to do things for your own good. Really, being a Christian is simple: All you have to do is make Jesus Lord of your life, follow the leading of the Holy Spirit, and do what God's Word tells you to do. You'll solve a lot of problems in your life by following those few simple steps.

    8a.   Concerning His will for your life, what doesn't God get into with you?
(Debates)

    8b.   God isn't going to argue with you about what you already what?
A. Think
B. Sample
C. Know
D. All of the above
E. None of the above
(C. Know)

    8c.   What is not the same thing as following God?
(Doing whatever you want and asking God to bless it as an afterthought)

    8d.   Being a Christian is simple because you'll solve a lot of problems in your life by following what simple steps?
(You have to make Jesus Lord of your life, follow the leading of the Holy Spirit, and do what God's Word tells you to do)

| Lesson 5 | How Do I Follow God? |

9. In order to remain sensitive to God's leading, you have to guard your heart against the negative philosophies that are being promoted in the world. Every time you watch a television program, read a book, listen to the radio, browse the internet, or watch a movie, you encounter ideas that are contrary to God's philosophy. Satan uses words to attack you through the way you think, and the modern media is the ideal way to push the world's philosophy. Every time you encounter those lies, you need to reject them. Isaiah says, **"No weapon that is formed against thee shall prosper; and every tongue that shall rise against thee in judgment thou shalt condemn. This is the heritage of the servants of the LORD, and their righteousness is of me, saith the LORD"** (Is. 54:17). The promise here is that attacks against you won't succeed. Notice that Isaiah then mentioned the words spoken against you. The number one weapon Satan uses against you is deceitful words. He steals from people through vain philosophies and lies. This scripture says you are to **"condemn"** the lies that rise against you. The word *condemn* is defined by *The Houghton Mifflin American Heritage Electronic Dictionary* (*HMAHED*) as "1. To express disapproval of; denounce. 2. a. To convict. b. To sentence to a punishment. 3. To declare unfit for use." You have to take the authority God has given you and condemn those negative words, philosophies, and thoughts. Anything that is contrary to God's Word must be rejected. This is more important than most Christians realize. Most people go through the day hardly paying attention to all of the garbage, unbelief, doubt, and complaining that come at them through the media and that wander through their minds. All of those words and thoughts will corrupt you. Scripture says, **"Be not deceived: evil communications corrupt good manners"** (1 Cor. 15:33). The truth of this scripture is demonstrated in the life of Lot and the infamous city of Sodom. Lot was a godly man and the evil of the society he lived in was a continual grief to him, but his association with the city of Sodom cost him dearly. He never participated in their sins, but he ended up losing his wife and daughters in the judgment that came against Sodom (2 Pet. 2:7-8). Lot is an example of the danger of trying to blend in and also of the mistake in thinking that the evil in society around you won't affect you. You have to condemn the negative things around you.

9a. What is the ideal way for Satan to attack you through pushing the world's philosophy?
(Modern media)

9b. Read Isaiah 54:17. How do you **"condemn"** the lies that rise against you?
(You have to take the authority God has given you and condemn those negative words, philosophies, and thoughts)

9c. Discussion Question: Read 1 Corinthians 15:33. Why shouldn't you think that the evil in society around you won't affect you?
(Discussion question)

10. Christians don't just wake up one morning and discover that they have a worldly philosophy; it happens slowly over time. You can see the process reflected in Satan's temptation of Eve. Satan didn't immediately call God a liar; he started out by questioning whether God had really told her not to eat of every tree in the Garden (Gen. 3:1). From there, he led Eve down a path of deceit until she was looking at things from his perspective and finally disobeyed God's command. It's like the story of putting a frog into a pot of boiling water: It will jump out of the hot water immediately, but if you put that same frog in lukewarm water and turn the heat up very slowly, you can boil it alive, and it will never try to escape—because it won't notice the gradual temperature change. This is how the devil works. He doesn't come at you all at once; instead, he drops little doubts here and there and attacks the integrity of God's Word piece by piece.

10a. Satan wants to get you to look at things from his perspective until you finally what?
A. Prosper financially
B. Live righteously
C. Proselytize others
D. Disobey God
E. Show respect
(D. Disobey God)

Lesson 5 — How Do I Follow God?

11. I heard a story one time about a father who was trying to protect his kids from the influence of the world by monitoring the movies and television they watched. One day, his daughter asked to go see an R-rated movie with her friends. "What's in the movie that makes it rated R?" he asked. She said, "I've heard there is a little nudity and some swearing, but not much. And it's supposed to be a great movie." "I'm sorry, honey, but I can't let you go see it," the father said. The daughter was angry, but her dad wouldn't budge, so she had her friends come over to the house that night instead. While she was hanging out with her friends and playing games, her father made everyone brownies. "Now, before you eat," he said, "I just want to let you know that I put a little bit of dog poop in the recipe this time. It's not much. You probably won't taste it, and it won't make you sick or anything—but it is in there. Don't worry about it, though—for the most part—these are really tasty brownies." I seriously doubt those kids ate any brownies. Why should we be any more tolerant of ungodliness in our entertainment? The world we live in is fallen and corrupt, but many of us have accepted the condition of the world and have grown tolerant of the ungodliness that surrounds us. We watch the same movies and television programs, read the same books, and listen to the same music—even though we know they aren't exactly right. We know they don't meet God's standard, but it's just a little bit of ungodliness—it's just a little nudity or profanity. Repeated exposure to that stuff leads to an increased tolerance for worldly viewpoints until, eventually, we are indulging attitudes and beliefs that are totally contrary to a godly perspective. Our great-grandparents would be shocked to see the things that are on television and in magazines today. My wife and I have had a subscription to *Reader's Digest* magazine for years, and traditionally, it has been a very wholesome, family-oriented publication. Recently they have begun including racy advertisements like those that feature the backs of nude women. It isn't nudity exactly, but it shows how the magazine is taking a step in the direction of more relaxed moral standards. Today many popular magazines feature ads that would have been considered pornography a few generations ago.

    11a. Discussion Question: Why should you not be tolerant of ungodliness in your entertainment?
(Discussion question)

    11b. Increased exposure to ungodliness leads to an increased tolerance for worldly viewpoints until what?
(Eventually, you are indulging attitudes and beliefs that are totally contrary to a godly perspective)

12. I don't watch a lot of television, but I have an hour drive from my house into the office, and I listen to the news on the radio. I don't listen to it for long, though, because most of it is false prophecy. They take a small event and blow it up by focusing on all of the negative things that *could* happen—usually with an emphasis on how it *will* happen, and maybe it will happen *to you*. You can ask anybody who rides in the car with me: I condemn the negative words that I hear over the radio. When the news broadcast comes on and says "It's flu season out there…Have you had your flu shot?" I say, "Oh, no, it isn't. In the name of Jesus, it's not flu season for me." To the commercial that asks "Are you having such-and-such medical problem? We can help," I say, "No. Thank You, Jesus, I'm not having that problem." I talk back to the radio and defend my belief system. I believe that when you hear a philosophy that is contrary to God's Word, you have to stand against it—that's what Eve should have done. When Satan asked "Did God really say…?" Eve should have said, "Yes, God did say, and He is not a liar—so go away." This might all sound a little weird, but it's just a component of guarding your heart. Scripture says you should guard your heart above everything else in life because it determines the course of your life (Prov. 4:23). Satan tries to come against you through the way you think, so when I hear a lie, I condemn it. *Condemn* means "to express disapproval of; denounce" (HMAHED). And that's what I do—I speak the truth from God's Word to counter the lie. It's a part of guarding my heart. When the media says sickness is rampant, I confess that by Jesus' stripes, I'm healed (Is. 53:5 and 1 Pet. 2:24). When the newspaper says the economy is in the toilet, I flush that thought and confess that God supplies all my needs according to His riches in glory (Phil. 4:19). When I fall short and thoughts of condemnation rise up, I confess that there is no longer condemnation for those who are in Christ Jesus and walk after the spirit (Rom. 8:1). Wherever and whenever the Enemy attacks God's Word with a lie, I counter the lie by speaking the truth (John 17:17).

    12a. Andrew believes that when you hear a philosophy that is contrary to God's Word, you have to do what?
(Stand against it)

    12b. Read Proverbs 4:23. Why should you guard your heart above all else?
(Because it determines the course of your life)

    12c. When you disapprove of or denounce a lie, what are you doing?
(Condemning it)

Lesson 5 — How Do I Follow God?

13. This is just a practical application of two philosophies I have been discussing. First, we have to believe that the Word of God is inspired and without error. Second, Jesus is Lord, and we shouldn't question His instructions. Those two philosophies will prevent Satan from having any access to us. Whenever we hear something that is contrary to God's Word, we should just reject it. The philosophy of making Jesus Lord means that when God tells you to do something, you just do it. Unfortunately, many Christians debate with God about whether or not they are going to do what He asks. For instance, Scripture says we're supposed to give, and the tithe (or 10 percent of your income) is just a starting place. Ten percent was the requirement under the Old Covenant. Nothing is required under the New Covenant of grace, but we should *desire* to give even more. God has promised that if we seek His kingdom first, He will freely give us the food, clothing, and shelter we need (Matt. 6:33). Most Christians give a little from the abundance of their wealth, but they don't give joyfully. Scripture says, **"Every man according as he purposeth in his heart, so let him give; not grudgingly, or of necessity: for God loveth a cheerful giver. And God is able to make all grace abound toward you; that ye, always having all sufficiency in all things, may abound to every good work"** (2 Cor. 9:7-8). A lot of people don't trust God to supply their needs, so they cling to money and material possessions as their safety net. They don't give joyfully, because they are afraid God won't come through on His promise to give back. We have to trust God that His Word is a sure promise. No marriage or friendship can thrive unless the partners trust one another, and relationship with God is no different in that respect. Following Jesus means trusting Him to do what He says He will do. But many people who say Jesus is Lord prove by their actions that they don't really trust Him. The Bible tells us to love our enemies, to bless those who curse us, to do good to those who hate us, and to pray for those who persecute us and despitefully use us (Matt. 5:44). We know we're supposed to turn the other cheek and we teach that principle to our children, but how many of us instantly slide into gossip and anger when someone comes against us? When we do that, we aren't submitting to Jesus as Lord of our lives. Our actions prove who is really sitting on the throne.

    13a.   What two philosophies will prevent Satan from having any access to you?
(First, you have to believe that the Word of God is inspired and without error. Second, Jesus is Lord, and you shouldn't question His instructions)

    13b.   True or false: Following Jesus means trusting Him to do what He says He will do.
(True)

    13c.   Many people who say Jesus is Lord prove what by their actions?
(That they don't really trust Him)

14. I'm not saying that we can be perfect after we submit to Jesus as Lord or that any failure in our lives means we haven't submitted to Jesus. It isn't possible for us to live perfectly. We're still going to make mistakes. Even though our spirits are perfect, our bodies and souls won't be perfected until the Lord comes back and gives us glorified bodies and new souls. But our desire should be to follow Jesus' commands perfectly. Whenever we recognize that we are doing something contrary to the Word, we need to humble ourselves and turn back to God. I certainly haven't lived perfectly. I've gossiped about people and said things in anger after someone has done something to hurt me. I've sinned plenty, but the moment I realize I am behaving contrary to God's instructions, I humble myself and turn away from whatever it was I was doing. My desire is that Jesus reigns as Lord of my life, and I follow His commands.

    14a.   Submitting to Jesus doesn't mean you are what?
(Perfect)

    14b.   What does Andrew do the moment he realizes he's behaving contrary to God's instructions?
(He humbles himself and turns away from whatever it was he was doing)

    14c.   Discussion Question: What are some examples of this?
(Discussion question)

15. We are in a battle. We win eternal life when we are born again, but in this world, we still have to fight the lies that come against us (Eph. 6:12-13). We win those battles by making the determination that Jesus will reign as Lord in our lives and by submitting to His leadership. When God leads us to do something, then we need to do it. The debate should end once God's will is clear in any area of our lives. No matter what the circumstances look like, we should follow God. The only way the Enemy can win is for us to consider and submit to his lies instead of following

Lesson 5 — How Do I Follow God?

God's leading. God didn't create us to run our own lives. He gave us the freedom to make our own choices in life, but He also told us that the right option is to choose life. The correct choice is to use our free will to make Jesus Lord and to follow His leading.

15a. What should you do, no matter what the circumstances look like?
(Follow God)

15b. Discussion Question: Why?
(Discussion question)

16. The great heroes of the Bible were people who followed God's way of thinking even when it meant putting their lives on the line. Shadrach, Meshach, and Abednego come immediately to mind. They were three young men who had been taken to Babylon during the captivity. After Daniel correctly interpreted one of King Nebuchadnezzar's dreams, they were elevated to positions of leadership within the king's government. After some time, the king made an idol of gold and instructed everyone to bow down and worship it. When Shadrach, Meshach, and Abednego refused, they were brought before the king to be punished. The king told them that if they bowed down and worshiped the image, he would let them live, but if they refused, he would throw them into a burning furnace. Then he challenged them by saying, "Who is the God who will deliver you from my hands then?" They replied, **"O Nebuchadnezzar, we are not careful to answer thee in this matter. If it be so, our God whom we serve is able to deliver us from the burning fiery furnace, and he will deliver us out of thine hand, O king. But if not, be it known unto thee, O king, that we will not serve thy gods, nor worship the golden image which thou hast set up"** (Dan. 3:16-18). Shadrach, Meshach, and Abednego knew God was capable of saving them, but they didn't have a specific promise that He *would*. Still, they were not afraid of the king's threats, so they told him that they were going to follow God, and they didn't care what he said or did about it. It didn't matter to them that the king was planning to roast them alive. They demonstrated that their commitment to God went beyond all other considerations, even the desire to live.

16a. Read Daniel 3:16-18. True or false: Shadrach, Meshach, and Abednego followed God because they knew He would save them.
(False)

17. Most Christians have not made such a strong commitment to God. Many will serve God and talk about the Gospel as long as they aren't persecuted, but as soon as someone starts making fun of them, they shrink back. When friends start deserting them and family members call them fanatics, they back off preaching the Gospel. As long as your philosophy allows for you to back down from your commitment to God, then the devil is going to have an inroad into your life. The Enemy will use your concern over other people's opinions to manipulate you into conforming to his worldview. All he will have to do to stop you from following God's will for your life is bring people along to make fun of you. That's why the Bible says, **"The fear of man bringeth a snare: but whoso putteth his trust in the Lord shall be safe"** (Prov. 29:25).

17a. Many will serve God and talk about the Gospel as long as they aren't _____.
(Persecuted)

17b. As long as your philosophy allows for you to back down from your commitment to God, then the devil is going to have an _____ into your life.
(Inroad)

18. Shadrach, Meshach, and Abednego maintained a philosophy that God is absolute Lord. He was the only one they would serve, and they would bow to no one else. Of course, their reply infuriated King Nebuchadnezzar. He was so angry that he ordered the furnace to be heated seven times hotter than usual. The king ordered the strongest men in his army to tie up Shadrach, Meshach, and Abednego and throw them into the fire—and it was so hot that the king's men were killed by the flames as they tossed the three Hebrews into the furnace. The king gazed into the flames, watching to see the three Israelites consumed by the fire, but he soon stood up in amazement and said, "Didn't we cast three men into the fire?" And his advisors said, "Certainly we did, sir." And the king said,

Lesson 5   How Do I Follow God?

"**Lo, I see four men loose, walking in the midst of the fire, and they have no hurt; and the form of the fourth is like the Son of God**" (Dan. 3:25). In astonishment, the king went near to the fiery furnace, calling the names of Shadrach, Meshach, and Abednego and ordering them to come out of the fire. They walked out from the middle of the flames, and Scripture says, "**The princes, governors, and captains, and the king's counsellors, being gathered together, saw these men, upon whose bodies the fire had no power, nor was an hair of their head singed, neither were their coats changed, nor the smell of fire had passed on them**" (Dan. 3:27). The flames that consumed the king's strongest men had zero effect upon the three Hebrews who were totally committed to God. Shadrach, Meshach, and Abednego refused to compromise and God preserved them. Daniel was preserved in the same way when he was thrown into a den of lions after refusing to follow a law that forbade praying to God (Dan. 6). These biblical stories illustrate that commitment to God can't be a negotiable issue. Whatever you have to compromise to keep or obtain, you will eventually lose. Compromise is the language of the devil. You need to make the decision that Jesus is Lord and that you are going to remain absolutely committed to Him no matter what anyone else says or does—it's a necessary step in becoming grounded in a Christian worldview.

    18a.   When did God preserve Shadrach, Meshach, and Abednego?
             (After they refused to compromise)

    18b.   You will eventually lose whatever you have to compromise to _____ or _____.
             A. Make/break
             B. Keep/obtain
             C. Sow/reap
             D. Buy/sell
             E. Promote/procure
             (B. Keep/obtain)

19. God should be our number one priority every day, but with many of us, He gets pushed to the end of our agenda. We should be seeking God about how to plan our days instead of planning our days and then seeing if we can squeeze in time for relationship with God. We should spend some time asking God, "What do *You* want me to do today?" We should present our calendars to God and say, "Here's my schedule, God. What would *You* like me to do?" This is how God intended for us to live when He created us. We should be allowing the Lord to direct our steps, not trying to figure out life with our limited understanding.

    19a.   Discussion Question: Why should you be seeking God about how to plan your day instead of planning your day and then seeing if you can squeeze in time for relationship with God?
             (Discussion question)

20. A common misconception in the church today is that only really devout Christians need to make a total commitment to God. You might think that what I'm suggesting is just for the minority of "super saints" whom God has given a special grace to excel in the Lord's work, but that isn't true. There are no super saints. All believers have received an abundance of grace to reign in this life as kings and queens (Rom. 5:17). Making Jesus Lord of your life and believing that the Word of God is the absolute authority are simply basic steps in establishing a godly perspective. These are simple ideas that are foundational components of a Christian philosophy, and adopting this philosophy will radically change your life.

    20a.   Thinking that only really devout Christians need to make a total commitment to God is a what?
             (A common misconception in the church today)

    20b.   Read Romans 5:17. What have all believers received?
             (An abundance of grace to reign in this life as kings and queens)

Lesson 5 — How Do I Follow God?

21. This may come as a surprise, but God's plans for your life are better than your plans for your life. You can trust Him. He desires good things for you (Jer. 29:11). The commands the Bible gives you about how to approach life are for your own good. It really simplifies life once you submit to Jesus as Lord and follow His commands regardless of what you think, feel, or see going on around you. Just make the decision that you are going to do what the Word says and follow the leadership of the Holy Spirit no matter what, and you will experience a drastic improvement in your quality of life.

    21a. The commands the Bible gives you about how to approach life are for what?
(Your own good)

    21b. What do you need to do in order to experience a drastic improvement in your quality of life?
(Just make the decision that you are going to do what the Word says and follow the leadership of the Holy Spirit no matter what)

Lesson 5 — How Do I Follow God?

DISCIPLESHIP QUESTIONS

1. Discussion Question: What should you do if God tells you to do something that involves more people than just you?

2. Your actions will be determined by your philosophy instead of by your environment or emotions, when what?

3. If God is telling you to do something, what could be the reasons?

4. Since some things can take a while to come to pass, what will God do?

5. Discussion Question: What does it mean to surrender to Jesus as Lord?

6. True or false: Having free will means you have to direct your own steps.

7. Discussion Question: Read Deuteronomy 30:19. Why does God tell you which option is best?

8. You're _____ to make Jesus your Lord and follow His guidance.

9. What didn't Adam and Eve determine?

SCRIPTURES TO USE WITH QUESTIONS

JEREMIAH 10:23
O Lord, I know that the way of man is not in himself: it is not in man that walketh to direct his steps.

DEUTERONOMY 30:19
I call heaven and earth to record this day against you, that I have set before you life and death, blessing and cursing: therefore choose life, that both thou and thy seed may live.

PROVERBS 3:5-6
Trust in the Lord with all thine heart; and lean not unto thine own understanding. **[6]** *In all thy ways acknowledge him, and he shall direct thy paths.*

LESSON 5 — HOW DO I FOLLOW GOD?

DISCIPLESHIP QUESTIONS

10. What does a solid Christian philosophy require?
    A. It requires making Jesus Lord of your life
    B. It requires knowing what the Bible says
    C. It requires believing in the Word of God as your supreme authority
    D. A and C
    E. A and B

11. Discussion Question: Why should you accept Jesus as Lord and not just Savior?

12. You have to _____ Jesus to direct your life.

13. Discussion Question: Why do you think submission to the Lord leads to a blessed life?

14. When should you decide to follow God's leading?

15. Concerning His will for your life, what doesn't God get into with you?

16. God isn't going to argue with you about what you already what?
    A. Think
    B. Sample
    C. Know
    D. All of the above
    E. None of the above

SCRIPTURES TO USE WITH QUESTIONS

MARK 10:17-22
And when he was gone forth into the way, there came one running, and kneeled to him, and asked him, Good Master, what shall I do that I may inherit eternal life? **[18]** *And Jesus said unto him, Why callest thou me good? there is none good but one, that is, God.* **[19]** *Thou knowest the commandments, Do not commit adultery, Do not kill, Do not steal, Do not bear false witness, Defraud not, Honour thy father and mother.* **[20]** *And he answered and said unto him, Master, all these have I observed from my youth.* **[21]** *Then Jesus beholding him loved him, and said unto him, One thing thou lackest: go thy way, sell whatsoever thou hast, and give to the poor, and thou shalt have treasure in heaven: and come, take up the cross, and follow me.* **[22]** *And he was sad at that saying, and went away grieved: for he had great possessions.*

ROMANS 10:9-10
That if thou shalt confess with thy mouth the Lord Jesus, and shalt believe in thine heart that God hath raised him from the dead, thou shalt be saved. **[10]** *For with the heart man believeth unto righteousness; and with the mouth confession is made unto salvation.*

Lesson 5 — How Do I Follow God?

DISCIPLESHIP QUESTIONS

17. What is not the same thing as following God?

18. Being a Christian is simple because you'll solve a lot of problems in your life by following what simple steps?

19. What is the ideal way for Satan to attack you through pushing the world's philosophy?

20. Read Isaiah 54:17. How do you **"condemn"** the lies that rise against you?

21. Discussion Question: Read 1 Corinthians 15:33. Why shouldn't you think that the evil in society around you won't affect you?

22. Satan wants to get you to look at things from his perspective until you finally what?
    A. Prosper financially
    B. Live righteously
    C. Proselytize others
    D. Disobey God
    E. Show respect

23. Discussion Question: Why should you not be tolerant of ungodliness in your entertainment?

24. Increased exposure to ungodliness leads to an increased tolerance for worldly viewpoints until what?

SCRIPTURES TO USE WITH QUESTIONS

ISAIAH 54:17
No weapon that is formed against thee shall prosper; and every tongue that shall rise against thee in judgment thou shalt condemn. This is the heritage of the servants of the Lord, and their righteousness is of me, saith the Lord.

1 CORINTHIANS 15:33
Be not deceived: evil communications corrupt good manners.

2 PETER 2:7-8
And delivered just Lot, vexed with the filthy conversation of the wicked: [8] (For that righteous man dwelling among them, in seeing and hearing, vexed his righteous soul from day to day with their unlawful deeds).

GENESIS 3:1
Now the serpent was more subtil than any beast of the field which the Lord God had made. And he said unto the woman, Yea, hath God said, Ye shall not eat of every tree of the garden?

LESSON 5 — HOW DO I FOLLOW GOD?

DISCIPLESHIP QUESTIONS

25. Andrew believes that when you hear a philosophy that is contrary to God's Word, you have to do what?

26. Read Proverbs 4:23. Why should you guard your heart above all else?

27. When you disapprove of or denounce a lie, what are you doing?

28. What two philosophies will prevent Satan from having any access to you?

29. True or false: Following Jesus means trusting Him to do what He says He will do.

30. Many people who say Jesus is Lord prove what by their actions?

31. Submitting to Jesus doesn't mean you are what?

32. What does Andrew do the moment he realizes he's behaving contrary to God's instructions?

33. Discussion Question: What are some examples of this?

SCRIPTURES TO USE WITH QUESTIONS

PROVERBS 4:23
Keep thy heart with all diligence; for out of it are the issues of life.

ISAIAH 53:5
But he was wounded for our transgressions, he was bruised for our iniquities: the chastisement of our peace was upon him; and with his stripes we are healed.

1 PETER 2:24
Who his own self bare our sins in his own body on the tree, that we, being dead to sins, should live unto righteousness: by whose stripes ye were healed.

PHILIPPIANS 4:19
But my God shall supply all your need according to his riches in glory by Christ Jesus.

ROMANS 8:1
There is therefore now no condemnation to them which are in Christ Jesus, who walk not after the flesh, but after the Spirit.

JOHN 17:17
Sanctify them through thy truth: thy word is truth.

MATTHEW 6:33
But seek ye first the kingdom of God, and his righteousness; and all these things shall be added unto you.

2 CORINTHIANS 9:7-8
Every man according as he purposeth in his heart, so let him give; not grudgingly, or of necessity: for God loveth a cheerful giver. **[8]** *And God is able to make all grace abound toward you; that ye, always having all sufficiency in all things, may abound to every good work.*

LESSON 5 — HOW DO I FOLLOW GOD?

DISCIPLESHIP QUESTIONS

34. What should you do, no matter what the circumstances look like?

35. Discussion Question: Why?

36. Read Daniel 3:16-18. True or false: Shadrach, Meshach, and Abednego followed God because they knew He would save them.

37. Many will serve God and talk about the Gospel as long as they aren't _____.

38. As long as your philosophy allows for you to back down from your commitment to God, then the devil is going to have an _____ into your life.

39. When did God preserve Shadrach, Meshach, and Abednego?

40. You will eventually lose whatever you have to compromise to _____ or _____.
    A. Make/break
    B. Keep/obtain
    C. Sow/reap
    D. Buy/sell
    E. Promote/procure

SCRIPTURES TO USE WITH QUESTIONS

MATTHEW 5:44
But I say unto you, Love your enemies, bless them that curse you, do good to them that hate you, and pray for them which despitefully use you, and persecute you.

EPHESIANS 6:12-13
For we wrestle not against flesh and blood, but against principalities, against powers, against the rulers of the darkness of this world, against spiritual wickedness in high places. [13] Wherefore take unto you the whole armour of God, that ye may be able to withstand in the evil day, and having done all, to stand.

DANIEL 3:16-18
Shadrach, Meshach, and Abednego, answered and said to the king, O Nebuchadnezzar, we are not careful to answer thee in this matter. [17] If it be so, our God whom we serve is able to deliver us from the burning fiery furnace, and he will deliver us out of thine hand, O king. [18] But if not, be it known unto thee, O king, that we will not serve thy gods, nor worship the golden image which thou hast set up.

PROVERBS 29:25
The fear of man bringeth a snare: but whoso putteth his trust in the LORD shall be safe.

DANIEL 3:25
He answered and said, Lo, I see four men loose, walking in the midst of the fire, and they have no hurt; and the form of the fourth is like the Son of God.

Lesson 5 — How Do I Follow God?

DISCIPLESHIP QUESTIONS

41. Discussion Question: Why should you be seeking God about how to plan your day instead of planning your day and then seeing if you can squeeze in time for relationship with God?

42. Thinking that only really devout Christians need to make a total commitment to God is a what?

43. Read Romans 5:17. What have all believers received?

44. The commands the Bible gives you about how to approach life are for what?

45. What do you need to do in order to experience a drastic improvement in your quality of life?

SCRIPTURES TO USE WITH QUESTIONS

DANIEL 3:27
And the princes, governors, and captains, and the king's counsellors, being gathered together, saw these men, upon whose bodies the fire had no power, nor was an hair of their head singed, neither were their coats changed, nor the smell of fire had passed on them.

ROMANS 5:17
For if by one man's offence death reigned by one; much more they which receive abundance of grace and of the gift of righteousness shall reign in life by one, Jesus Christ.

JEREMIAH 29:11
For I know the thoughts that I think toward you, saith the Lord, thoughts of peace, and not of evil, to give you an expected end.

LESSON 5 — How Do I Follow God?

ANSWER KEY

1. *Discussion question*
2. Your relationship with God should soak all the way down to the very core of your being
3. Either He wants you to do it now, or He wants you to start taking the necessary steps to get the ball rolling
4. He will give you instruction in advance
5. *Discussion question*
6. False
7. *Discussion question*
8. Meant
9. That they wouldn't lean to their own understanding
10. D. A and C
11. *Discussion question*
12. Allow
13. *Discussion question*
14. Ahead of time
15. Debates
16. C. Know
17. Doing whatever you want and asking God to bless it as an afterthought
18. You have to make Jesus Lord of your life, follow the leading of the Holy Spirit, and do what God's Word tells you to do
19. Modern media
20. You have to take the authority God has given you and condemn those negative words, philosophies, and thoughts
21. *Discussion question*
22. D. Disobey God
23. *Discussion question*
24. Eventually, you are indulging attitudes and beliefs that are totally contrary to a godly perspective
25. Stand against it
26. Because it determines the course of your life
27. Condemning it
28. First, you have to believe that the Word of God is inspired and without error. Second, Jesus is Lord, and you shouldn't question His instructions
29. True
30. That they don't really trust Him
31. Perfect
32. He humbles himself and turns away from whatever it was he was doing
33. *Discussion question*
34. Follow God
35. *Discussion question*
36. False
37. Persecuted
38. Inroad
39. After they refused to compromise
40. B. Keep/obtain
41. *Discussion question*
42. A common misconception in the church today
43. An abundance of grace to reign in this life as kings and queens
44. Your own good
45. Just make the decision that you are going to do what the Word says and follow the leadership of the Holy Spirit no matter what

Can I Really Know God?

When Satan tempted Adam and Eve, he didn't come right out and call God a liar; he started by questioning: "Did God really say…?" It wasn't until after he planted doubt in their minds that he accused God of lying to them. Satan told them that the real reason the Lord didn't want them to eat the fruit was because they would become like God (Gen. 3:5). The devil acted like God was being selfish, as if God didn't really love them and didn't have their best interests in mind. It was a total slander against the true nature and character of God.

Why didn't Adam and Eve recognize that Satan was lying to them? I believe that although they communed with God in ways that most of us would long for, they didn't truly know God. I know that sounds like a radical statement—I struggled with it at first too. After all, Adam and Eve were perfect before sin entered the world. They walked with God in the cool of the evening and talked with Him. They weren't exposed to the ungodliness that has hardened our hearts toward God since sin entered the world. Everything was perfect and nothing was blocking their relationship with God—but Adam and Eve didn't know the true nature and character of God as well as we can today. They didn't know God loved them so much that He would become a man Himself, suffer humiliation, and lay down His life to save them. They knew God as Lord, but they didn't know Him as Savior.

The Word reveals to us the depths of God's love. It shows how He has pursued mankind throughout history, how He has loved us and proven through His actions a love that Adam and Eve could not have imagined. True Christianity is the only religion on the face of the earth with the concept of God becoming a man and taking the punishment we deserved in order to redeem us back to a right relationship with Him.

Other religions may acknowledge a godlike entity, but they put the burden of salvation on the individual, on living a holy life and meeting certain standards of righteousness. The standards vary, but one consistent theme among all man-made religions is that there are specific instructions we must follow to appease an angry god. True Christianity is all about *what God has already done* for us. It's not about what we do, or how we live; it's all about what God has done to give us *His* righteousness. The Gospel of John sums it up by saying,

> *For God so loved the world, that he gave his only begotten Son, that whosoever believeth in him should not perish, but have everlasting life.*
>
> JOHN 3:16

LESSON 6 — CAN I REALLY KNOW GOD?

God demonstrated His love for us when He sent Jesus to suffer and die for our sins, and then He resurrected Him to give us His righteousness. It's a love that was impossible for Adam and Eve to understand. The sheer humility of God's plan of redemption is beyond human comprehension. No man could have conceived such a thing. Adam and Eve didn't know God's love to the extent that we can know and experience His love today. They had no idea that God would sacrifice His own Son so that they and their descendants could live forever. If they had known God that intimately, Satan would not have been able to deceive them into believing that God was holding out on them or trying to keep them from reaching their full potential.

A major part of having a Christian worldview is knowing God intimately, not from a distance. We can't just adopt other people's opinions about the nature and character of God; we need to have our own personal relationship with Him. The more we know the goodness of God, the less susceptible we will be to the lies of the devil. I fully believe that we succeed and experience victory in life to the degree that we have relationship with God. The good news is that we can know God better than Adam and Eve knew Him, because we have a much greater revelation of the extent to which God will go for us. Therefore, we don't have to fall prey to the lies of the devil. Once we know God intimately, Satan won't be able to discredit Him or convince us that God can't move in our lives. So, a close, intimate, personal relationship with God is an essential component of a Christian philosophy.

The heroes of Old Testament didn't understand God's love the way we can today. Prior to the Resurrection and the gift of the Holy Spirit, not even Jesus' disciples had the revelation of God that is given to us in Scripture. At the crucifixion, the disciples were expecting Jesus to come down from the cross and establish His kingdom on earth. They didn't understand what was happening. When Jesus was arrested, the disciples ran away in fear and hid (Matt. 26:56 and Mark 14:50). They knew Jesus was the Messiah, but they were expecting Him to establish a physical kingdom on earth—right then. As they stood and looked at Jesus hanging on the cross, they saw defeat. To them, it looked like all of the hope they had placed in Jesus to save mankind was wasted. It shocked them when Jesus rose from the dead, because they didn't know or understand God's plan of salvation (Mark 16:11; Luke 24:11; John 20:9, and 25).

In hindsight, through the record of Scripture, I now have a greater understanding of why Jesus sacrificed Himself on the cross than His disciples had prior to the coming of the Holy Spirit. Even after the establishment of the church, Peter—one of the Lord's closest disciples—still didn't fully understand grace or the dynamics of what had happened on the cross. He was trying to merge the Christian faith back into Jewish Law, and the Apostle Paul had to openly rebuke him for it (Gal. 2:11-14). Years later, Peter wrote in his second letter:

> *Our beloved brother Paul also according to the wisdom given unto him hath written unto you; As also in all his epistles, speaking in them of these things; in which are some things hard to be understood, which they that are unlearned and unstable wrest, as they do also the other scriptures, unto their own destruction.*
> 2 PETER 3:15B-16

Peter said right there that Paul's revelation of Jesus was superior to his own. Peter lived with Jesus for three-and-a-half years and Paul spent no time with Jesus while He was walking on earth, yet Paul had a greater revelation of who Jesus was and what He came to accomplish. The point is that Paul didn't get his revelation from other people; he received it through his spirit—the same way we receive revelation today. Paul has recorded for us the revelation God gave him in the letters he composed, which make up half of the New Testament. Through the Holy Spirit and the study of Scripture, we can know God's love for us to a degree that the disciples of Jesus did not understand while they were ministering with Him on earth. That's an amazing statement!

I have a greater revelation of the true nature of God than Abraham or Moses had—not because I'm better than they were, but because God's plan of redemption is complete, and I have a fuller picture of God than they did. If I could travel back in time and sit down with Moses to explain God's plan of redemption, he wouldn't understand it. He wouldn't understand that the system of animal sacrifice they practiced was only foreshadowing how God would send His Son to live in the flesh and become the Lamb who takes away the sins of the world. Moses did not anticipate that God would do away with the sacrificial system and tear down the veil that separated us from the holy of holies. He had no idea those things would happen.

Jesus said that John the Baptist was the greatest of those born of women, but **"he that is least in the kingdom of heaven is greater than he"** (Matt. 11:11b). Our born-again spirits make us greater than any of the Old Testament prophets: men like Moses, who spent forty days and nights in the presence of God and whose face, when he returned to the Israelites, was radiating the glory of God; Abraham, who believed God and became the father of faith; Elijah, who called down fire from heaven and never died but was taken up to heaven in a chariot of fire; Joshua, who led God's people into the Promised Land; and David, who was a man after God's own heart. We have access to a greater revelation of God's true nature than any of those men had.

Scripture says the Old Covenant, written and engraved in stone, led to death—but it was also glorious. When Moses presented the Law to the people of Israel, they couldn't bear to look at him, because of the brightness of God's glory that was reflected in his face. The old way was glorious, but what we have is much more glorious. Under the New Covenant, the Holy Spirit gives us life forever, which is infinitely better than the death that came through the Law (2 Cor. 3:6-11).

The revelation we have of God's love should cause us to trust Him. We shouldn't be susceptible to the lies of the devil in the same way that Adam and Eve were. Satan was able to slander God's character because Adam and Eve didn't really know God, but we *do* know Him. God has proven His love for us. The Apostle Paul wrote,

> *He that spared not his own Son, but delivered him up for us all, how shall he not with him also freely give us all things?*
>
> ROMANS 8:32

Once you truly understand the extent of God's love for you—demonstrated through the sacrifice of Jesus—you won't doubt His desire to freely give you all things. Jesus has completely redeemed you, and a full revelation of that truth will naturally lead you to believe how much God desires to bless you financially, heal you physically, and give you all that you need. The greater your revelation of God's love, the more successful you will be at resisting the attacks of the Enemy.

From what I can see, most Christians do not have an intimate relationship with the Lord. They know God from a distance, through the things they have heard from their pastors or someone else, but they don't know God for themselves. Before I understood that God loves me because His nature is love and not because I am lovely, I was always trying to do things to earn God's favor. When I was doing good, I felt close to God, but when I was falling short—which was most of the time—I didn't feel close to Him. All I could see was my own unworthiness. But once I got a revelation of how much God loves me, independent of my actions, everything that was holding me back from relationship with Him disappeared.

One of the greatest truths of Christianity is that your relationship with God is the key to everything. It's the key to having joy, peace, and abundance. It's the way to experiencing victory in life. Yet most believers aren't taking advantage of this amazing gift of relationship that is available to them.

After my encounter with God on March 23, 1968, I intuitively knew that God loved me completely separate from what I deserved, and it lit a fire under me to pursue relationship with Him even further. But even though I knew that God loved me, I didn't understand His love. I made a total commitment to God that day, but it took years for me to understand how a holy God could love me. I had spent my entire life trying to make myself righteous and acceptable to God, and I just couldn't get my mind around the fact that God's love and acceptance had nothing to do with my own efforts.

I was raised in a legalistic, works-oriented, religious system. My father died when I was twelve years old, and my church told me God killed him because it was His will for my father to die. I was taught that God put sickness, disease, poverty, and depression on me as punishments to make me a better person. I was told that the more I suffer, the holier I become. All of those ideas are absolutely false, but I didn't know any better back then. After my encounter with God's love, I was totally committed to God, but I had a wrong understanding of what God might do to make my relationship with Him deepen. It can be dangerous to be a living sacrifice—being totally submitted to the will of God—when you don't know what God's will includes! This is another reason it's important to renew your mind (Rom. 12:1-2).

I won't go into all of the details, but a few years after I made myself a living sacrifice, a traveling preacher came to my church and prophesied over me that God was going to put me into a coma. He told me that I was going to get sick and enter a vegetative state for years. He droned on and on about how God was going to use sickness to break me, but I would emerge as strong as the Apostle Paul after I came through it. I was ready to submit to what he said was God's will for me. Satan had me on the ropes. I was ready to accept whatever God wanted for me. But then the devil went too far. The so-called prophet told me that after I emerged from the coma, God was going to make me abstain from reading the Word for eight years.

I didn't know much, but I had a relationship with God, and I knew He would never tell me not to read His Word. As soon as the preacher said that, I knew it was all a lie. I stood up, renounced everything he had spoken over me, and walked away. I believe that if I had submitted to that false prophecy, I would have entered into a coma and died.

God doesn't use sickness to make people better; the devil uses sickness to steal, kill, and destroy (John 10:10). Scripture tells us to submit to God and resist the devil, and the devil will flee (James 4:7). But if we submit to the attacks of the Enemy and fail to resist evil, then the devil won't flee. I was able to resist the lies that were being spoken over me because I knew God. I had experienced the Word of God coming alive, God had spoken to me through it, and I knew He wouldn't take that away from me.

LESSON 6   CAN I REALLY KNOW GOD?

As New Covenant believers, we are able to understand the depths of God's love better than anyone did prior to the resurrection of Christ Jesus. Adam and Eve fell for Satan's temptation because they didn't know God well enough to realize that Satan was lying to them. If they had known God better, they would have recognized that He would never withhold good from them. Knowing God helps keep us from being deceived and from having our faith in God undermined by misunderstandings or wrong teaching.

I've been married to my wife, Jamie, since 1972. A lot of people may know Jamie, but I know her intimately. If someone were to tell me a story about Jamie that is totally inconsistent with her personality, I would know it wasn't true, because I know the kinds of things she would say and do. When you know someone well, it keeps you from being deceived by gossip or slander. But when you only know someone casually, you are more likely to believe the things you hear about them simply because you don't have any firsthand knowledge to judge by. The same is true of your relationship with God.

This analogy breaks down a little because people aren't perfect and sometimes they do things that are inconsistent with their normal behavior, but with God, there are no exceptions. God is the same yesterday, today, and forever (Heb. 13:8). God says, **"For I am the L**ORD**, I change not"** (Mal. 3:6). God is always the same. He doesn't make us righteous by grace one day and then judge us by our works the next. So, when religion tries to claim that God doesn't want to heal every person or that He puts sickness on people to teach them a lesson, we can know that those ideas are inconsistent with His nature. Jesus was the perfect representation of God (John 14:7, 9; and Heb. 1:3), and He went around doing good and healing *all* who were oppressed by the devil (Acts 10:38). We can know God's true nature because He reveals it to us in His Word.

People tend to think it would be great to have the same relationship with God that Old Testament kings and prophets had—like Adam and Eve, who walked with God in the cool of the evening, or Moses, who went up on a mountain and spent forty days in the presence of God. Those were awesome privileges, to be sure, but the revelation of God's true nature that has been given to us in Scripture is better than the revelation they had. We can actually know God better than they did. We can even know God better than the apostles knew Him prior to Jesus' resurrection and the gift of the Holy Spirit.

It's important for us to base our philosophy on the revelation of Jesus Christ and His grace, and not upon the traditions or ideas of man. Probably the most damaging tradition that is circulating in the body of Christ is the idea that nothing can happen unless God wills it to happen. It's a wrong philosophy, and it causes a lot of unnecessary pain. It isn't God's will for some babies to be born with deformities. God doesn't desire war, rape, or violence. God isn't behind any of the evil that we see in this world. Scripture says that God cannot be tempted with evil, and He doesn't tempt us with evil either (James 1:13). But if we think that God is sovereignly determining everything that happens in life, then we're going to be susceptible to bitterness and doubt toward Him. We'll either be mad at Him for making such a terrible mess of the world, or we'll lack confidence in Him for being unwilling to prevent it.

But God doesn't control everything. He gave us control, but mankind is too busy cooperating with the devil to fix what's wrong. God is all-powerful, but He has chosen to work through us (Eph. 3:20). God's will doesn't automatically come to pass. We have to cooperate with Him. If it was purely up to God, then everything on earth would be done the way it is in heaven (Matt. 6:10). There wouldn't be any sickness, crime, or sorrow. If God was controlling everything, our world wouldn't be in the mess it's in.

LESSON 6 — CAN I REALLY KNOW GOD?

Anyone who is upset with God has a wrong philosophy. They have been influenced by religion or other false doctrines that have misrepresented the Lord. One of the largest television networks in the United States is run by a man whose sister died when they were both very young. The church he attended told him it was God's will for her to die, and he decided that he didn't want anything to do with a God that would kill his sister. A wrong philosophy turned him against God, and he used his media influence to attack the Judeo-Christian ethic in the United States. I understand why he feels the way he does, but he has a wrong impression of God. Jesus said,

> *The thief cometh not, but for to steal, and to kill, and to destroy: I am come that they might have life, and that they might have it more abundantly.*
>
> JOHN 10:10

God doesn't kill anybody—it's the devil who takes lives. God comes to give us life in abundance. The Greek word used for **"life"** here is *zoe*, which means life that is "active and vigorous, devoted to God, blessed."[1] God is a good God! The Word also says,

> *Every good gift and every perfect gift is from above, and cometh down from the Father of lights, with whom is no variableness, neither shadow of turning.*
>
> JAMES 1:17

The simplest Christian theology is that if something is good, then it comes from God. If it's bad, then it's from the devil. God is not the cause of the tragedy in our lives. He doesn't take away our loved ones or cause disabilities, and He doesn't control and predetermine everything in life.[2] One reason is that God doesn't want to interfere with our free will, because doing so would cut off our only path to salvation. Another reason is that He has given us authority over the attacks of the Enemy, and He won't just step in and do things for us automatically. God uses people, so we need to cooperate with Him to allow His goodness and power to flow through us. Everything we need is already in our born-again spirits. When we cooperate with Him, His power flows from our spirits into our bodies and lives, bringing healing and victory.

God is your best friend—whether you recognize it or not. God is for you—He wants you to live a life full of joy and peace. Some people are afraid to seek God wholeheartedly because they think He might ask them to do something that would make them miserable—like move to the remotest corner of the globe and live under primitive conditions. They are afraid that God would suck all of the joy out of their lives, but He won't. God would never do something to hurt you—just the opposite. Once you start delighting in God, you will find that the desires of your heart are God's desires also (Ps. 37:4). So, if God were to lead you to go minister in a remote area, it's because you would fall in love with the people and love your work. God will always give you the grace to do what He calls you to do.

A life with God is an abundant, joyful life. The reason so many people are struggling today is that they don't really know the goodness of God. You can't base your relationship with God on what other people say or on their encounters with God. You have to know Him for yourself. God desires relationship with you, and relationship with God is the solution to any and every problem you might encounter.

---

[1] "Zoe," Blue Letter Bible, accessed January 7, 2011, http://www.blueletterbible.org/lang/lexicon/lexicon.cfm?Strongs=G2222&t=KJV.
[2] I have three, longer teachings that will give you a much deeper understanding in this area: *Spirit, Soul & Body*, *The Believer's Authority*, and *The True Nature of God*. Visit our website (www.awmi.net) and click on "Extras" to download free audio teachings, or order books from our online store.

LESSON 6 — CAN I REALLY KNOW GOD?

The importance of seeking God is often emphasized, but the truth is that God is seeking you more than you have ever sought Him. All you have to do is slow down a little and make a half turn toward God, and He will come into your life in a big way. You can know God personally—by intimate relationship—beyond mere knowledge *about* Him. Once you know God for yourself, you won't fall for the devil's schemes. The Enemy wants you to believe that life would be better if you had a bigger house, a nicer car, or a different spouse, but happiness is really found in relationship with the Lord.

God made us to desire relationship with Him, and people who don't know God try to satisfy that desire with substitute pleasures; they lust after sexual relationships, take drugs, or drink alcohol. They look for happiness in collecting material possessions and in the praise of others. They continually search for a sense of fulfillment in achieving the next big goal. None of those things are ultimately satisfying. What every human being needs is relationship with God.

After God created Adam, He breathed His Spirit into him. We were designed to be filled with God's presence, but when Adam and Eve rebelled, they kicked God out of their lives. God wasn't only talking about physical death when He commanded Adam not to eat of the forbidden fruit; the Lord said **"for in the day that thou eatest thereof thou shalt surely die"** (Gen. 2:17), but Adam and Eve lived on earth for many years after their rebellion. So, the death they experienced was spiritual, which eventually resulted in physical death. Adam and Eve's rebellion caused a God-shaped vacuum to be formed inside of every person. Sex, drugs, money, success, fame, and the other pursuits society is caught up in are just human attempts to fill the void caused by spiritual death.

We were made for relationship with God, and the only way to fill our spiritual void is to be born again and enter into relationship with Him. The reason I don't do drugs is that I'm not miserable. My born-again spirit allows me to enter into the presence of God and enjoy relationship with Him. In the presence of God is fullness of joy and pleasures forevermore (Ps. 16:11). We can get so full of God that we won't feel the need to be filled with anything else. The lust for other things will disappear. Once we have a real relationship with God, every day with Jesus can be sweeter than the day before.

Surface-level knowledge of God's love is not the same thing as plunging into the reality of His love. Real relationship with God involves going beyond a mere intellectual awareness of His love. Of all the things the Apostle Paul could have prayed for the Ephesians, he prayed for them to know the love of God. He said,

> *For this cause I bow my knees unto the Father of our Lord Jesus Christ, Of whom the whole family in heaven and earth is named, That he would grant you, according to the riches of his glory, to be strengthened with might by his Spirit in the inner man; That Christ may dwell in your hearts by faith; that ye, being rooted and grounded in love, May be able to comprehend with all saints what is the breadth, and length, and depth, and height; And to know the love of Christ, which passeth knowledge, that ye might be filled with all the fulness of God.*
>
> EPHESIANS 3:14-19

This passage of Scripture shows that God's love has multiple dimensions—it isn't merely a fact that you memorize like trivia. You can be overwhelmed by the height, depth, length, and breadth of God's love—so that it "passes knowledge" and becomes an experience of being filled with the grace and peace of God. It's one thing to say, "Oh, yeah, I know God loves me"; it's something else altogether to be filled with the fullness of God.

Lesson 6 — Can I Really Know God?

Do you know what it means to be filled with the fullness of God? God isn't depressed, discouraged, fearful, or anxious. He isn't poor or starving. The fullness of God is healing, prosperity, joy, peace, anointing, purpose, and total satisfaction. You get all of those things by *knowing* God experientially. In biblical language, "to know" is used to imply sexual intimacy, as in **"Adam knew Eve his wife; and she conceived, and bare Cain"** (Gen. 4:1). The Greek word Paul used in his prayer to the Ephesians is the same word used to describe how Joseph abstained from intimate relations with Mary until after the birth of Jesus (Matt. 1:25). Paul prayed for an intimate, personal knowledge of the love of Christ, one that passes mere knowledge, because that is how you get filled with the fullness of God.

Fear, loneliness, anger, frustration, poverty, sickness, and anxiety simply reflect a lack of the fullness of God. The remedy for those things is a revelation of how much God loves you. You just need a deeper relationship with God, one that allows you to experience the love of Christ beyond mere knowledge *about* Him. Of the thousands of people I counsel and pray for, nearly all of them are struggling because they lack a deep personal relationship with God.

Religion teaches people an approach to God that emphasizes personal effort, but no one can be perfect, and the frustration of failure leaves people feeling unlovable and separated from God. The Good News of Jesus Christ is that you don't have to *earn* relationship with God; Jesus earned it for you by dying on the cross and rising again. You were spiritually dead and couldn't save yourself, so Jesus came and died on your behalf to save you. He took your sin and gave you His righteousness. Salvation has nothing to do with what you deserve. God did this because He loves you and desires an intimate relationship with you.

Not every Christian has a deep personal relationship with God, but that isn't His fault. It's because they've been lied to. We've been taught that we have to earn relationship with God by living a holy life, going to church every week, paying a tithe, and studying the Word. Most of us are stuck on a treadmill of trying to live up to the requirements of being good Christians, falling short, and then getting back up to try harder. Our own hearts are condemning us and keeping us from entering into an intimate relationship. It's a wrong philosophy. Jesus paid for all of our sins—past, present, and future—and our shortcomings don't separate us from God. Scripture says,

> *For we through the Spirit wait for the hope of righteousness by faith. For in Jesus Christ neither circumcision availeth any thing, nor uncircumcision; but faith which worketh by love.*
> GALATIANS 5:5-6

Trying to earn God's love isn't going to get you anywhere. You're saved by faith, not by works. Once you rid yourself of the burden of thinking you have to be good enough and simply accept how much God loves you, your faith will go through the roof. Faith works by love, and faith is what releases the ability and the power of God. Knowing God's love will heal your body and bring peace to your mind. It will make your finances increase and your relationships flourish. Letting the love of God flow in you will bless you even beyond what you can imagine.

Maybe this sounds too good to be true—you might think there has to be more to it, some complicated step to perform, but it really is as simple as knowing God. Adam and Eve never experienced rejection or punishment from God prior to the Fall, but they never experienced the breadth, length, depth, and height of His love either. If they had known the fullness of God's love, then Satan would never have been able to tempt them.

LESSON 6 — CAN I REALLY KNOW GOD?

Before any of us can be tempted to sin, Satan first has to make us dissatisfied with what we already have. Adam and Eve were living in a sinless and perfect world, yet a talking snake convinced them God was holding out on them. Let's think about that. The temperature was perfect, the food was perfect, they didn't have any financial problems, and Adam and Eve were both perfect. They weren't constantly being bombarded by media reports of killing and strife all over the world. They couldn't even complain about each other. Everything was perfect. Yet Satan was able to make Adam and Eve feel discontent in the middle of paradise. Let's imagine, then, how easy it is for him to make people in our fallen world feel unhappy.

You live in a world where there is plenty to be displeased about, but the truth is that through Jesus, you can experience the love of God to a greater degree than Adam and Eve ever did. You can be filled with all the fullness of God and feel completely satisfied. What a powerful truth! All of the things you desire from God come freely through a heart that knows how wide, how long, how high, and how deep God's love is. Relationship with God is the pathway to everything He desires to give you.

Even though Adam and Eve were living in sinless perfection, they had a deficiency in their relationship with God—they didn't know how much He loved them. Today the shortages in our relationships with God are not because He hasn't communicated the depths of His love or His great desire to know us intimately; our problem is that most of us aren't entering into the intimacy God is calling us to. Often it's because we have a wrong philosophy and believe that we have to earn holiness in order to enter God's presence. The traditions and doctrines of man have made God's Word of no effect (Mark 7:13). Other times, we are simply too caught up in the things of this world to notice God calling us.

As a society, we are busy with many pursuits. So much stuff is being thrown at us every day that we don't have time to be still and know God (Ps. 46:10) and to know the greatness of His love for us. But it's within our power to change that: We can renew our minds and toss out the old religious philosophies that have damaged our relationship with God, and we can set aside time to spend with God and get to know His love. The promise of God's Word is that if we draw close to God, He will draw close to us (James 4:8). Jesus said,

> *Ask, and it shall be given you; seek, and ye shall find; knock, and it shall be opened unto you: For every one that asketh receiveth; and he that seeketh findeth; and to him that knocketh it shall be opened.*
>
> MATTHEW 7:7-8

God wants a relationship with you more than you desire a relationship with Him, so it's not a matter of you trying hard enough and forcing God to acknowledge you. It's simply a matter of allowing God to love you. God desires intimacy with you, but you have to let it happen, and you do that by seeking Him and yielding to His love. This understanding is essential to any Christian philosophy, and it will make a huge difference in the quality of life you experience.

LESSON 6 — CAN I REALLY KNOW GOD?

OUTLINE

I. When Satan tempted Adam and Eve, he didn't come right out and call God a liar; he started by questioning: "Did God really say…?"

    A. It wasn't until after he planted doubt in their minds that he accused God of lying to them.

    B. Satan told them that the real reason the Lord didn't want them to eat the fruit was because they would become like God (Gen. 3:5).

    C. The devil acted like God was being selfish, as if God didn't really love them and didn't have their best interests in mind.

    D. It was a total slander against the true nature and character of God.

    E. I believe that Adam and Eve didn't recognize that Satan was lying to them because although they communed with God in ways that most of us would long for, they didn't truly know God.

    F. I know that sounds like a radical statement—I struggled with it at first too. After all, Adam and Eve were perfect before sin entered the world.

    G. They walked with God in the cool of the evening and talked with Him.

    H. They weren't exposed to the ungodliness that has hardened our hearts toward God since sin entered the world.

    I. Everything was perfect and nothing was blocking their relationship with God—but Adam and Eve didn't know the true nature and character of God as well as we can today.

    J. They didn't know God loved them so much that He would become a man Himself, suffer humiliation, and lay down His life to save them.

    K. They knew God as Lord, but they didn't know Him as Savior.

II. The Word reveals to us the depths of God's love.

    A. It shows how He has pursued mankind throughout history, how He has loved us and proven through His actions a love that Adam and Eve could not have imagined.

    B. True Christianity is the only religion on the face of the earth with the concept of God becoming a man and taking the punishment we deserved in order to redeem us back to a right relationship with Him.

    C. Other religions may acknowledge a godlike entity, but they put the burden of salvation on the individual, on living a holy life and meeting certain standards of righteousness.

    D. The standards vary, but one consistent theme among all man-made religions is that there are specific instructions we must follow to appease an angry god.

    E. True Christianity is all about *what God has already done* for us.

    F. It's not about what we do, or how we live; it's all about what God has done to give us *His* righteousness.

    G. The Gospel of John sums it up by saying,

For God so loved the world, that he gave his only begotten Son, that whosoever believeth in him should not perish, but have everlasting life.

JOHN 3:16

- H. God demonstrated His love for us when He sent Jesus to suffer and die for our sins, and then He resurrected Him to give us His righteousness.
- I. It's a love that was impossible for Adam and Eve to understand.
- J. The sheer humility of God's plan of redemption is beyond human comprehension.
- K. No man could have conceived such a thing.
- L. Adam and Eve didn't know God's love to the extent that we can know and experience His love today.
- M. They had no idea that God would sacrifice His own Son so that they and their descendants could live forever.
- N. If they had known God that intimately, Satan would not have been able to deceive them into believing that God was holding out on them or trying to keep them from reaching their full potential.

III. A major part of having a Christian worldview is knowing God intimately, not from a distance.

- A. We can't just adopt other people's opinions about the nature and character of God; we need to have our own personal relationship with Him.
- B. The more we know the goodness of God, the less susceptible we will be to the lies of the devil.
- C. I fully believe that we succeed and experience victory in life to the degree that we have relationship with God.
- D. The good news is that we can know God better than Adam and Eve knew Him, because we have a much greater revelation of the extent to which God will go for us.
- E. Therefore, we don't have to fall prey to the lies of the devil.
- F. Once we know God intimately, Satan won't be able to discredit Him or convince us that God can't move in our lives.
- G. So, a close, intimate, personal relationship with God is an essential component of a Christian philosophy.

IV. The heroes of Old Testament didn't understand God's love the way we can today.

- A. Prior to the Resurrection and the gift of the Holy Spirit, not even Jesus' disciples had the revelation of God that is given to us in Scripture.
- B. At the crucifixion, the disciples were expecting Jesus to come down from the cross and establish His kingdom on earth.
- C. They didn't understand what was happening.
- D. When Jesus was arrested, the disciples ran away in fear and hid (Matt. 26:56 and Mark 14:50).
- E. They knew Jesus was the Messiah, but they were expecting Him to establish a physical kingdom on earth—right then.
- F. As they stood and looked at Jesus hanging on the cross, they saw defeat.
- G. To them, it looked like all of the hope they had placed in Jesus to save mankind was wasted.
- H. It shocked them when Jesus rose from the dead, because they didn't know or understand God's plan of salvation (Mark 16:11; Luke 24:11; John 20:9, and 25).

Lesson 6 — Can I Really Know God?

- I. In hindsight, through the record of Scripture, I now have a greater understanding of why Jesus sacrificed Himself on the cross than His disciples had prior to the coming of the Holy Spirit.

- J. Even after the establishment of the church, Peter—one of the Lord's closest disciples—still didn't fully understand grace or the dynamics of what had happened on the cross.

- K. He was trying to merge the Christian faith back into Jewish Law, and the Apostle Paul had to openly rebuke him for it (Gal. 2:11-14).

- L. Years later, Peter wrote in his second letter:

Our beloved brother Paul also according to the wisdom given unto him hath written unto you; As also in all his epistles, speaking in them of these things; in which are some things hard to be understood, which they that are unlearned and unstable wrest, as they do also the other scriptures, unto their own destruction.
2 PETER 3:15B-16

- M. Peter said right there that Paul's revelation of Jesus was superior to his own.

- N. Peter lived with Jesus for three-and-a-half years and Paul spent no time with Jesus while He was walking on earth, yet Paul had a greater revelation of who Jesus was and what He came to accomplish.

- O. The point is that Paul didn't get his revelation from other people; he received it through his spirit—the same way we receive revelation today.

- P. Paul has recorded for us the revelation God gave him in the letters he composed, which make up half of the New Testament.

- Q. Through the Holy Spirit and the study of Scripture, we can know God's love for us to a degree that the disciples of Jesus did not understand while they were ministering with Him on earth.

- R. That's an amazing statement!

V. I have a greater revelation of the true nature of God than Abraham or Moses had—not because I'm better than they were, but because God's plan of redemption is complete, and I have a fuller picture of God than they did.

- A. If I could travel back in time and sit down with Moses to explain God's plan of redemption, he wouldn't understand it.

- B. He wouldn't understand that the system of animal sacrifice they practiced was only foreshadowing how God would send His Son to live in the flesh and become the Lamb who takes away the sins of the world.

- C. Moses did not anticipate that God would do away with the sacrificial system and tear down the veil that separated us from the holy of holies.

- D. He had no idea those things would happen.

- E. Jesus said that John the Baptist was the greatest of those born of women, but **"he that is least in the kingdom of heaven is greater than he"** (Matt. 11:11b).

- F. Our born-again spirits make us greater than any of the Old Testament prophets: men like Moses, who spent forty days and nights in the presence of God and whose face, when he returned to the Israelites, was radiating the glory of God; Abraham, who believed God and became the father of faith; Elijah, who called down fire from heaven and never died but was taken up to heaven in a chariot of fire; Joshua, who led God's people into the Promised Land; and David, who was a man after God's own heart.

- G. We have access to a greater revelation of God's true nature than any of those men had.

- H. Scripture says the Old Covenant, written and engraved in stone, led to death—but it was also glorious.

Lesson 6 — Can I Really Know God?

    I. When Moses presented the Law to the people of Israel, they couldn't bear to look at him, because of the brightness of God's glory that was reflected in his face.

    J. The old way was glorious, but what we have is much more glorious.

    K. Under the New Covenant, the Holy Spirit gives us life forever, which is infinitely better than the death that came through the Law (2 Cor. 3:6-11).

VI. The revelation we have of God's love should cause us to trust Him.

    A. We shouldn't be susceptible to the lies of the devil in the same way that Adam and Eve were.

    B. Satan was able to slander God's character because Adam and Eve didn't really know God, but we *do* know Him.

    C. God has proven His love for us.

    D. The Apostle Paul wrote,

He that spared not his own Son, but delivered him up for us all, how shall he not with him also freely give us all things?

    ROMANS 8:32

    E. Once we truly understand the extent of God's love for us—demonstrated through the sacrifice of Jesus—we won't doubt His desire to freely give us all things.

    F. Jesus has completely redeemed us, and a full revelation of that truth will naturally lead us to believe how much God desires to bless us financially, heal us physically, and give us all that we need.

    G. The greater our revelation of God's love, the more successful we will be at resisting the attacks of the Enemy.

    H. From what I can see, most Christians do not have an intimate relationship with the Lord.

    I. They know God from a distance, through the things they have heard from their pastors or someone else, but they don't know God for themselves.

    J. Before I understood that God loves me because His nature is love and not because I am lovely, I was always trying to do things to earn God's favor.

    K. When I was doing good, I felt close to God, but when I was falling short—which was most of the time—I didn't feel close to Him.

    L. All I could see was my own unworthiness.

    M. But once I got a revelation of how much God loves me, independent of my actions, everything that was holding me back from relationship with Him disappeared.

VII. One of the greatest truths of Christianity is that your relationship with God is the key to everything.

    A. It's the key to having joy, peace, and abundance.

    B. It's the way to experiencing victory in life.

    C. Yet most believers aren't taking advantage of this amazing gift of relationship that is available to them.

    D. After my encounter with God on March 23, 1968, I intuitively knew that God loved me completely separate from what I deserved, and it lit a fire under me to pursue relationship with Him even further.

    E. But even though I knew that God loved me, I didn't understand His love.

LESSON 6 — CAN I REALLY KNOW GOD?

    F. I made a total commitment to God that day, but it took years for me to understand how a holy God could love me.

    G. I had spent my entire life trying to make myself righteous and acceptable to God, and I just couldn't get my mind around the fact that God's love and acceptance had nothing to do with my own efforts.

    H. I was raised in a legalistic, works-oriented, religious system.

    I. My father died when I was twelve years old, and my church told me God killed him because it was His will for my father to die.

    J. I was taught that God put sickness, disease, poverty, and depression on me as punishments to make me a better person.

    K. I was told that the more I suffer, the holier I become.

    L. All of those ideas are absolutely false, but I didn't know any better back then.

    M. After my encounter with God's love, I was totally committed to God, but I had a wrong understanding of what God might do to make my relationship with Him deepen.

    N. It can be dangerous to be a living sacrifice—being totally submitted to the will of God—when you don't know what God's will includes!

    O. This is another reason it's important to renew your mind (Rom. 12:1-2).

VIII. I won't go into all of the details, but a few years after I made myself a living sacrifice, a traveling preacher came to my church and prophesied over me that God was going to put me into a coma.

    A. He told me that I was going to get sick and enter a vegetative state for years.

    B. He droned on and on about how God was going to use sickness to break me, but I would emerge as strong as the Apostle Paul after I came through it.

    C. I was ready to submit to what he said was God's will for me.

    D. Satan had me on the ropes—I was ready to accept whatever God wanted for me.

    E. But then the devil went too far—the so-called prophet told me that after I emerged from the coma, God was going to make me abstain from reading the Word for eight years.

    F. I didn't know much, but I had a relationship with God, and I knew He would never tell me not to read His Word.

    G. As soon as the preacher said that, I knew it was all a lie.

    H. I stood up, renounced everything he had spoken over me, and walked away.

    I. I believe that if I had submitted to that false prophecy, I would have entered into a coma and died.

    J. God doesn't use sickness to make people better; the devil uses sickness to steal, kill, and destroy (John 10:10).

    K. Scripture tells us to submit to God and resist the devil, and the devil will flee (James 4:7).

    L. But if we submit to the attacks of the Enemy and fail to resist evil, then the devil won't flee.

    M. I was able to resist the lies that were being spoken over me because I knew God.

Lesson 6: Can I Really Know God?

- N. I had experienced the Word of God coming alive, God had spoken to me through it, and I knew He wouldn't take that away from me.
- O. If Adam and Eve had known God better, they would have recognized that He would never withhold good from them.
- P. Knowing God helps keep us from being deceived and from having our faith in God undermined by misunderstandings or wrong teaching.

IX. I've been married to my wife, Jamie, since 1972, and a lot of people may know Jamie, but I know her intimately.

- A. If someone were to tell me a story about Jamie that is totally inconsistent with her personality, I would know it wasn't true, because I know the kinds of things she would say and do.
- B. When you know someone well, it keeps you from being deceived by gossip or slander.
- C. But when you only know someone casually, you are more likely to believe the things you hear about them simply because you don't have any firsthand knowledge to judge by.
- D. The same is true of your relationship with God.
- E. This analogy breaks down a little because people aren't perfect and sometimes they do things that are inconsistent with their normal behavior, but with God, there are no exceptions.
- F. God is the same yesterday, today, and forever (Heb. 13:8).
- G. God says, **"For I am the Lord, I change not"** (Mal. 3:6)—He is always the same.
- H. He doesn't make you righteous by grace one day and then judge you by your works the next.
- I. So, when religion tries to claim that God doesn't want to heal every person or that He puts sickness on people to teach them a lesson, you can know that those ideas are inconsistent with His nature.
- J. Jesus was the perfect representation of God (John 14:7, 9; and Heb. 1:3), and He went around doing good and healing *all* who were oppressed by the devil (Acts 10:38).
- K. You can know God's true nature because He reveals it to us in His Word.
- L. It's important for you to base your philosophy on the revelation of Jesus Christ and His grace, and not upon the traditions or ideas of man.

X. Probably the most damaging tradition that is circulating in the body of Christ is the idea that nothing can happen unless God wills it to happen.

- A. It's a wrong philosophy, and it causes a lot of unnecessary pain.
- B. It isn't God's will for some babies to be born with deformities—He doesn't desire war, rape, or violence.
- C. God isn't behind any of the evil that we see in this world.
- D. Scripture says that God cannot be tempted with evil, and He doesn't tempt us with evil either (James 1:13).
- E. But if we think that God is sovereignly determining everything that happens in life, then we're going to be susceptible to bitterness and doubt toward Him.
- F. We'll either be mad at Him for making such a terrible mess of the world, or we'll lack confidence in Him for being unwilling to prevent it, but God doesn't control everything.
- G. He gave us control, but mankind is too busy cooperating with the devil to fix what's wrong.

H. God is all-powerful, but He has chosen to work through us (Eph. 3:20).

I. God's will doesn't automatically come to pass—we have to cooperate with Him.

J. If it was purely up to God, then everything on earth would be done the way it is in heaven (Matt. 6:10)—there wouldn't be any sickness, crime, or sorrow.

K. If God was controlling everything, our world wouldn't be in the mess it's in.

XI. Anyone who is upset with God has a wrong philosophy.

A. They have been influenced by religion or other false doctrines that have misrepresented the Lord.

B. One of the largest television networks in the United States is run by a man whose sister died when they were both very young.

C. The church he attended told him it was God's will for her to die, and he decided that he didn't want anything to do with a God that would kill his sister.

D. A wrong philosophy turned him against God, and he used his media influence to attack the Judeo-Christian ethic in the United States.

E. I understand why he feels the way he does, but he has a wrong impression of God.

F. Jesus said,

The thief cometh not, but for to steal, and to kill, and to destroy: I am come that they might have life, and that they might have it more abundantly.

JOHN 10:10

G. God doesn't kill anybody—it's the devil who takes lives.

H. God comes to give us life in abundance.

I. The Greek word used for **"life"** here is *zoe*, which means life that is "active and vigorous, devoted to God, blessed."[1]

XII. God is a good God!

A. The Word also says,

Every good gift and every perfect gift is from above, and cometh down from the Father of lights, with whom is no variableness, neither shadow of turning.

JAMES 1:17

B. The simplest Christian theology is that if something is good, then it comes from God—if it's bad, then it's from the devil.

C. God doesn't take away our loved ones or cause disabilities, and He doesn't control and predetermine everything in life.[2]

D. One reason is that God doesn't want to interfere with our free will, because doing so would cut off our only path to salvation.

E. Another reason is that He has given us authority over the attacks of the Enemy, and He won't just step in and do things for us automatically.

---

[1] "Zoe," Blue Letter Bible, accessed January 7, 2011, http://www.blueletterbible.org/lang/lexicon/lexicon.cfm?Strongs=G2222&t=KJV.
[2] I have three, longer teachings that will give you a much deeper understanding in this area: *Spirit, Soul & Body*, *The Believer's Authority*, and *The True Nature of God*. Visit our website (www.awmi.net) and click on "Extras" to download free audio teachings, or order books from our online store.

Lesson 6 — Can I Really Know God?

- F. God uses people, so we need to cooperate with Him to allow His goodness and power to flow through us.
- G. Everything we need is already in our born-again spirits.
- H. When we cooperate with Him, His power flows from our spirits into our bodies and lives, bringing healing and victory.

XIII. God is your best friend—whether you recognize it or not.

- A. God is for you—He wants you to live a life full of joy and peace.
- B. Some people are afraid to seek God wholeheartedly because they think He might ask them to do something that would make them miserable—like move to the remotest corner of the globe and live under primitive conditions.
- C. They are afraid that God would suck all of the joy out of their lives, but He won't.
- D. God would never do something to hurt you—just the opposite.
- E. Once you start delighting in God, you will find that the desires of your heart are God's desires also (Ps. 37:4).
- F. So, if God were to lead you to go minister in a remote area, it's because you would fall in love with the people and love your work.
- G. God will always give you the grace to do what He calls you to do.
- H. A life with God is an abundant, joyful life.
- I. The reason so many people are struggling today is that they don't really know the goodness of God.
- J. You can't base your relationship with God on what other people say or on their encounters with God.
- K. You have to know Him for yourself.
- L. God desires relationship with you, and relationship with God is the solution to any and every problem you might encounter.
- M. The importance of seeking God is often emphasized, but the truth is that God is seeking you more than you have ever sought Him.
- N. All you have to do is slow down a little and make a half turn toward God, and He will come into your life in a big way.
- O. You can know God personally—by intimate relationship—beyond mere knowledge *about* Him.
- P. Once you know God for yourself, you won't fall for the devil's schemes.
- Q. The Enemy wants you to believe that life would be better if you had a bigger house, a nicer car, or a different spouse, but happiness is really found in relationship with the Lord.

XIV. God made us to desire relationship with Him, and people who don't know God try to satisfy that desire with substitute pleasures; they lust after sexual relationships, take drugs, or drink alcohol.

- A. They look for happiness in collecting material possessions and in the praise of others.
- B. They continually search for a sense of fulfillment in achieving the next big goal.
- C. None of those things are ultimately satisfying. What every human being needs is relationship with God.
- D. After God created Adam, He breathed His Spirit into him.

LESSON 6 — CAN I REALLY KNOW GOD?

E. We were designed to be filled with God's presence, but when Adam and Eve rebelled, they kicked God out of their lives.

F. God wasn't only talking about physical death when He commanded Adam not to eat of the forbidden fruit.

G. The Lord said **"for in the day that thou eatest thereof thou shalt surely die"** (Gen. 2:17), but Adam and Eve lived on earth for many years after their rebellion. So, the death they experienced was spiritual, which eventually resulted in physical death.

H. Adam and Eve's rebellion caused a God-shaped vacuum to be formed inside of every person.

I. Sex, drugs, money, success, fame, and the other pursuits society is caught up in are just human attempts to fill the void caused by spiritual death.

J. We were made for relationship with God, and the only way to fill our spiritual void is to be born again and enter into relationship with Him.

K. The reason I don't do drugs is that I'm not miserable.

L. My born-again spirit allows me to enter into the presence of God and enjoy relationship with Him.

M. In the presence of God is fullness of joy and pleasures forevermore (Ps. 16:11).

N. We can get so full of God that we won't feel the need to be filled with anything else—the lust for other things will disappear.

O. Once we have a real relationship with God, every day with Jesus can be sweeter than the day before.

XV. Surface-level knowledge of God's love is not the same thing as plunging into the reality of His love.

A. Real relationship with God involves going beyond a mere intellectual awareness of His love.

B. Of all the things the Apostle Paul could have prayed for the Ephesians, he prayed for them to know the love of God.

C. He said,

For this cause I bow my knees unto the Father of our Lord Jesus Christ, Of whom the whole family in heaven and earth is named, That he would grant you, according to the riches of his glory, to be strengthened with might by his Spirit in the inner man; That Christ may dwell in your hearts by faith; that ye, being rooted and grounded in love, May be able to comprehend with all saints what is the breadth, and length, and depth, and height; And to know the love of Christ, which passeth knowledge, that ye might be filled with all the fulness of God.

EPHESIANS 3:14-19

D. This passage of Scripture shows that God's love has multiple dimensions—it isn't merely a fact that you memorize like trivia.

E. You can be overwhelmed by the height, depth, length, and breadth of God's love—so that it "passes knowledge" and becomes an experience of being filled with the grace and peace of God.

F. It's one thing to say, "Oh, yeah, I know God loves me"; it's something else altogether to be filled with the fullness of God.

G. God isn't depressed, discouraged, fearful, or anxious—He isn't poor or starving.

H. The fullness of God is healing, prosperity, joy, peace, anointing, purpose, and total satisfaction.

I. You get all of those things by *knowing* God experientially.

LESSON 6   CAN I REALLY KNOW GOD?

    J. In biblical language, "to know" is used to imply sexual intimacy, as in **"Adam knew Eve his wife; and she conceived, and bare Cain"** (Gen. 4:1).

    K. The Greek word Paul used in his prayer to the Ephesians is the same word used to describe how Joseph abstained from intimate relations with Mary until after the birth of Jesus (Matt. 1:25).

    L. Paul prayed for an intimate, personal knowledge of the love of Christ, one that passes mere knowledge, because that is how you get filled with the fullness of God.

    M. Fear, loneliness, anger, frustration, poverty, sickness, and anxiety simply reflect a lack of the fullness of God.

    N. The remedy for those things is a revelation of how much God loves you.

    O. You just need a deeper relationship with God, one that allows you to experience the love of Christ beyond mere knowledge *about* Him.

    P. Of the thousands of people I counsel and pray for, nearly all of them are struggling because they lack a deep personal relationship with God.

XVI. Religion teaches people an approach to God that emphasizes personal effort, but no one can be perfect, and the frustration of failure leaves people feeling unlovable and separated from God.

    A. The Good News of Jesus Christ is that we don't have to *earn* relationship with God; Jesus earned it for us by dying on the cross and rising again.

    B. We were spiritually dead and couldn't save ourselves, so Jesus came and died on our behalf to save us.

    C. He took our sin and gave us His righteousness.

    D. Salvation has nothing to do with what we deserve.

    E. God did this because He loves us and desires an intimate relationship with us.

    F. Not every Christian has a deep personal relationship with God, but that isn't His fault—it's because they've been lied to.

    G. We've been taught that we have to earn relationship with God by living a holy life, going to church every week, paying a tithe, and studying the Word.

    H. Most of us are stuck on a treadmill of trying to live up to the requirements of being good Christians, falling short, and then getting back up to try harder.

    I. Our own hearts are condemning us and keeping us from entering into an intimate relationship.

    J. It's a wrong philosophy, because Jesus paid for all of our sins—past, present, and future—and our shortcomings don't separate us from God.

    K. Scripture says,

For we through the Spirit wait for the hope of righteousness by faith. For in Jesus Christ neither circumcision availeth any thing, nor uncircumcision; but faith which worketh by love.
                                                               GALATIANS 5:5-6

    L. Trying to earn God's love isn't going to get us anywhere.

    M. We're saved by faith, not by works.

    N. Once we rid ourselves of the burden of thinking we have to be good enough and simply accept how much God loves us, our faith will go through the roof.

Lesson 6 — Can I Really Know God?

- O. Faith works by love, and faith is what releases the ability and the power of God.
- P. Knowing God's love will heal our bodies and bring peace to our minds.
- Q. It will make our finances increase and our relationships flourish.
- R. Letting the love of God flow in us will bless us even beyond what we can imagine.

XVII. Maybe this sounds too good to be true—you might think there has to be more to it, some complicated step to perform, but it really is as simple as knowing God.

- A. Adam and Eve never experienced rejection or punishment from God prior to the Fall, but they never experienced the breadth, length, depth, and height of His love either.
- B. If they had known the fullness of God's love, then Satan would never have been able to tempt them.
- C. Before you can be tempted to sin, Satan first has to make you dissatisfied with what you already have.
- D. Adam and Eve were living in a sinless and perfect world, yet a talking snake convinced them God was holding out on them.
- E. Think about that: The temperature was perfect, the food was perfect, they didn't have any financial problems, and Adam and Eve were both perfect.
    - i. They weren't constantly being bombarded by media reports of killing and strife all over the world.
    - ii. They couldn't even complain about each other.
- F. Yet Satan was able to make Adam and Eve feel discontent in the middle of paradise.
- G. Imagine, then, how easy it is for him to make people in a fallen world feel unhappy.
- H. You live in a world where there is plenty to be displeased about, but the truth is that through Jesus, you can experience the love of God to a greater degree than Adam and Eve ever did.
- I. You can be filled with all the fullness of God and feel completely satisfied.
- J. What a powerful truth!
- K. All of the things you desire from God come freely through a heart that knows how wide, how long, how high, and how deep God's love is.
- L. Relationship with God is the pathway to everything He desires to give you.

XVIII. Today the shortages in our relationships with God are not because He hasn't communicated the depths of His love or His great desire to know us intimately.

- A. Our problem is that most of us aren't entering into the intimacy God is calling us to.
- B. Often it's because we have a wrong philosophy and believe that we have to earn holiness in order to enter God's presence.
- C. The traditions and doctrines of man have made God's Word of no effect (Mark 7:13).
- D. Other times, we are simply too caught up in the things of this world to notice God calling us.
- E. As a society, we are busy with many pursuits.

F. So much stuff is being thrown at us every day that we don't have time to be still and know God (Ps. 46:10) and to know the greatness of His love for us.

G. But it's within our power to change that: We can renew our minds and toss out the old religious philosophies that have damaged our relationship with God, and we can set aside time to spend with God and get to know His love.

XIX. The promise of God's Word is that if you draw close to God, He will draw close to you (James 4:8).

A. Jesus said,

Ask, and it shall be given you; seek, and ye shall find; knock, and it shall be opened unto you: For every one that asketh receiveth; and he that seeketh findeth; and to him that knocketh it shall be opened.
MATTHEW 7:7-8

B. God wants a relationship with you more than you desire a relationship with Him, so it's not a matter of you trying hard enough and forcing God to acknowledge you.

C. It's simply a matter of allowing God to love you.

D. God desires intimacy with you, but you have to let it happen, and you do that by seeking Him and yielding to His love.

E. This understanding is essential to any Christian philosophy, and it will make a huge difference in the quality of life you experience.

LESSON 6 — CAN I REALLY KNOW GOD?

TEACHER'S GUIDE

1. When Satan tempted Adam and Eve, he didn't come right out and call God a liar; he started by questioning: "Did God really say…?" It wasn't until after he planted doubt in their minds that he accused God of lying to them. Satan told them that the real reason the Lord didn't want them to eat the fruit was because they would become like God (Gen. 3:5). The devil acted like God was being selfish, as if God didn't really love them and didn't have their best interests in mind. It was a total slander against the true nature and character of God. I believe that Adam and Eve didn't recognize that Satan was lying to them because although they communed with God in ways that most of us would long for, they didn't truly know God. I know that sounds like a radical statement—I struggled with it at first too. After all, Adam and Eve were perfect before sin entered the world. They walked with God in the cool of the evening and talked with Him. They weren't exposed to the ungodliness that has hardened our hearts toward God since sin entered the world. Everything was perfect and nothing was blocking their relationship with God—but Adam and Eve didn't know the true nature and character of God as well as we can today. They didn't know God loved them so much that He would become a man Himself, suffer humiliation, and lay down His life to save them. They knew God as Lord, but they didn't know Him as Savior.

- 1a. It's possible to commune with God and not really _____ Him.
   (Know)

- 1b. Discussion Question: Why is it important to know God as Savior and not just Lord?
   (Discussion question)

2. The Word reveals to us the depths of God's love. It shows how He has pursued mankind throughout history, how He has loved us and proven through His actions a love that Adam and Eve could not have imagined. True Christianity is the only religion on the face of the earth with the concept of God becoming a man and taking the punishment we deserved in order to redeem us back to a right relationship with Him. Other religions may acknowledge a godlike entity, but they put the burden of salvation on the individual, on living a holy life and meeting certain standards of righteousness. The standards vary, but one consistent theme among all man-made religions is that there are specific instructions we must follow to appease an angry god. True Christianity is all about *what God has already done* for us. It's not about what we do, or how we live; it's all about what God has done to give us *His* righteousness. The Gospel of John sums it up by saying, **"For God so loved the world, that he gave his only begotten Son, that whosoever believeth in him should not perish, but have everlasting life"** (John 3:16). God demonstrated His love for us when He sent Jesus to suffer and die for our sins, and then He resurrected Him to give us His righteousness. It's a love that was impossible for Adam and Eve to understand. The sheer humility of God's plan of redemption is beyond human comprehension. No man could have conceived such a thing. Adam and Eve didn't know God's love to the extent that we can know and experience His love today. They had no idea that God would sacrifice His own Son so that they and their descendants could live forever. If they had known God that intimately, Satan would not have been able to deceive them into believing that God was holding out on them or trying to keep them from reaching their full potential.

- 2a. Other religions may acknowledge a godlike entity, but they put the _____ of salvation on the individual, on living a holy life and meeting certain standards of righteousness.
   (Burden)

- 2b. Read John 3:16. What is true Christianity about?
   (It's all about what God has already done for us. It's not about what we do, or how we live; it's all about what God has done to give us His righteousness)

- 2c. Why did God resurrect Jesus?
   (To give us His righteousness)

- 2d. What do you need if you're not going to be deceived into believing that God is holding out on you or trying to keep you from reaching your full potential?
   A. To read the Bible
   B. To serve at church
   C. To know God intimately
   D. All of the above
   E. None of the above
   (C. To know God intimately)

LESSON 6   CAN I REALLY KNOW GOD?

3. A major part of having a Christian worldview is knowing God intimately, not from a distance. We can't just adopt other people's opinions about the nature and character of God; we need to have our own personal relationship with Him. The more we know the goodness of God, the less susceptible we will be to the lies of the devil. I fully believe that we succeed and experience victory in life to the degree that we have relationship with God. The good news is that we can know God better than Adam and Eve knew Him, because we have a much greater revelation of the extent to which God will go for us. Therefore, we don't have to fall prey to the lies of the devil. Once we know God intimately, Satan won't be able to discredit Him or convince us that God can't move in our lives. So, a close, intimate, personal relationship with God is an essential component of a Christian philosophy.

    3a.   Knowing God intimately is a _____ part of having a Christian worldview.
            (Major)

    3b.   Discussion Question: What hinders you from knowing God intimately?
            (Discussion question)

4. The heroes of Old Testament didn't understand God's love the way we can today. Prior to the Resurrection and the gift of the Holy Spirit, not even Jesus' disciples had the revelation of God that is given to us in Scripture. At the crucifixion, the disciples were expecting Jesus to come down from the cross and establish His kingdom on earth. They didn't understand what was happening. When Jesus was arrested, the disciples ran away in fear and hid (Matt. 26:56 and Mark 14:50). They knew Jesus was the Messiah, but they were expecting Him to establish a physical kingdom on earth—right then. As they stood and looked at Jesus hanging on the cross, they saw defeat. To them, it looked like all of the hope they had placed in Jesus to save mankind was wasted. It shocked them when Jesus rose from the dead, because they didn't know or understand God's plan of salvation (Mark 16:11; Luke 24:11; John 20:9, and 25). In hindsight, through the record of Scripture, I now have a greater understanding of why Jesus sacrificed Himself on the cross than His disciples had prior to the coming of the Holy Spirit. Even after the establishment of the church, Peter—one of the Lord's closest disciples—still didn't fully understand grace or the dynamics of what had happened on the cross. He was trying to merge the Christian faith back into Jewish Law, and the Apostle Paul had to openly rebuke him for it (Gal. 2:11-14). Years later, Peter wrote in his second letter: **"Our beloved brother Paul also according to the wisdom given unto him hath written unto you; As also in all his epistles, speaking in them of these things; in which are some things hard to be understood, which they that are unlearned and unstable wrest, as they do also the other scriptures, unto their own destruction"** (2 Pet. 3:15b-16). Peter said right there that Paul's revelation of Jesus was superior to his own. Peter lived with Jesus for three-and-a-half years and Paul spent no time with Jesus while He was walking on earth, yet Paul had a greater revelation of who Jesus was and what He came to accomplish. The point is that Paul didn't get his revelation from other people; he received it through his spirit—the same way we receive revelation today. Paul has recorded for us the revelation God gave him in the letters he composed, which make up half of the New Testament. Through the Holy Spirit and the study of Scripture, we can know God's love for us to a degree that the disciples of Jesus did not understand while they were ministering with Him on earth. That's an amazing statement!

    4a.   Not even who had the revelation of God that is given to you in Scripture?
            A. Paul
            B. Apollos
            C. Agabus
            D. Jesus' disciples
            E. The church
            (D. Jesus' disciples)

    4b.   Why was Paul's revelation of Jesus superior to Peter's?
            (Because Paul didn't get his revelation from other people; he received it through his spirit)

5. I have a greater revelation of the true nature of God than Abraham or Moses had—not because I'm better than they were, but because God's plan of redemption is complete, and I have a fuller picture of God than they did. If I could travel back in time and sit down with Moses to explain God's plan of redemption, he wouldn't understand it. He wouldn't understand that the system of animal sacrifice they practiced was only foreshadowing how God would send His Son to live in the flesh and become the Lamb who takes away the sins of the world. Moses did not anticipate that God would do away with the sacrificial system and tear down the veil that separated us from the

LESSON 6   CAN I REALLY KNOW GOD?

holy of holies. He had no idea those things would happen. Jesus said that John the Baptist was the greatest of those born of women, but **"he that is least in the kingdom of heaven is greater than he"** (Matt. 11:11b). Our born-again spirits make us greater than any of the Old Testament prophets: men like Moses, who spent forty days and nights in the presence of God and whose face, when he returned to the Israelites, was radiating the glory of God; Abraham, who believed God and became the father of faith; Elijah, who called down fire from heaven and never died but was taken up to heaven in a chariot of fire; Joshua, who led God's people into the Promised Land; and David, who was a man after God's own heart. We have access to a greater revelation of God's true nature than any of those men had. Scripture says the Old Covenant, written and engraved in stone, led to death—but it was also glorious. When Moses presented the Law to the people of Israel, they couldn't bear to look at him, because of the brightness of God's glory that was reflected in his face. The old way was glorious, but what we have is much more glorious. Under the New Covenant, the Holy Spirit gives us life forever, which is infinitely better than the death that came through the Law (2 Cor. 3:6-11).

    5a.   What makes you greater than the Old Testament prophets?
             (Your born-again spirit)

    5b.   Read 2 Corinthians 3:6-11. True or false: Life came through the Law.
             (False)

6. The revelation we have of God's love should cause us to trust Him. We shouldn't be susceptible to the lies of the devil in the same way that Adam and Eve were. Satan was able to slander God's character because Adam and Eve didn't really know God, but we *do* know Him. God has proven His love for us. The Apostle Paul wrote, **"He that spared not his own Son, but delivered him up for us all, how shall he not with him also freely give us all things?"** (Rom. 8:32). Once we truly understand the extent of God's love for us—demonstrated through the sacrifice of Jesus—we won't doubt His desire to freely give us all things. Jesus has completely redeemed us, and a full revelation of that truth will naturally lead us to believe how much God desires to bless us financially, heal us physically, and give us all that we need. The greater our revelation of God's love, the more successful we will be at resisting the attacks of the Enemy. From what I can see, most Christians do not have an intimate relationship with the Lord. They know God from a distance, through the things they have heard from their pastors or someone else, but they don't know God for themselves. Before I understood that God loves me because His nature is love and not because I am lovely, I was always trying to do things to earn God's favor. When I was doing good, I felt close to God, but when I was falling short—which was most of the time—I didn't feel close to Him. All I could see was my own unworthiness. But once I got a revelation of how much God loves me, independent of my actions, everything that was holding me back from relationship with Him disappeared.

    6a.   Read Romans 8:32. What do you need so you won't doubt God's desire to freely give you all things?
             (To truly understand the extent of God's love for you—demonstrated through the sacrifice of Jesus)

    6b.   How can you become more successful at resisting the attacks of the Enemy?
             A. By listening to more sermons
             B. By getting a greater revelation of God's love
             C. By putting more effort into it
             D. By binding and loosing
             E. By strengthening your will power
             (B. By getting a greater revelation of God's love)

    6c.   True or false: It's important to know God through the things you have heard from your pastor or someone else.
             (False)

    6d.   Discussion Question: Why should you know God for yourself?
             (Discussion question)

    6e.   Before Andrew understood that God loves him because His nature is love and not because he is lovely, he was always trying to do things to _____ God's favor.
             (Earn)

    6f.   True or false: Sometimes it's good to try to earn God's favor.
             (False)

LESSON 6 — CAN I REALLY KNOW GOD?

7. One of the greatest truths of Christianity is that your relationship with God is the key to everything. It's the key to having joy, peace, and abundance. It's the way to experiencing victory in life. Yet most believers aren't taking advantage of this amazing gift of relationship that is available to them. After my encounter with God on March 23, 1968, I intuitively knew that God loved me completely separate from what I deserved, and it lit a fire under me to pursue relationship with Him even further. But even though I knew that God loved me, I didn't understand His love. I made a total commitment to God that day, but it took years for me to understand how a holy God could love me. I had spent my entire life trying to make myself righteous and acceptable to God, and I just couldn't get my mind around the fact that God's love and acceptance had nothing to do with my own efforts. I was raised in a legalistic, works-oriented, religious system. My father died when I was twelve years old, and my church told me God killed him because it was His will for my father to die. I was taught that God put sickness, disease, poverty, and depression on me as punishments to make me a better person. I was told that the more I suffer, the holier I become. All of those ideas are absolutely false, but I didn't know any better back then. After my encounter with God's love, I was totally committed to God, but I had a wrong understanding of what God might do to make my relationship with Him deepen. It can be dangerous to be a living sacrifice—being totally submitted to the will of God—when you don't know what God's will includes! This is another reason it's important to renew your mind (Rom. 12:1-2).

    7a.   What is one of the greatest truths to Christianity?
            (That your relationship with God is the key to everything; e.g., joy, peace, and abundance)

    7b.   Read Romans 12:1-2. What's one reason it's important to renew your mind?
            (So you'll know what God's will includes)

8. I won't go into all of the details, but a few years after I made myself a living sacrifice, a traveling preacher came to my church and prophesied over me that God was going to put me into a coma. He told me that I was going to get sick and enter a vegetative state for years. He droned on and on about how God was going to use sickness to break me, but I would emerge as strong as the Apostle Paul after I came through it. I was ready to submit to what he said was God's will for me. Satan had me on the ropes. I was ready to accept whatever God wanted for me. But then the devil went too far. The so-called prophet told me that after I emerged from the coma, God was going to make me abstain from reading the Word for eight years. I didn't know much, but I had a relationship with God, and I knew He would never tell me not to read His Word. As soon as the preacher said that, I knew it was all a lie. I stood up, renounced everything he had spoken over me, and walked away. I believe that if I had submitted to that false prophecy, I would have entered into a coma and died. God doesn't use sickness to make people better; the devil uses sickness to steal, kill, and destroy (John 10:10). Scripture tells us to submit to God and resist the devil, and the devil will flee (James 4:7). But if we submit to the attacks of the Enemy and fail to resist evil, then the devil won't flee. I was able to resist the lies that were being spoken over me because I knew God. I had experienced the Word of God coming alive, God had spoken to me through it, and I knew He wouldn't take that away from me. If Adam and Eve had known God better, they would have recognized that He would never withhold good from them. Knowing God helps keep us from being deceived and from having our faith in God undermined by misunderstandings or wrong teaching.

    8a.   True or false: God would never tell you to stop reading His Word.
            (True)

    8b.   Knowing God keeps you from what?
            (Being deceived and from having your faith in God undermined by misunderstandings or wrong teaching)

9. I've been married to my wife, Jamie, since 1972. A lot of people may know Jamie, but I know her intimately. If someone were to tell me a story about Jamie that is totally inconsistent with her personality, I would know it wasn't true, because I know the kinds of things she would say and do. When you know someone well, it keeps you from being deceived by gossip or slander. But when you only know someone casually, you are more likely to believe the things you hear about them simply because you don't have any firsthand knowledge to judge by. The same is true of your relationship with God. This analogy breaks down a little because people aren't perfect and sometimes they do things that are inconsistent with their normal behavior, but with God, there are no exceptions. God is the same yesterday, today, and forever (Heb. 13:8). God says, **"For I am the Lord, I change not"** (Mal. 3:6). God is always the same. He doesn't make you righteous by grace one day and then judge you by your works the next. So, when

LESSON 6 — CAN I REALLY KNOW GOD?

religion tries to claim that God doesn't want to heal every person or that He puts sickness on people to teach them a lesson, you can know that those ideas are inconsistent with His nature. Jesus was the perfect representation of God (John 14:7, 9; and Heb. 1:3), and He went around doing good and healing *all* who were oppressed by the devil (Acts 10:38). You can know God's true nature because He reveals it to us in His Word. It's important for you to base your philosophy on the revelation of Jesus Christ and His grace, and not upon the traditions or ideas of man.

9a. Read Hebrews 13:8 and Malachi 3:6. God doesn't make you righteous by _____ one day and then judge you by your _____ the next.
(Grace/works)

9b. Read John 14:7, 9; and Hebrews 1:3. Jesus was the _____ representation of God.
(Perfect)

9c. Discussion Question: What does this mean to you?
(Discussion question)

9d. It's important for you to base your philosophy on what?
(The revelation of Jesus Christ and His grace, and not upon the traditions or ideas of man)

10. Probably the most damaging tradition that is circulating in the body of Christ is the idea that nothing can happen unless God wills it to happen. It's a wrong philosophy, and it causes a lot of unnecessary pain. It isn't God's will for some babies to be born with deformities. God doesn't desire war, rape, or violence. God isn't behind any of the evil that we see in this world. Scripture says that God cannot be tempted with evil, and He doesn't tempt us with evil either (James 1:13). But if we think that God is sovereignly determining everything that happens in life, then we're going to be susceptible to bitterness and doubt toward Him. We'll either be mad at Him for making such a terrible mess of the world, or we'll lack confidence in Him for being unwilling to prevent it. But God doesn't control everything. He gave us control, but mankind is too busy cooperating with the devil to fix what's wrong. God is all-powerful, but He has chosen to work through us (Eph. 3:20). God's will doesn't automatically come to pass. We have to cooperate with Him. If it was purely up to God, then everything on earth would be done the way it is in heaven (Matt. 6:10). There wouldn't be any sickness, crime, or sorrow. If God was controlling everything, our world wouldn't be in the mess it's in.

10a. What is probably the most damaging tradition that is circulating in the body of Christ?
(The idea that nothing can happen unless God wills it to happen)

10b. According to James 1:13, what can't God be tempted with?
A. Evil
B. Food
C. Money
D. All of the above
E. None of the above
(A. Evil)

10c. If you think that God is sovereignly determining everything that happens in life, what will you be?
(Susceptible to bitterness and doubt toward Him, mad at Him for making such a terrible mess of the world, or you'll lack confidence in Him for being unwilling to prevent it)

10d. Read Ephesians 3:20. Even though God is all-powerful, He has chosen to work through whom?
A. Only leaders
B. You
C. The devil
D. Those worthy enough
E. Angels
(B. You)

10e. Discussion Question: How do you know that God's will doesn't automatically come to pass?
(Discussion question)

LESSON 6   CAN I REALLY KNOW GOD?

11. Anyone who is upset with God has a wrong philosophy. They have been influenced by religion or other false doctrines that have misrepresented the Lord. One of the largest television networks in the United States is run by a man whose sister died when they were both very young. The church he attended told him it was God's will for her to die, and he decided that he didn't want anything to do with a God that would kill his sister. A wrong philosophy turned him against God, and he used his media influence to attack the Judeo-Christian ethic in the United States. I understand why he feels the way he does, but he has a wrong impression of God. Jesus said, **"The thief cometh not, but for to steal, and to kill, and to destroy: I am come that they might have life, and that they might have it more abundantly"** (John 10:10). God doesn't kill anybody—it's the devil who takes lives. God comes to give us life in abundance. The Greek word used for **"life"** here is *zoe*, which means life that is "active and vigorous, devoted to God, blessed."[1]

     11a. _____ who is upset with God has a wrong philosophy.
           (Anyone)

     11b. Read John 10:10. The Greek word used for **"life"** here is *zoe*, which means what?
           (Life that is "active and vigorous, devoted to God, blessed")

12. God is a good God! The Word also says, **"Every good gift and every perfect gift is from above, and cometh down from the Father of lights, with whom is no variableness, neither shadow of turning"** (James 1:17). The simplest Christian theology is that if something is good, then it comes from God. If it's bad, then it's from the devil. God doesn't take away our loved ones or cause disabilities, and He doesn't control and predetermine everything in life.[2] One reason is that God doesn't want to interfere with our free will, because doing so would cut off our only path to salvation. Another reason is that He has given us authority over the attacks of the Enemy, and He won't just step in and do things for us automatically. God uses people, so we need to cooperate with Him to allow His goodness and power to flow through us. Everything we need is already in our born-again spirits. When we cooperate with Him, His power flows from our spirits into our bodies and lives, bringing healing and victory.

     12a. Read James 1:17. What is the simplest theology?
           (If something is good, then it comes from God. If it's bad, then it's from the devil)

     12b. Discussion Question: Give an example of how God steps in and does things for you automatically.
           (Discussion question)

13. God is your best friend—whether you recognize it or not. God is for you—He wants you to live a life full of joy and peace. Some people are afraid to seek God wholeheartedly because they think He might ask them to do something that would make them miserable—like move to the remotest corner of the globe and live under primitive conditions. They are afraid that God would suck all of the joy out of their lives, but He won't. God would never do something to hurt you—just the opposite. Once you start delighting in God, you will find that the desires of your heart are God's desires also (Ps. 37:4). So, if God were to lead you to go minister in a remote area, it's because you would fall in love with the people and love your work. God will always give you the grace to do what He calls you to do. A life with God is an abundant, joyful life. The reason so many people are struggling today is that they don't really know the goodness of God. You can't base your relationship with God on what other people say or on their encounters with God. You have to know Him for yourself. God desires relationship with you, and relationship with God is the solution to any and every problem you might encounter. The importance of seeking God is often emphasized, but the truth is that God is seeking you more than you have ever sought Him. All you have to do is slow down a little and make a half turn toward God, and He will come into your life in a big way. You can know God personally—by intimate relationship—beyond mere knowledge *about* Him. Once you know God for yourself, you won't fall for the devil's schemes. The Enemy wants you to believe that life would be better if you had a bigger house, a nicer car, or a different spouse, but happiness is really found in relationship with the Lord.

     13a. Read Psalm 37:4. What happens when you delight in God?
           (You will find that the desires of your heart are God's desires also)

---

[1]   "Zoe," Blue Letter Bible, accessed January 7, 2011, http://www.blueletterbible.org/lang/lexicon/lexicon.cfm?Strongs=G2222&t=KJV.
[2]   I have three, longer teachings that will give you a much deeper understanding in this area: *Spirit, Soul & Body*, *The Believer's Authority*, and *The True Nature of God*. Visit our website (www.awmi.net) and click on "Extras" to download free audio teachings, or order books from our online store.

Lesson 6 — Can I Really Know God?

13b. So many people are struggling today because they don't know the _____ of God.
(Goodness)

13c. Discussion Question: How do you know that relationship with God is the solution to any and every problem you might encounter?
(Discussion question)

13d. Happiness is found in relationship with the Lord, not in what?
(A bigger house, a nicer car, or a different spouse)

14. God made us to desire relationship with Him, and people who don't know God try to satisfy that desire with substitute pleasures; they lust after sexual relationships, take drugs, or drink alcohol. They look for happiness in collecting material possessions and in the praise of others. They continually search for a sense of fulfillment in achieving the next big goal. None of those things are ultimately satisfying. What every human being needs is relationship with God. After God created Adam, He breathed His Spirit into him. We were designed to be filled with God's presence, but when Adam and Eve rebelled, they kicked God out of their lives. God wasn't only talking about physical death when He commanded Adam not to eat of the forbidden fruit; the Lord said **"for in the day that thou eatest thereof thou shalt surely die"** (Gen. 2:17), but Adam and Eve lived on earth for many years after their rebellion. So, the death they experienced was spiritual, which eventually resulted in physical death. Adam and Eve's rebellion caused a God-shaped vacuum to be formed inside of every person. Sex, drugs, money, success, fame, and the other pursuits society is caught up in are just human attempts to fill the void caused by spiritual death. We were made for relationship with God, and the only way to fill our spiritual void is to be born again and enter into relationship with Him. The reason I don't do drugs is that I'm not miserable. My born-again spirit allows me to enter into the presence of God and enjoy relationship with Him. In the presence of God is fullness of joy and pleasures forevermore (Ps. 16:11). We can get so full of God that we won't feel the need to be filled with anything else. The lust for other things will disappear. Once we have a real relationship with God, every day with Jesus can be sweeter than the day before.

14a. What were you designed for?
(To be filled with God's presence)

14b. What did spiritual death cause in people?
A. A stirring
B. An unction
C. A void
D. All of the above
E. None of the above
(C. A void)

14c. What is the only way to fill your spiritual void?
(By being born again and entering into relationship with God)

14d. The lust for other things will disappear when what?
A. When you get more things
B. When you make more money
C. When you have more control of circumstances
D. When you become a stronger Christian
E. When you get full of God
(E. When you get full of God)

15. Surface-level knowledge of God's love is not the same thing as plunging into the reality of His love. Real relationship with God involves going beyond a mere intellectual awareness of His love. Of all the things the Apostle Paul could have prayed for the Ephesians, he prayed for them to know the love of God. He said, **"For this cause I bow my knees unto the Father of our Lord Jesus Christ, Of whom the whole family in heaven and earth is named, That he would grant you, according to the riches of his glory, to be strengthened with might by his Spirit in the inner man; That Christ may dwell in your hearts by faith; that ye, being rooted and grounded in**

Lesson 6 — Can I Really Know God?

love, May be able to comprehend with all saints what is the breadth, and length, and depth, and height; And to know the love of Christ, which passeth knowledge, that ye might be filled with all the fulness of God" (Eph. 3:14-19). This passage of Scripture shows that God's love has multiple dimensions—it isn't merely a fact that you memorize like trivia. You can be overwhelmed by the height, depth, length, and breadth of God's love—so that it "passes knowledge" and becomes an experience of being filled with the grace and peace of God. It's one thing to say, "Oh, yeah, I know God loves me"; it's something else altogether to be filled with the fullness of God. God isn't depressed, discouraged, fearful, or anxious. He isn't poor or starving. The fullness of God is healing, prosperity, joy, peace, anointing, purpose, and total satisfaction. You get all of those things by *knowing* God experientially. In biblical language, "to know" is used to imply sexual intimacy, as in **"Adam knew Eve his wife; and she conceived, and bare Cain"** (Gen. 4:1). The Greek word Paul used in his prayer to the Ephesians is the same word used to describe how Joseph abstained from intimate relations with Mary until after the birth of Jesus (Matt. 1:25). Paul prayed for an intimate, personal knowledge of the love of Christ, one that passes mere knowledge, because that is how you get filled with the fullness of God. Fear, loneliness, anger, frustration, poverty, sickness, and anxiety simply reflect a lack of the fullness of God. The remedy for those things is a revelation of how much God loves you. You just need a deeper relationship with God, one that allows you to experience the love of Christ beyond mere knowledge *about* Him. Of the thousands of people I counsel and pray for, nearly all of them are struggling because they lack a deep personal relationship with God.

15a. Discussion Question: Read Ephesians 3:14-19. Why do you think Paul prayed what he did for the Ephesians?
(Discussion question)

15b. When you're filled with God, you aren't what?
A. Depressed
B. Discouraged
C. Fearful
D. All of the above
E. None of the above
(D. All of the above)

15c. Paul prayed for an intimate, personal knowledge of the love of Christ, one that passes mere knowledge, because that is how you get what?
(Filled with the fullness of God)

16. Religion teaches people an approach to God that emphasizes personal effort, but no one can be perfect, and the frustration of failure leaves people feeling unlovable and separated from God. The Good News of Jesus Christ is that we don't have to *earn* relationship with God; Jesus earned it for us by dying on the cross and rising again. We were spiritually dead and couldn't save ourselves, so Jesus came and died on our behalf to save us. He took our sin and gave us His righteousness. Salvation has nothing to do with what we deserve. God did this because He loves us and desires an intimate relationship with us. Not every Christian has a deep personal relationship with God, but that isn't His fault. It's because they've been lied to. We've been taught that we have to earn relationship with God by living a holy life, going to church every week, paying a tithe, and studying the Word. Most of us are stuck on a treadmill of trying to live up to the requirements of being good Christians, falling short, and then getting back up to try harder. Our own hearts are condemning us and keeping us from entering into an intimate relationship. It's a wrong philosophy. Jesus paid for all of our sins—past, present, and future—and our shortcomings don't separate us from God. Scripture says, **"For we through the Spirit wait for the hope of righteousness by faith. For in Jesus Christ neither circumcision availeth any thing, nor uncircumcision; but faith which worketh by love"** (Gal. 5:5-6). Trying to earn God's love isn't going to get us anywhere. We're saved by faith, not by works. Once we rid ourselves of the burden of thinking we have to be good enough and simply accept how much God loves us, our faith will go through the roof. Faith works by love, and faith is what releases the ability and the power of God. Knowing God's love will heal our bodies and bring peace to our minds. It will make our finances increase and our relationships flourish. Letting the love of God flow in us will bless us even beyond what we can imagine.

16a. Discussion Question: Why is the Good News of Jesus Christ good news for you?
(Discussion question)

16b. True or false: Salvation has something to do with what you deserve.
(False)

Lesson 6 — Can I Really Know God?

16c. A wrong philosophy keeps you from having what?
A. A deep personal relationship with God
B. Consistent failure in life
C. Being better at sports
D. All of the above
E. None of the above
(A. A deep personal relationship with God)

16d. Read Galatians 5:5-6. How do you get your faith to go through the roof?
(By ridding yourself of the burden of thinking you have to be good enough and simply accept how much God loves you)

16e. What will knowing God's love and letting it flow through you do for you?
(It will heal your body and bring peace to your mind. It will make your finances increase and your relationships flourish. It will bless you even beyond what you can imagine)

17. Maybe this sounds too good to be true—you might think there has to be more to it, some complicated step to perform, but it really is as simple as knowing God. Adam and Eve never experienced rejection or punishment from God prior to the Fall, but they never experienced the breadth, length, depth, and height of His love either. If they had known the fullness of God's love, then Satan would never have been able to tempt them. Before you can be tempted to sin, Satan first has to make you dissatisfied with what you already have. Adam and Eve were living in a sinless and perfect world, yet a talking snake convinced them God was holding out on them. Think about that. The temperature was perfect, the food was perfect, they didn't have any financial problems, and Adam and Eve were both perfect. They weren't constantly being bombarded by media reports of killing and strife all over the world. They couldn't even complain about each other. Yet Satan was able to make Adam and Eve feel discontent in the middle of paradise. Imagine, then, how easy it is for him to make people in a fallen world feel unhappy. You live in a world where there is plenty to be displeased about, but the truth is that through Jesus, you can experience the love of God to a greater degree than Adam and Eve ever did. You can be filled with all the fullness of God and feel completely satisfied. What a powerful truth! All of the things you desire from God come freely through a heart that knows how wide, how long, how high, and how deep God's love is. Relationship with God is the pathway to everything He desires to give you.

17a. What has to happen before you are tempted with sin?
(Satan first has to make you dissatisfied with what you already have)

17b. Discussion Question: What are some ways you can better understand God's love?
(Discussion question)

18. Today the shortages in our relationships with God are not because He hasn't communicated the depths of His love or His great desire to know us intimately; our problem is that most of us aren't entering into the intimacy God is calling us to. Often it's because we have a wrong philosophy and believe that we have to earn holiness in order to enter God's presence. The traditions and doctrines of man have made God's Word of no effect (Mark 7:13). Other times, we are simply too caught up in the things of this world to notice God calling us. As a society, we are busy with many pursuits. So much stuff is being thrown at us every day that we don't have time to be still and know God (Ps. 46:10) and to know the greatness of His love for us. But it's within our power to change that: We can renew our minds and toss out the old religious philosophies that have damaged our relationship with God, and we can set aside time to spend with God and get to know His love.

18a. Since God has communicated His love, why is there still a deficiency in people's relationship with God?
(They aren't entering into the intimacy God is calling them to)

18b. What are two reasons for this?
(They believe they have to earn holiness in order to enter God's presence or they are simply too caught up in the things of this world to notice God calling them)

Lesson 6 — Can I Really Know God?

18c. How can you change that in your life?
(You can renew your mind and toss out the old religious philosophies that have damaged your relationship with God, and you can set aside time to spend with God and get to know His love)

19. The promise of God's Word is that if you draw close to God, He will draw close to you (James 4:8). Jesus said, **"Ask, and it shall be given you; seek, and ye shall find; knock, and it shall be opened unto you: For every one that asketh receiveth; and he that seeketh findeth; and to him that knocketh it shall be opened"** (Matt. 7:7-8). God wants a relationship with you more than you desire a relationship with Him, so it's not a matter of you trying hard enough and forcing God to acknowledge you. It's simply a matter of allowing God to love you. God desires intimacy with you, but you have to let it happen, and you do that by seeking Him and yielding to His love. This understanding is essential to any Christian philosophy, and it will make a huge difference in the quality of life you experience.

19a. Read James 4:7. How do you draw close to God?
(You have seek Him and yield to His love)

LESSON 6 — CAN I REALLY KNOW GOD?

DISCIPLESHIP QUESTIONS

1. It's possible to commune with God and not really _____ Him.

2. Discussion Question: Why is it important to know God as Savior and not just Lord?

3. Other religions may acknowledge a godlike entity, but they put the _____ of salvation on the individual, on living a holy life and meeting certain standards of righteousness.

4. Read John 3:16. What is true Christianity about?

5. Why did God resurrect Jesus?

6. What do you need if you're not going to be deceived into believing that God is holding out on you or trying to keep you from reaching your full potential?
   A. To read the Bible
   B. To serve at church
   C. To know God intimately
   D. All of the above
   E. None of the above

7. Knowing God intimately is a _____ part of having a Christian worldview.

SCRIPTURES TO USE WITH QUESTIONS

GENESIS 3:5
For God doth know that in the day ye eat thereof, then your eyes shall be opened, and ye shall be as gods, knowing good and evil.

JOHN 3:16
For God so loved the world, that he gave his only begotten Son, that whosoever believeth in him should not perish, but have everlasting life.

MATTHEW 26:56
But all this was done, that the scriptures of the prophets might be fulfilled. Then all the disciples forsook him, and fled.

MARK 14:50
And they all forsook him, and fled.

MARK 16:11
And they, when they had heard that he was alive, and had been seen of her, believed not.

LUKE 24:11
And their words seemed to them as idle tales, and they believed them not.

JOHN 20:9
For as yet they knew not the scripture, that he must rise again from the dead.

JOHN 20:25
The other disciples therefore said unto him, We have seen the Lord. But he said unto them, Except I shall see in his hands the print of the nails, and put my finger into the print of the nails, and thrust my hand into his side, I will not believe.

LESSON 6 — CAN I REALLY KNOW GOD?

DISCIPLESHIP QUESTIONS

8. Discussion Question: What hinders you from knowing God intimately?

9. Not even who had the revelation of God that is given to you in Scripture?
    A. Paul
    B. Apollos
    C. Agabus
    D. Jesus' disciples
    E. The church

10. Why was Paul's revelation of Jesus superior to Peter's?

11. What makes you greater than the Old Testament prophets?

SCRIPTURES TO USE WITH QUESTIONS

GALATIANS 2:11-14
But when Peter was come to Antioch, I withstood him to the face, because he was to be blamed. [12] For before that certain came from James, he did eat with the Gentiles: but when they were come, he withdrew and separated himself, fearing them which were of the circumcision. [13] And the other Jews dissembled likewise with him; insomuch that Barnabas also was carried away with their dissimulation. [14] But when I saw that they walked not uprightly according to the truth of the gospel, I said unto Peter before them all, If thou, being a Jew, livest after the manner of Gentiles, and not as do the Jews, why compellest thou the Gentiles to live as do the Jews?

2 PETER 3:15-16
And account that the longsuffering of our Lord is salvation; even as our beloved brother Paul also according to the wisdom given unto him hath written unto you; [16] As also in all his epistles, speaking in them of these things; in which are some things hard to be understood, which they that are unlearned and unstable wrest, as they do also the other scriptures, unto their own destruction.

MATTHEW 11:11
Verily I say unto you, Among them that are born of women there hath not risen a greater than John the Baptist: notwithstanding he that is least in the kingdom of heaven is greater than he.

LESSON 6 — CAN I REALLY KNOW GOD?

DISCIPLESHIP QUESTIONS

12. Read 2 Corinthians 3:6-11. True or false: Life came through the Law.

13. Read Romans 8:32. What do you need so you won't doubt God's desire to freely give you all things?

14. How can you become more successful at resisting the attacks of the Enemy?
    A. By listening to more sermons
    B. By getting a greater revelation of God's love
    C. By putting more effort into it
    D. By binding and loosing
    E. By strengthening your will power

15. True or false: It's important to know God through the things you have heard from your pastor or someone else.

16. Discussion Question: Why should you know God for yourself?

17. Before Andrew understood that God loves him because His nature is love and not because he is lovely, he was always trying to do things to _____ God's favor.

18. True or false: Sometimes it's good to try to earn God's favor.

19. What is one of the greatest truths to Christianity?

SCRIPTURES TO USE WITH QUESTIONS

2 CORINTHIANS 3:6-11
Who also hath made us able ministers of the new testament; not of the letter, but of the spirit: for the letter killeth, but the spirit giveth life. **[7]** *But if the ministration of death, written and engraven in stones, was glorious, so that the children of Israel could not stedfastly behold the face of Moses for the glory of his countenance; which glory was to be done away:* **[8]** *How shall not the ministration of the spirit be rather glorious?* **[9]** *For if the ministration of condemnation be glory, much more doth the ministration of righteousness exceed in glory.* **[10]** *For even that which was made glorious had no glory in this respect, by reason of the glory that excelleth.* **[11]** *For if that which is done away was glorious, much more that which remaineth is glorious.*

ROMANS 8:32
He that spared not his own Son, but delivered him up for us all, how shall he not with him also freely give us all things?

LESSON 6 — CAN I REALLY KNOW GOD?

DISCIPLESHIP QUESTIONS

20. Read Romans 12:1-2. What's one reason it's important to renew your mind?

21. True or false: God would never tell you to stop reading His Word.

22. Knowing God keeps you from what?

23. Read Hebrews 13:8 and Malachi 3:6. God doesn't make you righteous by _____ one day and then judge you by your _____ the next.

24. Read John 14:7, 9; and Hebrews 1:3. Jesus was the _____ representation of God.

25. Discussion Question: What does this mean to you?

26. It's important for you to base your philosophy on what?

27. What is probably the most damaging tradition that is circulating in the body of Christ?

SCRIPTURES TO USE WITH QUESTIONS

ROMANS 12:1-2
I beseech you therefore, brethren, by the mercies of God, that ye present your bodies a living sacrifice, holy, acceptable unto God, which is your reasonable service. [2] And be not conformed to this world: but be ye transformed by the renewing of your mind, that ye may prove what is that good, and acceptable, and perfect, will of God.

HEBREWS 13:8
Jesus Christ the same yesterday, and to day, and for ever.

MALACHI 3:6
For I am the Lord, I change not; therefore ye sons of Jacob are not consumed.

JOHN 14:7
If ye had known me, ye should have known my Father also: and from henceforth ye know him, and have seen him.

JOHN 14:9
Jesus saith unto him, Have I been so long time with you, and yet hast thou not known me, Philip? he that hath seen me hath seen the Father; and how sayest thou then, Shew us the Father?

HEBREWS 1:3
Who being the brightness of his glory, and the express image of his person, and upholding all things by the word of his power, when he had by himself purged our sins, sat down on the right hand of the Majesty on high.

ACTS 10:38
How God anointed Jesus of Nazareth with the Holy Ghost and with power: who went about doing good, and healing all that were oppressed of the devil; for God was with him.

LESSON 6 — CAN I REALLY KNOW GOD?

DISCIPLESHIP QUESTIONS

28. According to James 1:13, what can't God be tempted with?
    A. Evil
    B. Food
    C. Money
    D. All of the above
    E. None of the above

29. If you think that God is sovereignly determining everything that happens in life, what will you be?

30. Read Ephesians 3:20. Even though God is all-powerful, He has chosen to work through whom?
    A. Only leaders
    B. You
    C. The devil
    D. Those worthy enough
    E. Angels

31. Discussion Question: How do you know that God's will doesn't automatically come to pass?

32. _____ who is upset with God has a wrong philosophy.

33. Read John 10:10. The Greek word used for **"life"** here is *zoe*, which means what?

34. Read James 1:17. What is the simplest theology?

SCRIPTURES TO USE WITH QUESTIONS

JAMES 1:13
Let no man say when he is tempted, I am tempted of God: for God cannot be tempted with evil, neither tempteth he any man.

EPHESIANS 3:20
Now unto him that is able to do exceeding abundantly above all that we ask or think, according to the power that worketh in us.

JOHN 10:10
The thief cometh not, but for to steal, and to kill, and to destroy: I am come that they might have life, and that they might have it more abundantly.

MATTHEW 6:10
Thy kingdom come. Thy will be done in earth, as it is in heaven.

JAMES 1:17
Every good gift and every perfect gift is from above, and cometh down from the Father of lights, with whom is no variableness, neither shadow of turning.

LESSON 6 — CAN I REALLY KNOW GOD?

DISCIPLESHIP QUESTIONS

35. Discussion Question: Give an example of how God steps in and does things for you automatically.

36. Read Psalm 37:4. What happens when you delight in God?

37. So many people are struggling today because they don't know the _____ of God.

38. Discussion Question: How do you know that relationship with God is the solution to any and every problem you might encounter?

39. Happiness is found in relationship with the Lord, not in what?

40. What were you designed for?

41. What did spiritual death cause in people?
    A. A stirring
    B. An unction
    C. A void
    D. All of the above
    E. None of the above

42. What is the only way to fill your spiritual void?

SCRIPTURES TO USE WITH QUESTIONS

PSALM 37:4
*Delight thyself also in the L*ORD*; and he shall give thee the desires of thine heart.*

GENESIS 2:17
But of the tree of the knowledge of good and evil, thou shalt not eat of it: for in the day that thou eatest thereof thou shalt surely die.

PSALM 16:11
Thou wilt shew me the path of life: in thy presence is fulness of joy; at thy right hand there are pleasures for evermore.

LESSON 6 — CAN I REALLY KNOW GOD?

DISCIPLESHIP QUESTIONS

43. The lust for other things will disappear when what?
    A. When you get more things
    B. When you make more money
    C. When you have more control of circumstances
    D. When you become a stronger Christian
    E. When you get full of God

44. Discussion Question: Read Ephesians 3:14-19. Why do you think Paul prayed what he did for the Ephesians?

45. When you're filled with God, you aren't what?
    A. Depressed
    B. Discouraged
    C. Fearful
    D. All of the above
    E. None of the above

46. Paul prayed for an intimate, personal knowledge of the love of Christ, one that passes mere knowledge, because that is how you get what?

47. Discussion Question: Why is the Good News of Jesus Christ good news for you?

48. True or false: Salvation has something to do with what you deserve.

49. A wrong philosophy keeps you from having what?
    A. A deep personal relationship with God
    B. Consistent failure in life
    C. Being better at sports
    D. All of the above
    E. None of the above

SCRIPTURES TO USE WITH QUESTIONS

EPHESIANS 3:14-19
For this cause I bow my knees unto the Father of our Lord Jesus Christ, [15] Of whom the whole family in heaven and earth is named, [16] That he would grant you, according to the riches of his glory, to be strengthened with might by his Spirit in the inner man; [17] That Christ may dwell in your hearts by faith; that ye, being rooted and grounded in love, [18] May be able to comprehend with all saints what is the breadth, and length, and depth, and height; [19] And to know the love of Christ, which passeth knowledge, that ye might be filled with all the fulness of God.

GENESIS 4:1
And Adam knew Eve his wife; and she conceived, and bare Cain, and said, I have gotten a man from the LORD.

MATTHEW 1:25
And knew her not till she had brought forth her firstborn son: and he called his name Jesus.

LESSON 6 — CAN I REALLY KNOW GOD?

DISCIPLESHIP QUESTIONS

50. Read Galatians 5:5-6. How do you get your faith to go through the roof?

51. What will knowing God's love and letting it flow through you do for you?

52. What has to happen before you are tempted with sin?

53. Discussion Question: What are some ways you can better understand God's love?

54. Since God has communicated His love, why is there still a deficiency in people's relationship with God?

55. What are two reasons for this?

56. How can you change that in your life?

57. Read James 4:7. How do you draw close to God?

SCRIPTURES TO USE WITH QUESTIONS

GALATIANS 5:5-6
For we through the Spirit wait for the hope of righteousness by faith. [6] For in Jesus Christ neither circumcision availeth any thing, nor uncircumcision; but faith which worketh by love.

MARK 7:13
Making the word of God of none effect through your tradition, which ye have delivered: and many such like things do ye.

PSALM 46:10
Be still, and know that I am God: I will be exalted among the heathen, I will be exalted in the earth.

MATTHEW 7:7-8
Ask, and it shall be given you; seek, and ye shall find; knock, and it shall be opened unto you: [8] For every one that asketh receiveth; and he that seeketh findeth; and to him that knocketh it shall be opened.

JAMES 4:7-8
Submit yourselves therefore to God. Resist the devil, and he will flee from you. [8] Draw nigh to God, and he will draw nigh to you. Cleanse your hands, ye sinners; and purify your hearts, ye double minded.

LESSON 6 — CAN I REALLY KNOW GOD?

ANSWER KEY

1. Know

2. *Discussion question*

3. Burden

4. It's all about what God has already done for us. It's not about what we do, or how we live; it's all about what God has done to give us His righteousness

5. To give us His righteousness

6. C. To know God intimately

7. Major

8. *Discussion question*

9. D. Jesus' disciples

10. Because Paul didn't get his revelation from other people; he received it through his spirit

11. Your born-again spirit

12. False

13. To truly understand the extent of God's love for you—demonstrated through the sacrifice of Jesus

14. B. By getting a greater revelation of God's love

15. False

16. *Discussion question*

17. Earn

18. False

19. That your relationship with God is the key to everything; e.g., joy, peace, and abundance

20. So you'll know what God's will includes

21. True

22. Being deceived and from having your faith in God undermined by misunderstandings or wrong teaching

23. Grace/works

24. Perfect

25. *Discussion question*

26. The revelation of Jesus Christ and His grace, and not upon the traditions or ideas of man

27. The idea that nothing can happen unless God wills it to happen

28. A. Evil

29. Susceptible to bitterness and doubt toward Him, mad at Him for making such a terrible mess of the world, or you'll lack confidence in Him for being unwilling to prevent it

30. B. You

31. *Discussion question*

32. Anyone

33. Life that is "active and vigorous, devoted to God, blessed"

34. If something is good, then it comes from God. If it's bad, then it's from the devil

35. *Discussion question*

36. You will find that the desires of your heart are God's desires also

37. Goodness

38. *Discussion question*

39. A bigger house, a nicer car, or a different spouse

40. To be filled with God's presence

41. C. A void

42. By being born again and entering into relationship with God

43. E. When you get full of God

44. *Discussion question*

LESSON 6 — CAN I REALLY KNOW GOD?

ANSWER KEY

45. D. All of the above

46. Filled with the fullness of God

47. *Discussion question*

48. False

49. A. A deep personal relationship with God

50. By ridding yourself of the burden of thinking you have to be good enough and simply accept how much God loves you

51. It will heal your body and bring peace to your mind. It will make your finances increase and your relationships flourish. It will bless you even beyond what you can imagine

52. Satan first has to make you dissatisfied with what you already have

53. *Discussion question*

54. They aren't entering into the intimacy God is calling them to

55. They believe they have to earn holiness in order to enter God's presence or they are simply too caught up in the things of this world to notice God calling them

56. You can renew your mind and toss out the old religious philosophies that have damaged your relationship with God, and you can set aside time to spend with God and get to know His love

57. You have seek Him and yield to His love

Is God Angry with Me?

I remember watching an old game show on television when I was a kid, called *To Tell the Truth*. Three guests sat in front of a panel of four celebrity judges. All three of the guests claimed the same identity, but only one of them was the real person—the other two people were imposters trying to confuse the judges. For instance, all three of them would claim to be Joe Smith, a heavyweight boxer. One of the guests really would be Joe Smith, but the other two were just acting. After the judges asked a lot of questions, they would make guesses about which one of the guests they thought was telling the truth. When the judges were done guessing, the announcer would say, "Would the real Joe Smith please stand up!" They would always have one person start to stand up and then another, and finally, the real Joe Smith would stand.

I think that God is being represented in so many contrasting ways by so many different groups in society, that many people are frustrated and confused. They want to say, "Would the real God please stand up!" They read Old Testament scriptures that talk about God smiting people with leprosy, then they hear someone like me say God is love and He would never use evil against us, and they wonder, *Which one is the real God?* They wonder if God is schizophrenic or something, but God has never changed. He has always been the same loving God we see manifested in the life and ministry of Jesus.

God is on our side, yet a lot of people think of Him as an old man with a long grey beard, leaning over a banister in heaven with a lightning bolt in His hand, ready to sock it to us the minute we step out of line. They imagine a harsh and angry God who is eager to judge us for the wrong we've done. Religion is even teaching that suffering and disease are a blessing in disguise—they say that God uses evil to teach us a lesson (Is. 5:20). None of that is true, but many people are confused about what the truth really is.

To begin with, we have to understand the difference between the way God dealt with people under the Old Covenant and the way He deals with us as born-again believers under the New Covenant. God revealed a mercy and grace through Jesus that isn't seen in the Old Testament scriptures—but God hasn't changed; He has just changed the way He relates to mankind because of the transformation in *us*.

The Gospel of John tells the story of a woman who was caught in adultery by the Pharisees and brought to Jesus for judgment. John 8:1-5 says,

> *Jesus went unto the mount of Olives. And early in the morning he came again into the temple, and all the people came unto him; and he sat down, and taught them. And the scribes and Pharisees brought unto him a woman taken in adultery; and when they had set her in the midst, They say unto him, Master, this woman was taken in adultery, in the very act. Now Moses in the law commanded us, that such should be stoned: but what sayest thou?*

Lesson 7 — Is God Angry with Me?

On the surface, the Pharisees appeared to have been seeking justice by bringing the adulteress before Jesus, but they were really just trying to entrap Him. It's interesting that the woman was caught in the act of adultery, yet the Pharisees didn't apprehend the man she was with. Although we don't know for sure, I can think of two possible reasons for this. First, the man might have been someone the Pharisees enlisted to help capture the woman in the middle of the act—specifically for the purpose of setting this trap for Jesus. So, they let the man escape because he was part of the deal. Second, if it really was a randomly discovered act of adultery, maybe they only brought the woman because we tend to be easier on women when it comes to sentencing people to death. The Old Testament Law said that a person caught in adultery should be stoned to death (Lev. 20:10 and Deut. 22:22), and they might have thought bringing just the woman suited their purpose of entrapment better—figuring it would be harder for Jesus to condemn a woman than a man.

Jesus had been preaching and teaching the mercy of God, and He wanted to set people free from the bondage of religious tradition. Jesus ate meals with sinners (Matt. 9:11, Mark 2:16, and Luke 15:2) and associated with outcasts. One of His disciples was a hated tax collector (Matt. 10:3), and a formerly demon-possessed woman cooked for Him (Luke 8:2). His life and teaching were in complete contrast to the harsh, judgmental God that the religious leaders of the day were portraying.

By bringing this woman to Jesus for judgment, they were trying to make Him choose between obeying the Law and demonstrating the mercy He had been preaching. Either way, they thought Jesus was trapped. If He demonstrated mercy and let the woman go, then He Himself would be subject to stoning for failing to enforce the Law of Moses. Yet if Jesus followed the Law and condemned the woman to death, then He would be going against the message of mercy He had been teaching, and the people would think He was a hypocrite. The Pharisees thought it was a win-win situation.

Of course, the Pharisees' trap wasn't as good as they thought. Jesus immediately recognized what they were up to, so when the Pharisees threw the woman down before Him and demanded His judgment, Jesus simply bent down and wrote in the dirt with His finger. When the Pharisees continued to press Him for an answer, He stood up and said, **"He that is without sin among you, let him first cast a stone at her"** (John 8:7). Then Jesus bent over again and continued writing on the ground. We don't know what He was writing, but whatever it was, it appears to have convicted the accusers of their own sins. One by one, they walked away until only the woman was left standing before Jesus. When Jesus looked up and saw only the woman, He said,

> *Woman, where are those thine accusers? hath no man condemned thee? She said, No man, Lord. And Jesus said unto her, Neither do I condemn thee: go, and sin no more.*
> JOHN 8:10-11

Jesus didn't tell her that it was okay to commit adultery. He didn't lower the standard of righteousness. Some people today are trying to reconcile God's love and holiness by saying everything is okay—drunkenness, adultery, homosexuality, drugs, and other harmful lifestyle choices—but that isn't how Jesus responded. He didn't deny that the woman's act was wrong or imply that it would be okay for her to continue committing adultery. No, He said, **"Go, and sin no more."** Jesus admitted that she had sinned, but He didn't condemn her—He showed mercy.

LESSON 7   IS GOD ANGRY WITH ME?

Adultery was punishable by death under the Old Covenant, but Jesus didn't enforce the punishment. If someone was caught in adultery under the Law of Moses, then they were stoned to death—it wasn't negotiable. As a matter of fact, the very first person who was punished for breaking the Old Testament Law was a man who gathered sticks on the Sabbath (Num. 15:32-36). After he was caught gathering sticks, the Israelites turned him over to Moses and Aaron because no one knew what the punishment should be. The Lord told Moses that the man should be taken outside the camp and stoned to death. He was killed for gathering sticks to make a fire!

Some people hear these stories and wonder, *Why the change?* In a nutshell, God held people accountable for sin under the Old Covenant, so He punished them for it. But under the New Covenant, our sins have all been paid for by Jesus, and God isn't holding sin against us anymore. God has changed the way He deals with us because the price for sin has been paid—and that single change makes everything brand new. After putting our faith in Jesus, we become new creatures (2 Cor. 5:17), and God can deal with us differently than He could deal with people under the Old Covenant (Heb. 8:12-13).

Jesus changed everything, and nothing has been the same since. A helpful illustration is to consider how we change the way we relate to our own children as they mature. Young children often have to be physically restrained from doing wrong. I know that many people today reject spanking children as being harmful, but leaving children to themselves is what's harmful. The Scripture says, **"The rod and reproof give wisdom: but a child left to himself bringeth his mother to shame"** (Prov. 29:15). So, it's a godly thing to use corporal punishment to train young children. Two year olds don't understand that the devil is inspiring their selfish actions. If we try to tell them it's the devil who leads them to take their siblings' toys, they will just look at us with blank stares. They don't get it. But when the devil gives them those selfish thoughts of taking their siblings' toys, we can tell them, "If you do that again, I'm going to give you a spanking." They may not know about resisting the devil (James 4:7), but I guarantee, when that thought comes again, they will resist it because they don't want the punishment. Sometimes kids need to be spanked—not to hurt them, but to deter them from doing what is wrong.

Even so, spanking is not a long-term solution. You only use physical restraint for a short period of time, until your children grow up and you can teach them by instruction. You don't spank your twenty-, thirty-, or forty-year-old children! Likewise, the Old Testament revealed God's wrath against sin, and He put punishments in place to deter the Israelites from sinning, until His plan of redemption could unfold. When the time was right, Jesus came and paid for everyone's sin. Until Jesus made a new way for everyone, the Israelites were kept under the Law, waiting for saving faith in Christ to appear (Gal. 3:23). The Apostle Paul said it this way:

> *Wherefore the law was our schoolmaster to bring us unto Christ, that we might be justified by faith. But after that faith is come, we are no longer under a schoolmaster.*
>
> GALATIANS 3:24-25

The Law was just a training tool God used to guide His children until they could be saved by faith. You could say that the human race was in its infancy until Jesus came and revealed the true nature of God. Before Jesus came, God dealt with sin harshly in order to keep the Israelites out of trouble. But now, God no longer deals with His children in the same way. You aren't under the Law that the Israelites were under (Rom. 6:14). You have a different covenant, a New Covenant of salvation by grace through faith in Jesus (Eph. 2:8). You are a different kind of person from the Old Covenant believer—a new creature entirely—and God deals with you differently.

It's true that God inflicted people with leprosy and destroyed entire cities under the Old Covenant, but those actions have to be understood within the context of how God was able to deal with humanity. Jesus changed all that. He made it possible for you to be spiritually reborn. In much the same way that you can't reason with an infant, God couldn't reason with humanity prior to Jesus. In the Old Testament, God released His wrath on people, but in the New Testament, Jesus changed how God relates to you.

Scripture says that Jesus is the exact representation of God the Father (Heb. 1:3). The Old Testament prophets revealed some truths about God, but Jesus gave us a complete view of the Father. The writer of Hebrews said, **"How shall we escape, if we neglect so great salvation; which at the first began to be spoken by the Lord, and was confirmed unto us by them that heard him"** (Heb. 2:3). Jesus revealed God in a way that superseded all previous revelation. In Jesus, we see a kind and compassionate God who gave Himself over to a cruel death in order to give us the hope of new life.

Jesus' disciples tried to reenact a story from the Old Testament once, and His response to them dramatically illustrates the difference between the Old and the New Covenants. The story revolves around the ungodly King Ahaziah, the son of Ahab and Jezebel. Ahaziah fell seriously ill, but instead of seeking the Lord for healing, he sent messengers to inquire of the false god Baalzebub, the god of the neighboring people of Ekron. God told the prophet Elijah what King Ahaziah was doing and sent him to intercept the messengers. Elijah said to them, **"Is it not because there is not a God in Israel, that ye go to enquire of Baalzebub the god of Ekron? Now therefore thus saith the Lord, Thou shalt not come down from that bed on which thou art gone up, but shalt surely die"** (2 Kin. 1:3b-4).

When the messengers heard this, they returned to Ahaziah and reported what Elijah had said. Although Elijah didn't identify himself to the messengers, he had a long history with Ahaziah's family, and the king knew right away who it was that had spoken to them. After hearing Elijah's warning, the king sent out a captain with fifty soldiers to capture him. The captain found Elijah on top of a hill and commanded him to come down. Elijah replied, **"If I be a man of God, then let fire come down from heaven, and consume thee and thy fifty"** (2 Kin. 1:10). After saying this, fire came down from heaven and consumed the captain and his fifty soldiers.

Undeterred, the king sent out another captain with fifty soldiers. Elijah called down fire from heaven again, and the second captain and his men were also killed. So, the king sent out a third captain with fifty soldiers, but this time, the captain fell down on his knees before Elijah and begged for his life. At that, the angel of the Lord spoke to Elijah, told him not to be afraid, and to go with the soldiers to see King Ahaziah. Elijah went with the men, delivered a message to the king, and that was the end of the matter.

This story comes up again in the New Testament while Jesus and His disciples were passing through Samaria. The Jews looked down upon the Samaritans because they had stayed behind in the land of Israel and intermarried with Gentiles during the time the Jews were taken into captivity. As a result of the intermarrying, the Samaritans adopted pagan beliefs and mixed them with their Jewish religious tradition. Because of the Samaritans' mixed religion, the Jews forbade them from worshiping in Jerusalem—even though they were worshiping the God of Israel. The mutual hatred between the Jews

Lesson 7 — Is God Angry with Me?

and the Samaritans was both religious and racial, and we need to keep the extreme prejudice between them in mind as we read the New Testament story.

> *And it came to pass, when the time was come that he should be received up, he stedfastly set his face to go to Jerusalem, And sent messengers before his face: and they went, and entered into a village of the Samaritans, to make ready for him. And they did not receive him, because his face was as though he would go to Jerusalem.*
> LUKE 9:51-53

We know that Jesus had already taught in Samaria, because the Gospel of John tells the story of Jesus ministering to the woman at the well (John 4). After Jesus ministered to the woman, she went and got the entire village to go hear Him, and they all accepted Him as the Messiah. On this occasion, Jesus was on His way to Jerusalem, but instead of going around Samaria the way the strict Jews did, He went right through Samaria. Before arriving, Jesus sent some men ahead to find lodging for Him, but once the Samaritans knew that Jesus was on His way to celebrate a feast in Jerusalem, they rejected Him and wouldn't even give Him a place to stay. They hated the Jews so much that it offended them that Jesus was planning to go worship in Jerusalem.

These were people who already acknowledged Jesus as the Messiah! They were willing to accept Jesus as God's anointed Savior, but they were unable to overcome their religious prejudice against the Jewish worship, so when Jesus identified Himself with the Jews in Jerusalem, they rejected Him. They didn't snub Jesus due to ignorance—they knew He was sent by God—they rejected Him because He was associating with a group of people they didn't like. They intentionally rejected God's anointed Savior because they couldn't get over their racial and religious hatred.

The Samaritans' rejection of Jesus was much worse than anything the army captains did to Elijah in the Old Testament story. The army captains were just obeying orders by trying to bring Elijah to King Ahaziah, but the Samaritans were rejecting the Messiah. When the disciples saw how the Samaritans were acting, they asked Jesus, **"Lord, wilt thou that we command fire to come down from heaven, and consume them, even as** [Elijah] **did?"** (Luke 9:54, brackets mine).

The disciples wanted to imitate Elijah by calling down fire to kill the Samaritans, and you could argue that what the Samaritans had done was more deserving of judgment than anything the soldiers did. Yet Jesus reproached the disciples:

> *But he turned, and rebuked them, and said, Ye know not what manner of spirit ye are of. For the Son of man is not come to destroy men's lives, but to save them. And they went to another village.*
> LUKE 9:55-56

Someone who looks at this casually might think that God was being inconsistent, but the difference here is actually the difference between the Old Covenant and the New Covenant. Prior to the Law being given through Moses, which was approximately 2,000 years *after* the fall of Adam and Eve, God wasn't holding people responsible for their sin (Rom. 5:13). He was dealing with people in mercy and grace, but people began to take God's lack of punishment as an indication that He didn't care whether they lived holy lives or not. They didn't understand that even though God wasn't punishing sin, Satan was taking advantage of sinful actions and corrupting the whole human race. So, God had to restrain sin. He had to get people to turn away from sin and the damage it was causing.

Lesson 7 — Is God Angry with Me?

Before the Law, God wasn't punishing sin. For example, He actually protected the first murderer (Gen. 4). After Cain killed Abel, God set a mark on Cain to protect him from any vigilante-style attempts to exact justice by taking Cain's life. God didn't approve of the murder Cain committed—it was wrong and it had consequences—but God didn't punish Cain for his sinful action. God's grace toward Cain stands in sharp contrast to the punishment exacted upon the first person to violate the Law—a man who was picking up sticks on the Sabbath to make a fire (Num. 15:32-36). The difference in God's reaction to these sins was that prior to the giving of the Law, God wasn't holding people accountable for their sin (Rom. 5:13); He was dealing with people in grace.

The way God turned people away from sin under the Old Covenant Law was by bringing judgment on sin and using punishment. When the Law was given, it held people accountable for sin. The Law made people realize that God wasn't indifferent to the way they were acting. It revealed God's standard of righteousness, and it made the Israelites fearful of God's wrath against sin. As a result, they turned away from sin. So, the Law limited the amount of sin, but it also had the effect of making people feel guilty and unworthy. The Law was part of God's plan for redemption, but it was only a temporary measure put in place until Jesus should come:

> *But before faith came, we were kept under the law, shut up unto the faith which should afterwards be revealed. Wherefore the law was our schoolmaster to bring us unto Christ, that we might be justified by faith. But after that faith is come, we are no longer under a schoolmaster.*
>
> GALATIANS 3:23-25

Just as the giving of the Law brought judgment for sin, the sacrifice of Jesus brought a return to grace. Now that we have been transferred to the kingdom of Christ, we're no longer under a schoolmaster (Gal. 3:24-25). Jesus Christ fulfilled the Law, and God isn't imputing our sins against us any longer (2 Cor. 5:19). Under the Old Covenant, Elijah called down fire from heaven, and it consumed 102 soldiers, but Jesus rebuked His disciples for wanting to do the same thing, because He was ushering in a transition to the New Covenant of grace.

I believe that if Jesus had been on earth in His physical body when Elijah was calling fire down out of heaven, Jesus would have rebuked Elijah. Elijah got away with calling down fire because he was under the ministry of the Law, which was holding people's sins against them, but it was never the true nature of God to deal with people that way. It's the way He had to deal with people to restrain sin and rein them in, but it was only a temporary way of dealing with humanity. Now that grace has come through Jesus, we're no longer under the Law.

Under the Old Covenant, there were very harsh punishments for sin. The Lord often commanded to kill all the men, women, children, and even the animals when the Israelites conquered other nations (Josh. 6:17-21, 10:40, and 11:11-14). There was even a commandment for people to kill their own children if they were persistently stubborn and rebellious (Deut. 21:18-21). This was because they couldn't be cured or healed, so they were taken out of society—in much the same way that doctors cut out a cancerous tumor to save the rest of the body. It wasn't possible for anyone to be born again, and God didn't want foreign peoples infecting the children of Israel with demonic beliefs or behavior.

But under our New and better Covenant (Heb. 8:6 and 13), we don't kill our rebellious children or people who are committing ungodly acts, because they can be born again and changed. Praise God for the vast change that Jesus made. Under the Old Covenant, God's judgment against evil was mercy to the rest of God's people, but under the New Covenant, we can be delivered from evil. There is no need to judge individuals in order to save the rest of society. Today we minister the love of God to anyone who is caught up in sin and share the Good News about Jesus Christ. This difference should help us understand the harshness of the Old Testament and why we now have a better covenant through Jesus.

Some make the mistake of thinking that the transformation in how God has related to mankind over time reflects some sort of conversion in God, which isn't true. God declares, **"I am the LORD, I change not"** (Mal. 3:6a), and **"Jesus Christ is the same yesterday, today, and forever"** (Heb. 13:8, *New King James Version*). God hasn't changed; we have—and the way He relates to us under the New Covenant has changed as a result.

> *Wherefore henceforth know we no man after the flesh: yea, though we have known Christ after the flesh, yet now henceforth know we him no more.*
>
> 2 CORINTHIANS 5:16

At first, the disciples related to Christ through His physical presence and attributes, but now that He has risen from the dead and ascended into heaven, we relate to Him through the Holy Spirit. In the same way, we shouldn't look at ourselves only from a physical perspective. We have a spiritual identity that completely changed when we were born again, and we need to know who we are in the spirit—the part of us that is created new in the image of Christ.

> *Therefore if any man be in Christ, he is a new creature: old things are passed away; behold, all things are become new.*
>
> 2 CORINTHIANS 5:17

This is a startling statement! When you are in Christ, old things have passed away and *all* things have become new. Not some things—all things—and they aren't in the process of transforming into something new; they *are* new.

A lot of people struggle with this scripture because they don't feel completely new and don't see anything new in themselves. They say, "I still get angry. I still have some of the same bad habits. I feel like I'm getting better, but I'm not there yet." They struggle with accepting the idea that they are already new, because they don't understand that this scripture isn't talking about their physical bodies or their personalities. Being born again doesn't cause obesity to disappear, and it doesn't automatically change your personality. The Holy Spirit can help you improve and you can change, but it isn't automatic. Your thoughts and memories don't immediately change, but in the spirit, you become a totally brand-new person—instantly.

The reason you don't see a totally new person when you look in the mirror is that you are looking at your physical appearance or searching your mental and emotional makeup, but the changes in your spirit cannot be perceived by your natural senses. Your spirit is the part of you that becomes completely new. Look at how the *Amplified Bible* translates 2 Corinthians 5:17 –

> *Therefore if any person is [ingrafted] in Christ (the Messiah) he is a new creation (a new creature altogether); the old [previous moral and spiritual condition] has passed away. Behold, the fresh and new has come!*

Lesson 7 — Is God Angry with Me?

In the spirit, your salvation is perfect. You have been united with Christ, and your spirit is as perfect, pure, and holy as it ever will be. The moment you are born again, your spirit is transformed into the new creation you will be for all of eternity. Your spirit will never change. You will get a new heavenly body, and your soul will be renewed so that you know all things even as you are known (1 Cor. 13:12), but your spirit is changed forever the moment you are born again. The next verses say,

> *And all things are of God, who hath reconciled us to himself by Jesus Christ, and hath given to us the ministry of reconciliation; To wit, that God was in Christ, reconciling the world unto himself, not imputing their trespasses unto them; and hath committed unto us the word of reconciliation.*
> 2 CORINTHIANS 5:18-19

God has already—past tense—reconciled us to Himself through Jesus Christ. More specifically, God was in Christ reconciling the sins of the entire human race. "Reconcile" is a term we don't use every day, but it just means to reestablish a close relationship between, or to settle or resolve. God took away all of the discord that sin caused, and He harmonized our relationship with Him again.

Second Corinthians 5:19 also says God is not **"imputing"** your sins anymore, which means to attribute responsibility for. It is a term used in bookkeeping to describe charging or accrediting fees to an account. For instance, when you use a credit card to purchase something, you are really asking the seller to give you the item and charge the fee to your account. The item isn't actually paid for until you pay off your credit card. You didn't pay for it when you gave the seller your credit card; you just had the cost imputed to your account. If you don't believe that, just refuse to pay the credit card bill when it comes, and see if they think you've already paid.

When Scripture says that God reconciled the world unto Himself, not imputing our trespasses unto us, it means that God didn't charge sin to our account. He went ahead and paid the debt for us—a balance that was impossible for us to settle—so that He could reestablish a close relationship with us.

> *For he hath made him to be sin for us, who knew no sin; that we might be made the righteousness of God in him.*
> 2 CORINTHIANS 5:21

God took the sins of all humanity and charged it to the account of Jesus, and He was also in Jesus on Calvary. God didn't just turn His head and pretend sin never happened. No, sin had a cost—death—that had to be paid (Rom. 6:23). God's pure, holy, and righteous nature wouldn't allow Him to look the other way, yet He loves us and desires a relationship with us. So, He decided to pay for sin Himself. Sin was still imputed, but instead of charging us, God charged it to His Son.

Going back to the credit-card illustration, it's as if you were to roll a cartload of computer gear to the checkout in an electronics store, and just as you are about to be charged, a man steps up and says "Let me get that for you" and puts it all on his credit card. That's very different from the store clerk saying to you, "Don't worry about it—everything is free today." The items aren't free—someone had to pay for them. Similarly, I give away a lot of my materials for free, but it isn't because I have unlimited resources. Everything I give away has a cost. It's just that I absorb the expense. I pay the cost to help those who can't afford to buy materials.

God didn't say, "Oh, let's just forget sin. Let's not impute sin anymore." No, sin had a cost that had to be paid—a price we couldn't possibly pay—so God charged it to His own account. He put all of our sin upon His Son, the Lord Jesus. He made Jesus, who never sinned, become sin for us, and He took the sin of the entire human race (2 Cor. 5:21). The Apostle John wrote,

And he is the propitiation for our sins: and not for ours only, but also for the sins of the whole world.
1 JOHN 2:2

Jesus didn't just die for a select number of people who would later accept Him. No, Jesus paid for the sins of the whole world, even the people who reject Him. Adolf Hitler's sins, for example, were paid for—Jesus took the murder of six million Jews and the responsibility for a World War upon Himself. Jesus suffered shame, hurt, and degradation on Hitler's behalf. All of that evil was charged to Jesus. Jesus suffered all of the humiliation and depression that results from sin for every person who has ever lived—billions and billions of people.

That doesn't mean Hitler was saved, because as far as we know, Hitler didn't accept the salvation that Jesus provided. All of his actions indicate he was in rebellion toward the Lord and in union with the devil. We have to humble ourselves and make Jesus our Lord (Rom. 10:9) so that what He did for us is credited to our account.

Once you truly understand the significance of Jesus' sacrifice, then you can understand why God dealt with people differently under the New Covenant than He did under the Old Covenant. God didn't change—God never changes—but the atoning sacrifice of Jesus changed everything. Under the Old Covenant, the payment for sin had not been made, and people bore their own sins. People bore the wrath and the punishment of God.

You can find a limited amount of mercy under the Old Covenant, but only to the degree that people understood God's grace nature and operated in it. King David is a good example. When he committed adultery with Bathsheba, according to the Old Testament Law, he should have been stoned to death. Yet God showed him mercy because David understood the true nature of God. In a sense, he was able to reach into the future by faith and appropriate some of the grace that we live under in the New Covenant. We can see this reflected in the psalm David wrote when he said, "Against you, and you only, Lord, have I sinned and done this evil in your sight" (Ps. 51:4, paraphrase mine). David showed his understanding of God's true nature when he went on to say that he would offer a sacrifice, but he knew that sacrifice is not what God really wants (Ps. 51:16). Under the Old Covenant, David was supposed to offer a blood sacrifice, but by his own admission, he knew it wasn't what God really wanted. David broke free from the Old Testament system and offered the sacrifice of a contrite heart.

Instead of David being killed in the way the Law prescribed, God showed him mercy. But we also see the Old Covenant punishment for sin in how the child that was born to Bathsheba was killed in judgment. We don't see that kind of judgment under the New Covenant. God has always desired to relate to us by grace, but He couldn't under the Old Covenant, because of humanity's hardness of heart. Fortunately, the debt of sin has been paid now, and God is free to be just and merciful.

Jesus coming to this earth made a pivotal difference in the way God deals with mankind. Without the sacrifice of Jesus, humanity would still be living under God's wrath against sin. Instead, God poured out all of His wrath against sin on Jesus (John 12:32). God isn't judging our sin now, because the judgment for all sin, for all time, was put on Jesus.

> *Who his own self bare our sins in his own body on the tree, that we, being dead to sins, should live unto righteousness: by whose stripes ye were healed.*
>
> 1 PETER 2:24

Does that mean we are free to go live however we want? Of course not. Sin has negative consequences that are purely natural, and it gives Satan an inroad into our individual lives—and into our society (Rom. 6:16). When our societies promote ungodly principles and make morality a completely private issue, then it gives Satan an opportunity to destroy nations (Prov. 14:34). Society cannot continue to seek the immorality it promotes and succeed in the long run, but the consequences of sin are not a punishment from God.

LESSON 7 — Is God Angry with Me?

OUTLINE

I. I think that God is being represented in so many contrasting ways by so many different groups in society, that many people are frustrated and confused.

  A. They read Old Testament scriptures that talk about God smiting people with leprosy, then they hear someone like me say God is love and He would never use evil against us, and they wonder, *Which one is the real God?*

  B. But God has always been the same loving God we see manifested in the life and ministry of Jesus.

  C. God is on our side, yet a lot of people think of Him as a harsh and angry God who is eager to judge us for the wrong we've done.

  D. Religion is even teaching that suffering and disease are a blessing in disguise—they say that God uses evil to teach us a lesson (Is. 5:20).

  E. None of that is true, but many people are confused about what the truth really is.

  F. We have to understand the difference between the way God dealt with people under the Old Covenant and the way He deals with us as born-again believers under the New Covenant.

  G. He has changed the way He relates to mankind because of the transformation in *us*.

II. The Gospel of John tells the story of a woman who was caught in adultery by the Pharisees and brought to Jesus for judgment.

  A. John 8:1-5 says,

  Jesus went unto the mount of Olives. And early in the morning he came again into the temple, and all the people came unto him; and he sat down, and taught them. And the scribes and Pharisees brought unto him a woman taken in adultery; and when they had set her in the midst, They say unto him, Master, this woman was taken in adultery, in the very act. Now Moses in the law commanded us, that such should be stoned: but what sayest thou?

  B. It's interesting that the woman was caught in the act of adultery, yet the Pharisees didn't apprehend the man she was with.

  C. I can think of two possible reasons for this:

   i. First, the man might have been someone the Pharisees enlisted to help capture the woman in the middle of the act, so they let the man escape because he was part of the deal.

   ii. Second, if it really was a randomly discovered act of adultery, maybe they only brought the woman because we tend to be easier on women when it comes to sentencing people to death. The Old Testament Law said that a person caught in adultery should be stoned to death (Lev. 20:10 and Deut. 22:22), and they might have thought bringing just the woman suited their purpose of entrapment better—figuring it would be harder for Jesus to condemn a woman than a man.

  D. By bringing this woman to Jesus for judgment, they were trying to make Him choose between obeying the Law and demonstrating the mercy He had been preaching.

  E. Either way, they thought Jesus was trapped: If He demonstrated mercy and let the woman go, then He Himself would be subject to stoning for failing to enforce the Law of Moses. Yet if Jesus followed the Law and condemned the woman to death, then He would be going against the message of mercy He had been teaching, and the people would think He was a hypocrite.

F. Jesus immediately recognized what they were up to, so He simply bent down and wrote in the dirt with His finger.

G. When the Pharisees continued to press Him for an answer, He stood up and said **"He that is without sin among you, let him first cast a stone at her"** (John 8:7) and bent over again and continued writing on the ground.

H. We don't know what He was writing, but whatever it was, it appears to have convicted the accusers of their own sins.

I. One by one, they walked away until only the woman was left standing before Jesus.

J. When Jesus looked up and saw only the woman, He didn't tell her that it was okay to commit adultery—He didn't lower the standard of righteousness—He said, **"Go, and sin no more"** (John 8:11).

K. Jesus admitted that she had sinned, but He didn't condemn her—He showed mercy.

III. The very first person who was punished for breaking the Old Testament Law was a man who gathered sticks on the Sabbath (Num. 15:32-36).

   A. The Lord told Moses that the man should be taken outside the camp and stoned to death for gathering sticks to make a fire!

   B. Some people hear these stories and wonder, *Why the change?*

   C. In a nutshell, God held people accountable for sin under the Old Covenant, so He punished them for it, but under the New Covenant, our sins have all been paid for by Jesus, and God isn't holding sin against us anymore.

   D. After putting our faith in Jesus, we become new creatures (2 Cor. 5:17), and God can deal with us differently than He could deal with people under the Old Covenant (Heb. 8:12-13).

   E. Jesus changed everything, and nothing has been the same since.

   F. A helpful illustration is to consider how we change the way we relate to our own children as they mature:

      i. Young children often have to be physically restrained from doing wrong.

      ii. I know that many people today reject spanking children as being harmful, but the Scripture says, *"The rod and reproof give wisdom: but a child left to himself bringeth his mother to shame"* (Prov. 29:15).

      iii. So, it's a godly thing to use corporal punishment to train young children.

      iv. If we try to tell two year olds it's the devil who leads them to take their siblings' toys, they will just look at us with blank stares.

      v. But when the devil gives them those selfish thoughts of taking their siblings' toys, we can tell them, "If you do that again, I'm going to give you a spanking."

      vi. They may not know about resisting the devil (James 4:7), but I guarantee, when that thought comes again, they will resist it because they don't want the punishment.

      vii. Even so, spanking is not a long-term solution—you only use physical restraint for a short period of time, until your children grow up and you can teach them by instruction.

      viii. Likewise, the Old Testament revealed God's wrath against sin, and He put punishments in place to deter the Israelites from sinning, until His plan of redemption could unfold.

IV. Until Jesus made a new way for everyone, the Israelites were kept under the Law, waiting for saving faith in Christ to appear (Gal. 3:23).

Lesson 7 — Is God Angry with Me?

A. The Apostle Paul said it this way:

Wherefore the law was our schoolmaster to bring us unto Christ, that we might be justified by faith. But after that faith is come, we are no longer under a schoolmaster.

GALATIANS 3:24-25

B. The Law was just a training tool God used to guide His children until they could be saved by faith.

C. You could say that the human race was in its infancy until Jesus came and revealed the true nature of God.

D. Before Jesus came, God dealt with sin harshly in order to keep the Israelites out of trouble, but now, He no longer deals with His children in the same way.

E. You have a different covenant, a New Covenant of salvation by grace through faith in Jesus (Eph. 2:8).

V. Scripture says that Jesus is the exact representation of God the Father (Heb. 1:3).

A. The Old Testament prophets revealed some truths about God, but Jesus gave us a complete view of the Father.

B. The writer of Hebrews said, **"How shall we escape, if we neglect so great salvation; which at the first began to be spoken by the Lord, and was confirmed unto us by them that heard him"** (Heb. 2:3).

C. Jesus revealed God in a way that superseded all previous revelation.

D. In Jesus, we see a kind and compassionate God who gave Himself over to a cruel death in order to give us the hope of new life.

VI. Jesus' disciples tried to reenact a story from the Old Testament once, and His response to them dramatically illustrates the difference between the Old and the New Covenants.

A. The story revolves around the ungodly King Ahaziah, who fell seriously ill but instead of seeking the Lord for healing, he sent messengers to inquire of the false god Baalzebub.

B. God told the prophet Elijah what King Ahaziah was doing, and he intercepted the messengers and said to them, **"Is it not because there is not a God in Israel, that ye go to enquire of Baalzebub the god of Ekron? Now therefore thus saith the Lord, Thou shalt not come down from that bed on which thou art gone up, but shalt surely die"** (2 Kin. 1:3b-4).

C. Although Elijah didn't identify himself to the messengers, he had a long history with Ahaziah's family, so when the messengers returned to Ahaziah and reported what Elijah had said, the king knew right away who it was that had spoken to the messengers.

D. After hearing Elijah's warning, the king sent out a captain with fifty soldiers to capture him, and when they found Elijah, the captain commanded him to come down.

E. Elijah replied **"If I be a man of God, then let fire come down from heaven, and consume thee and thy fifty"** (2 Kin. 1:10), and fire came down from heaven and consumed the captain and his fifty soldiers.

F. Undeterred, the king sent out another captain with fifty soldiers, Elijah called down fire from heaven again, and the second captain and his men were also killed.

G. So, the king sent out a third captain with fifty soldiers, but this time, the captain fell down on his knees before Elijah and begged for his life, and the angel of the Lord spoke to Elijah, told him not to be afraid, and to go with the soldiers to see King Ahaziah.

H. This story comes up again in the New Testament while Jesus and His disciples were passing through Samaria.

I. The mutual hatred between the Jews and the Samaritans was both religious and racial, and we need to keep the extreme prejudice between them in mind as we read the New Testament story:

And it came to pass, when the time was come that he should be received up, he stedfastly set his face to go to Jerusalem, And sent messengers before his face: and they went, and entered into a village of the Samaritans, to make ready for him. And they did not receive him, because his face was as though he would go to Jerusalem.
LUKE 9:51-53

J. We know that Jesus had already taught in Samaria, because the Gospel of John tells the story of Jesus ministering to the woman at the well (John 4).

K. These were people who already acknowledged Jesus as the Messiah!

L. They were willing to accept Jesus as God's anointed Savior, but they were unable to overcome their religious prejudice against the Jewish worship, so when Jesus identified Himself with the Jews in Jerusalem, they rejected Him.

M. In the Old Testament story, the army captains were just obeying orders by trying to bring Elijah to King Ahaziah, but the Samaritans were rejecting the Messiah.

N. When the disciples saw how the Samaritans were acting, they asked Jesus, **"Lord, wilt thou that we command fire to come down from heaven, and consume them, even as** [Elijah] **did?"** (Luke 9:54, brackets mine).

O. The disciples wanted to imitate Elijah by calling down fire to kill the Samaritans, and it could be argued that what the Samaritans had done was more deserving of judgment than anything the soldiers did.

P. Yet Jesus reproached the disciples:

But he turned, and rebuked them, and said, Ye know not what manner of spirit ye are of. For the Son of man is not come to destroy men's lives, but to save them. And they went to another village.
LUKE 9:55-56

Q. Someone who looks at this casually might think that God was being inconsistent, but the difference here is actually the difference between the Old Covenant and the New Covenant.

VII. Prior to the Law being given through Moses, which was approximately 2,000 years *after* the fall of Adam and Eve, God was dealing with people in mercy and grace (Rom. 5:13), but people began to take God's lack of punishment as an indication that He didn't care whether they lived holy lives or not.

A. They didn't understand that even though God wasn't punishing sin, Satan was taking advantage of sinful actions and corrupting the whole human race.

B. So, God had to restrain sin—He had to get people to turn away from sin and the damage it was causing.

C. Before the Law, God actually protected the first murderer (Gen. 4).

D. After Cain killed Abel, God set a mark on Cain to protect him from any vigilante-style attempts to exact justice by taking Cain's life.

E. God didn't approve of the murder Cain committed—it was wrong and it had consequences—but God didn't punish Cain for his sinful action.

F. God's grace toward Cain stands in sharp contrast to the punishment exacted upon the first person to violate the Law.

G. The way God turned people away from sin under the Old Covenant Law was by bringing judgment on sin and using punishment.

H. When the Law was given, it held people accountable for sin.

LESSON 7 — IS GOD ANGRY WITH ME?

I. The Law made people realize that God wasn't indifferent to the way they were acting.

J. It revealed God's standard of righteousness, and it made the Israelites fearful of God's wrath against sin.

K. As a result, they turned away from sin, but the Law also had the effect of making people feel guilty and unworthy.

L. The Law was part of God's plan for redemption, but it was only a temporary measure put in place until Jesus should come:

But before faith came, we were kept under the law, shut up unto the faith which should afterwards be revealed. Wherefore the law was our schoolmaster to bring us unto Christ, that we might be justified by faith. But after that faith is come, we are no longer under a schoolmaster.
GALATIANS 3:23-25

M. Just as the giving of the Law brought judgment for sin, the sacrifice of Jesus brought a return to grace.

N. I believe that if Jesus had been on earth in His physical body when Elijah was calling fire down out of heaven, Jesus would have rebuked Elijah.

O. Elijah got away with calling down fire because he was under the ministry of the Law, which was holding people's sins against them, but it was never the true nature of God to deal with people that way.

P. Now that grace has come through Jesus, we're no longer under the Law.

VIII. Under the Old Covenant, there were very harsh punishments for sin.

    A. The Lord often commanded to kill all the men, women, children, and even the animals when the Israelites conquered other nations (Josh. 6:17-21, 10:40, and 11:11-14).

    B. There was even a commandment for people to kill their own children if they were persistently stubborn and rebellious (Deut. 21:18-21).

        i. This was because they couldn't be cured or healed, so they were taken out of society—in much the same way that doctors cut out a cancerous tumor to save the rest of the body.

    C. It wasn't possible for anyone to be born again, and God didn't want foreign peoples infecting the children of Israel with demonic beliefs or behavior.

    D. But under our New and better Covenant (Heb. 8:6 and 13), we don't kill our rebellious children or people who are committing ungodly acts, because they can be born again and changed.

    E. Praise God for the vast change that Jesus made.

    F. Under the Old Covenant, God's judgment against evil was mercy to the rest of God's people, but under the New Covenant, we can be delivered from evil.

    G. Today we minister the love of God to anyone who is caught up in sin and share the Good News about Jesus Christ.

    H. This difference should help us understand the harshness of the Old Testament and why we now have a better covenant through Jesus.

    I. Some make the mistake of thinking that the transformation in how God has related to mankind over time reflects some sort of conversion in God, which isn't true.

    J. God declares, **"I am the Lord, I change not"** (Mal. 3:6a), and **"Jesus Christ is the same yesterday, today, and forever"** (Heb. 13:8, *New King James Version*).

Lesson 7 — Is God Angry with Me?

    K. God hasn't changed; we have—and the way He relates to us under the New Covenant has changed as a result.

IX. At first, the disciples related to Christ through His physical presence and attributes, but now that He has risen from the dead and ascended into heaven, you relate to Him through the Holy Spirit (2 Cor. 5:16).

    A. In the same way, you shouldn't look at yourself only from a physical perspective—you have a spiritual identity that completely changed when you were born again, and you need to know who you are in the spirit—the part of you that is created new in the image of Christ.

    B. When you are in Christ, old things have passed away and *all* things have become new (2 Cor. 5:17), not some things.

    C. A lot of people struggle with this scripture because they don't feel completely new and don't see anything new in themselves.

        i. They say, "I still get angry. I still have some of the same bad habits. I feel like I'm getting better, but I'm not there yet."

    D. They struggle with accepting the idea that they are already new, because they don't understand that this scripture isn't talking about their physical bodies or their personalities.

    E. Being born again doesn't cause obesity to disappear, and it doesn't automatically change your personality—the Holy Spirit can help you improve and you can change, but it isn't automatic.

    F. Your thoughts and memories don't immediately change, but in the spirit, you become a totally brand-new person—instantly.

    G. The reason you don't see a totally new person when you look in the mirror is that you are looking at your physical appearance or searching your mental and emotional makeup, but the changes in your spirit cannot be perceived by your natural senses.

    H. Your spirit is the part of you that becomes completely new. Look at how the *Amplified Bible* translates 2 Corinthians 5:17 -

Therefore if any person is [ingrafted] in Christ (the Messiah) he is a new creation (a new creature altogether); the old [previous moral and spiritual condition] has passed away. Behold, the fresh and new has come!

    I. In the spirit, your salvation is perfect.

    J. You have been united with Christ, and your spirit is as perfect, pure, and holy as it ever will be.

    K. The moment you are born again, your spirit is transformed into the new creation you will be for all of eternity.

    L. You will get a new heavenly body, and your soul will be renewed so that you know all things even as you are known (1 Cor. 13:12), but your spirit is changed forever the moment you are born again.

X. God has already—past tense—reconciled us to Himself through Jesus Christ:

And all things are of God, who hath reconciled us to himself by Jesus Christ, and hath given to us the ministry of reconciliation; To wit, that God was in Christ, reconciling the world unto himself, not imputing their trespasses unto them; and hath committed unto us the word of reconciliation.

        2 CORINTHIANS 5:18-19

    A. More specifically, God was in Christ reconciling the sins of the entire human race.

    B. "Reconcile" is a term people don't use every day, but it just means to reestablish a close relationship between, or to settle or resolve.

Lesson 7 — Is God Angry with Me?

    C. God took away all of the discord that sin caused, and He harmonized your relationship with Him again.

    D. Second Corinthians 5:19 also says God is not **"imputing"** your sins anymore, which means to attribute responsibility for.

    E. It is a term used in bookkeeping to describe charging or accrediting fees to an account.

    F. For instance, when you use a credit card to purchase something, you are really asking the seller to give you the item and charge the fee to your account.

    G. The item isn't actually paid for until you pay off your credit card.

    H. You didn't pay for it when you gave the seller your credit card; you just had the cost imputed to your account.

    I. If you don't believe that, just refuse to pay the credit card bill when it comes, and see if they think you've already paid.

    J. When Scripture says that God reconciled the world unto Himself, not imputing your trespasses unto you, it means that God didn't charge sin to your account.

    K. He went ahead and paid the debt for you—a balance that was impossible for you to settle—so that He could reestablish a close relationship with you.

    L. God took the sins of all humanity and charged it to the account of Jesus, and He was also in Jesus on Calvary.

XI. God didn't just turn His head and pretend sin never happened—His pure, holy, and righteous nature wouldn't allow Him to look the other way.

    A. Yet He loves us and desires a relationship with us, so He decided to pay for sin Himself.

    B. Sin was still imputed, but instead of charging us, God charged it to His Son.

    C. Going back to the credit-card illustration, it's as if you were to roll a cartload of computer gear to the checkout in an electronics store, and just as you are about to be charged, a man steps up and says "Let me get that for you" and puts it all on his credit card.

        i. That's very different from the store clerk saying to you, "Don't worry about it—everything is free today."

        ii. The items aren't free—someone had to pay for them.

    D. God put all of our sin upon His Son, the Lord Jesus.

    E. He made Jesus, who never sinned, become sin for us, and He took the sin of the entire human race (2 Cor. 5:21).

XII. Jesus didn't just die for a select number of people who would later accept Him—He paid for the sins of the whole world, even the people who reject Him (1 John 2:2).

    A. Adolf Hitler's sins, for example, were paid for—Jesus took the murder of six million Jews and the responsibility for a World War upon Himself.

    B. Jesus suffered shame, hurt, and degradation on Hitler's behalf—all of that evil was charged to Jesus.

    C. That doesn't mean Hitler was saved, because, as far as we know, Hitler didn't accept the salvation that Jesus provided.

    D. We have to humble ourselves and make Jesus our Lord (Rom. 10:9) so that what He did for us is credited to our account.

E. Once we truly understand the significance of Jesus' sacrifice, then we can understand why God dealt with people differently under the New Covenant than He did under the Old Covenant.

XIII. You can find a limited amount of mercy under the Old Covenant, but only to the degree that people understood God's grace nature and operated in it.

   A. King David is a good example.

      i. When he committed adultery with Bathsheba, according to the Old Testament Law, he should have been stoned to death.

      ii. Yet God showed him mercy because David understood the true nature of God.

      iii. In a sense, he was able to reach into the future by faith and appropriate some of the grace that we live under in the New Covenant.

      iv. We can see this reflected in the psalm David wrote when he said, "Against you, and you only, Lord, have I sinned and done this evil in your sight" (Ps. 51:4, paraphrase mine).

      v. David showed his understanding of God's true nature when he went on to say that he would offer a sacrifice, but he knew that sacrifice is not what God really wants (Ps. 51:16).

      vi. Under the Old Covenant, David was supposed to offer a blood sacrifice, but by his own admission, he knew it wasn't what God really wanted.

      vii. David broke free from the Old Testament system and offered the sacrifice of a contrite heart.

      viii. Instead of David being killed in the way the Law prescribed, God showed him mercy.

      ix. But we also see the Old Covenant punishment for sin in how the child that was born to Bathsheba was killed in judgment.

      x. We don't see that kind of judgment under the New Covenant.

   B. God has always desired to relate to us by grace, but He couldn't under the Old Covenant, because of humanity's hardness of heart.

   C. Fortunately, the debt of sin has been paid now, and God is free to be just and merciful.

XIV. Jesus coming to this earth made a pivotal difference in the way God deals with mankind.

   A. Without the sacrifice of Jesus, humanity would still be living under God's wrath against sin.

   B. Instead, God poured out all of His wrath against sin on Jesus (John 12:32).

   C. God isn't judging our sin now, because the judgment for all sin, for all time, was put on Jesus.

   Who his own self bare our sins in his own body on the tree, that we, being dead to sins, should live unto righteousness: by whose stripes ye were healed.

   1 PETER 2:24

   D. Of course that doesn't mean we are free to go live however we want.

   E. Sin has negative consequences that are purely natural, and it gives Satan an inroad into our individual lives—and into our society (Rom. 6:16).

   F. When our societies promote ungodly principles and make morality a completely private issue, then it gives Satan an opportunity to destroy nations (Prov. 14:34).

   G. Society cannot continue to seek the immorality it promotes and succeed in the long run, but the consequences of sin are not a punishment from God.

| LESSON 7 | IS GOD ANGRY WITH ME? |

TEACHER'S GUIDE

1. I think that God is being represented in so many contrasting ways by so many different groups in society, that many people are frustrated and confused. They read Old Testament scriptures that talk about God smiting people with leprosy, then they hear someone like me say God is love and He would never use evil against us, and they wonder, *Which one is the real God?* But God has always been the same loving God we see manifested in the life and ministry of Jesus. God is on our side, yet a lot of people think of Him as a harsh and angry God who is eager to judge us for the wrong we've done. Religion is even teaching that suffering and disease are a blessing in disguise—they say that God uses evil to teach us a lesson (Is. 5:20). None of that is true, but many people are confused about what the truth really is. We have to understand the difference between the way God dealt with people under the Old Covenant and the way He deals with us as born-again believers under the New Covenant. He has changed the way He relates to mankind because of the transformation in *us*.

1a. Why are many people frustrated and confused about God?
(Because He's being represented in so many contrasting ways by so many different groups in society)

1b. Discussion Question: How do you know that God is not the harsh and angry God who is eager to judge you for the wrong you've done?
(Discussion question)

1c. True or false: God has changed the way He relates to mankind because of the transformation in society.
(False)

2. The Gospel of John tells the story of a woman who was caught in adultery by the Pharisees and brought to Jesus for judgment. John 8:1-5 says,

> *Jesus went unto the mount of Olives. And early in the morning he came again into the temple, and all the people came unto him; and he sat down, and taught them. And the scribes and Pharisees brought unto him a woman taken in adultery; and when they had set her in the midst, They say unto him, Master, this woman was taken in adultery, in the very act. Now Moses in the law commanded us, that such should be stoned: but what sayest thou?*

It's interesting that the woman was caught in the act of adultery, yet the Pharisees didn't apprehend the man she was with. I can think of two possible reasons for this: First, the man might have been someone the Pharisees enlisted to help capture the woman in the middle of the act, so they let the man escape because he was part of the deal. Second, if it really was a randomly discovered act of adultery, maybe they only brought the woman because we tend to be easier on women when it comes to sentencing people to death. The Old Testament Law said that a person caught in adultery should be stoned to death (Lev. 20:10 and Deut. 22:22), and they might have thought bringing just the woman suited their purpose of entrapment better—figuring it would be harder for Jesus to condemn a woman than a man. By bringing this woman to Jesus for judgment, they were trying to make Him choose between obeying the Law and demonstrating the mercy He had been preaching. Either way, they thought Jesus was trapped: If He demonstrated mercy and let the woman go, then He Himself would be subject to stoning for failing to enforce the Law of Moses. Yet if Jesus followed the Law and condemned the woman to death, then He would be going against the message of mercy He had been teaching, and the people would think He was a hypocrite. Jesus immediately recognized what they were up to, so He simply bent down and wrote in the dirt with His finger. When the Pharisees continued to press Him for an answer, He stood up and said **"He that is without sin among you, let him first cast a stone at her"** (John 8:7) and bent over again and continued writing on the ground. We don't know what He was writing, but whatever it was, it appears to have convicted the accusers of their own sins. One by one, they walked away until only the woman was left standing before Jesus. When Jesus looked up and saw only the woman, He didn't tell her that it was okay to commit adultery—He didn't lower the standard of righteousness—He said, **"Go, and sin no more"** (John 8:11). Jesus admitted that she had sinned, but He didn't condemn her—He showed mercy.

2a. Read John 8:1-5. Why did the Jews think they had Jesus trapped?
(Because if Jesus demonstrated mercy and let the woman go, then He Himself would be subject to stoning for failing to enforce the Law of Moses. Yet if He followed the Law and condemned the woman to death, then He would be going against the message of mercy He had been teaching, and the people would think He was a hypocrite)

Lesson 7   Is God Angry with Me?

2b. According to John 8:7, what did Jesus say?
*("**He that is without sin among you, let him first cast a stone at her**")*

2c. After everyone left but Jesus and the woman, what did Jesus do?
A. He picked up a stone to exact justice on the woman
B. He endorsed the woman's sin
C. He told the woman to go get her husband and come back
D. He denied that the woman had even sinned
E. He admitted that the woman had sinned, but He showed mercy
(E. He admitted that the woman had sinned, but He showed mercy)

3. The very first person who was punished for breaking the Old Testament Law was a man who gathered sticks on the Sabbath (Num. 15:32-36). The Lord told Moses that the man should be taken outside the camp and stoned to death for gathering sticks to make a fire! Some people hear these stories and wonder, *Why the change?* In a nutshell, God held people accountable for sin under the Old Covenant, so He punished them for it, but under the New Covenant, our sins have all been paid for by Jesus, and God isn't holding sin against us anymore. After putting our faith in Jesus, we become new creatures (2 Cor. 5:17), and God can deal with us differently than He could deal with people under the Old Covenant (Heb. 8:12-13). Jesus changed everything, and nothing has been the same since. A helpful illustration is to consider how we change the way we relate to our own children as they mature: Young children often have to be physically restrained from doing wrong. I know that many people today reject spanking children as being harmful, but the Scripture says, "**The rod and reproof give wisdom: but a child left to himself bringeth his mother to shame**" (Prov. 29:15). So, it's a godly thing to use corporal punishment to train young children. If we try to tell two year olds it's the devil who leads them to take their siblings' toys, they will just look at us with blank stares. But when the devil gives them those selfish thoughts of taking their siblings' toys, we can tell them, "If you do that again, I'm going to give you a spanking." They may not know about resisting the devil (James 4:7), but I guarantee, when that thought comes again, they will resist it because they don't want the punishment. Even so, spanking is not a long-term solution—you only use physical restraint for a short period of time, until your children grow up and you can teach them by instruction. Likewise, the Old Testament revealed God's wrath against sin, and He put punishments in place to deter the Israelites from sinning, until His plan of redemption could unfold.

3a. Who held people accountable for sin in the Old Testament?
A. Moses
B. The priests
C. God
D. A. and C.
E. All of the above
(C. God)

3b. Read 2 Corinthians 5:17 and Hebrews 8:12-13. Why can God deal with us differently than He could deal with people under the Old Covenant?
(Because after putting our faith in Jesus, we've become new creatures)

3c. What is a helpful illustration to consider?
(How you change the way you relate to your own children as they mature: you use physical restraint for a short period of time)

3d. Why?
(Because until they grow up, you can't teach your children by instruction)

4. Until Jesus made a new way for everyone, the Israelites were kept under the Law, waiting for saving faith in Christ to appear (Gal. 3:23). The Apostle Paul said it this way:

> *Wherefore the law was our schoolmaster to bring us unto Christ, that we might be justified by faith. But after that faith is come, we are no longer under a schoolmaster.*
>
> GALATIANS 3:24-25

LESSON 7   IS GOD ANGRY WITH ME?

The Law was just a training tool God used to guide His children until they could be saved by faith. You could say that the human race was in its infancy until Jesus came and revealed the true nature of God. Before Jesus came, God dealt with sin harshly in order to keep the Israelites out of trouble, but now, He no longer deals with His children in the same way. You have a different covenant, a New Covenant of salvation by grace through faith in Jesus (Eph. 2:8).

4a. Read Galatians 3:23-25. What did God use the Law for?
(A training tool to guide His children until they could be saved by faith)

4b. Salvation is by grace through faith in _____.
(Jesus)

5. Scripture says that Jesus is the exact representation of God the Father (Heb. 1:3). The Old Testament prophets revealed some truths about God, but Jesus gave us a complete view of the Father. The writer of Hebrews said, **"How shall we escape, if we neglect so great salvation; which at the first began to be spoken by the Lord, and was confirmed unto us by them that heard him"** (Heb. 2:3). Jesus revealed God in a way that superseded all previous revelation. In Jesus, we see a kind and compassionate God who gave Himself over to a cruel death in order to give us the hope of new life.

5a. Read Hebrews 1:3. Jesus is the exact representation of whom?
A. God
B. The Law
C. The prophets
D. All of the above
E. None of the above
(A. God)

5b. According to Hebrews 2:3, the Lord was first to speak of what?
(So great salvation)

6. Jesus' disciples tried to reenact a story from the Old Testament once, and His response to them dramatically illustrates the difference between the Old and the New Covenants. The story revolves around the ungodly King Ahaziah, who fell seriously ill but instead of seeking the Lord for healing, he sent messengers to inquire of the false god Baalzebub. God told the prophet Elijah what King Ahaziah was doing, and he intercepted the messengers and said to them, **"Is it not because there is not a God in Israel, that ye go to enquire of Baalzebub the god of Ekron? Now therefore thus saith the LORD, Thou shalt not come down from that bed on which thou art gone up, but shalt surely die"** (2 Kin. 1:3b-4). Although Elijah didn't identify himself to the messengers, he had a long history with Ahaziah's family, so when the messengers returned to Ahaziah and reported what Elijah had said, the king knew right away who it was that had spoken to the messengers. After hearing Elijah's warning, the king sent out a captain with fifty soldiers to capture him, and when they found Elijah, the captain commanded him to come down. Elijah replied **"If I be a man of God, then let fire come down from heaven, and consume thee and thy fifty"** (2 Kin. 1:10), and fire came down from heaven and consumed the captain and his fifty soldiers. Undeterred, the king sent out another captain with fifty soldiers, Elijah called down fire from heaven again, and the second captain and his men were also killed. So, the king sent out a third captain with fifty soldiers, but this time, the captain fell down on his knees before Elijah and begged for his life, and the angel of the Lord spoke to Elijah, told him not to be afraid, and to go with the soldiers to see King Ahaziah. This story comes up again in the New Testament while Jesus and His disciples were passing through Samaria. The mutual hatred between the Jews and the Samaritans was both religious and racial, and we need to keep the extreme prejudice between them in mind as we read the New Testament story:

> *And it came to pass, when the time was come that he should be received up, he stedfastly set his face to go to Jerusalem, And sent messengers before his face: and they went, and entered into a village of the Samaritans, to make ready for him. And they did not receive him, because his face was as though he would go to Jerusalem.*
> LUKE 9:51-53

We know that Jesus had already taught in Samaria, because the Gospel of John tells the story of Jesus ministering to the woman at the well (John 4). These were people who already acknowledged Jesus as the Messiah! They were

Lesson 7 — Is God Angry with Me?

willing to accept Jesus as God's anointed Savior, but they were unable to overcome their religious prejudice against the Jewish worship, so when Jesus identified Himself with the Jews in Jerusalem, they rejected Him. In the Old Testament story, the army captains were just obeying orders by trying to bring Elijah to King Ahaziah, but the Samaritans were rejecting the Messiah. When the disciples saw how the Samaritans were acting, they asked Jesus, **"Lord, wilt thou that we command fire to come down from heaven, and consume them, even as [Elijah] did?"** (Luke 9:54, brackets mine). The disciples wanted to imitate Elijah by calling down fire to kill the Samaritans, and it could be argued that what the Samaritans had done was more deserving of judgment than anything the soldiers did. Yet Jesus reproached the disciples:

> *But he turned, and rebuked them, and said, Ye know not what manner of spirit ye are of. For the Son of man is not come to destroy men's lives, but to save them. And they went to another village.*
>
> LUKE 9:55-56

Someone who looks at this casually might think that God was being inconsistent, but the difference here is actually the difference between the Old Covenant and the New Covenant.

    6a.   Discussion Question: How do 2 Kings 1 and Luke 9 speak of the difference between the Old Covenant and the New Covenant?
(Discussion question)

7. Prior to the Law being given through Moses, which was approximately 2,000 years *after* the fall of Adam and Eve, God was dealing with people in mercy and grace (Rom. 5:13), but people began to take God's lack of punishment as an indication that He didn't care whether they lived holy lives or not. They didn't understand that even though God wasn't punishing sin, Satan was taking advantage of sinful actions and corrupting the whole human race. So, God had to restrain sin—He had to get people to turn away from sin and the damage it was causing. Before the Law, God actually protected the first murderer (Gen. 4). After Cain killed Abel, God set a mark on Cain to protect him from any vigilante-style attempts to exact justice by taking Cain's life. God didn't approve of the murder Cain committed—it was wrong and it had consequences—but God didn't punish Cain for his sinful action. God's grace toward Cain stands in sharp contrast to the punishment exacted upon the first person to violate the Law. The way God turned people away from sin under the Old Covenant Law was by bringing judgment on sin and using punishment. When the Law was given, it held people accountable for sin. The Law made people realize that God wasn't indifferent to the way they were acting. It revealed God's standard of righteousness, and it made the Israelites fearful of God's wrath against sin. As a result, they turned away from sin, but the Law also had the effect of making people feel guilty and unworthy. The Law was part of God's plan for redemption, but it was only a temporary measure put in place until Jesus should come:

> *But before faith came, we were kept under the law, shut up unto the faith which should afterwards be revealed. Wherefore the law was our schoolmaster to bring us unto Christ, that we might be justified by faith. But after that faith is come, we are no longer under a schoolmaster.*
>
> GALATIANS 3:23-25

Just as the giving of the Law brought judgment for sin, the sacrifice of Jesus brought a return to grace. I believe that if Jesus had been on earth in His physical body when Elijah was calling fire down out of heaven, Jesus would have rebuked Elijah. Elijah got away with calling down fire because he was under the ministry of the Law, which was holding people's sins against them, but it was never the true nature of God to deal with people that way. Now that grace has come through Jesus, we're no longer under the Law.

    7a.   True or false: The Law was given through Moses approximately 2,000 years after the fall of Adam and Eve.
(True)

    7b.   True or false: God's lack of punishment is an indication that He doesn't care whether you live a holy life or not.
(False)

LESSON 7 — IS GOD ANGRY WITH ME?

7c. Why did God extend grace toward the first murderer, Cain, but pronounce judgment on the first person to violate the Law?
A. Because God has favorites and liked Cain better
B. Because God changes what He's like sometimes
C. Because Cain's act of murder was before the Law
D. Because the Law held people accountable for sin
E. C. and D.
(E. C. and D.)

7d. What effect(s) did the Law have on people?
A. It made people turn away from sin
B. It made people feel guilty
C. It made people feel unworthy
D. All of the above
E. None of the above
(D. All of the above)

7e. The sacrifice of Jesus brought a return to what?
(Grace)

7f. Why does Andrew believe that if Jesus had been on earth in His physical body when Elijah was calling fire down out of heaven, He would have rebuked Elijah?
(Because if Jesus had been on the earth in His physical body when Elijah was calling fire down out of heaven, Elijah wouldn't have been under the Law)

8. Under the Old Covenant, there were very harsh punishments for sin. The Lord often commanded to kill all the men, women, children, and even the animals when the Israelites conquered other nations (Josh. 6:17-21, 10:40, and 11:11-14). There was even a commandment for people to kill their own children if they were persistently stubborn and rebellious (Deut. 21:18-21). This was because they couldn't be cured or healed, so they were taken out of society—in much the same way that doctors cut out a cancerous tumor to save the rest of the body. It wasn't possible for anyone to be born again, and God didn't want foreign peoples infecting the children of Israel with demonic beliefs or behavior. But under our New and better Covenant (Heb. 8:6 and 13), we don't kill our rebellious children or people who are committing ungodly acts, because they can be born again and changed. Praise God for the vast change that Jesus made. Under the Old Covenant, God's judgment against evil was mercy to the rest of God's people, but under the New Covenant, we can be delivered from evil. Today we minister the love of God to anyone who is caught up in sin and share the Good News about Jesus Christ. This difference should help us understand the harshness of the Old Testament and why we now have a better covenant through Jesus. Some make the mistake of thinking that the transformation in how God has related to mankind over time reflects some sort of conversion in God, which isn't true. God declares, **"I am the Lord, I change not"** (Mal. 3:6a), and **"Jesus Christ is the same yesterday, today, and forever"** (Heb. 13:8, *New King James Version*). God hasn't changed; we have—and the way He relates to us under the New Covenant has changed as a result.

8a. In the Old Covenant, what was God's judgment against evil?
A. A blessing in disguise
B. God's way of humbling those who sinned
C. What the people wanted
D. Mercy to the rest of God's people
E. God's ultimate plan for mankind
(D. Mercy to the rest of God's people)

8b. Today what do you do to people who are caught up in sin?
(Minister the love of God to them and share the Good News about Jesus Christ)

8c. What should this difference help you understand?
(The harshness of the Old Testament and why you now have a better covenant through Jesus)

Lesson 7 — Is God Angry with Me?

8d. Why doesn't this reflect some kind of conversion in God?
(Because Malachi 3:6a and Hebrews 13:8 say that God never changes)

8e. Who and what have changed?
(You have and the way God relates to you has changed)

9. At first, the disciples related to Christ through His physical presence and attributes, but now that He has risen from the dead and ascended into heaven, you relate to Him through the Holy Spirit (2 Cor. 5:16). In the same way, you shouldn't look at yourself only from a physical perspective—you have a spiritual identity that completely changed when you were born again, and you need to know who you are in the spirit—the part of you that is created new in the image of Christ. When you are in Christ, old things have passed away and *all* things have become new (2 Cor. 5:17), not some things. A lot of people struggle with this scripture because they don't feel completely new and don't see anything new in themselves. They say, "I still get angry. I still have some of the same bad habits. I feel like I'm getting better, but I'm not there yet." They struggle with accepting the idea that they are already new, because they don't understand that this scripture isn't talking about their physical bodies or their personalities. Being born again doesn't cause obesity to disappear, and it doesn't automatically change your personality—the Holy Spirit can help you improve and you can change, but it isn't automatic. Your thoughts and memories don't immediately change, but in the spirit, you become a totally brand-new person—instantly. The reason you don't see a totally new person when you look in the mirror is that you are looking at your physical appearance or searching your mental and emotional makeup, but the changes in your spirit cannot be perceived by your natural senses. Your spirit is the part of you that becomes completely new. Look at how the *Amplified Bible* translates 2 Corinthians 5:17 –

> *Therefore if any person is [ingrafted] in Christ (the Messiah) he is a new creation (a new creature altogether); the old [previous moral and spiritual condition] has passed away. Behold, the fresh and new has come!*

In the spirit, your salvation is perfect. You have been united with Christ, and your spirit is as perfect, pure, and holy as it ever will be. The moment you are born again, your spirit is transformed into the new creation you will be for all of eternity. You will get a new heavenly body, and your soul will be renewed so that you know all things even as you are known (1 Cor. 13:12), but your spirit is changed forever the moment you are born again.

9a. Read 2 Corinthians 5:16. How do you relate to Christ?
(Through the Holy Spirit)

9b. Read 2 Corinthians 5:17. When you are in Christ, _____ things have passed away and _____ things have become new.
(Old/all)

9c. True or false: When you're born again, what changes?
A. Your IQ
B. Your body
C. Your personality
D. Your spirit
E. Nothing
(D. Your spirit)

9d. Discussion Question: Why is it important to know what changed?
(Discussion question)

9e. Your spirit is where what is perfect?
(Everything)

10. God has already—past tense—reconciled us to Himself through Jesus Christ:

Lesson 7 — Is God Angry with Me?

And all things are of God, who hath reconciled us to himself by Jesus Christ, and hath given to us the ministry of reconciliation; To wit, that God was in Christ, reconciling the world unto himself, not imputing their trespasses unto them; and hath committed unto us the word of reconciliation.

2 CORINTHIANS 5:18-19

More specifically, God was in Christ reconciling the sins of the entire human race. "Reconcile" is a term people don't use every day, but it just means to reestablish a close relationship between, or to settle or resolve. God took away all of the discord that sin caused, and He harmonized your relationship with Him again. Second Corinthians 5:19 also says God is not **"imputing"** your sins anymore, which means to attribute responsibility for. It is a term used in bookkeeping to describe charging or accrediting fees to an account. For instance, when you use a credit card to purchase something, you are really asking the seller to give you the item and charge the fee to your account. The item isn't actually paid for until you pay off your credit card. You didn't pay for it when you gave the seller your credit card; you just had the cost imputed to your account. If you don't believe that, just refuse to pay the credit card bill when it comes, and see if they think you've already paid. When Scripture says that God reconciled the world unto Himself, not imputing your trespasses unto you, it means that God didn't charge sin to your account. He went ahead and paid the debt for you—a balance that was impossible for you to settle—so that He could reestablish a close relationship with you. God took the sins of all humanity and charged it to the account of Jesus, and He was also in Jesus on Calvary.

10a. Discussion Question: Read 2 Corinthians 5:18-19. What does the phrase **"reconciling the world unto himself"** mean to you?
(Discussion question)

10b. Discussion Question: What does **"not imputing their trespasses unto them"** mean to you?
(Discussion question)

10c. God went ahead and paid the _____ for you—a balance that was _____ for you to settle—so that He could _____ a close relationship with you.
(Debt/impossible/reestablish)

11. God didn't just turn His head and pretend sin never happened—His pure, holy, and righteous nature wouldn't allow Him to look the other way. Yet He loves us and desires a relationship with us, so He decided to pay for sin Himself. Sin was still imputed, but instead of charging us, God charged it to His Son. Going back to the credit-card illustration, it's as if you were to roll a cartload of computer gear to the checkout in an electronics store, and just as you are about to be charged, a man steps up and says "Let me get that for you" and puts it all on his credit card. That's very different from the store clerk saying to you, "Don't worry about it—everything is free today." The items aren't free—someone had to pay for them. God put all of our sin upon His Son, the Lord Jesus. He made Jesus, who never sinned, become sin for us, and He took the sin of the entire human race (2 Cor. 5:21).

11a. True or false: God didn't pretend that sin never happened.
(True)

11b. Why?
(Because of His pure, holy, and righteous nature)

11c. Because God loves you and desires relationship with you, what did He decide to do?
A. Make the angels pay
B. Restart creation
C. Pay for sin Himself
D. All of the above
E. None of the above
(C. Pay for sin Himself)

11d. Read 2 Corinthians 5:21. He made Jesus, who never sinned, _____ sin for you, and He took the sin of the entire human race.
(Become)

12. Jesus didn't just die for a select number of people who would later accept Him—He paid for the sins of the whole world, even the people who reject Him (1 John 2:2). Adolf Hitler's sins, for example, were paid for—Jesus took the murder of six million Jews and the responsibility for a World War upon Himself. Jesus suffered shame, hurt, and degradation on Hitler's behalf—all of that evil was charged to Jesus. That doesn't mean Hitler was saved, because as far as we know, Hitler didn't accept the salvation that Jesus provided. We have to humble ourselves and make Jesus our Lord (Rom. 10:9) so that what He did for us is credited to our account. Once we truly understand the significance of Jesus' sacrifice, then we can understand why God dealt with people differently under the New Covenant than He did under the Old Covenant.

    12a. Read 1 John 2:2. True or false: Jesus died for a select number of people who would later accept Him.
(False)

    12b. Since Jesus paid for the sins of the whole world, why isn't everyone saved?
(Because they have to humble themselves and make Jesus their Lord [Rom. 10:9] so that what He did for them is credited to their account)

    12c. What happens once you truly understand the significance of Jesus' sacrifice?
(Then you can understand why God dealt with people differently under the New Covenant than He did under the Old Covenant)

13. You can find a limited amount of mercy under the Old Covenant, but only to the degree that people understood God's grace nature and operated in it. King David is a good example. When he committed adultery with Bathsheba, according to the Old Testament Law, he should have been stoned to death. Yet God showed him mercy because David understood the true nature of God. In a sense, he was able to reach into the future by faith and appropriate some of the grace that we live under in the New Covenant. We can see this reflected in the psalm David wrote when he said, "Against you, and you only, Lord, have I sinned and done this evil in your sight" (Ps. 51:4, paraphrase mine). David showed his understanding of God's true nature when he went on to say that he would offer a sacrifice, but he knew that sacrifice is not what God really wants (Ps. 51:16). Under the Old Covenant, David was supposed to offer a blood sacrifice, but by his own admission, he knew it wasn't what God really wanted. David broke free from the Old Testament system and offered the sacrifice of a contrite heart. Instead of David being killed in the way the Law prescribed, God showed him mercy. But we also see the Old Covenant punishment for sin in how the child that was born to Bathsheba was killed in judgment. We don't see that kind of judgment under the New Covenant. God has always desired to relate to us by grace, but He couldn't under the Old Covenant, because of humanity's hardness of heart. Fortunately, the debt of sin has been paid now, and God is free to be just and merciful.

    13a. True or false: Under the Old Covenant, only those who understood God's grace nature and operated in it had mercy.
(True)

    13b. Read Psalm 51:16. What did David understand that God really wanted?
(A contrite heart)

    13c. God has always desired to relate to us by what?
(Grace)

14. Jesus coming to this earth made a pivotal difference in the way God deals with mankind. Without the sacrifice of Jesus, humanity would still be living under God's wrath against sin. Instead, God poured out all of His wrath against sin on Jesus (John 12:32). God isn't judging our sin now, because the judgment for all sin, for all time, was put on Jesus.

> *Who his own self bare our sins in his own body on the tree, that we, being dead to sins, should live unto righteousness: by whose stripes ye were healed.*
>
> 1 PETER 2:24

LESSON 7 — IS GOD ANGRY WITH ME?

Of course that doesn't mean we are free to go live however we want. Sin has negative consequences that are purely natural, and it gives Satan an inroad into our individual lives—and into our society (Rom. 6:16). When our societies promote ungodly principles and make morality a completely private issue, then it gives Satan an opportunity to destroy nations (Prov. 14:34). Society cannot continue to seek the immorality it promotes and succeed in the long run, but the consequences of sin are not a punishment from God.

14a. Without the sacrifice of Jesus, what would man still be living under?
(God's wrath against sin)

14b. What was put on Jesus?
(The judgment for all sin, for all time)

14c. Why doesn't that mean you are free to live however you want?
(Because sin has negative consequences that are purely natural, and it gives Satan an inroad into our individual lives—and into our society)

14d. Discussion Question: Read Proverbs 14:34. Why can't society continue to seek the immorality it promotes and succeed in the long run?
(Discussion question)

LESSON 7 — Is God Angry with Me?

DISCIPLESHIP QUESTIONS

1. Why are many people frustrated and confused about God?

2. Discussion Question: How do you know that God is not the harsh and angry God who is eager to judge you for the wrong you've done?

3. True or false: God has changed the way He relates to mankind because of the transformation in society.

4. Read John 8:1-5. Why did the Jews think they had Jesus trapped?

SCRIPTURES TO USE WITH QUESTIONS

ISAIAH 5:20
Woe unto them that call evil good, and good evil; that put darkness for light, and light for darkness; that put bitter for sweet, and sweet for bitter!

JOHN 8:1-5
Jesus went unto the mount of Olives. [2] And early in the morning he came again into the temple, and all the people came unto him; and he sat down, and taught them. [3] And the scribes and Pharisees brought unto him a woman taken in adultery; and when they had set her in the midst, [4] They say unto him, Master, this woman was taken in adultery, in the very act. [5] Now Moses in the law commanded us, that such should be stoned: but what sayest thou?

LEVITICUS 20:10
And the man that committeth adultery with another man's wife, even he that committeth adultery with his neighbour's wife, the adulterer and the adulteress shall surely be put to death.

DEUTERONOMY 22:22
If a man be found lying with a woman married to an husband, then they shall both of them die, both the man that lay with the woman, and the woman: so shalt thou put away evil from Israel.

MATTHEW 9:11
And when the Pharisees saw it, they said unto his disciples, Why eateth your Master with publicans and sinners?

MARK 2:16
And when the scribes and Pharisees saw him eat with publicans and sinners, they said unto his disciples, How is it that he eateth and drinketh with publicans and sinners?

Lesson 7 — Is God Angry with Me?

DISCIPLESHIP QUESTIONS

5. According to John 8:7, what did Jesus say?

6. After everyone left but Jesus and the woman, what did Jesus do?
   - A. He picked up a stone to exact justice on the woman
   - B. He endorsed the woman's sin
   - C. He told the woman to go get her husband and come back
   - D. He denied that the woman had even sinned
   - E. He admitted that the woman had sinned, but He showed mercy

7. Who held people accountable for sin in the Old Testament?
   - A. Moses
   - B. The priests
   - C. God
   - D. A. and C.
   - E. All of the above

SCRIPTURES TO USE WITH QUESTIONS

LUKE 15:2
And the Pharisees and scribes murmured, saying, This man receiveth sinners, and eateth with them.

MATTHEW 10:3
Philip, and Bartholomew; Thomas, and Matthew the publican; James the son of Alphaeus, and Lebbaeus, whose surname was Thaddaeus.

LUKE 8:2
And certain women, which had been healed of evil spirits and infirmities, Mary called Magdalene, out of whom went seven devils.

JOHN 8:7
So when they continued asking him, he lifted up himself, and said unto them, He that is without sin among you, let him first cast a stone at her.

JOHN 8:10-11
When Jesus had lifted up himself, and saw none but the woman, he said unto her, Woman, where are those thine accusers? hath no man condemned thee? [11] *She said, No man, Lord. And Jesus said unto her, Neither do I condemn thee: go, and sin no more.*

NUMBERS 15:32-36
And while the children of Israel were in the wilderness, they found a man that gathered sticks upon the sabbath day. [33] *And they that found him gathering sticks brought him unto Moses and Aaron, and unto all the congregation.* [34] *And they put him in ward, because it was not declared what should be done to him.* [35] *And the L*ORD *said unto Moses, The man shall be surely put to death: all the congregation shall stone him with stones without the camp.* [36] *And all the congregation brought him without the camp, and stoned him with stones, and he died; as the L*ORD *commanded Moses.*

Lesson 7 — Is God Angry with Me?

DISCIPLESHIP QUESTIONS

8. Read 2 Corinthians 5:17 and Hebrews 8:12-13. Why can God deal with us differently than He could deal with people under the Old Covenant?

9. What is a helpful illustration to consider?

10. Why?

SCRIPTURES TO USE WITH QUESTIONS

2 CORINTHIANS 5:16-19
Wherefore henceforth know we no man after the flesh: yea, though we have known Christ after the flesh, yet now henceforth know we him no more. [17] Therefore if any man be in Christ, he is a new creature: old things are passed away; behold, all things are become new. [18] And all things are of God, who hath reconciled us to himself by Jesus Christ, and hath given to us the ministry of reconciliation; [19] To wit, that God was in Christ, reconciling the world unto himself, not imputing their trespasses unto them; and hath committed unto us the word of reconciliation.

2 CORINTHIANS 5:17 (AMPLIFIED BIBLE)
Therefore if any person is [ingrafted] in Christ (the Messiah) he is a new creation (a new creature altogether); the old [previous moral and spiritual condition] has passed away. Behold, the fresh and new has come!

HEBREWS 8:12-13
For I will be merciful to their unrighteousness, and their sins and their iniquities will I remember no more. [13] In that he saith, A new covenant, he hath made the first old. Now that which decayeth and waxeth old is ready to vanish away.

PROVERBS 29:15
The rod and reproof give wisdom: but a child left to himself bringeth his mother to shame.

JAMES 4:7
Submit yourselves therefore to God. Resist the devil, and he will flee from you.

LESSON 7 — Is God Angry with Me?

DISCIPLESHIP QUESTIONS

11. Read Galatians 3:23-25. What did God use the Law for?

12. Salvation is by grace through faith in _____.

13. Read Hebrews 1:3. Jesus is the exact representation of whom?
    A. God
    B. The Law
    C. The prophets
    D. All of the above
    E. None of the above

14. According to Hebrews 2:3, the Lord was first to speak of what?

SCRIPTURES TO USE WITH QUESTIONS

GALATIANS 3:23-25
But before faith came, we were kept under the law, shut up unto the faith which should afterwards be revealed. [24] Wherefore the law was our schoolmaster to bring us unto Christ, that we might be justified by faith. [25] But after that faith is come, we are no longer under a schoolmaster.

ROMANS 6:14
For sin shall not have dominion over you: for ye are not under the law, but under grace.

EPHESIANS 2:8
For by grace are ye saved through faith; and that not of yourselves: it is the gift of God.

HEBREWS 1:3
Who being the brightness of his glory, and the express image of his person, and upholding all things by the word of his power, when he had by himself purged our sins, sat down on the right hand of the Majesty on high.

HEBREWS 2:3
How shall we escape, if we neglect so great salvation; which at the first began to be spoken by the Lord, and was confirmed unto us by them that heard him.

LESSON 7 — Is God Angry with Me?

DISCIPLESHIP QUESTIONS

15. Discussion Question: How do 2 Kings 1 and Luke 9 speak of the difference between the Old Covenant and the New Covenant?

16. True or false: The Law was given through Moses approximately 2,000 years after the fall of Adam and Eve.

17. True or false: God's lack of punishment is an indication that He doesn't care whether you live a holy life or not.

18. Why did God extend grace toward the first murderer, Cain, but pronounce judgment on the first person to violate the Law?
    A. Because God has favorites and liked Cain better
    B. Because God changes what He's like sometimes
    C. Because Cain's act of murder was before the Law
    D. Because the Law held people accountable for sin
    E. C. and D.

19. What effect(s) did the Law have on people?
    A. It made people turn away from sin
    B. It made people feel guilty
    C. It made people feel unworthy
    D. All of the above
    E. None of the above

20. The sacrifice of Jesus brought a return to what?

21. Why does Andrew believe that if Jesus had been on earth in His physical body when Elijah was calling fire down out of heaven, He would have rebuked Elijah?

SCRIPTURES TO USE WITH QUESTIONS

2 KINGS 1:3-4
But the angel of the LORD said to Elijah the Tishbite, Arise, go up to meet the messengers of the king of Samaria, and say unto them, Is it not because there is not a God in Israel, that ye go to enquire of Baalzebub the god of Ekron? [4] Now therefore thus saith the LORD, Thou shalt not come down from that bed on which thou art gone up, but shalt surely die. And Elijah departed.

2 KINGS 1:10
And Elijah answered and said to the captain of fifty, If I be a man of God, then let fire come down from heaven, and consume thee and thy fifty. And there came down fire from heaven, and consumed him and his fifty.

LUKE 9:51-56
And it came to pass, when the time was come that he should be received up, he stedfastly set his face to go to Jerusalem, [52] And sent messengers before his face: and they went, and entered into a village of the Samaritans, to make ready for him. [53] And they did not receive him, because his face was as though he would go to Jerusalem. [54] And when his disciples James and John saw this, they said, Lord, wilt thou that we command fire to come down from heaven, and consume them, even as Elias did? [55] But he turned, and rebuked them, and said, Ye know not what manner of spirit ye are of. [56] For the Son of man is not come to destroy men's lives, but to save them. And they went to another village.

ROMANS 5:13
For until the law sin was in the world: but sin is not imputed when there is no law.

LESSON 7 — Is God Angry with Me?

DISCIPLESHIP QUESTIONS

22. In the Old Covenant, what was God's judgment against evil?
    A. A blessing in disguise
    B. God's way of humbling those who sinned
    C. What the people wanted
    D. Mercy to the rest of God's people
    E. God's ultimate plan for mankind

23. Today what do you do to people who are caught up in sin?

24. What should this difference help you understand?

25. Why doesn't this reflect some kind of conversion in God?

26. Who and what have changed?

SCRIPTURES TO USE WITH QUESTIONS

JOSHUA 6:17-21
*And the city shall be accursed, even it, and all that are therein, to the L*ORD*: only Rahab the harlot shall live, she and all that are with her in the house, because she hid the messengers that we sent.* **[18]** *And ye, in any wise keep yourselves from the accursed thing, lest ye make yourselves accursed, when ye take of the accursed thing, and make the camp of Israel a curse, and trouble it.* **[19]** *But all the silver, and gold, and vessels of brass and iron, are consecrated unto the L*ORD*: they shall come into the treasury of the L*ORD*.* **[20]** *So the people shouted when the priests blew with the trumpets: and it came to pass, when the people heard the sound of the trumpet, and the people shouted with a great shout, that the wall fell down flat, so that the people went up into the city, every man straight before him, and they took the city.* **[21]** *And they utterly destroyed all that was in the city, both man and woman, young and old, and ox, and sheep, and ass, with the edge of the sword.*

JOSHUA 10:40
*So Joshua smote all the country of the hills, and of the south, and of the vale, and of the springs, and all their kings: he left none remaining, but utterly destroyed all that breathed, as the L*ORD *God of Israel commanded.*

Lesson 7 — Is God Angry with Me?

DISCIPLESHIP QUESTIONS

27. Read 2 Corinthians 5:16. How do you relate to Christ?

28. Read 2 Corinthians 5:17. When you are in Christ, _____ things have passed away and _____ things have become new.

29. True or false: When you're born again, what changes?
    A. Your IQ
    B. Your body
    C. Your personality
    D. Your spirit
    E. Nothing

30. DISCIPLESHIP QUESTION: Why is it important to know what changed?

31. Your spirit is where what is perfect?

32. DISCIPLESHIP QUESTION: Read 2 Corinthians 5:18-19. What does the phrase **"reconciling the world unto himself"** mean to you?

33. DISCIPLESHIP QUESTION: What does **"not imputing their trespasses unto them"** mean to you?

SCRIPTURES TO USE WITH QUESTIONS

2 CORINTHIANS 5:16-19
Wherefore henceforth know we no man after the flesh: yea, though we have known Christ after the flesh, yet now henceforth know we him no more. [17] Therefore if any man be in Christ, he is a new creature: old things are passed away; behold, all things are become new. [18] And all things are of God, who hath reconciled us to himself by Jesus Christ, and hath given to us the ministry of reconciliation; [19] To wit, that God was in Christ, reconciling the world unto himself, not imputing their trespasses unto them; and hath committed unto us the word of reconciliation.

JOSHUA 11:11-14
And they smote all the souls that were therein with the edge of the sword, utterly destroying them: there was not any left to breathe: and he burnt Hazor with fire. [12] And all the cities of those kings, and all the kings of them, did Joshua take, and smote them with the edge of the sword, and he utterly destroyed them, as Moses the servant of the LORD commanded. [13] But as for the cities that stood still in their strength, Israel burned none of them, save Hazor only; that did Joshua burn. [14] And all the spoil of these cities, and the cattle, the children of Israel took for a prey unto themselves; but every man they smote with the edge of the sword, until they had destroyed them, neither left they any to breathe.

Lesson 7 — Is God Angry with Me?

DISCIPLESHIP QUESTIONS

34. God went ahead and paid the _____ for you—a balance that was _____ for you to settle—so that He could _____ a close relationship with you.

35. True or false: God didn't pretend that sin never happened.

36. Why?

37. Because God loves you and desires relationship with you, what did He decide to do?
    A. Make the angels pay
    B. Restart creation
    C. Pay for sin Himself
    D. All of the above
    E. None of the above

SCRIPTURES TO USE WITH QUESTIONS

DEUTERONOMY 21:18-21
If a man have a stubborn and rebellious son, which will not obey the voice of his father, or the voice of his mother, and that, when they have chastened him, will not hearken unto them: **[19]** *Then shall his father and his mother lay hold on him, and bring him out unto the elders of his city, and unto the gate of his place;* **[20]** *And they shall say unto the elders of his city, This our son is stubborn and rebellious, he will not obey our voice; he is a glutton, and a drunkard.* **[21]** *And all the men of his city shall stone him with stones, that he die: so shalt thou put evil away from among you; and all Israel shall hear, and fear.*

HEBREWS 8:6
But now hath he obtained a more excellent ministry, by how much also he is the mediator of a better covenant, which was established upon better promises.

HEBREWS 8:13
In that he saith, A new covenant, he hath made the first old. Now that which decayeth and waxeth old is ready to vanish away.

MALACHI 3:6
*For I am the L*ORD*, I change not; therefore ye sons of Jacob are not consumed.*

HEBREWS 13:8 (NEW KING JAMES VERSION)
Jesus Christ is the same yesterday, today, and forever.

1 CORINTHIANS 13:12
For now we see through a glass, darkly; but then face to face: now I know in part; but then shall I know even as also I am known.

Lesson 7 — Is God Angry with Me?

DISCIPLESHIP QUESTIONS

38. Read 2 Corinthians 5:21. He made Jesus, who never sinned, _____ sin for you, and He took the sin of the entire human race.

39. Read 1 John 2:2. True or false: Jesus died for a select number of people who would later accept Him.

40. Since Jesus paid for the sins of the whole world, why isn't everyone saved?

41. What happens once you truly understand the significance of Jesus' sacrifice?

42. True or false: Under the Old Covenant, only those who understood God's grace nature and operated in it had mercy.

43. Read Psalm 51:16. What did David understand that God really wanted?

44. God has always desired to relate to us by what?

45. Without the sacrifice of Jesus, what would man still be living under?

SCRIPTURES TO USE WITH QUESTIONS

2 CORINTHIANS 5:21
For he hath made him to be sin for us, who knew no sin; that we might be made the righteousness of God in him.

ROMANS 6:23
For the wages of sin is death; but the gift of God is eternal life through Jesus Christ our Lord.

1 JOHN 2:2
And he is the propitiation for our sins: and not for ours only, but also for the sins of the whole world.

ROMANS 10:9
That if thou shalt confess with thy mouth the Lord Jesus, and shalt believe in thine heart that God hath raised him from the dead, thou shalt be saved.

PSALM 51:4
Against thee, thee only, have I sinned, and done this evil in thy sight: that thou mightest be justified when thou speakest, and be clear when thou judgest.

PSALM 51:16
For thou desirest not sacrifice; else would I give it: thou delightest not in burnt offering.

JOHN 12:32
And I, if I be lifted up from the earth, will draw all men unto me.

1 PETER 2:24
Who his own self bare our sins in his own body on the tree, that we, being dead to sins, should live unto righteousness: by whose stripes ye were healed.

LESSON 7 — Is God Angry with Me?

DISCIPLESHIP QUESTIONS

46. What was put on Jesus?

47. Why doesn't that mean you are free to live however you want?

48. Discussion Question: Read Proverbs 14:34. Why can't society continue to seek the immorality it promotes and succeed in the long run?

SCRIPTURES TO USE WITH QUESTIONS

ROMANS 6:16
Know ye not, that to whom ye yield yourselves servants to obey, his servants ye are to whom ye obey; whether of sin unto death, or of obedience unto righteousness?

PROVERBS 14:34
Righteousness exalteth a nation: but sin is a reproach to any people.

Lesson 7 — Is God Angry with Me?

ANSWER KEY

1. Because He's being represented in so many contrasting ways by so many different groups in society

2. *Discussion question*

3. False

4. Because if Jesus demonstrated mercy and let the woman go, then He Himself would be subject to stoning for failing to enforce the Law of Moses. Yet if He followed the Law and condemned the woman to death, then He would be going against the message of mercy He had been teaching, and the people would think He was a hypocrite

5. **"He that is without sin among you, let him first cast a stone at her"**

6. E. He admitted that the woman had sinned, but He showed mercy

7. C. God

8. Because after putting our faith in Jesus, we've become new creatures

9. How you change the way you relate to your own children as they mature: you use physical restraint for a short period of time

10. Because until they grow up, you can't teach your children by instruction

11. A training tool to guide His children until they could be saved by faith

12. Jesus

13. A. God

14. So great salvation

15. *Discussion question*

16. True

17. False

18. E. C. and D.

19. D. All of the above

20. Grace

21. Because if Jesus had been on the earth in His physical body when Elijah was calling fire down out of heaven, Elijah wouldn't have been under the Law

22. D. Mercy to the rest of God's people

23. Minister the love of God to them and share the Good News about Jesus Christ

24. The harshness of the Old Testament and why you now have a better covenant through Jesus

25. Because Malachi 3:6a and Hebrews 13:8 say that God never changes

26. You have and the way God relates to you has changed

27. Through the Holy Spirit

28. Old/all

29. D. Your spirit

30. *Discussion question*

31. Everything

32. *Discussion question*

33. *Discussion question*

34. Debt/impossible/reestablish

35. True

36. Because of His pure, holy, and righteous nature

37. C. Pay for sin Himself

38. Become

39. False

40. Because they have to humble themselves and make Jesus their Lord (Rom. 10:9) so that what He did for them is credited to their account

ANSWER KEY

41. Then you can understand why God dealt with people differently under the New Covenant than He did under the Old Covenant

42. True

43. A contrite heart

44. Grace

45. God's wrath against sin

46. The judgment for all sin, for all time

47. Because sin has negative consequences that are purely natural, and it gives Satan an inroad into our individual lives—and into our society

48. *Discussion question*

What about Suffering?

Certain Bible verses dealing with suffering have frequently been misinterpreted and are sometimes used to suggest that God uses suffering to teach us a lesson or to help us grow spiritually. I believe that those interpretations are harmful and that they cause people to have a wrong understanding of God's true nature. One of the frequently misinterpreted passages of Scripture says,

My brethren, count it all joy when ye fall into divers temptations; Knowing this, that the trying of your faith worketh patience. But let patience have her perfect work, that ye may be perfect and entire, wanting nothing.

JAMES 1:2-4

These verses have been used by many to imply that praying for patience means that God will put trials and temptations in our way in order to teach us patience. We've all heard someone say, "Be careful what you pray for," as if problems are actually the work of God intended to bring us to maturity. The church I grew up in talked about problems as "heavenly sandpaper" that rubbed off all of our rough edges and made us better people.

Let me make an obvious statement: If suffering and problems are what make you a better person, then the people who have suffered the most should be the holiest, godliest people on earth—but that isn't the case. In fact, the opposite is usually true. The people who have suffered the most are often bitter, angry people whose lives are a mess. It simply is not an observable truth to say that suffering produces holiness.

On the other hand, it is true to say that when you respond to hardship by trusting in God, then it brings to the surface things that God has placed on the inside of you. As you depend on God's strength, then you become stronger in your faith—but the hardships aren't what make you better. What makes you stronger is exercising your faith in God and trusting in Him. It's the improvement of your relationship with God that comes from seeking Him, so hardship might cause you to seek God, but suffering doesn't make you a better person.

The Vietnam War was a trying situation for my faith, and I came out of it much stronger than when I went in—but God didn't organize the war to make me holy. God didn't have people criticize me for my stance on Christianity or put me in a bunker that was wallpapered with pictures of nude women. The Lord didn't do those things to make me stronger, but I did become stronger through those trials because I kept my faith and trust in God.

LESSON 8 — WHAT ABOUT SUFFERING?

When I was drafted into the Army, they taught me how to fire a rifle, how to throw grenades, plant mines, and defend myself in hand-to-hand combat. The Army spent six months training me to fight in a war, and then they sent me to Vietnam. But training and information are not equal to experience. After I had been in Vietnam for a short period of time, I learned to be wary of new recruits who had just arrived in country, because they were dangerous. Officers were particularly dangerous because they could arrive straight from school—with no combat experience—and start ordering people around.

I remember being on bunker guard one night with a brand-new guy and a bunch of other soldiers who had been in Vietnam for a while. We were sitting around eating our C-rations, and the new guy said, "Can I throw a hand grenade? Can I fire my rifle?" On the fire-support base I was at, we did those things all the time. It was a normal part of pulling bunker guard. We would just randomly fire outside the perimeter to deter the enemy from sneaking up on us. The new guy was all excited to blow some stuff up, so we told him to go ahead. He pulled the pin on a grenade, and as he did, the grenade came out of his hand and bounced down between my feet. The way we all scattered, you'd have thought the grenade exploded, but it didn't. Luckily, it was a new style of grenade with an extra safety on it. The point is that the new guy was dangerous because he had knowledge but lacked experience.

Becoming a good soldier involves putting into practice all of the things you learn through training, so you do become a better soldier after you have engaged in combat. You learn things through experience that you can't learn from a book. But it would be insane to embrace the enemy when they attack you, as if their purpose is to make you a better soldier. The enemy isn't there to make you better—they're there to kill you. Only by resisting the enemy and overcoming them will you live through the attack and become a better soldier.

Likewise, God doesn't send problems into your life to make you a better person—the Enemy tries to create problems in order to cause suffering. It would be crazy to embrace trials and tribulations as if they are a good thing. Afflictions and persecutions come to steal the Word of God out of your heart (Mark 4:17). They come to discourage you and to undermine your faith. Sickness comes to defeat you. Financial problems come to cause anxiety and to limit what you can do for the kingdom of God. To embrace those problems as if they are sent by God to make you a better person is crazy. But if, through faith, you continue to trust in God's promises and resist the Enemy, then you will overcome the challenges and prosper in spite of them.

Going through hardship and using your faith in God are going to make you a stronger Christian on the other side, but I am not encouraging anybody to accept hardship as a blessing from God. Hardship is not a blessing. It's a curse from the Enemy. You are only made stronger through hardship by resisting it and standing in faith.

> *Let no man say when he is tempted, I am tempted of God: for God cannot be tempted with evil, neither tempteth he any man: But every man is tempted, when he is drawn away of his own lust, and enticed.*
> JAMES 1:13-14

Scripture couldn't be any clearer in saying that suffering and temptation are not from God, yet many religious traditions continue to blame God. The foundation of this teaching on Christian philosophy is the Apostle Paul's warning for us not to be spoiled through philosophy (Col. 2:8). This teaching that God sends hardships to make us better is a religious tradition that has spoiled untold numbers of Christians. They believe that God is orchestrating the problems in their lives and using suffering for some redemptive purpose. That attitude will make us passive because it takes away our desire to resist problems.

If it was God's will for you to have cancer, why would you go to the doctor and try to get out of His will? If God wants you to be sick, why would you fight against Him by trying to get better? The more sincere your desire to please God, the more likely you are to give up in the face of hardship, if you believe that God is behind your problems. Believing that God will send problems into your life is a false teaching that will keep you from having a positive relationship with Him. It's impossible to really trust someone and have a healthy relationship with them if you are constantly wondering whether they might hurt you—even if they are supposedly doing it for your own good.

What would you think of me if I was personally responsible for every baby born with a deformity or disability? How much would you like me if you knew that I was responsible for every death, disease, hardship, and tragedy in the world? Would you want to be my friend or spend any time with me? Who in their right mind would want to get close to me if having a relationship with me might mean that I would "bless" you with some incurable disease or kill the people you love most? I can guarantee you that if I was guilty of all the things people are blaming God for, society would lock me up and throw away the key.

Just as Satan convinced Adam and Eve that the Lord wasn't all good but that He had withheld His best from them, so religion (which is the devil's creation) has put forth the lie that the Lord is responsible for all the bad things in our lives. That just isn't so.

Many people have misunderstood the true nature of God, and they are proclaiming that nothing happens without God's permission. Therefore, they say, He must be responsible for all of the suffering in our world. Then they try to defend their position by saying that God is sending the evil for our own good. It's a total misrepresentation of who God is and how He relates to us.

I know a number of people who are running from God because they think He is responsible for the evil in the world. One of their main arguments is, "How could a good God allow all of this to happen?" But God is not the source of the suffering in our world. God does not tempt us with hardship, there is no shadow of evil in Him, and He only blesses us with good things.

> *Do not err, my beloved brethren. Every good gift and every perfect gift is from above, and cometh down from the Father of lights, with whom is no variableness, neither shadow of turning.*
> JAMES 1:16-17

"Do not err" is another way of saying, "Unless you believe what I'm saying, you're wrong." The simplest Christian philosophy you can have is that if something is good, then it's from God, and if it's bad, then it's from the devil. Only good and perfect gifts come down from the heavenly Father—sickness, hardship, and suffering are not good and perfect gifts.

The goodness of God has to be the trump card against all arguments and circumstances in your life. No matter what is going on, you have to know absolutely that God is a good God. The moment someone starts trying to tell you that God gave you a sickness or put hardship in your life, the absolute certainty of God's goodness should rise up within you and immediately reject what they are saying.

LESSON 8 — WHAT ABOUT SUFFERING?

Unfortunately, a lot of religious teaching portrays God in a very bad light. They are trying to say that God is dangling people over hell by a thin thread—that He is angry with you and out to get you. I've even heard people say that if you don't tithe, God is going to punish you by taking the money from you in doctors' bills. Other preachers say that if you leave their church, you are departing from God's will, and the wrath of God will descend on you by destroying your family, by you contracting some disease, or by you having some other tragedy. A lot of those teachers are trying to drive people to God through fear of punishment, but Scripture says it is the goodness of God that leads people to repentance (Rom. 2:4). They should be telling people about the extravagant goodness of God, not threatening them.

God doesn't send problems into your life, but if you believe He does, then it is going to be hard for you to believe that He is truly good. It is easy to say God is a good God in theory, but if you don't really believe it, then your relationship is going to be hindered. Every time someone you love becomes ill or tragedy strikes, it is going to chip away at your resolve that God only wants good things for you. Look at this passage of Scripture:

> *But after that the kindness and love of God our Saviour toward man appeared, Not by works of righteousness which we have done, but according to his mercy he saved us, by the washing of regeneration, and renewing of the Holy Ghost; Which he shed on us abundantly through Jesus Christ our Saviour.*
> TITUS 3:4-6

God's kindness and love toward you have nothing to do with any righteousness on your part. Too many people are preaching that you have to earn God's favor and that He is only good toward you when you deserve it, but that isn't true. If you think you have to earn God's love, then you will never believe that God is good, because your conscience will always condemn you. It doesn't matter how holy you live, you are always going to fall short of God's standard of holiness, which will leave you feeling separated from God. Your righteousness comes from God, so if you are depending on your own righteousness to make you feel worthy of God's love, then you are never going to feel worthy.

The summer before Oral Roberts died, I was privileged to have the opportunity to meet with him in his home. While I was there, people were asking him questions about all of the things God had done in his life. Oral's response was that he didn't understand how or why God had used him. He said that there was nothing special about him, except that God had touched his life. The same thing is true of every Christian.

When I look at all of the things God has done for me, I am overwhelmed by His goodness. God has sought after me more than I have searched for Him. My life could have turned out a lot differently than it has if it wasn't for the goodness of God. For instance, one of my sons was dead for five hours. My wife, Jamie, and I prayed that God would raise him from the dead, and out of His mercy and love, God did raise him back to life, but it wasn't because of anything I deserved. I have a granddaughter that I wouldn't have had if it wasn't for the goodness of God.

My father died when I was twelve years old—and he was only fifty-four at the time. I don't believe it was God's will for him to die. I have never believed that God took my father, even though my pastor told me that he died because God needed him in heaven. It wasn't God's fault that my father died, but God was with me, and He blessed me through the ordeal. I remember the Sunday morning our pastor came to our house to talk to my brother and me about our father's death. Immediately, a supernatural peace of God came over me, and the Lord brought to my remembrance a scripture from Psalm 27: **"When my**

LESSON 8 — WHAT ABOUT SUFFERING?

father and my mother forsake me, then the LORD will take me up" (verse 10). From that moment on, God took me up. He became my Father and my best friend. Even though it wasn't God's will for my father to die, I can look back and see the goodness of God blessing me through that experience.

So many aspects of my life have been affected by the goodness of God. I believe that we can all look back on our lives and see how God worked to bless us, despite the tragedy we may have endured. I remember the Holy Spirit giving me supernatural knowledge about a woman at one of my meetings who had suffered a history of abuse. Terrible things had been done to her, but God had saved her life. He delivered her from the hands of the abusers whose plan was to kill her. Through the gifts of the Holy Spirit, I began to help her see that God had blessed her. She had a husband and a wonderful family, and God had been good to her. She went from being focused on the horrors of the abuse to seeing how God had intervened in her life with mercy and love. In the same way, each one of us can see the goodness of God in our lives, even if we have suffered tragedy.

> *And we know that all things work together for good to them that love God, to them who are the called according to his purpose.*
>
> ROMANS 8:28

Most people have heard this scripture used as a blanket statement to convey that whatever happens must be God's will—that God works all things together for good, so there must be some purpose behind the tragedies in our lives. But just because God can bring good out of tragedy doesn't mean He caused the tragedy or wants us to endure suffering. It's true that exercising our faith through trials causes us to emerge stronger on the other side, but this verse does not say that God causes everything that happens in our lives.

God works all things together for good, but He doesn't cause all things—and things don't work together for good for every person. It's pretty obvious when you look around that not everything that happens ultimately works out for good. Some people have tragic lives that end in bitterness, anger, and destitution. A life of destructive choices often adds up to a disastrous ending, so there are some qualifications on exactly how **"all things work together for good."**

This scripture doesn't say that all things end well for all people; it says that things work together for good for **"them that love God."** That single qualification dramatically limits the number of people this scripture applies to, because the majority of people do not love God.

I can remember being at a Full Gospel Business Men's meeting a long time ago when the speaker used this scripture to talk about God working everything together for good. He had just come from conducting the funeral of a teenage boy and girl who died in a vehicle accident. They had been drinking and were speeding down the roadway in a rainstorm. The car went into a turn too fast, the driver lost control, and they crashed into a telephone pole—killing both of them. Neither of them were known to be Christian, so as far as we know, they didn't go straight to the arms of Jesus—they went to eternal punishment. Clearly, there was nothing good about the accident, and if they did end up in hell, then zero redemptive value came out of it.

Yet this minister used Romans 8:28 to say that God had a purpose in this tragedy, and it was working together for good. That's not right. God didn't do this. I'm sure the Lord convicted these teenagers that

Lesson 8 — What about Suffering?

what they were doing was wrong, and He tried to sway them from that path. But God doesn't control us like pawns. We have free will, and He won't force us to make the right choices.

It should be clear that good doesn't come out of every situation for every person. If you don't love God, then things aren't necessarily going to work together for good. The reason I'm stressing this point is because if you believe that God controls every single thing that happens, then you are going to get the impression that God isn't a good God. If you think that God caused those two kids to get drunk and drive too fast on a wet road, and killed them and sent them to hell, then you aren't going to believe God is a good God.

Some people can see that God doesn't cause suffering, but they think that He "allows" it to happen, but Scripture says that God reveals Himself **"against all ungodliness and unrighteousness of men"** (Rom. 1:18). In the case of the two teenagers who died in the car accident, I believe that God gave them an intuitive knowledge of right and wrong and convicted them that what they were doing was wrong. I believe that God spoke to them hundreds of times before they crashed the car and died—not just on the night of the accident, but in all the years leading up to it. God didn't "allow" the accident to happen in the sense that He didn't intervene in any way to stop it. It's more like there was a mountain of obstacles that God put in their way, but they persisted and climbed over all of the things God was doing to save them.

Don't we all want the best for our children? Scripture says that if we—being the imperfect and sinful people that we are—can wish good for our children, then how much more will our heavenly Father do good for us when we ask Him (Matt. 7:9-11). Anyone who goes to hell has to ignore the thousands and thousands of times God has tried to convict them and draw them into His love. Going to hell isn't a one-time decision; it is the result of rejecting God countless times. Our God is a good God, and He desires good things for us—even more than we desire good for our children.

Not only does the scripture in the book of Romans say that things work together for good for those who love God; it also says for **"them who are the called according to his purpose"** (Rom. 8:28). God's purposes are redemptive. The Bible says that Jesus came to earth to destroy the works of the devil (1 John 3:8), so to be called according to His purpose means that you are resisting the works of the devil (James 4:7). If you are rebelling against God and chasing sin, then the tragedy that occurs in your life is not necessarily going to work together for good.

Another qualification on this scripture appears in the verses before Romans 8:28. The scripture begins, **"And we know that all things work together for good."** *And* is a conjunction linking the statement about good to the previous sentences, which talk about the Holy Spirit making intercession through you (Rom. 8:26-27). The Holy Spirit doesn't pray without you, but when you start to pray, the Holy Spirit comes alongside you and pleads your cause. When you have that kind of Spirit-led intercession working in your life, then things are going to work together for good.

Those are three major qualifications on things working together for good: You have to love God, you have to be resisting the works of the devil, and you have to pray—allowing the Holy Spirit to help you make intercession. Scripture does not say that God is orchestrating everything that happens in your life, and if you aren't trying to meet those three qualifications, then everything isn't necessarily going to work together for good.

Lesson 8 — What about Suffering?

God is not the cause of all the evil in the world. He isn't killing people because He loves them so much. He is a good God. His plans for your life are peace and victory (Jer. 29:11), but God's will doesn't come to pass automatically; you have to cooperate with Him. Once you believe that God is only good, your faith will abound, and you will see better results in your life. You can cooperate with God, and all things *will* work together for good.

A lot of negative things happen in life: People we love die, children get sick, jobs are lost, and tragedy strikes when we least expect it. It's easy to look at the circumstances in life and wonder why the all-powerful God doesn't prevent suffering, which can lead you to think that God is responsible for it, but Scripture reveals that God has nothing to do with evil.

When God created the heavens and the earth, everything was perfect. God told Adam not to eat of the Tree of the Knowledge of Good and Evil, because in the day that he did, he would die. Adam rejected God's instructions, and the result was that sin entered creation. Every one of us has leaned unto our own understanding rather than depending on God, and our rebellion is what has released evil on earth. Satan is the cause of suffering. He roams around seeking whom he may devour—he steals, kills, and destroys (1 Pet. 5:8 and John 10:10). God is not the source of the tragedy in our lives!

The Bible is full of proof that God is a good God. The ultimate testimony is that Jesus came to this earth and suffered, not only on the cross, but even just by humbling Himself and taking on human form for thirty-three years. Jesus suffered by being confined to a physical human body when He was God. Solomon said, **"The heaven and heaven of heavens cannot contain thee; how much less this house that I have [built]?"** (1 Kin. 8:27, brackets mine). God is infinite—even the universe can't contain Him—yet He limited Himself to a physical body. He was despised and rejected by men, and He ultimately took the punishment for your sins. If God loved you enough to suffer and die for you, He loves you enough to do anything for you.

> *Let them shout for joy, and be glad, that favour my righteous cause: yea, let them say continually,*
> *Let the LORD be magnified, which hath pleasure in the prosperity of his servant.*
> PSALM 35:27

God is pleased when you prosper. He wants to see you succeed. Nobody is pulling for you more than God is—which might not be what you are used to hearing, but it's the message the Bible teaches. God is love (1 John 4:7-8). God doesn't just love some people or have a little love for all. He *is* love.

> *In this was manifested the love of God toward us, because that God sent his only begotten Son into the world, that we might live through him. Herein is love, not that we loved God, but that he loved us, and sent his Son to be the propitiation for our sins.*
> 1 JOHN 4:9-10

God showed you His love by sending Jesus. I am convinced that if you focus on God sending Jesus to earth, instead of just hearing the words, you will experience the fruit of God's peace and joy. If God's love isn't impacting you or how you feel about life, then take time to be still and meditate on this truth that God showed His love by sending His Son. God's love will be revealed to you by focusing on Jesus coming to earth and becoming the payment for your sin.

LESSON 8   WHAT ABOUT SUFFERING?

Salvation isn't about us loving God first and then, because we initiate relationship with Him, God extends love to us in return. God's loving nature is revealed in that He reached out to us while we were rejecting Him. Christ died for us while we were still living in sin:

> *But God commendeth his love toward us, in that, while we were yet sinners, Christ died for us.*
> ROMANS 5:8

God has already given you His Son—why wouldn't He give you joy, peace, health, and prosperity (Rom. 8:32)? It would be totally inconsistent for me to be willing to die for you but be unwilling to give you some money. God not only has the ability to heal and prosper you; *He desires to do it*. Faith works by love, and if you trust and believe in God's love—by focusing on what He has already done for you—your faith will rise.

Jesus didn't have to suffer death on a cross; He chose to. He could have called down an army of angels (Matt. 26:53), but He humbly submitted to a humiliating death instead. Jesus allowed the scribes and Pharisees to mock Him. They spit in His face, slapped Him, insulted Him, beat Him, and finally killed Him. Jesus took all of that because He loved us and wanted to save us.

The life, death, and resurrection of Jesus were a physical manifestation of God's love pursuing us, and when Jesus ascended into heaven, He gave us the Holy Spirit to continue His ministry on earth until He returns. The Holy Spirit is our Teacher and Helper. He leads us into all truth, and He is the eyes of the Lord that search the whole earth seeking to show Himself strong on behalf of those who love God (2 Chr. 16:9).

The Lord is looking for you. He isn't hiding from you. You don't have to pursue Him; you just need to slow down and unplug from the distractions of the world for a little bit. You can't make a connection with God in the three minutes between your two favorite television shows. You need to find time to be still and know God (Ps. 46:10)—not just physical stillness, but stillness in your mind, which just means not being completely occupied with other thoughts. God wants to reveal His love for you more than you desire to know it, but He isn't going to force His way into your life. You have to take time and give God the opportunity to show you His love.

> *Behold, I stand at the door, and knock: if any man hear my voice, and open the door, I will come in to him, and will sup with him, and he with me.*
> REVELATION 3:20

This verse has been used to talk about being born again—which isn't wrong—but this letter was written to Christians. Jesus was saying this to people who were already born again. He is asking if you will let Him into your life. Will you give Him your attention? Will you unplug from the distractions of life that keep you from hearing the voice of God, and simply focus on His voice? The results of knowing God's love are tremendous. Knowing His love is worth sacrificing a little entertainment in front of the television to sit quietly in the presence of the Lord.

I can't tell you how many people come to me in fear of the circumstances in their lives. They are fearful over the future, the economy, kids, relationships, health, and all kinds of other things. A lot of people today are living in fear, but God's love will push the fear out of your life. Scripture says there is no fear in love (1 John 4:18). When you spend time in the presence of God, the experience of His love kills your fears. It is impossible for fear to thrive where God's love dwells.

During the Vietnam War, I visited a forward fire-support base that was overrun by the enemy just hours after I left. Before I was evacuated by helicopter, I remember seeing the muzzle flashes from the rifle fire of the enemy as they charged up the hill toward our position, but I wasn't afraid. I was worshiping God. I was actually thinking, *Lord, today could be the day I come to meet You!* I had supernatural compassion for the people who were rushing to kill me. I had no fear of dying. All I experienced was love and excitement about the possibility of going to be with the Lord.

Once you know God and understand how good He is, you can become like the Apostle Paul, who said, **"For to me to live is Christ, and to die is gain"** (Phil. 1:21). This is normal Christianity. It sounds a little extreme by the world's standards, but this is the attitude you should have.

The suffering of this life is not worthy of being compared with the glory that will be revealed in us (Rom. 8:18). We have something so awesome prepared for us in the presence of God that we won't give a second thought to the heartache and rejection we experienced in this life. Nobody in heaven is grieving over the things that happened to them during their lives on earth. If we were to really think about this, we wouldn't have any fear of poverty, sickness, or failure. Whatever this world has to throw at us, God has something greater in store.

God has been misrepresented as causing the tragedy in our world, and I believe that is the number one reason people are not seeking relationship with Him. If you think God is causing the problems in your life, then you'll want to keep Him at arm's length—even if you are a Christian. It's a natural response to try to avoid people and situations that might hurt you. But God isn't causing the suffering in the world. In fact, God has nothing to do with it.

God loves you and He desires good things for you, but experiencing the love of God passes mere knowledge about His love (Eph. 3:19). Once you understand how good God is and begin having a real relationship with Him, you open yourself to receiving His love and being filled with all the fullness of God. The blessings of God will come upon you and overtake you, and it will cause everything to work out for good in your life.

Lesson 8 — What about Suffering?

OUTLINE

I. Certain Bible verses dealing with suffering have frequently been misinterpreted and are sometimes used to suggest that God uses suffering to teach us a lesson or to help us grow spiritually.

   A. I believe that those interpretations are harmful and that they cause people to have a wrong understanding of God's true nature.

   B. One of the frequently misinterpreted passages of Scripture says,

   My brethren, count it all joy when ye fall into divers temptations; Knowing this, that the trying of your faith worketh patience. But let patience have her perfect work, that ye may be perfect and entire, wanting nothing.
   JAMES 1:2-4

   C. These verses have been used by many to imply that praying for patience means that God will put trials and temptations in our way in order to teach us patience.

   D. We've all heard someone say, "Be careful what you pray for," as if problems are actually the work of God intended to bring us to maturity.

   E. The church I grew up in talked about problems as "heavenly sandpaper" that rubbed off all of our rough edges and made us better people.

   F. Let me make an obvious statement: If suffering and problems are what make us better people, then the people who have suffered the most should be the holiest, godliest people on earth—but that isn't the case.

   G. In fact, the opposite is usually true—the people who have suffered the most are often bitter, angry people whose lives are a mess.

   H. It simply is not an observable truth to say that suffering produces holiness.

   I. On the other hand, it is true to say that when we respond to hardship by trusting in God, then it brings to the surface things that God has placed on the inside of us.

   J. As we depend on God's strength, then we become stronger in our faith—but the hardships aren't what make us better.

   K. What makes us stronger is exercising our faith in God and trusting in Him.

   L. It's the improvement of our relationship with God that comes from seeking Him, so hardship might cause us to seek God, but suffering doesn't make us better people.

II. The Vietnam War was a trying situation for my faith, and I came out of it much stronger than when I went in—but God didn't organize the war to make me holy.

   A. Becoming a good soldier involves putting into practice all of the things you learn through training, so you do become a better soldier after you have engaged in combat.

   B. You learn things through experience that you can't learn from a book, but it would be insane to embrace the enemy when they attack you, as if their purpose is to make you a better soldier.

   C. The enemy isn't there to make you better—they're there to kill you.

   D. Only by resisting the enemy and overcoming them will you live through the attack and become a better soldier.

   E. Likewise, God doesn't send problems into your life to make you a better person—the Enemy tries to create problems in order to cause suffering.

Lesson 8 — What about Suffering?

- F. Afflictions and persecutions come to steal the Word of God out of your heart (Mark 4:17).
    - i. They come to discourage you and to undermine your faith.
    - ii. Sickness comes to defeat you.
    - iii. Financial problems come to cause anxiety and to limit what you can do for the kingdom of God.
- G. To embrace those problems as if they are sent by God to make you a better person is crazy.
- H. But if, through faith, you continue to trust in God's promises and resist the Enemy, then you will overcome the challenges and prosper in spite of them.
- I. Going through hardship and using your faith in God are going to make you a stronger Christian on the other side, but I am not encouraging anybody to accept hardship as a blessing from God.
- J. Hardship is not a blessing—it's a curse from the Enemy.
- K. You are only made stronger through hardship by resisting it and standing in faith.

III. Scripture couldn't be any clearer in saying that suffering and temptation are not from God (James 1:13-14), yet many religious traditions continue to blame God.

- A. The foundation of this teaching on Christian philosophy is the Apostle Paul's warning you not to be spoiled through philosophy (Col. 2:8).
- B. This teaching that God sends hardships to make you better is a religious tradition that has spoiled untold numbers of Christians.
- C. They believe that God is orchestrating the problems in their lives and using suffering for some redemptive purpose.
- D. That attitude will make you passive because it takes away your desire to resist problems.
- E. If God wants you to be sick, why would you fight against Him by trying to get better?
- F. The more sincere your desire to please God, the more likely you are to give up in the face of hardship, if you believe that God is behind your problems.
- G. Believing that God will send problems into your life is a false teaching that will keep you from having a positive relationship with Him.
- H. It's impossible to really trust someone and have a healthy relationship with them if you are constantly wondering whether they might hurt you—even if they are supposedly doing it for your own good.
    - i. What would you think of me if I was personally responsible for every baby born with a deformity or disability?
    - ii. How much would you like me if you knew that I was responsible for every death, disease, hardship, and tragedy in the world?
    - iii. Would you want to be my friend or spend any time with me?
    - iv. Who in their right mind would want to get close to me if having a relationship with me might mean that I would "bless" you with some incurable disease or kill the people you love most?
    - v. I can guarantee you that if I was guilty of all the things people are blaming God for, society would lock me up and throw away the key.

Lesson 8 — What about Suffering?

IV. Just as Satan convinced Adam and Eve that the Lord wasn't all good but that He had withheld His best from them, so religion (which is the devil's creation) has put forth the lie that the Lord is responsible for all the bad things in your life, but that just isn't so.

   A. Many people have misunderstood the true nature of God, and they are proclaiming that nothing happens without God's permission.

   B. Therefore, they say, He must be responsible for all of the suffering in the world.

   C. Then they try to defend their position by saying that God is sending the evil for your own good.

   D. It's a total misrepresentation of who God is and how He relates to you.

   E. I know a number of people who are running from God because they think He is responsible for the evil in the world.

   F. One of their main arguments is, "How could a good God allow all of this to happen?"

   G. But God is not the source of the suffering in the world.

   H. God does not tempt you with hardship, there is no shadow of evil in Him, and He only blesses you with good things.

   Do not err, my beloved brethren. Every good gift and every perfect gift is from above, and cometh down from the Father of lights, with whom is no variableness, neither shadow of turning.
   JAMES 1:16-17

   I. **"Do not err"** is another way of saying, "Unless you believe what I'm saying, you're wrong."

   J. The simplest Christian philosophy you can have is that if something is good, then it's from God, and if it's bad, then it's from the devil.

   K. Only good and perfect gifts come down from the heavenly Father—sickness, hardship, and suffering are not good and perfect gifts.

   L. The goodness of God has to be the trump card against all arguments and circumstances in your life.

   M. No matter what is going on, you have to know absolutely that God is a good God.

   N. The moment someone starts trying to tell you that God gave you a sickness or put hardship in your life, the absolute certainty of God's goodness should rise up within you and immediately reject what they are saying.

   O. Unfortunately, a lot of religious teaching portrays God in a very bad light.

   P. They are trying to say that God is dangling people over hell by a thin thread—that He is angry with you and out to get you.

   Q. I've even heard people say that if you don't tithe, God is going to punish you by taking the money from you in doctors' bills.

   R. Other preachers say that if you leave their church, you are departing from God's will, and the wrath of God will descend on you by destroying your family, by you contracting some disease, or by you having some other tragedy.

   S. A lot of those teachers are trying to drive people to God through fear of punishment, but Scripture says it is the goodness of God that leads people to repentance (Rom. 2:4).

Lesson 8 — What about Suffering?

T. They should be telling people about the extravagant goodness of God, not threatening them. God doesn't send problems into your life, but if you believe He does, then it is going to be hard for you to believe that He is truly good.

V. It is easy to say God is a good God in theory, but if you don't really believe it, then your relationship is going to be hindered.

- A. Every time someone you love becomes ill or tragedy strikes, it is going to chip away at your resolve that God only wants good things for you.

- B. Look at this passage of Scripture:

But after that the kindness and love of God our Saviour toward man appeared, Not by works of righteousness which we have done, but according to his mercy he saved us, by the washing of regeneration, and renewing of the Holy Ghost; Which he shed on us abundantly through Jesus Christ our Saviour.

TITUS 3:4-6

- C. God's kindness and love toward you have nothing to do with any righteousness on your part.

- D. Too many people are preaching that you have to earn God's favor and that He is only good toward you when you deserve it, but that isn't true.

- E. If you think you have to earn God's love, then you will never believe that God is good, because your conscience will always condemn you.

- F. It doesn't matter how holy you live, you are always going to fall short of God's standard of holiness, which will leave you feeling separated from God.

- G. Your righteousness comes from God, so if you are depending on your own righteousness to make you feel worthy of God's love, then you are never going to feel worthy.

VI. When I look at all of the things God has done for me, I am overwhelmed by His goodness.

- A. God has sought after me more than I have searched for Him.

- B. My life could have turned out a lot differently than it has if it wasn't for the goodness of God.

- C. For instance, one of my sons was dead for five hours.

- D. My wife, Jamie, and I prayed that God would raise him from the dead, and out of His mercy and love, God did raise him back to life.

- E. I have a granddaughter that I wouldn't have had if it wasn't for the goodness of God.

- F. My father died when I was twelve years old, and when our pastor came to our house to talk to my brother and me about our father's death, a supernatural peace of God came over me, and the Lord brought to my remembrance a scripture from Psalm 27: **"When my father and my mother forsake me, then the Lord will take me up"** (verse 10).

- G. From that moment on, God took me up. He became my Father and my best friend.

- H. Even though it wasn't God's will for my father to die, I can look back and see the goodness of God blessing me through that experience.

- I. So many aspects of my life have been affected by the goodness of God.

- J. I believe that we can all look back on our lives and see how God worked to bless us, despite the tragedy we may have endured.

Lesson 8 — What about Suffering?

- K. I remember the Holy Spirit giving me supernatural knowledge about a woman at one of my meetings who had suffered a history of abuse.

- L. Terrible things had been done to her, but God had saved her life. He delivered her from the hands of the abusers whose plan was to kill her.

- M. Through the gifts of the Holy Spirit, I began to help her see that God had blessed her.

- N. She had a husband and a wonderful family, and God had been good to her.

- O. She went from being focused on the horrors of the abuse to seeing how God had intervened in her life with mercy and love.

- P. In the same way, each one of us can see the goodness of God in our lives, even if we have suffered tragedy.

VII. Most people have heard Romans 8:28 used as a blanket statement to convey that whatever happens must be God's will—that God works all things together for good, so there must be some purpose behind the tragedies in our lives.

- A. But just because God can bring good out of tragedy doesn't mean He caused the tragedy or wants us to endure suffering.

- B. It's true that exercising our faith through trials causes us to emerge stronger on the other side, but this verse does not say that God causes everything that happens in our lives.

- C. God works all things together for good, but He doesn't cause all things—and things don't work together for good for every person.
    - i. Some people have tragic lives that end in bitterness, anger, and destitution.
    - ii. A life of destructive choices often adds up to a disastrous ending, so there are some qualifications on exactly how **"all things work together for good."**

- D. This scripture says that things work together for good for **"them that love God."**

- E. That single qualification dramatically limits the number of people this scripture applies to, because the majority of people do not love God.

- F. I can remember being at a Full Gospel Business Men's meeting a long time ago when the speaker used this scripture to talk about God working everything together for good.
    - i. He had just come from conducting the funeral of a teenage boy and girl who died in a vehicle accident.
    - ii. Neither of them were known to be Christian, so as far as we know, they didn't go straight to the arms of Jesus—they went to eternal punishment.
    - iii. Clearly, there was nothing good about the accident, and if they did end up in hell, then zero redemptive value came out of it.
    - iv. Yet this minister used Romans 8:28 to say that God had a purpose in this ragedy, and it was working together for good.

- G. That's not right—God didn't do this.

- H. But God doesn't control us like pawns—we have free will, and He won't force us to make the right choices.

- I. It should be clear that good doesn't come out of every situation for every person.

- J. If we don't love God, then things aren't necessarily going to work together for good.

Lesson 8 — What about Suffering?

K. The reason I'm stressing this point is because if we believe that God controls every single thing that happens, then we are going to get the impression that God isn't a good God.

L. Some people can see that God doesn't cause suffering, but they think that He "allows" it to happen, but Scripture says that God reveals Himself **"against all ungodliness and unrighteousness of men"** (Rom. 1:18).

M. In the case of the two teenagers who died in the car accident, I believe that God gave them an intuitive knowledge of right and wrong and convicted them that what they were doing was wrong.

N. I believe that God spoke to them hundreds of times before they crashed the car and died—not just on the night of the accident, but in all the years leading up to it.

O. God didn't "allow" the accident to happen in the sense that He didn't intervene in any way to stop it.

P. It's more like there was a mountain of obstacles that God put in their way, but they persisted and climbed over all of the things God was doing to save them.

Q. Anyone who goes to hell has to ignore the thousands and thousands of times God has tried to convict them and draw them into His love.

R. Going to hell isn't a one-time decision; it is the result of rejecting God countless times.

S. Our God is a good God, and He desires good things for us—even more than we desire good for our children.

T. Not only does the scripture in the book of Romans say that things work together for good for those who love God; it also says for **"them who are the called according to his purpose"** (Rom. 8:28).

U. The Bible says that Jesus came to earth to destroy the works of the devil (1 John 3:8), so to be called according to His purpose means that we are resisting the works of the devil (James 4:7).

    i. If we are rebelling against God and chasing sin, then the tragedy that occurs in our lives is not necessarily going to work together for good.

V. Another qualification on this scripture appears in the verses before Romans 8:28, which talk about the Holy Spirit making intercession through us (Rom. 8:26-27).

W. The Holy Spirit doesn't pray without us, but when we start to pray, the Holy Spirit comes alongside us and pleads our cause.

X. When we have that kind of Spirit-led intercession working in our lives, then things are going to work together for good.

Y. Those are three major qualifications on things working together for good: We have to love God, we have to be resisting the works of the devil, and we have to pray—allowing the Holy Spirit to help us make intercession.

Z. If we aren't trying to meet those three qualifications, then everything isn't necessarily going to work together for good.

VIII. God is not the cause of all the evil in our world.

    A. He isn't killing people because He loves them so much—He is a good God.

    B. His plans for our lives are peace and victory (Jer. 29:11), but God's will doesn't come to pass automatically; we have to cooperate with Him.

    C. Once we believe that God is only good, our faith will abound, and we will see better results in our lives.

LESSON 8 — WHAT ABOUT SUFFERING?

    D. We can cooperate with God, and all things *will* work together for good.

    E. A lot of negative things happen in life: People we love die, children get sick, jobs are lost, and tragedy strikes when we least expect it.

    F. It's easy to look at the circumstances in life and wonder why the all-powerful God doesn't prevent suffering, which can lead us to think that God is responsible for it, but Scripture reveals that God has nothing to do with evil.

    G. When God created the heavens and the earth, everything was perfect.

    H. God told Adam not to eat of the Tree of the Knowledge of Good and Evil, because in the day that he did, he would die.

    I. Adam rejected God's instructions, and the result was that sin entered creation.

    J. Every one of us has leaned unto our own understanding rather than depending on God, and our rebellion is what has released evil on earth.

    K. Satan is the cause of suffering: he roams around seeking whom he may devour—he steals, kills, and destroys (1 Pet. 5:8 and John 10:10).

    L. God is not the source of the tragedy in our lives!

IX. The Bible is full of proof that God is a good God.

    A. The ultimate testimony is that Jesus came to this earth and suffered, not only on the cross, but even just by humbling Himself and taking on human form for thirty-three years.

    B. Jesus suffered by being confined to a physical human body when He was God.

    C. Solomon said, **"The heaven and heaven of heavens cannot contain thee; how much less this house that I have** [built]**?"** (1 Kin. 8:27, brackets mine).

    D. God is infinite—even the universe can't contain Him—yet He limited Himself to a physical body.

    E. He was despised and rejected by men, and He ultimately took the punishment for your sins.

    F. If God loved you enough to suffer and die for you, He loves you enough to do anything for you.

Let them shout for joy, and be glad, that favour my righteous cause: yea, let them say continually, Let the Lord be magnified, which hath pleasure in the prosperity of his servant.

PSALM 35:27

    G. God is pleased when you prosper—He wants to see you succeed.

    H. Nobody is pulling for you more than God is—which might not be what you are used to hearing, but it's the message the Bible teaches.

    I. God is love (1 John 4:7-8). God doesn't just love some people or have a little love for all. He *is* love.

X. God showed you His love by sending Jesus (1 John 4:9-10).

    A. I am convinced that if you focus on God sending Jesus to earth, instead of just hearing the words, you will experience the fruit of God's peace and joy.

    B. If God's love isn't impacting you or how you feel about life, then take time to be still and meditate on this truth that God showed His love by sending His Son.

Lesson 8 — What about Suffering?

C. God's love will be revealed to you by focusing on Jesus coming to earth and becoming the payment for your sin.

D. Salvation isn't about you loving God first and then, because you initiate relationship with Him, God extends love to you in return.

E. God's loving nature is revealed in that He reached out to you while you were rejecting Him.

F. Christ died for you while you were still living in sin:

But God commendeth his love toward us, in that, while we were yet sinners, Christ died for us.
ROMANS 5:8

G. God has already given you His Son—why wouldn't He give you joy, peace, health, and prosperity (Rom. 8:32)?

H. It would be totally inconsistent for me to be willing to die for you but be unwilling to give you some money.

I. God not only has the ability to heal and prosper you; *He desires to do it.*

J. Faith works by love, and if you trust and believe in God's love—by focusing on what He has already done for you—your faith will rise.

K. Jesus didn't have to suffer death on a cross; He chose to.

L. He could have called down an army of angels (Matt. 26:53), but He humbly submitted to a humiliating death instead.

M. Jesus allowed the scribes and Pharisees to mock Him.

N. They spit in His face, slapped Him, insulted Him, beat Him, and finally killed Him.

O. Jesus took all of that because He loved you and wanted to save you.

P. The life, death, and resurrection of Jesus were a physical manifestation of God's love pursuing you, and when Jesus ascended into heaven, He gave you the Holy Spirit to continue His ministry on earth until He returns.

Q. The Holy Spirit is your Teacher and Helper.

R. He leads you into all truth, and He is the eyes of the Lord that search the whole earth seeking to show Himself strong on behalf of those who love God (2 Chr. 16:9).

S. The Lord is looking for you—He isn't hiding from you.

T. You don't have to pursue Him; you just need to slow down and unplug from the distractions of the world for a little bit.

U. You can't make a connection with God in the three minutes between your two favorite television shows.

V. You need to find time to be still and know God (Ps. 46:10)—not just physical stillness, but stillness in your mind, which just means not being completely occupied with other thoughts.

W. God wants to reveal His love for you more than you desire to know it, but He isn't going to force His way into your life.

X. You have to take time and give God the opportunity to show you His love.

Lesson 8 — What about Suffering?

XI. Revelation 3:20 has been used to talk about being born again—which isn't wrong—but this letter was written to Christians.

    A. Jesus was saying this to people who were already born again.

    B. He is asking if you will let Him into your life.

        i. Will you give Him your attention?

        ii. Will you unplug from the distractions of life that keep you from hearing the voice of God, and simply focus on His voice?

    C. The results of knowing God's love are tremendous.

    D. Knowing His love is worth sacrificing a little entertainment in front of the television to sit quietly in the presence of the Lord.

    E. I can't tell you how many people come to me in fear of the circumstances in their lives.

    F. They are fearful over the future, the economy, kids, relationships, health, and all kinds of other things.

    G. A lot of people today are living in fear, but God's love will push the fear out of your life.

    H. Scripture says there is no fear in love (1 John 4:18).

    I. When you spend time in the presence of God, the experience of His love kills your fears.

    J. It is impossible for fear to thrive where God's love dwells.

    K. During the Vietnam War, I visited a forward fire-support base that was overrun by the enemy just hours after I left.

        i. Before I was evacuated by helicopter, I remember seeing the muzzle flashes from the rifle fire of the enemy as they charged up the hill toward our position, but I wasn't afraid.

        ii. I was worshiping God, thinking, *Lord, today could be the day I come to meet You!*

        iii. I had supernatural compassion for the people who were rushing to kill me.

        iv. All I experienced was love and excitement about the possibility of going to be with the Lord.

    L. Once you know God and understand how good He is, you can become like the Apostle Paul, who said, **"For to me to live is Christ, and to die is gain"** (Phil. 1:21).

    M. This is normal Christianity—it sounds a little extreme by the world's standards, but this is the attitude you should have.

    N. The suffering of this life is not worthy of being compared with the glory that will be revealed in you (Rom. 8:18).

    O. You have something so awesome prepared for you in the presence of God that you won't give a second thought to the heartache and rejection you experienced in this life.

    P. Nobody in heaven is grieving over the things that happened to them during their lives on earth.

    Q. If you were to really think about this, you wouldn't have any fear of poverty, sickness, or failure.

    R. Whatever this world has to throw at you, God has something greater in store.

XII. God has been misrepresented as causing the tragedy in our world, and I believe that is the number one reason people are not seeking relationship with Him.

   A. If you think God is causing the problems in your life, then you'll want to keep Him at arm's length—even if you are a Christian.

   B. It's a natural response to try to avoid people and situations that might hurt you.

   C. But God isn't causing the suffering in the world—in fact, He has nothing to do with it.

   D. God loves you and He desires good things for you, but experiencing the love of God passes mere knowledge about His love (Eph. 3:19).

   E. Once you understand how good God is and begin having a real relationship with Him, you open yourself to receiving His love and being filled with all the fullness of God.

   F. The blessings of God will come upon you and overtake you, and it will cause everything to work out for good in your life.

LESSON 8 — WHAT ABOUT SUFFERING?

TEACHER'S GUIDE

1. Certain Bible verses dealing with suffering have frequently been misinterpreted and are sometimes used to suggest that God uses suffering to teach us a lesson or to help us grow spiritually. I believe that those interpretations are harmful and that they cause people to have a wrong understanding of God's true nature. One of the frequently misinterpreted passages of Scripture says,

> *My brethren, count it all joy when ye fall into divers temptations; Knowing this, that the trying of your faith worketh patience. But let patience have her perfect work, that ye may be perfect and entire, wanting nothing.*
> JAMES 1:2-4

These verses have been used by many to imply that praying for patience means that God will put trials and temptations in our way in order to teach us patience. We've all heard someone say, "Be careful what you pray for," as if problems are actually the work of God intended to bring us to maturity. The church I grew up in talked about problems as "heavenly sandpaper" that rubbed off all of our rough edges and made us better people. Let me make an obvious statement: If suffering and problems are what make us better people, then the people who have suffered the most should be the holiest, most godliest people on earth—but that isn't the case. In fact, the opposite is usually true. The people who have suffered the most are often bitter, angry people whose lives are a mess. It simply is not an observable truth to say that suffering produces holiness. On the other hand, it is true to say that when we respond to hardship by trusting in God, then it brings to the surface things that God has placed on the inside of us. As we depend on God's strength, then we become stronger in our faith—but the hardships aren't what make us better. What makes us stronger is exercising our faith in God and trusting in Him. It's the improvement of our relationship with God that comes from seeking Him, so hardship might cause us to seek God, but suffering doesn't make us better people.

1a. What is sometimes used to suggest that God uses suffering to teach you a lesson or to help you grow spiritually?
(Certain Bible verses dealing with suffering)

1b. Read James 1:2-4. True or false: Problems are actually the work of God intended to bring you to maturity.
(False)

1c. Discussion Question: How is it true that when you respond to hardship by trusting in God, then it brings to the surface things that God has placed on the inside of you?
(Discussion question)

1d. What makes you stronger?
A. Getting plenty of sunlight
B. Staying away from garlic
C. Horseradish
D. Hearing more sermons
E. Exercising your faith in God and trusting in Him
(E. Exercising your faith in God and trusting in Him)

1e. The improvement of your relationship with God comes from what?
(Seeking Him)

2. The Vietnam War was a trying situation for my faith, and I came out of it much stronger than when I went in—but God didn't organize the war to make me holy. Becoming a good soldier involves putting into practice all of the things you learn through training, so you do become a better soldier after you have engaged in combat. You learn things through experience that you can't learn from a book. But it would be insane to embrace the enemy when they attack you, as if their purpose is to make you a better soldier. The enemy isn't there to make you better—they're there to kill you. Only by resisting the enemy and overcoming them will you live through the attack and become a better soldier. Likewise, God doesn't send problems into your life to make you a better person—the Enemy tries to create problems in order to cause suffering. Afflictions and persecutions come to steal the Word of God out of your heart (Mark 4:17). They come to discourage you and to undermine your faith. Sickness comes to defeat you. Financial problems come to cause anxiety and to limit what you can do for the kingdom of God. To embrace those problems as if they are sent by God to make you a better person is crazy. But if, through faith, you continue to trust

Lesson 8 — What about Suffering?

in God's promises and resist the Enemy, then you will overcome the challenges and prosper in spite of them. Going through hardship and using your faith in God are going to make you a stronger Christian on the other side, but I am not encouraging anybody to accept hardship as a blessing from God. Hardship is not a blessing. It's a curse from the Enemy. You are only made stronger through hardship by resisting it and standing in faith.

- 2a. You learn things through _____ that you can't learn from a _____.
  (Experience/book)

- 2b. Read Mark 4:17. Why do afflictions and persecutions come?
  (To steal the Word of God out of your heart—they come to discourage you and undermine your faith)

3. Scripture couldn't be any clearer in saying that suffering and temptation are not from God (James 1:13-14), yet many religious traditions continue to blame God. The foundation of this teaching on Christian philosophy is the Apostle Paul's warning you not to be spoiled through philosophy (Col. 2:8). This teaching that God sends hardships to make you better is a religious tradition that has spoiled untold numbers of Christians. They believe that God is orchestrating the problems in their lives and using suffering for some redemptive purpose. That attitude will make you passive because it takes away your desire to resist problems. If God wants you to be sick, why would you fight against Him by trying to get better? The more sincere your desire to please God, the more likely you are to give up in the face of hardship, if you believe that God is behind your problems. Believing that God will send problems into your life is a false teaching that will keep you from having a positive relationship with Him. It's impossible to really trust someone and have a healthy relationship with them if you are constantly wondering whether they might hurt you—even if they are supposedly doing it for your own good. What would you think of me if I was personally responsible for every baby born with a deformity or disability? How much would you like me if you knew that I was responsible for every death, disease, hardship, and tragedy in the world? Would you want to be my friend or spend any time with me? Who in their right mind would want to get close to me if having a relationship with me might mean that I would "bless" you with some incurable disease or kill the people you love most? I can guarantee you that if I was guilty of all the things people are blaming God for, society would lock me up and throw away the key.

- 3a. Read James 1:13-14. What is Scripture clear in saying?
  (That suffering and temptation are not from God)

- 3b. If you believe that God is orchestrating the problems in your life and using suffering for some redemptive purpose, what will that make you?
  A. Thankful and more trusting of God
  B. Passive because it takes away your desire to resist problems
  C. The holiest person in your church
  D. All of the above
  E. None of the above
  (B. Passive because it takes away your desire to resist problems)

- 3c. Discussion Question: Even if they are supposedly doing it for your own good, why is it impossible to really trust someone and have a healthy relationship with them if you are constantly wondering whether they might hurt you?
  (Discussion question)

4. Just as Satan convinced Adam and Eve that the Lord wasn't all good but that He had withheld His best from them, so religion (which is the devil's creation) has put forth the lie that the Lord is responsible for all the bad things in your life. That just isn't so. Many people have misunderstood the true nature of God, and they are proclaiming that nothing happens without God's permission. Therefore, they say, He must be responsible for all of the suffering in the world. Then they try to defend their position by saying that God is sending the evil for your own good. It's a total misrepresentation of who God is and how He relates to you. I know a number of people who are running from God because they think He is responsible for the evil in the world. One of their main arguments is, "How could a good God allow all of this to happen?" But God is not the source of the suffering in the world. God does not tempt you with hardship, there is no shadow of evil in Him, and He only blesses you with good things.

Lesson 8 — What about Suffering?

Do not err, my beloved brethren. Every good gift and every perfect gift is from above, and cometh down from the Father of lights, with whom is no variableness, neither shadow of turning.

JAMES 1:16-17

"Do not err" is another way of saying, "Unless you believe what I'm saying, you're wrong." The simplest Christian philosophy you can have is that if something is good, then it's from God, and if it's bad, then it's from the devil. Only good and perfect gifts come down from the heavenly Father—sickness, hardship, and suffering are not good and perfect gifts. The goodness of God has to be the trump card against all arguments and circumstances in your life. No matter what is going on, you have to know absolutely that God is a good God. The moment someone starts trying to tell you that God gave you a sickness or put hardship in your life, the absolute certainty of God's goodness should rise up within you and immediately reject what they are saying. Unfortunately, a lot of religious teaching portrays God in a very bad light. They are trying to say that God is dangling people over hell by a thin thread—that He is angry with you and out to get you. I've even heard people say that if you don't tithe, God is going to punish you by taking the money from you in doctors' bills. Other preachers say that if you leave their church, you are departing from God's will, and the wrath of God will descend on you by destroying your family, by you contracting some disease, or by you having some other tragedy. A lot of those teachers are trying to drive people to God through fear of punishment, but Scripture says it is the goodness of God that leads people to repentance (Rom. 2:4). They should be telling people about the extravagant goodness of God, not threatening them. God doesn't send problems into your life, but if you believe He does, then it is going to be hard for you to believe that He is truly good.

4a. True or false: Nothing happens without God's permission.
(False)

4b. Read James 1:16-17. What is the simplest Christian philosophy you can have?
(That if something is good, then it's from God, and if it's bad, then it's from the devil)

4c. No matter what is going on, what do you have to know absolutely?
(That God is a good God)

4d. True or false: The moment someone starts trying to tell you that God gave you a sickness or put hardship in your life, the absolute certainty of God's goodness should rise up within you and consider what they are saying.
(False)

4e. You should be telling people about the _____ goodness of God, not _____ them.
(Extravagant/threatening)

5. It is easy to say God is a good God in theory, but if you don't really believe it, then your relationship is going to be hindered. Every time someone you love becomes ill or tragedy strikes, it is going to chip away at your resolve that God only wants good things for you. Look at this passage of Scripture:

But after that the kindness and love of God our Saviour toward man appeared, Not by works of righteousness which we have done, but according to his mercy he saved us, by the washing of regeneration, and renewing of the Holy Ghost; Which he shed on us abundantly through Jesus Christ our Saviour.

TITUS 3:4-6

God's kindness and love toward you have nothing to do with any righteousness on your part. Too many people are preaching that you have to earn God's favor and that He is only good toward you when you deserve it, but that isn't true. If you think you have to earn God's love, then you will never believe that God is good, because your conscience will always condemn you. It doesn't matter how holy you live, you are always going to fall short of God's standard of holiness, which will leave you feeling separated from God. Your righteousness comes from God, so if you are depending on your own righteousness to make you feel worthy of God's love, then you are never going to feel worthy.

5a. It is easy to say God is a good God in theory, but if you don't really believe it, why will your relationship be hindered?
(Because every time someone you love becomes ill or tragedy strikes, it is going to chip away at your resolve that God only wants good things for you)

Lesson 8 — What about Suffering?

5b. Read Titus 3:4-6. True or false: God is good to you even though you don't deserve it.
(True)

5c. Discussion Question: When you've thought that you have to earn God's love, how has your conscience condemned you?
(Discussion question)

5d. If you are depending on your own righteousness to make you feel worthy of God's love, then you are never going to what?
A. Feel worthy
B. Sing loudly
C. Attend church
D. Trust others
E. Pray constantly
(A. Feel worthy)

6. When I look at all of the things God has done for me, I am overwhelmed by His goodness. God has sought after me more than I have searched for Him. My life could have turned out a lot differently than it has if it wasn't for the goodness of God. For instance, one of my sons was dead for five hours. My wife, Jamie, and I prayed that God would raise him from the dead, and out of His mercy and love, God did raise him back to life. I have a granddaughter that I wouldn't have had if it wasn't for the goodness of God. My father died when I was twelve years old, and when our pastor came to our house to talk to my brother and me about our father's death, a supernatural peace of God came over me, and the Lord brought to my remembrance a scripture from Psalm 27 – **"When my father and my mother forsake me, then the Lord will take me up"** (verse 10). From that moment on, God took me up. He became my Father and my best friend. Even though it wasn't God's will for my father to die, I can look back and see the goodness of God blessing me through that experience. So many aspects of my life have been affected by the goodness of God. I believe that we can all look back on our lives and see how God worked to bless us, despite the tragedy we may have endured. I remember the Holy Spirit giving me supernatural knowledge about a woman at one of my meetings who had suffered a history of abuse. Terrible things had been done to her, but God had saved her life. He delivered her from the hands of the abusers whose plan was to kill her. Through the gifts of the Holy Spirit, I began to help her see that God had blessed her. She had a husband and a wonderful family, and God had been good to her. She went from being focused on the horrors of the abuse to seeing how God had intervened in her life with mercy and love. In the same way, each one of us can see the goodness of God in our lives, even if we have suffered tragedy.

6a. Discussion Question: How have you seen the goodness of God in your life, even through tragedy?
(Discussion question)

7. Most people have heard Romans 8:28 used as a blanket statement to convey that whatever happens must be God's will—that God works all things together for good, so there must be some purpose behind the tragedies in our lives. But just because God can bring good out of tragedy doesn't mean He caused the tragedy or wants us to endure suffering. It's true that exercising our faith through trials causes us to emerge stronger on the other side, but this verse does not say that God causes everything that happens in our lives. God works all things together for good, but He doesn't cause all things—and things don't work together for good for *every person*. Some people have tragic lives that end in bitterness, anger, and destitution. A life of destructive choices often adds up to a disastrous ending, so there are some qualifications on exactly how **"all things work together for good."** This scripture says that things work together for good for **"them that love God."** That single qualification dramatically limits the number of people this scripture applies to, because the majority of people do not love God. I can remember being at a Full Gospel Business Men's meeting a long time ago when the speaker used this scripture to talk about God working everything together for good. He had just come from conducting the funeral of a teenage boy and girl who died in a vehicle accident. Neither of them were known to be Christian, so as far as we know, they didn't go straight to the arms of Jesus—they went to eternal punishment. Clearly, there was nothing good about the accident, and if they did end up in hell, then zero redemptive value came out of it. Yet this minister used Romans 8:28 to say that God had a purpose in this tragedy, and it was working together for good. That's not right. God didn't do this. But God doesn't control us like pawns. We have free will, and He won't force us to make the right choices. It should be clear that good doesn't come out of every situation for every person. If we don't love God, then things

Lesson 8 — What about Suffering?

aren't necessarily going to work together for good. The reason I'm stressing this point is because if we believe that God controls every single thing that happens, then we are going to get the impression that God isn't a good God. Some people can see that God doesn't cause suffering, but they think that He "allows" it to happen, but Scripture says that God reveals Himself **"against all ungodliness and unrighteousness of men"** (Rom. 1:18). In the case of the two teenagers who died in the car accident, I believe that God gave them an intuitive knowledge of right and wrong and convicted them that what they were doing was wrong. I believe that God spoke to them hundreds of times before they crashed the car and died—not just on the night of the accident, but in all the years leading up to it. God didn't "allow" the accident to happen in the sense that He didn't intervene in any way to stop it. It's more like there was a mountain of obstacles that God put in their way, but they persisted and climbed over all of the things God was doing to save them. Anyone who goes to hell has to ignore the thousands and thousands of times God has tried to convict them and draw them into His love. Going to hell isn't a one-time decision; it is the result of rejecting God countless times. Our God is a good God, and He desires good things for us—even more than we desire good for our children. Not only does the scripture in the book of Romans say that things work together for good for those who love God; it also says for **"them who are the called according to his purpose"** (Rom. 8:28). The Bible says that Jesus came to earth to destroy the works of the devil (1 John 3:8), so to be called according to His purpose means that we are resisting the works of the devil (James 4:7). If we are rebelling against God and chasing sin, then the tragedy that occurs in our lives is not necessarily going to work together for good. Another qualification on this scripture appears in the verses before Romans 8:28, which talk about the Holy Spirit making intercession through us (Rom. 8:26-27). The Holy Spirit doesn't pray without us, but when we start to pray, the Holy Spirit comes alongside us and pleads our cause. When we have that kind of Spirit-led intercession working in our lives, then things are going to work together for good. Those are three major qualifications on things working together for good: We have to love God, we have to be resisting the works of the devil, and we have to pray—allowing the Holy Spirit to help us make intercession. If we aren't trying to meet those three qualifications, then everything isn't necessarily going to work together for good.

7a. Read Romans 8:28. What has this verse been used as?
(A blanket statement to convey that whatever happens must be God's will)

7b. Just because God can bring good out of tragedy doesn't mean He _____ the tragedy or wants us to endure suffering.
(Caused)

7c. True or false: Romans 8:28 says that all things work together for good for every person.
(False)

7d. Read Romans 1:18. How do you know that God doesn't allow suffering?
*(Because God reveals Himself **"against all ungodliness and unrighteousness of men"**)*

7e. Read 1 John 3:8, James 4:7, and Romans 8:26-27. What are the three qualifications on exactly how **"all things work together for good"**?
(You have to love God, you have to be resisting the works of the devil, and you have to pray—allowing the Holy Spirit to help you make intercession)

8. God is not the cause of all the evil in our world. He isn't killing people because He loves them so much. He is a good God. His plans for our lives are peace and victory (Jer. 29:11), but God's will doesn't come to pass automatically; we have to cooperate with Him. Once we believe that God is only good, our faith will abound, and we will see better results in our lives. We can cooperate with God, and all things *will* work together for good. A lot of negative things happen in life: People we love die, children get sick, jobs are lost, and tragedy strikes when we least expect it. It's easy to look at the circumstances in life and wonder why the all-powerful God doesn't prevent suffering, which can lead us to think that God is responsible for it, but Scripture reveals that God has nothing to do with evil. When God created the heavens and the earth, everything was perfect. God told Adam not to eat of the Tree of the Knowledge of Good and Evil, because in the day that he did, he would die. Adam rejected God's instructions, and the result was that sin entered creation. Every one of us has leaned unto our own understanding rather than depending on God, and our rebellion is what has released evil on earth. Satan is the cause of suffering. He roams around seeking whom he may devour—he steals, kills, and destroys (1 Pet. 5:8 and John 10:10). God is not the source of the tragedy in our lives!

Lesson 8 — What about Suffering?

8a. Since God loves people, that means He won't what?
   A. Help them
   B. Convict them
   C. Kill them
   D. All of the above
   E. None of the above
   (C. Kill them)

8b. Discussion Question: Can you give some examples of how God's will doesn't come to pass automatically?
   (Discussion question)

8c. What is easy to do when you look at the circumstances in life?
   (Wonder why the all-powerful God doesn't prevent suffering)

8d. If you lean unto your own understanding rather than depend on God, your _____ will release evil on earth.
   (Rebellion)

8e. How do you know that Satan is the cause of suffering, roaming around seeking whom he may devour and stealing, killing, and destroying?
   (Because 1 Peter 5:8 and John 10:10 say so)

9. The Bible is full of proof that God is a good God. The ultimate testimony is that Jesus came to this earth and suffered, not only on the cross, but even just by humbling Himself and taking on human form for thirty-three years. Jesus suffered by being confined to a physical human body when He was God. Solomon said, **"The heaven and heaven of heavens cannot contain thee; how much less this house that I have** [built]**?"** (1 Kin. 8:27, brackets mine). God is infinite—even the universe can't contain Him—yet He limited Himself to a physical body. He was despised and rejected by men, and He ultimately took the punishment for your sins. If God loved you enough to suffer and die for you, He loves you enough to do anything for you.

> *Let them shout for joy, and be glad, that favour my righteous cause: yea, let them say continually, Let the LORD be magnified, which hath pleasure in the prosperity of his servant.*
> PSALM 35:27

God is pleased when you prosper. He wants to see you succeed. Nobody is pulling for you more than God is—which might not be what you are used to hearing, but it's the message the Bible teaches. God is love (1 John 4:7-8). God doesn't just love some people or have a little love for all. He *is* love.

9a. What is full of proof that God is a good God?
   A. Your bank account
   B. A new teaching
   C. The Bible
   D. A storybook
   E. The news
   (C. The Bible)

9b. If God loved you enough to suffer and die for you, He loves you enough to do what for you?
   A. Nothing else
   B. Anything
   C. One other thing
   D. All of the above
   E. None of the above
   (B. Anything)

9c. According to Psalm 35:27, God is _____ when you prosper.
   (Pleased)

9d. Who pulls for you more than God?
   (No one)

Lesson 8 — What about Suffering?

10. God showed you His love by sending Jesus (1 John 4:9-10). I am convinced that if you focus on God sending Jesus to earth, instead of just hearing the words, you will experience the fruit of God's peace and joy. If God's love isn't impacting you or how you feel about life, then take time to be still and meditate on this truth that God showed His love by sending His Son. God's love will be revealed to you by focusing on Jesus coming to earth and becoming the payment for your sin. Salvation isn't about you loving God first and then, because you initiate relationship with Him, God extends love to you in return. God's loving nature is revealed in that He reached out to you while you were rejecting Him. Christ died for you while you were still living in sin:

> *But God commendeth his love toward us, in that, while we were yet sinners, Christ died for us.*
> ROMANS 5:8

God has already given you His Son—why wouldn't He give you joy, peace, health, and prosperity (Rom. 8:32)? It would be totally inconsistent for me to be willing to die for you but be unwilling to give you some money. God not only has the ability to heal and prosper you; *He desires to do it*. Faith works by love, and if you trust and believe in God's love—by focusing on what He has already done for you—your faith will rise. Jesus didn't have to suffer death on a cross; He chose to. He could have called down an army of angels (Matt. 26:53), but He humbly submitted to a humiliating death instead. Jesus allowed the scribes and Pharisees to mock Him. They spit in His face, slapped Him, insulted Him, beat Him, and finally killed Him. Jesus took all of that because He loved you and wanted to save you. The life, death, and resurrection of Jesus were a physical manifestation of God's love pursuing you, and when Jesus ascended into heaven, He gave you the Holy Spirit to continue His ministry on earth until He returns. The Holy Spirit is your Teacher and Helper. He leads you into all truth, and He is the eyes of the Lord that search the whole earth seeking to show Himself strong on behalf of those who love God (2 Chr. 16:9). The Lord is looking for you. He isn't hiding from you. You don't have to pursue Him; you just need to slow down and unplug from the distractions of the world for a little bit. You can't make a connection with God in the three minutes between your two favorite television shows. You need to find time to be still and know God (Ps. 46:10)—not just physical stillness, but stillness in your mind, which just means not being completely occupied with other thoughts. God wants to reveal His love for you more than you desire to know it, but He isn't going to force His way into your life. You have to take time and give God the opportunity to show you His love.

10a. Andrew is convinced that if you focus on God sending Jesus to earth, instead of just hearing the words, you will experience what?
(The fruit of God's peace and joy)

10b. What should you do if God's love isn't impacting you or how you feel about life?
(Take time to be still and meditate on this truth that God showed His love by sending His Son)

10c. Read Romans 5:8. How is God's loving nature revealed?
A. By God fixing all your circumstances
B. By God taking you to the store and buying you something
C. By God giving you a great big hug
D. By God just telling you He loves you
E. By Christ dying for you while you were still living in sin
(E. By Christ dying for you while you were still living in sin)

10d. If you trust and believe in God's love—by focusing on what He has already done for you—what will rise?
(Your faith)

10e. Discussion Question: What do you think about the fact that Jesus chose to suffer death on a cross because He loved you and wanted to save you?
(Discussion question)

10f. True or false: God is pursuing you.
(True)

10g. What more did Jesus do for you after He ascended into heaven?
(Gave you the Holy Spirit to continue His ministry on earth until He returns)

10h. Read Psalm 46:10. What kind of stillness do you need?
(Not just physical stillness, but stillness in your mind, which just means not being completely occupied with other thoughts)

Lesson 8 — What about Suffering?

10i. God wants to reveal His love for you _____ than you desire to know it, but He isn't going to _____ His way into your life.
(More/force)

11. Revelation 3:20 has been used to talk about being born again—which isn't wrong—but this letter was written to Christians. Jesus was saying this to people who were already born again. He is asking if you will let Him into your life. Will you give Him your attention? Will you unplug from the distractions of life that keep you from hearing the voice of God, and simply focus on His voice? The results of knowing God's love are tremendous. Knowing His love is worth sacrificing a little entertainment in front of the television to sit quietly in the presence of the Lord. I can't tell you how many people come to me in fear of the circumstances in their lives. They are fearful over the future, the economy, kids, relationships, health, and all kinds of other things. A lot of people today are living in fear, but God's love will push the fear out of your life. Scripture says there is no fear in love (1 John 4:18). When you spend time in the presence of God, the experience of His love kills your fears. It is impossible for fear to thrive where God's love dwells. During the Vietnam War, I visited a forward fire-support base that was overrun by the enemy just hours after I left. Before I was evacuated by helicopter, I remember seeing the muzzle flashes from the rifle fire of the enemy as they charged up the hill toward our position, but I wasn't afraid. I was worshiping God. I was actually thinking, *Lord, today could be the day I come to meet You!* I had supernatural compassion for the people who were rushing to kill me. All I experienced was love and excitement about the possibility of going to be with the Lord. Once you know God and understand how good He is, you can become like the Apostle Paul, who said, **"For to me to live is Christ, and to die is gain"** (Phil. 1:21). This is normal Christianity. It sounds a little extreme by the world's standards, but this is the attitude you should have. The suffering of this life is not worthy of being compared with the glory that will be revealed in you (Rom. 8:18). You have something so awesome prepared for you in the presence of God that you won't give a second thought to the heartache and rejection you experienced in this life. Nobody in heaven is grieving over the things that happened to them during their lives on earth. If you were to really think about this, you wouldn't have any fear of poverty, sickness, or failure. Whatever this world has to throw at you, God has something greater in store.

11a. Read Revelation 3:20. What is Jesus asking here?
(If you will let Him into your life, give Him your attention, unplug from the distractions of life that keep you from hearing the voice of God, and simply focus on His voice)

11b. Read 1 John 4:18. What will push the fear out of your life?
(God's love)

11c. You can become like the Apostle Paul, who said, **"For to me to live is Christ, and to die is gain"** (Phil. 1:21) when you what?
A. Starting giving more to your church
B. Just fast and pray a little more than you do
C. Know God and understand how good He is
D. All of the above
E. None of the above
(C. Know God and understand how good He is)

11d. Read Romans 8:18. Whatever this world has to throw at you, God has something _____ in store.
(Greater)

12. God has been misrepresented as causing the tragedy in our world, and I believe that is the number one reason people are not seeking relationship with Him. If you think God is causing the problems in your life, then you'll want to keep Him at arm's length—even if you are a Christian. It's a natural response to try to avoid people and situations that might hurt you. But God isn't causing the suffering in the world. In fact, God has nothing to do with it. God loves you and He desires good things for you, but experiencing the love of God passes mere knowledge about His love (Eph. 3:19). Once you understand how good God is and begin having a real relationship with Him, you open yourself to receiving His love and being filled with all the fullness of God. The blessings of God will come upon you and overtake you, and it will cause everything to work out for good in your life.

Lesson 8 — What about Suffering?

12a. Read Ephesians 3:19. God loves you and He desires good things for you, but experiencing the love of God passes what about His love?
A. Past experience
B. Your opinion
C. Mere knowledge
D. Worship songs
E. All of the above
(E. All of the above)

12b. Discussion Question: Once you'd opened yourself to receiving His love and being filled with all of His fullness, what are some examples in your life of how the blessings of God have come upon you and overtaken you, and how it caused everything to work out for good in your life?
(Discussion question)

LESSON 8 — WHAT ABOUT SUFFERING?

DISCIPLESHIP QUESTIONS

1. What is sometimes used to suggest that God uses suffering to teach you a lesson or to help you grow spiritually?

2. Read James 1:2-4. True or false: Problems are actually the work of God intended to bring you to maturity.

3. Discussion Question: How is it true that when you respond to hardship by trusting in God, then it brings to the surface things that God has placed on the inside of you?

4. What makes you stronger?
    A. Getting plenty of sunlight
    B. Staying away from garlic
    C. Horseradish
    D. Hearing more sermons
    E. Exercising your faith in God and trusting in Him

5. The improvement of your relationship with God comes from what?

6. You learn things through _____ that you can't learn from a _____.

7. Read Mark 4:17. Why do afflictions and persecutions come?

8. Read James 1:13-14. What is Scripture clear in saying?

SCRIPTURES TO USE WITH QUESTIONS

JAMES 1:2-4
My brethren, count it all joy when ye fall into divers temptations; **[3]** *Knowing this, that the trying of your faith worketh patience.* **[4]** *But let patience have her perfect work, that ye may be perfect and entire, wanting nothing.*

MARK 4:17
And have no root in themselves, and so endure but for a time: afterward, when affliction or persecution ariseth for the word's sake, immediately they are offended.

JAMES 1:13-14
Let no man say when he is tempted, I am tempted of God: for God cannot be tempted with evil, neither tempteth he any man: **[14]** *But every man is tempted, when he is drawn away of his own lust, and enticed.*

LESSON 8 — WHAT ABOUT SUFFERING?

DISCIPLESHIP QUESTIONS

9. If you believe that God is orchestrating the problems in your life and using suffering for some redemptive purpose, what will that make you?
   A. Thankful and more trusting of God
   B. Passive because it takes away your desire to resist problems
   C. The holiest person in your church
   D. All of the above
   E. None of the above

10. Discussion Question: Even if they are supposedly doing it for your own good, why is it impossible to really trust someone and have a healthy relationship with them if you are constantly wondering whether they might hurt you?

11. True or false: Nothing happens without God's permission.

12. Read James 1:16-17. What is the simplest Christian philosophy you can have?

13. No matter what is going on, what do you have to know absolutely?

14. True or false: The moment someone starts trying to tell you that God gave you a sickness or put hardship in your life, the absolute certainty of God's goodness should rise up within you and consider what they are saying.

15. You should be telling people about the _____ goodness of God, not _____ them.

SCRIPTURES TO USE WITH QUESTIONS

COLOSSIANS 2:8
Beware lest any man spoil you through philosophy and vain deceit, after the tradition of men, after the rudiments of the world, and not after Christ.

JAMES 1:16-17
Do not err, my beloved brethren. [17] Every good gift and every perfect gift is from above, and cometh down from the Father of lights, with whom is no variableness, neither shadow of turning.

ROMANS 2:4
Or despisest thou the riches of his goodness and forbearance and longsuffering; not knowing that the goodness of God leadeth thee to repentance?

Lesson 8 — What about Suffering?

DISCIPLESHIP QUESTIONS

16. It is easy to say God is a good God in theory, but if you don't really believe it, why will your relationship be hindered?

17. Read Titus 3:4-6. True or false: God is good to you even though you don't deserve it.

18. Discussion Question: When you've thought that you have to earn God's love, how has your conscience condemned you?

19. If you are depending on your own righteousness to make you feel worthy of God's love, then you are never going to what?
    A. Feel worthy
    B. Sing loudly
    C. Attend church
    D. Trust others
    E. Pray constantly

20. Discussion Question: How have you seen the goodness of God in your life, even through tragedy?

21. Read Romans 8:28. What has this verse been used as?

22. Just because God can bring good out of tragedy doesn't mean He _____ the tragedy or wants us to endure suffering.

SCRIPTURES TO USE WITH QUESTIONS

TITUS 3:4-6
But after that the kindness and love of God our Saviour toward man appeared, [5] Not by works of righteousness which we have done, but according to his mercy he saved us, by the washing of regeneration, and renewing of the Holy Ghost; [6] Which he shed on us abundantly through Jesus Christ our Saviour.

PSALM 27:10
When my father and my mother forsake me, then the Lord will take me up.

ROMANS 8:26-28
Likewise the Spirit also helpeth our infirmities: for we know not what we should pray for as we ought: but the Spirit itself maketh intercession for us with groanings which cannot be uttered. [27] And he that searcheth the hearts knoweth what is the mind of the Spirit, because he maketh intercession for the saints according to the will of God. [28] And we know that all things work together for good to them that love God, to them who are the called according to his purpose.

LESSON 8

WHAT ABOUT SUFFERING?

DISCIPLESHIP QUESTIONS

23. True or false: Romans 8:28 says that all things work together for good for every person.

24. Read Romans 1:18. How do you know that God doesn't allow suffering?

25. Read 1 John 3:8, James 4:7, and Romans 8:26-27. What are the three qualifications on exactly how **"all things work together for good"**?

26. Since God loves people, that means He won't what?
    A. Help them
    B. Convict them
    C. Kill them
    D. All of the above
    E. None of the above

27. Discussion Question: Can you give some examples of how God's will doesn't come to pass automatically?

28. What is easy to do when you look at the circumstances in life?

29. If you lean unto your own understanding rather than depend on God, your _____ will release evil on earth.

30. How do you know that Satan is the cause of suffering, roaming around seeking whom he may devour and stealing, killing, and destroying?

SCRIPTURES TO USE WITH QUESTIONS

ROMANS 1:18
For the wrath of God is revealed from heaven against all ungodliness and unrighteousness of men, who hold the truth in unrighteousness.

MATTHEW 7:9-11
Or what man is there of you, whom if his son ask bread, will he give him a stone? **[10]** *Or if he ask a fish, will he give him a serpent?* **[11]** *If ye then, being evil, know how to give good gifts unto your children, how much more shall your Father which is in heaven give good things to them that ask him?*

1 JOHN 3:8
He that committeth sin is of the devil; for the devil sinneth from the beginning. For this purpose the Son of God was manifested, that he might destroy the works of the devil.

JAMES 4:7
Submit yourselves therefore to God. Resist the devil, and he will flee from you.

ROMANS 8:26-28
Likewise the Spirit also helpeth our infirmities: for we know not what we should pray for as we ought: but the Spirit itself maketh intercession for us with groanings which cannot be uttered. **[27]** *And he that searcheth the hearts knoweth what is the mind of the Spirit, because he maketh intercession for the saints according to the will of God.* **[28]** *And we know that all things work together for good to them that love God, to them who are the called according to his purpose.*

JEREMIAH 29:11
For I know the thoughts that I think toward you, saith the LORD, thoughts of peace, and not of evil, to give you an expected end.

Lesson 8 — What about Suffering?

DISCIPLESHIP QUESTIONS

31. What is full of proof that God is a good God?
    A. Your bank account
    B. A new teaching
    C. The Bible
    D. A storybook
    E. The news

32. If God loved you enough to suffer and die for you, He loves you enough to do what for you?
    A. Nothing else
    B. Anything
    C. One other thing
    D. All of the above
    E. None of the above

33. According to Psalm 35:27, God is _____ when you prosper.

34. Who pulls for you more than God?

35. Andrew is convinced that if you focus on God sending Jesus to earth, instead of just hearing the words, you will experience what?

36. What should you do if God's love isn't impacting you or how you feel about life?

37. Read Romans 5:8. How is God's loving nature revealed?
    A. By God fixing all your circumstances
    B. By God taking you to the store and buying you something
    C. By God giving you a great big hug
    D. By God just telling you He loves you
    E. By Christ dying for you while you were still living in sin

SCRIPTURES TO USE WITH QUESTIONS

1 PETER 5:8
Be sober, be vigilant; because your adversary the devil, as a roaring lion, walketh about, seeking whom he may devour.

JOHN 10:10
The thief cometh not, but for to steal, and to kill, and to destroy: I am come that they might have life, and that they might have it more abundantly.

1 KINGS 8:27
But will God indeed dwell on the earth? behold, the heaven and heaven of heavens cannot contain thee; how much less this house that I have builded?

PSALM 35:27
Let them shout for joy, and be glad, that favour my righteous cause: yea, let them say continually, Let the Lord be magnified, which hath pleasure in the prosperity of his servant.

1 JOHN 4:7-10
Beloved, let us love one another: for love is of God; and every one that loveth is born of God, and knoweth God. [8] He that loveth not knoweth not God; for God is love. [9] In this was manifested the love of God toward us, because that God sent his only begotten Son into the world, that we might live through him. [10] Herein is love, not that we loved God, but that he loved us, and sent his Son to be the propitiation for our sins.

ROMANS 5:8
But God commendeth his love toward us, in that, while we were yet sinners, Christ died for us.

LESSON 8 — WHAT ABOUT SUFFERING?

DISCIPLESHIP QUESTIONS

38. If you trust and believe in God's love—by focusing on what He has already done for you—what will rise?

39. Discussion Question: What do you think about the fact that Jesus chose to suffer death on a cross because He loved you and wanted to save you?

40. True or false: God is pursuing you.

41. What more did Jesus do for you after He ascended into heaven?

42. Read Psalm 46:10. What kind of stillness do you need?

43. God wants to reveal His love for you _____ than you desire to know it, but He isn't going to _____ His way into your life.

44. Read Revelation 3:20. What is Jesus asking here?

45. Read 1 John 4:18. What will push the fear out of your life?

SCRIPTURES TO USE WITH QUESTIONS

ROMANS 8:32
He that spared not his own Son, but delivered him up for us all, how shall he not with him also freely give us all things?

MATTHEW 26:53
Thinkest thou that I cannot now pray to my Father, and he shall presently give me more than twelve legions of angels?

2 CHRONICLES 16:9
For the eyes of the L<small>ORD</small> run to and fro throughout the whole earth, to shew himself strong in the behalf of them whose heart is perfect toward him. Herein thou hast done foolishly: therefore from henceforth thou shalt have wars.

PSALM 46:10
Be still, and know that I am God: I will be exalted among the heathen, I will be exalted in the earth.

REVELATION 3:20
Behold, I stand at the door, and knock: if any man hear my voice, and open the door, I will come in to him, and will sup with him, and he with me.

1 JOHN 4:18
There is no fear in love; but perfect love casteth out fear: because fear hath torment. He that feareth is not made perfect in love.

Lesson 8 — What about Suffering?

DISCIPLESHIP QUESTIONS

46. You can become like the Apostle Paul, who said, **"For to me to live is Christ, and to die is gain"** (Phil. 1:21) when you what?
    A. Starting giving more to your church
    B. Just fast and pray a little more than you do
    C. Know God and understand how good He is
    D. All of the above
    E. None of the above

47. Read Romans 8:18. Whatever this world has to throw at you, God has something _____ in store.

48. Read Ephesians 3:19. God loves you and He desires good things for you, but experiencing the love of God passes what about His love?
    A. Past experience
    B. Your opinion
    C. Mere knowledge
    D. Worship songs
    E. All of the above

49. Discussion Question: Once you'd opened yourself to receiving His love and being filled with all of His fullness, what are some examples in your life of how the blessings of God have come upon you and overtaken you, and how it caused everything to work out for good in your life?

SCRIPTURES TO USE WITH QUESTIONS

PHILIPPIANS 1:21
For to me to live is Christ, and to die is gain.

ROMANS 8:18
For I reckon that the sufferings of this present time are not worthy to be compared with the glory which shall be revealed in us.

EPHESIANS 3:19
And to know the love of Christ, which passeth knowledge, that ye might be filled with all the fulness of God.

LESSON 8 — WHAT ABOUT SUFFERING?

ANSWER KEY

1. Certain Bible verses dealing with suffering
2. False
3. *Discussion question*
4. E. Exercising your faith in God and trusting in Him
5. Seeking Him
6. Experience/book
7. To steal the Word of God out of your heart—they come to discourage you and undermine your faith
8. That suffering and temptation are not from God
9. B. Passive because it takes away your desire to resist problems
10. *Discussion question*
11. False
12. That if something is good, then it's from God, and if it's bad, then it's from the devil
13. That God is a good God
14. False
15. Extravagant/threatening
16. Because every time someone you love becomes ill or tragedy strikes, it is going to chip away at your resolve that God only wants good things for you
17. True
18. *Discussion question*
19. A. Feel worthy
20. *Discussion question*
21. A blanket statement to convey that whatever happens must be God's will
22. Caused
23. False
24. Because God reveals Himself **"against all ungodliness and unrighteousness of men"**
25. You have to love God, you have to be resisting the works of the devil, and you have to pray—allowing the Holy Spirit to help you make intercession
26. C. Kill them
27. *Discussion question*
28. Wonder why the all-powerful God doesn't prevent suffering
29. Rebellion
30. Because 1 Peter 5:8 and John 10:10 say so
31. C. The Bible
32. B. Anything
33. Pleased
34. No one
35. The fruit of God's peace and joy
36. Take time to be still and meditate on this truth that God showed His love for us by sending His Son
37. E. By Christ dying for you while you were still living in sin
38. Your faith
39. *Discussion question*
40. True
41. Gave you the Holy Spirit to continue His ministry on earth until He returns
42. Not just physical stillness, but stillness in your mind, which just means not being completely occupied with other thoughts
43. More/force

Lesson 8 — What about Suffering?

ANSWER KEY

44. If you will let Him into your life, give Him your attention, unplug from the distractions of life that keep you from hearing the voice of God, and simply focus on His voice

45. God's love

46. C. Know God and understand how good He is

47. Greater

48. E. All of the above

49. *Discussion question*

SOCIAL ISSUES: CHRISTIANS MUST SPEAK UP

Before we start looking at the biblical perspective on social issues and how to apply our Christian philosophy, I want to establish my right as a minister to discuss current affairs. I feel like this is necessary because many people have adopted the attitude that ministers can say all they want—as long as they stay in church. Much of society thinks that Christianity should be a privately held conviction that never gets talked about publicly.

In America, the notion of "separation of church and state" has been misunderstood and misapplied. Contrary to popular belief, the phrase does not appear anywhere in the Constitution of the United States but was used in a private letter written by Thomas Jefferson in reference to state-sponsored religion. He was against the government mandating the religion of its citizens—his statement had nothing to do with Christianity being totally removed from the public arena. There is a big difference between the two.

Critics have used the phrase "separation of church and state" to beat Christians into retreat. Unbelievers want us to withdraw into the walls of church buildings and not speak out on moral issues, but we can't separate Christianity from current affairs. The very notion of "worldview" means that our lives are influenced—if not determined—by what we believe. We cannot compartmentalize our lives into a separation of religious conviction and political affiliation. Who we are, what we believe, and how we act in everyday life are inseparable. Jesus said that a house divided won't stand for long (Mark 3:25), so we're headed for trouble when we try to divide our lives into parts that relate to God and parts that don't.

Christian ministers have every right to speak out on current affairs because the stance you take on social issues is as relevant to your relationship with God as church affairs. If your position on social issues is in opposition to God's revealed will, then you are creating a division in yourself that will, at the very least, make you insensitive to God's leading. The Bible has a lot to say about moral issues in society, and ministers need to talk about morality so Christians understand the biblical perspective.

One reason ungodliness is advancing in our culture is that a lot of Christians have retreated from the public forum. They have been intimidated into silence, but we shouldn't draw back from those who oppose God. Scripture says,

> *Thou shalt not hate thy brother in thine heart: thou shalt in any wise rebuke thy neighbour, and not suffer sin upon him. Thou shalt not avenge, nor bear any grudge against the children of thy people, but thou shalt love thy neighbour as thyself: I am the Lord.*
>
> LEVITICUS 19:17-18

Lesson 9 — Social Issues: Christians Must Speak Up

Jesus quoted this passage when He said that the two greatest commandments are to love God and to love your neighbor as yourself (Matt. 22:37-40). This passage in Leviticus says that loving your neighbor can mean letting them know when they are wrong, by not allowing them to live in sin ignorantly. Actually, the command to rebuke your neighbor is given as the opposite of hating your neighbor in your heart—by allowing them to live in sin without any reproach. Remaining silent while the world around you revels in sin isn't loving your neighbor; it's esteeming yourself above your neighbor.

It's true that the moment you speak out against immorality, people who disagree with you are going to say things to try to shut you up, like calling you intolerant or close-minded, but you can't let criticism and persecution keep you from speaking the truth in love. Despite what some think, morality isn't relative to the circumstances. Certain things are always wrong, and Christians should speak out against those things. You can't keep quiet about immorality because you are afraid of criticism.

I have received a lot of criticism over the years for speaking out on social issues. My television program has been removed from television stations, and the broadcasting channel in one country has edited out material they considered provocative. They do this not because I'm saying mean or offensive things but because some biblical positions are not considered politically correct enough to mention on television. I don't like rejection and criticism, but I'm not going to stop speaking the truth just because some people don't want to hear it.

Sometimes loving your neighbors means telling them when they are wrong, so it isn't hate speech to tell someone the truth. The Word says, **"Thou shalt not hate thy brother in thine heart: thou shalt in any wise rebuke thy neighbour, and not suffer sin upon him"** (Lev. 19:17). When you know something is wrong but refuse to talk about it because you don't want to be criticized, then your behavior shows hate toward the person who is engaged in wrongdoing.

I believe it is especially important for ministers to speak out on moral issues because a lot of Christians honestly don't know what the Word of God says about some of the things happening today. Many Christians have been listening to worldly perspectives for so long that they have taken on worldly attitudes. Their moral compasses are completely out of whack.

I'm going to give you the scriptural perspective on current social issues such as evolution, abortion, and homosexuality, but I'm also going to discuss the natural evidence that supports those biblical positions. I'm satisfied just knowing what the Word of God says, but I know that many Christians who have adopted worldly viewpoints are going to want evidence from other sources, so I'm going to present the natural evidence.

The issues I will discuss are subjects about which I believe many Christians are confused. My hope is that you will discover truths you aren't aware of, and it will reinforce your trust in the Word of God. With God, there is forgiveness, and your job as a Christian is to minister love to people lost in sin, so my motivation for speaking out against immorality is not to hurt anyone. I am not against sinners—but I am against sin, and the pain it causes.

I live in the mountains of Colorado, and a number of years ago, I was driving home on a foggy night with really poor visibility. A car passed me just as I was going into a sharp turn, and almost as soon as the car pulled in front of me, its brake lights came on and the car jerked violently. I immediately slammed

Lesson 9   Social Issues: Christians Must Speak Up

on my brakes and swerved right to avoid hitting the car. I ended up stopping on the shoulder of the road right beside the other car, which had struck a horse. The car was seriously damaged as a result of the collision, and it was sitting in the middle of the road.

As I sat there wondering what to do, a large sport utility vehicle came around the corner behind me and had to swerve to avoid the car stuck in the middle of the road. As it swerved, the SUV ran over the horse carcass, and the driver of the SUV was also injured.

At that point, both lanes of the curve were blocked on a dark foggy night, and people were driving sixty miles per hour heading into the curve. I knew more people were going to get hurt if I didn't do something to warn the oncoming traffic. I didn't have a flashlight or anything, so the only thing I could do was stand out in the road and try to flag people down. The problem was it was so foggy that drivers couldn't see me until they were so close, it was dangerous. I was jumping out in front of cars going sixty miles per hour, and they were slamming on their brakes and skidding all over the road.

A couple of people pulled over and got out of their vehicles to cuss me out. I'm sure they were pretty ticked off at me for scaring them, but I guarantee you that as soon as they came around the next corner and saw the wreck, they realized I was trying to help them. It was better for them to dodge a pedestrian attempting to slow them down than to go full speed around the corner and plow into another vehicle.

It took the police thirty minutes to arrive at the accident and take control of the traffic. I don't know how many people I stopped from speeding around the corner and getting into an accident, but it was a lot. People could have been killed. I risked bodily injury and criticism, but it was the right thing to do. It would have been selfish for me to get myself to safety and then stand by and watch car after car speed around the corner and crash into each other—just because I didn't want to get involved or anger oncoming drivers by trying to flag them down.

I believe that speaking out on moral issues is a similar situation. The Word of God speaks against immoral behaviors because they are destructive. It would be selfish of me not to warn others of the dangers of destructive behavior just because I don't want to be criticized. I know some people are going to call me intolerant and close-minded, but I am not discussing these things to make anyone angry. I'm speaking out on social issues to save lives and prevent injury, and I'm not going to let criticism or rejection prevent me from speaking the truth in love, because I believe it is not only the right of ministers to speak out on immoral trends in society but our duty as well.

LESSON 9 — SOCIAL ISSUES: CHRISTIANS MUST SPEAK UP

SCRIPTURES

MARK 3:25
And if a house be divided against itself, that house cannot stand.

LEVITICUS 19:17-18
Thou shalt not hate thy brother in thine heart: thou shalt in any wise rebuke thy neighbour, and not suffer sin upon him. **[18]** *Thou shalt not avenge, nor bear any grudge against the children of thy people, but thou shalt love thy neighbour as thyself: I am the LORD.*

MATTHEW 22:37-40
Jesus said unto him, Thou shalt love the Lord thy God with all thy heart, and with all thy soul, and with all thy mind. **[38]** *This is the first and great commandment.* **[39]** *And the second is like unto it, Thou shalt love thy neighbour as thyself.* **[40]** *On these two commandments hang all the law and the prophets.*

Creation vs. Evolution

Dr. Richard Von Sternberg, an evolutionary biologist, is a former editor of a prominent scientific journal associated with the Smithsonian Museum of Natural History. After an article that Dr. Von Sternberg chose to publish for the journal was printed, he was immediately pressured to resign, and an investigation into his political and religious beliefs was conducted. Halfway across the country at Baylor University, science professor Robert Marks, who was approaching tenure in his position at the university, suddenly had his professional website shut down by the university and was forced to return research grant money to the school.[1]

What horrible crime did these two well-respected scientists commit that sparked such outrage and drastic action to be taken against them? They dared to mention, within their sphere of influence, an evolutionist's two most-feared words: *intelligent design*. Even the consideration of life being created instead of the result of random chance is considered heretical by evolutionists.

In Dr. Von Sternberg's case, he published an article by another scientist who merely suggested that intelligent design might be able to explain how life began. Those in the scientific community were so upset about the article, Von Sternberg was thereafter labeled as an "intellectual terrorist."

As Professor Marks learned, even at some institutes of higher learning that carry a Christian label, like Baylor, being associated with any concept other than evolution can cost you your career. When the university discovered a link between Marks' research and intelligent design, they completely ostracized him. For Marks, who used his website to promote himself and his research in order to obtain grant money, it was devastating, both financially and professionally. Professor Marks was shocked by Baylor's reaction to his work. "I have never been treated like this in my thirty years of academia," he stated.[1]

Dr. Von Sternberg and Professor Marks are only two examples of the kind of treatment a person can expect to receive when going against the tide of evolution. Hundreds, if not thousands, of excellent and well-loved professors have been fired or forced to resign for simply making a comment about intelligent design in their classrooms, even in those schools that pride themselves on having "healthy debate" and a "diversity of opinions." And many scientists have found themselves blackballed from the scientific community, essentially ending their careers, because of research they've conducted that even hints at intelligent design.

---

1   Nathan Frankowski, Kevin Miller, & Ben Stein. *Expelled: No Intelligence Allowed* DVD. Premise Media Corporation and Rampant Films. 2008.

But there are others—many others—who have evolved, so to speak, from believing in evolution to now believing in intelligent design, or creationism, yet they do not dare to openly confess their new way of thinking. Hidden in our universities, high schools, and research labs are ex-atheists, ex-agnostics, and ex-evolutionists who have discovered the lie behind evolution. Unfortunately, they must keep their discoveries to themselves.

So, it makes you wonder—what is it that the scientific and educational institutions are so afraid of? Why do they try so hard to squelch even the thought that something other than evolution is responsible for life?

I believe it's because pure evolution promotes a completely godless philosophy, or view of the earth and humanity. Satan has worked very hard and has been quite successful at keeping God out of our classrooms and other institutions. When humanists teach evolution as a fact and don't allow any other viewpoints on the subject of creation, they close the door for any possible seeds to be planted in people's minds—and hearts—that God exists.

Ironically, at the Scopes "monkey trial" in 1925, where evolutionists were granted the right to present evolution as a theory in American classrooms, it was said to be a travesty of justice that only one theory of life origin—which at that time was creationism—should be taught. Yet that is exactly what is happening today, except the single theory now being taught is evolution.

Dr. Carl Baugh, founder of the Creation Evidence Museum in Glen Rose, Texas, is an ex-atheist who became a Christian and creationist. He also believes that evolution is a spiritual battleground. "It's not only a battle for the minds of men; it's a battle for their souls."[2] Another atheist-turned-creationist, Dr. Grady McMurtry, who developed Creation Worldview Ministries, adds, "Without the doctrine of creation, there is no Christianity.... If you start with Genesis…then take a look at John chapter 1 and Revelation 14:6 and 7, it is creation which is the foundation of Christianity. Without [creation] there is no Christianity."[3]

> *In the beginning was the Word, and the Word was with God, and the Word was God. The same was in the beginning with God. All things were made by him; and without him was not any thing made that was made. In him was life; and the life was the light of men. And the light shineth in darkness; and the darkness comprehended it not.*
>
> JOHN 1:1-5

> *And I saw another angel fly in the midst of heaven, having the everlasting gospel to preach unto them that dwell on the earth, and to every nation, and kindred, and tongue, and people, Saying with a loud voice, Fear God, and give glory to him; for the hour of his judgment is come: and worship him that made heaven, and earth, and the sea, and the fountains of waters.*
>
> REVELATION 14:6-7

Being totally pro-evolution allows people to deaden their hearts to the voice of creation. According to Psalm 19, creation is shouting out to us:

---

[2] Dr. Carl Baugh, interview with Andrew Wommack, March 6, 2012, Creation Evidence Museum, Glen Rose, TX.
[3] Dr. Grady McMurtry, interview with Andrew Wommack, June 8, 2012, Woodland Park, CO.

Lesson 10   Creation vs. Evolution

The heavens declare the glory of God; and the firmament sheweth his handywork. Day unto day uttereth speech, and night unto night sheweth knowledge. There is no speech nor language, where their voice is not heard. Their line is gone out through all the earth, and their words to the end of the world.

PSALM 19:1-4

Every day, people everywhere—even in the farthest reaches of this planet—are within shouting distance for creation to let them know there's a Creator. But people want to believe in evolution because it eliminates that voice, therefore eliminating accountability to a Creator. If we evolved from slime and are nothing but evolved animals, then we can live like animals. And when we die, it's over—period. We didn't come from anywhere and aren't going anywhere, so we can do whatever we want. People who think this way conclude they can do whatever they want as long as they don't get caught or suffer any consequences. They simply establish their own morality.

However, the Bible is filled with stories of God holding people accountable for their actions. God often pronounced judgment and punishment because people went against His commands. We, as His creation, are responsible to Him. One example is when the Lord became upset at mankind and wiped out everyone except Noah and his family (Gen. 6).

So many places in Scripture prove that we didn't evolve and that God is not some disinterested person out "there" who just wound the earth up like a clock and let it run. He created everything we see. He created us. His fingerprints are everywhere, and all of creation screams that at us. I believe evolution is being so heavily pushed down people's throats because it's an attempt to drown out that voice of creation.

Dr. McMurtry believes that "according to evolutionists, we're only thinking animals…. Evolution is absolutely a religion. It is not science. It's a religion of convenience, meaning, if it's not convenient, it doesn't fit my religion…. [Evolutionists] want to believe it because it's the only way in which they can intellectually justify that they can lead a sinless life without Jesus Christ….this is what justifies the homosexual lifestyle, abortion, euthanasia, racism, pornography, all of our social ills…. These social issues are merely the branches. The tree trunk is secular humanism, and evolution is the tap root."[3]

It's dangerous for anyone to fall into the evolution trap because it keeps that person from God. But it's especially hard to understand a Christian falling for it. The fundamental problem with evolution, like any other secular philosophy, is that it violates the Word of God. If, as a Christian, you embrace evolution and believe it to be true, you are ultimately going to disbelieve God's Word. Evolution is not compatible with the Bible.

I know there are some of you Christians reading this who believe in evolution because that's what you've been taught. You've drunk the Kool-Aid without ever questioning its content. It's been reinforced millions and millions of times, and it seems like all of the movers and shakers of our world believe it, so you should too. But at the same time, you'll claim that you believe the Bible. You can't have it both ways. If you truly believe in evolution, then you're going to have to believe that the Word of God is not accurate. By believing in evolution, you lose confidence in the authority that God's Word holds, which in turn will destroy your faith.

---

[3]   Dr. Grady McMurtry, interview with Andrew Wommack, June 8, 2012, Woodland Park, CO.

There is not one particular theory of evolution; there are many different theories. This is another problem with the whole evolution argument, because even among evolutionists, they can't agree on which theory is correct. In general, there are two categories of theories: Anti-theistic theories, which basically state that our universe is here by a random accident and not because an intelligent being created it; and theistic theories, which hold that God did create the universe but that evolution was still part of the equation. Yet another theory is intelligent design, which claims that there was some sort of being—not necessarily God—who created life.

Biblical creationism, which views creation as a literal six-day event, and anti-theistic evolution are polar opposites of one another, while all these other theories create an evolution spectrum in between. Sadly, many Christians believe in one of the many non-biblical theories of evolution, holding creationism views that have subtlety evolved away from the truth of Scripture.

One of Satan's greatest tactics is to mix just enough truth with lies that we fall for the lies and into deception. Over time, he has masterfully created hybrids between evolution and creationism—theistic evolutionary theories—to the point where many Christians no longer have an untainted biblical view of how and when God formed the earth.

An example of theistic evolution is the thought that God was responsible for the Big Bang but that living beings evolved from that point. Another is that God did form each creature, including humans, as individual and unique entities, but He did so millions of years ago. One version of this theory is called the gap theory, which states that there are actually millions of years of time between Genesis 1:1 (**"In the beginning God created the heaven and the earth."**) and Genesis 1:2 (**"And the earth was without form, and void; and darkness was upon the face of the deep. And the Spirit of God moved upon the face of the waters."**).

I've got friends, who love God and love His Word, who have bought into this theory, but I can't subscribe to it. They believe that prior to Genesis 1:2, hundreds of millions of years existed, and during that time, all of the dinosaurs were alive and there was an entire pre-Adamic civilization. They believe that what Genesis is explaining is actually a re-creation, not an original creation, of the earth.

Some Christians believe that there was a civilization in which Lucifer, whom we now call Satan, populated this earth and ruled over it. Lucifer then rebelled against God, and God destroyed the demonic civilization, causing the earth to become vain and void (Gen. 1:2). They believe that when God told Adam and Eve to replenish the earth (Gen. 1:28), the word *replenish* indicates that the earth was once vibrant, that it was once full of life but then was destroyed. To those who believe this, Genesis 1:28 is describing the re-creation where Adam and Eve had to replenish—or refill—the earth.

I admit that the word *replenish* can mean to fill again, but this word is used a number of times in Scripture, and it's not talking about filling again; it simply means "to fill" (*American Heritage Dictionary*). In fact, all of the main translations of the Bible interpret this verse as "Be fruitful and fill the earth." It doesn't imply any of the meaning of refilling as some think.

Too many people, including Christians, won't stand and speak against evolution because they've been told that it's an established fact. They're taught that evolution has been proven over and over. So often, people are afraid to stand up and say anything about it. I was shocked to read an article that showed only a slight majority of pastors believe in biblical creationism. But even among those who do believe it, the vast majority won't teach it, because they fear how their people will respond.

But there are currently thousands upon thousands of scientists who don't buy into the lie of evolution. Some believe in intelligent design and others believe in biblical creationism. Even though we're all told that evolution is an established fact, they understand that it's not. It's merely a theory—and one with many holes.

I believe in biblical creationism because I believe the Bible. The Word of God is sufficient for me to settle the issue of evolution versus creationism. But I also realize that there are many Christians, even some of you reading this book, who may honor God's Word to a degree, but you also—maybe even more so—honor the natural and secular views you've been taught through the educational system. For this reason, I also want to approach this topic from a place of logic and science, using experts in the field who've discovered evidence supporting biblical creationism, to showcase the multitude of problems surrounding the theory of evolution.

First, let me share some things from Scripture. I encourage you to read through Genesis 1 on your own. Do so with an open mind and an open heart, and allow the Holy Spirit to speak to you through the scriptures. You'll see in Genesis that the Bible clearly states how God created the heavens and the earth:

> *In the beginning God created the heaven and the earth. And the earth was without form, and void; and darkness was upon the face of the deep. And the Spirit of God moved upon the face of the waters. And God said, Let there be light: and there was light.... And God said, Let there be lights in the firmament of the heaven to divide the day from the night; and let them be for signs, and for seasons, and for days, and years: And let them be for lights in the firmament of the heaven to give light upon the earth: and it was so. And God made two great lights; the greater light to rule the day, and the lesser light to rule the night: he made the stars also.*
>
> GENESIS 1:1-3 AND 14-16

In verse 3, God spoke light into existence. He spoke light into existence before He created the sun, moon, or stars. That's what the Bible says. In other words, He spoke light into existence before there was a place for light to come from (verse 16). This by itself totally disproves the Big Bang theory. These verses refute that theory because there was light before there was the sun, moon, and stars. The earth existed before the sun existed. There wasn't a bunch of matter that was just flung out in space. God created the earth, and then on the third day, He made the sun, moon, and stars and placed them in the heavens to give light to the earth. If you believe the Bible's account of creation, there isn't room to believe evolution.

Even if you believe there was a God who made the process of evolution happen, things didn't happen in the sequence that evolutionists say they did. The earth was created first. It was totally covered by water, and God spoke light into existence. It wasn't until the third day when He created the sun, moon, and stars. This is hard to understand because if you need light, you flip a light switch or grab a flashlight. The light comes from that source. But Romans 4:17 tells us that God **"calleth those things which be not as though they were."**

God simply speaks things into existence. God spoke light into existence before He created a source for light. I know that's hard for our little peanut brains to wrap around and understand, but it doesn't disprove it. Just because we can't understand how God did something and because it's not the way we would've done it doesn't mean it isn't true.

Lesson 10   Creation vs. Evolution

Dr. Baugh once reported on a graduate project conducted at UCLA where the students used a flask of water and a boom box from which they could control the sound frequencies. They discovered that when they generated certain frequencies, a small bubble appeared in the center of a flask of water. They later found by experimentation that the bubble heated to 100,000 degrees yet was self-insulating. As it heated, a full spectrum of light was emitted out the other side of the bubble.

Commenting on these results, Dr. Baugh said, "What happened in this experiment totally verifies Scripture. God said in the presence of that sphere of water that He had just created, 'Let there be light,' and there was light…from sound."[2]

We know that physicists have learned that at the base of every physical entity are cells made of atoms, which in turn are made of subatomic particles. All of these subatomic particles are vibrating. They have discovered that at the base of that vibration is sound. This confirms exactly what the Bible says! Everything we see was created by words, is maintained by words, and responds to words.

One big problem I've always had with the pro-evolution argument is that it's based on the assumption that the universe goes from disorder to order and from simple to complex. But this is the exact opposite of what really happens in nature, as stated in the Second Law of Thermodynamics. In fact, the popular evolutionist and anti-creationist Isaac Asimov admitted: "The Second Law of Thermodynamics states that the amount of available work you can get out of the energy of the universe is constantly decreasing…. This is true for everything in general, the universe all over.[4] Another way of stating the second law then is, 'The universe is constantly getting more disorderly!' Viewed that way we can see the second law all about us. …everything deteriorates, collapses, breaks down, wears out, all by itself—and that is what the second law is all about."[5]

This is totally contrary to the theory of evolution. In evolution, everything goes from very simple to incredibly complex and sophisticated. This is not observable anywhere in nature.

Dr. Baugh adds, "Basic life forms are more complicated than evolution can ever hope to address. Evolutionists like to say that changes take place over time. What they don't say is that that change has boundaries. So, they slip in the concept that a tadpole can ultimately become a monkey that can ultimately become a PhD. But that change has limitations, and that change never leads to a higher order. It never increases the complexity. It might isolate the gene pool to get a superior product temporarily, but you have not increased the complexity. You have only limited the viability…. Change over time is limited, and the final product is always downhill."[1]

To put this concept in simple terms, you can breed dogs, horses, and cows and get changes within those species, but at the end of the day, they are still dogs, horses, and cows. Mankind, with all its intelligence, can't breed a dog to become a cow, or a monkey to become a man. Change is limited to variations within that specific species. If it can't be done on purpose with intelligent thought and design, then it certainly can't happen accidentally.

Scripture backs this up. The Lord said in Genesis 1:11 that the grass and herbs were to bring forth after their kind. In Genesis 1:21, all the sea creatures and fowl of the air **"brought forth…after their kind."** Genesis 1:24-25 states:

---
4   Isaac Asimov, "The Origin of the Universe" *ORIGINS: How the World Came to Be* DVD, Eden Communications, 1983.
5   Isaac Asimov, "In the Game of Energy and Thermodynamics You Can't Even Break Even," *Smithsonian Institution Journal* (June 1970), 6.

LESSON 10 CREATION VS. EVOLUTION

And God said, Let the earth bring forth the living creature after his kind, cattle, and creeping thing, and beast of the earth after his kind: and it was so. And God made the beast of the earth after his kind, and cattle after their kind, and every thing that creepeth upon the earth after his kind: and God saw that it was good.

Scripture clearly teaches that each species reproduces after its own kind. According to the command of God, it's impossible for one species to evolve into another species. For those who believe in the authority of the Bible, that kills evolution. But sadly, many Christians don't let the Bible get in the way of what they believe.

I believe in devolution. I can see in nature, and I see in the Bible, where humanity and other life forms have gone from complex to simple and from order to disorder. For instance, I believe that Adam was incredibly smart. It is said that people only use about 10 percent of their brain. I have no way of knowing how they came to that conclusion. I think these people may use a lot less than 10 percent! But I do believe that Adam was hitting on all cylinders. God created man to be incredibly smart.

Adam was able to name every animal on earth. Their names are so descriptive of their function and how they live; this shows incredible intelligence on Adam's part. I believe that Adam and Eve were super smart, and I believe that we've all evolved downward from there. Evolution says that people came from apes, and they started out as cavemen who had no sophistication. Yet if you look at the oldest skeletons we have of mankind, they show incredible sophistication.

I also believe that we used to have a much deeper revelation of God. Adam and Eve walked with God in perfection, and Adam lived to be 930 years old. Adam had an intimate relationship with God and saw the creation in its perfection. Then he began to see the animals start to prey upon each other, where in the beginning they were all herbivorous. Enoch also walked with God and had such a close relationship with Him that he was literally caught up into the heavens (Gen. 5:24). He never died. He lived for over 300 years. The revelation of God that Adam and Enoch passed on impacted people!

People started out knowing God. Cain, when he killed Abel, spoke directly to God (Gen. 4:9-16). They were having an audible, face-to-face confrontation. People started out knowing that there was a God, but we have devolved. When people say there is no God, that's reverse evolution. It's foolish! It goes against their intuitive knowledge (Rom. 1:18-20).

*The fool hath said in his heart, There is no God. They are corrupt, they have done abominable works, there is none that doeth good. The L*ORD *looked down from heaven upon the children of men, to see if there were any that did understand, and seek God. They are all gone aside, they are all together become filthy: there is none that doeth good, no, not one.*

PSALM 14:1-3

According to verse 1, which is repeated in Psalm 53, only a fool would say there is no God. Only a fool could look at creation and not figure out that this incredible complexity could not possibly evolve.

Take one of the simplest things in nature—a single blade of grass. If you pooled all the intellectual and financial resources of mankind, we could not produce a single, living blade of grass. We could produce something that looks like grass; it might have the same texture and chemical makeup, but it couldn't reproduce itself. It wouldn't be alive.

Lesson 10 — Creation vs. Evolution

If man, with all his intelligence, can't do that which is least, then how can anyone possibly believe that the incredible complexity of nature could happen randomly? That defies logic. The chances of evolution happening randomly are impossible.

The chances of a 747 jet being perfectly assembled and able to fly as the result of a bomb going off at the Boeing Aircraft factory are infinitely more probable than the chances of evolution. The chances of an explosion in a print shop creating perfectly printed, bound, and stacked Bibles are infinitely more probable than the chances of evolution.

If spacecraft discovered a house on Mars, I guarantee that people would see this as proof that there was once life on that planet. They wouldn't think this house just evolved. Only an intelligent creature could create something like that. Yet so-called "intellectuals" look at the complexity of nature and think it just evolved. That's foolish.

Perhaps you're reading this and acknowledging that you don't fully believe in evolution to the point where you think the earth is here by accident, but you have bought into some of the other theistic theories of evolution. In this case, you still have mixed truth with lies and have adopted a secular worldview of how the earth was made. This is damaging to your faith. If you can't accept the Word at face value but instead mix other ingredients with it, your faith will become compromised. Satan can then easily get you to doubt the integrity of the rest of God's Word. This puts everything you believe about the Bible at risk.

Biblical creationism, which follows the whole truth of Scripture, is also called the Young Earth Theory by scientists. It holds that the earth and every living creature were made by a Creator in a period of six days, just as stated in Genesis 1. Based on these verses, creation covered a span of six days—literal days, because each had a morning and an evening and because this is the same type of day referred to in Exodus 20:8-11, where the Sabbath is discussed. Jesus confirmed that humans were created at the same time as the earth (without millions of years separating them) when He said, **"From the beginning of the creation God made them male and female"** (Mark 10:6). Any other view of creation is, in some form, a compromise of what Scripture teaches.

Dr. Grady McMurtry wholeheartedly believes in a Young Earth Theory. But this was not always the case. Dr. McMurtry grew up learning evolution in the public schools of Berkeley, California. He also spent time in the paleontology labs of University of California, Berkeley, learning about dinosaur fossils and evolutionary theory as a child. He learned so much that when he was only eight years old, teachers started "borrowing" him from one classroom to another to teach other kids! He ultimately went on to earn an MS from State University of New York in evolutionary theory, which he later taught.

But when McMurtry was twenty-seven, the Holy Spirit guided him through Scripture and proved to him that Jesus was who He said He was, and he became a Christian. He immediately recognized that he couldn't reconcile what he was reading in the Bible about creation with his evolution background. *After sixteen months of study and research, he came to the conclusion that there is not one law of science or one natural process that sufficiently supports evolution, whereas every natural law, every natural process, and all of the earth's physical evidence supports creation.*

Now, after decades of continued research, McMurtry travels the world educating people on the case for a young earth. "Whether you look in the earth, on the earth, or outside of the earth in space, there is plenty of evidence to show the earth is young," he argues.[6] In fact, McMurtry states that there are over 270 geochronometers, or earth time clocks, that demonstrate a recent creation of the universe.

For example, minerals and gemstones found inside the earth are said by evolutionists to take millions of years to form. But Dr. McMurtry has found evidence of gold being formed in fewer than five hours, and states that in 2006, it was discovered how to produce flawless diamonds in fewer than twelve hours.[6] McMurtry also points to stalagmites—which supposedly take millions of years to grow—having formed on Mayan pottery made in A.D. 700, as evidence of a young earth.[6]

My own study found that granite contains a radioactive particle called polonium 214, having a half-life of 0.000164 seconds. That means this radioactive particle dissipates in less than one one-thousandth of a second. If it took more than one one-thousandth of a second for granite to form, polonium 214 wouldn't be trapped in the rock.

Dr. McMurtry also views the decay of the earth's magnetic field as further evidence of a young earth. Earth's decay has been measurable since the early 1800s. The earth decays in the same way that radioactive material does, meaning it has a half-life. The half-life of the earth's magnetic field is 1,400 years. So, every 1,400 years, one half of the strength of the magnetic field decays. Going back in time 1,400 years, the strength of this field would double. Our magnetic field bends the sun's radiation at the poles, and without it, everything on earth would die. Ten thousand years ago, the strength of the field would have killed all life on earth; therefore, living beings couldn't have been here millions of years ago, as Old Earth theorists claim.

Yet the further we move ahead in time, the weaker the field becomes. Within 2,000 years, our current magnetic field will be gone. As Dr. McMurtry put it, "We live in a very narrow band of time. This is why we know that Jesus is coming back soon, because when He comes there will still be people on earth. That means the field has to still be strong enough to shield the earth from the sun's radiation. God never intended the earth to last a long time once it became flawed due to human sin."[6]

What absolutely convinces Dr. McMurtry of a young earth is the evidence he's seen in the world's rock formations, along with sediment that has formed in the mouths of rivers across the globe. He thoroughly believes these things point to a global event of catastrophic proportions that very quickly changed the face of the earth—an event that perfectly harmonizes with the Flood in the Bible. The following is taken from an interview I conducted with Dr. McMurtry where he explains his findings.[3]

●────────────────────────────●

Let's start with day three of creation to show how Noah's Flood is related to the way God made the earth. On day three, God caused the dry land to rise out of the water, and He gathered the seas, which are shallow—only up to a mile deep. He gathered the water into one place, and dry land appeared. There are separations of waters above and below, and in this firmament God made what we call the earth's crust, but it's more like an eggshell. Ten miles underneath is a layer of water one mile deep, which we found evidence of in 1909. We now know that there are large pockets of water down there that never came up the first time and that there is at least five to six times more water in the crust than on the crust. At ten miles of depth, the earth warms at 90 degrees per mile initially, so that water is 900 degrees Fahrenheit.

---
[6] Dr. Grady McMurty, *Why I Believe in a Young Creation DVD*, Creation Worldview Ministries, 2009.
[3] Dr. Grady McMurtry, interview with Andrew Wommack, June 8, 2012, Woodland Park, CO.

At this temperature, the water is liquid steam, the same thing that causes volcanic eruptions. God put it down there, knowing He'd need it 1,656 years later. Genesis 7:11 says that the fountains of the great deep, or the springs of waters, burst forth or broke open. The actual Hebrew word used is cleave. Cleave means to come into a knife edge. The waters knifed through from below to start the Flood. The World Ocean Floor Map (Fig. 1) shows the exact places where the waters knifed through. It also shows how the continents were separated by this water bursting forth. They floated rapidly because they're on a layer of water. Although the continents are in one piece to start with, when they were knifed through, they broke into smaller pieces.

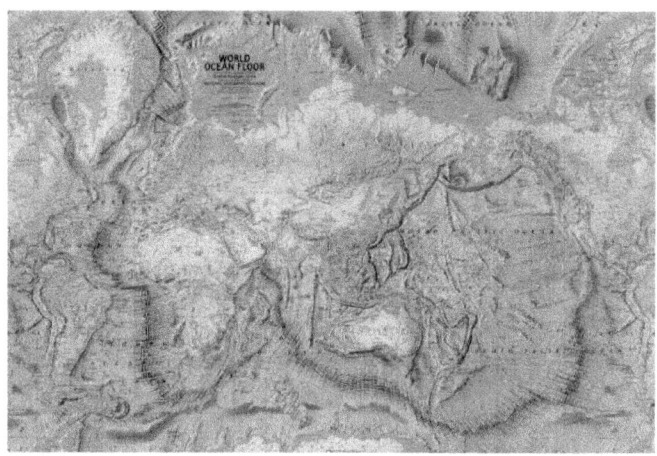

FIG. 1

During earthquakes, land cracks open, presenting an opportunity for hot rock and hot water to come up from below. Initially the water is trapped, but when the earth breaks open, the waters knife through the crack. Caesarea Philippi is where the land crack of the Flood began. It started very, very tight, which is what will happen with tremendous pressure at one point. From there, the crack went down to what is now the Jordan River and then to the Red Sea. It continued underneath the ocean into the Indian Ocean, going around the world 40,000 miles, breaking all three continents from the others. This one continuous crack shows it was the result of one specific occurrence and not separate events.

The significance of the crack starting at Caesarea Philippi is beyond belief. This is where Jesus led His disciples and asked them, "Who do men say the Son of Man is?" Then He asked one of the two most important questions in the entire New Testament: "Who do *you* say that I am?" He asked that at the very spot where the crack started and broke off three continents. It's the very place where the Jordan River starts as clear living water coming out of a rock. This is not a coincidence. Jesus knew exactly where He was. He was there before the crack was!

Evolutionists talk about Pangaea, or how all the continents used to fit together, which is a biblical concept. You can see on the Pangaea Globe (Fig. 2)—although you can tell better on a round globe—how the continental shelf of Greenland perfectly fits the continental shelf of Norway. It's like two pieces of a jigsaw puzzle. Then there's a crack going up the middle where the eruption of hot rock and hot water took place when the waters cleaved from below. You can also see how the western continental shelf of New Zealand perfectly fits the eastern continental shelf of Australia.

Lesson 10 — Creation vs. Evolution

FIG. 2

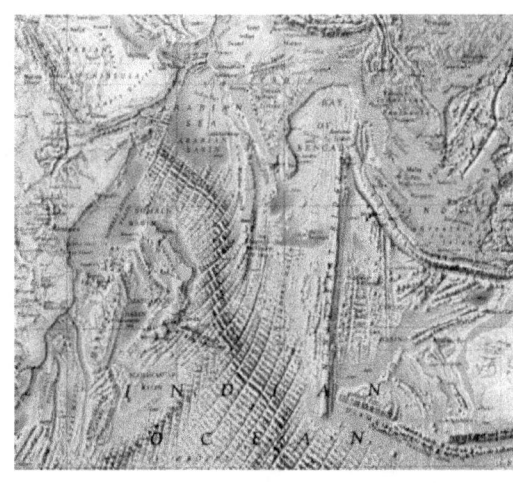

FIG. 3

And, you can see stretch marks in the Indian Ocean (Fig. 3), which only happen when something occurs quickly, like during a nine-month pregnancy. If evolution was true and it took hundreds of millions of years, you wouldn't see the stretch marks because there would be deep layers of mud due to years and years of rain washing sediment off the continents. But we do see stretch marks, and we have what are called abyssal plains, or flat sand bottoms, right up against the side of the continents. This proves that mud never came into the Atlantic in the first place, meaning this all formed in a short period of time.

Now, the mountains before the Flood were up to 5,000 feet high but were capable of being covered with one mile of water. The water eroded those mountains that existed from creation to the Flood and created the wet mud layers—the sedimentary rock layers—that were re-deposited. Seventy-five to eighty percent of the earth's land surface is covered with dried-out mud layers, or sedimentary rock, containing trillions of dead plants and animals that all drowned. That should be proof enough of a worldwide flood, not a slow and gradual accumulation.

After the Flood ended, the layers eroded, and other layers were lifted and folded by tectonic forces, the moving of continents and so forth. This occurs while the layers are still wet, and then only after they have been folded do they dry into hard rock. We see these folded layers all over the world, showing how everything was deposited very quickly and proving a rapid formation. We also know that fossilization is rapid, and to form a fossil, something has to be buried rapidly. Otherwise, it would decay. Yet we have fossils all through these mud layers.

Experiments in Colorado State University's sedimentation laboratory prove that all layers form at the same time and merely extend in the direction of water flow. With moving water, the bottom and top layers form at the same time but extend as the water flows in that direction. The layer in the bottom is the same age as the layer on the top, which totally disproves evolution.

The layers in the Rocky Mountains (Fig. 4) are easy to see. If evolution was true, these layers should be flat because water seeks its own level and lays down flat. But instead of flat layers, there are undulations or wavelike layers, again showing a rapid formation. More evidence is the erosion material at the bottom. If those mountains are 300 million years old, there's not nearly enough erosion material. The erosion material present only supports a formation time of a few thousand years.

FIG. 4

In the Grand Canyon (Fig. 5), there are Redwall Limestone and Cambrian Muav layers interlaced. There's one, then another, then another, going back and forth, showing that the canyon was not clean cut like evolutionists say it should be if the layers have different ages. Rather, it reflects water currents depositing layer after layer of material as the currents moved back and forth. And we even have layers that are missing according to evolutionary thinking (Fig. 6). Sometimes there are smooth flat lines, but there are ten million years missing.

FIG. 5

FIG. 6

Also, if—as evolutionists claim—the layers were deposited at different times, there had to be some period during which each layer was exposed before the next layer was deposited. But there are no soil horizons, or places where rock eroded into soil, in between the layers. There also are no V-shape erosion marks, which occur when the layers are exposed to rain. Those erosion marks should be filled in by the next layer of mud, but evidence of that is not there. And there are no animal holes or root holes. The lack of these things shows that all these layers were deposited at one time in a really big flood, and they were not exposed one after another after another.

We can also look at the eruption of Mount St. Helens in 1980 to show how the Grand Canyon was formed quickly. During the initial nine hours of eruption on May 18, twenty-five feet of ash were laid down in one layer. The second layer is actually comprised of several layers that formed during a second eruption over a period of five hours. Again, these layers are about twenty-five feet deep. The top layer, also about twenty-five feet, formed in fewer than twenty-four hours. There were three distinct events during the time of the eruptions from 1980 to 1982. But all three layers—a total of seventy-five feet—came into existence in fewer than three days. This shows that geological features form quite rapidly.

We have eyewitness documentation and photographic evidence to prove the time frame in which these layers developed (Fig. 7). The ash formed a seventy-five-foot cliff with three separate "zones," each twenty-five feet deep. Evolutionists would believe that this material came into existence at the rate of one inch every thousand to ten thousand years by the erosion of prior rock material. Therefore, to an evolutionist, this cliff would represent one million years' worth of history. In reality, it represents three days.

FIG. 7

Evolutionists would also want you to believe that all the layers of the Grand Canyon came about slowly and gradually over millions of years and that the Colorado River cut the canyon just as slowly and gradually. The first problem with that is a river that small could not cut such a big canyon. Second, we have another example from Mount St. Helens to prove how fast a canyon can be cut (Fig. 8). This 125-foot-deep canyon was cut in one day by mudflow. This just shows that massive amounts of water or mud moving very quickly all at once can do a tremendous amount of work. There's no reason an event such as Noah's Flood could not have carved the Grand Canyon in less than a year.

FIG. 8

We can also look at mud accumulation at the mouths of the world's rivers to prove the earth has only been around for about 6,000 years. One example is the Mississippi River (Fig. 9). The Gulf of Mexico is a big empty hole in the ground with a flat sand surface on the bottom. Only 4,500 years' worth of mud has collected at the mouth of the Mississippi. If the Mississippi were millions of years old, the entire Gulf of Mexico would be filled in. This is one of the simplest and easiest ways to see that the earth is young. And every major river in the world is the same way. The Amazon, the Colorado River that goes all the way into the Baja, the Indus Ganges, and so forth—all of them only have 4,500 years' worth of mud at their mouths, showing that the earth has only been eroding since the time of Noah's Flood.

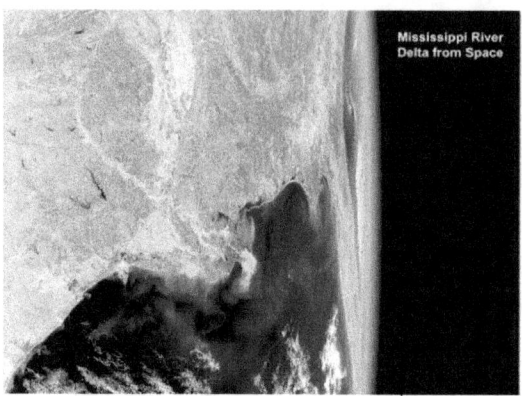

FIG. 9

It's obvious that Dr. McMurtry has compiled quite a bit of research that goes a long way toward validating biblical creationism while also demonstrating many of the problems with the pro-evolution argument. But whenever evolution versus creationism is discussed, people always want to know about the fossils, especially the dinosaurs. In addition to Dr. McMurtry, I've also spent considerable time with Dr. Carl Baugh, who has personally excavated many, many fossils during his time in paleontology.

Like Dr. McMurtry, Dr. Baugh is an ex-atheist who used to teach evolution. He has doctorate degrees in education, theology, and biblical archaeology. His most recent work has been in the paleontological field where he has discovered and directed the excavation of sixteen different dinosaurs. The following information is what Dr. Baugh discussed with me as he presented his case for a young earth.[2]

Dr. Ernst Mayr, who's considered to be the world's leading evolutionary biologist, said if there's proof that man and dinosaur lived at the same time, evolution is destroyed. Well, I found that proof in 1982 when my excavation team unearthed a dinosaur footprint and a human footprint only seventeen inches apart. But, not surprisingly, none of the scientists or media would even look at the findings because they assumed it was a hoax.

We discovered a very large acrocanthosaurus along the banks of the Paluxy River in Texas, and the other dinosaurs we found in northwestern Colorado. But the one along the Paluxy completely shattered my entire paradigm, because coming into that excavation, I was an old-age creationist. I had heard but didn't believe that there were human footprints right along with dinosaur footprints near the Paluxy

River. In 1982, I came out to direct the excavation. I assimilated a team, and we excavated one dinosaur footprint. Then, over the course of four days, we excavated another eighteen footprints.

I still didn't believe we'd find human footprints because I adhered to the view of evolution in which the last dinosaur died out sixty-four million years ago, and the first human didn't appear, even in primitive form, until two and a half million years ago. I was what you could call a progressive creationist. But then, one day as we were peeling back the layers of rock, I discovered a human footprint only seventeen-and-a-half inches from a dinosaur footprint. It completely blew my mind. We continued excavating and discovered a total of four of these human prints.

In this trail of dinosaur and human footprints, the dinosaur stepped on two of the human footprints and pushed its print back into the heel of the human print, compressing it. You can see the heel, the toes, the compression. The dinosaur actually pushed the mud into the human print. And then it stepped on another one and cut it off (Figs. 10 and 11).

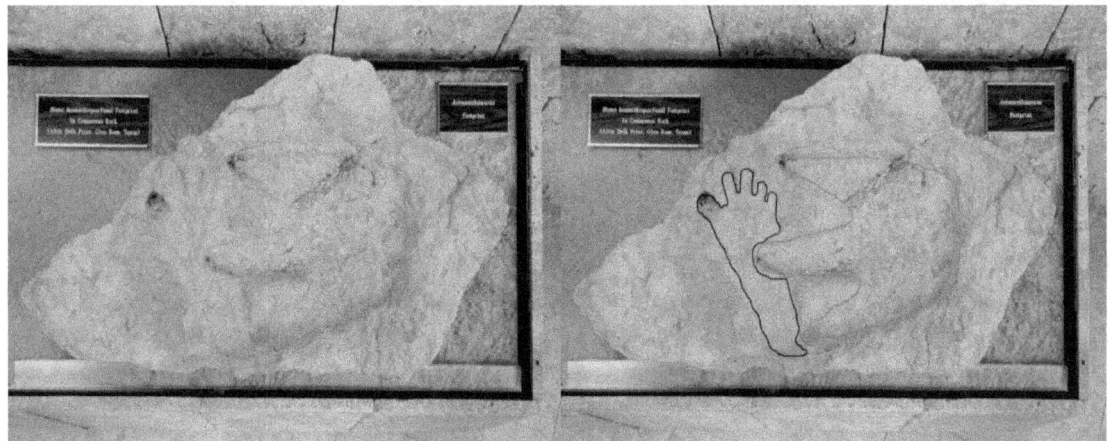

FIG. 10   FIG. 11 (PRINTS OUTLINED)

[Author's note: I personally saw these fossils at the Creation Evidence Museum in Glen Rose, Texas, when I was interviewing Dr. Baugh. They are very clearly human and dinosaur prints side by side and on top of each other. It's somewhat hard to determine from these photos, but I can personally verify that they are clearly visible.]

On another occasion, we found a series of human footprints from the Lueders Formation in the Permian Basin in West Texas. According to evolution, the hard sandstone of the Permian Basin is about 230 million years old, so there shouldn't be any human prints in it. We took those prints to two separate laboratories and ran spiral CAT scan analyses on them, which reads through the rock to determine if the print is genuine. Every one of these footprints had compression density under it and to its side, mimicking the way a real foot would move (Fig. 12).

Lesson 10　　　　　　　　　　　　Creation vs. Evolution

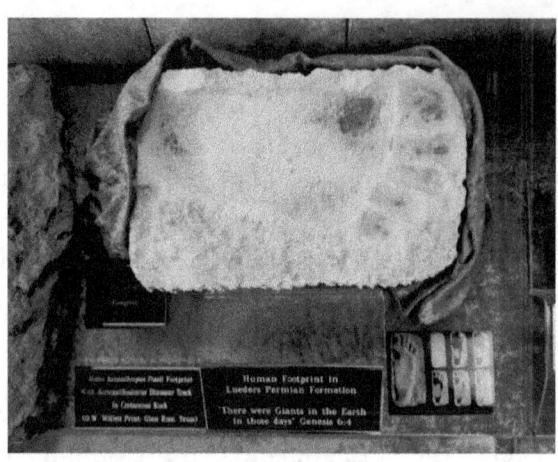

FIG. 12

[Author's note: I'm aware that many people, even some creation scientists, have discounted these footprints because there was a man in Glen Rose, Texas, who carved dinosaur and human footprints together to make money during the Great Depression. Therefore, all evidence from Glen Rose is considered to be false. But as Dr. Baugh explained to me, these spiral CAT scans can detect compression density; they can determine if the imprint was carved or made by the weight of an actual foot. All of Dr. Baugh's samples have been proven to be actual prints made by humans and dinosaurs.]

Although the media who've come to view our discoveries always find a way to explain away what they're seeing with their own eyes, we've had many evolutionists come who leave as creationists. Recently a leading evolutionary scholar became a creationist, and one of my friends said to him, "I thought you were an evolutionist and taught evolution."

He said, "I was, and I did."

"What changed you?" my friend asked.

"Well," he said, "I kept watching and reading about the evidence that Carl Baugh in Glen Rose, Texas, presented, and I couldn't ignore it."

Even Dr. Antony Flew—one of the world's leading atheists—a few years ago, turned his back on evolution after visiting our friends at The Institute for Creation Research. Dr. Flew admitted in writing that he has taught atheism and was one of the world's leading atheists, but The Institute for Creation Research exposed enough information that he can no longer deny that living systems are so complex, they require a designer. These examples prove that when people have an open mind, the evidence will speak for itself.

Aside from discovering dinosaur and human prints in the Permian Basin, we've found man-made artifacts saturated throughout this system of rock layers. According to evolutionists, these rock layers would have been here millions of years before man even existed. One artifact we found was a human sandal print with stitching around its sides. The stitching proves this was from a developed man. This sandal even has wear on the heel from the transference of weight when we walk (Fig. 13).

Lesson 10　　　　　　　　　　Creation vs. Evolution

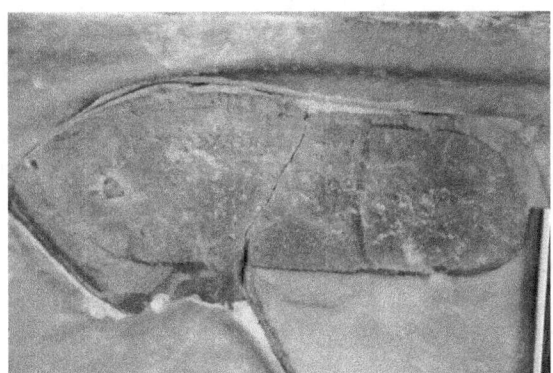

Fig. 13

What's even more interesting about this sandal is that it has a three-lobed sea bug pressed into the heel and another pressed into the toe. These sea bugs are supposedly around 550 million years old, and evolutionists put them at the bottom of the geological column because they're considered to be simple life forms. But some types of these bugs have compound eyes more sophisticated than any of today's most advanced cameras. And these bugs were found at the exact same time and place as a human sandal print!

Once I saw actual evidence that man and dinosaur lived contemporaneously, I searched for additional evidence. Over a period of time, I've discovered a long series of artifacts, supposedly from the bottom of the geologic column, that are scattered throughout the geologic column. The director of a leading museum in Austria once called me to say that it's come to his attention that we have more out-of-place artifacts that destroy evolutionary theory than all other entities combined. And he's right!

Another discovery worth noting is a cup that was found encased in coal. It was found by Frank Kinard in 1928 as he was working in the Sulphur City Water Works, shoveling coal to use as electricity for the town. He had a huge chunk of coal that he couldn't fit into the furnace, so he took a sledgehammer to it, and it fell apart. A man-made cup fell out of it. Coal is said by evolutionists to take nearly 400 million years to form. Yet we see evidence of coal and a man-made cup that are the same age (Fig. 14). Similarly, a man-made hammer was found buried in early Cretaceous rock, once again showing that humans were alive at the same time as these rock layers (Fig. 14).

Fig. 14

Lesson 10 — Creation vs. Evolution

I believe that all this evidence, along with other evidence that has been discovered over the years, absolutely disproves any form of evolution and decidedly points to a Young-Earth, biblical creationism. But again, I don't have to have scientists help me reach this conclusion—I have the Word of God. You were created by God. If you truly believe that you somehow evolved, you will believe anything! If you can swallow that lie, I don't know what the limit would be on what you would believe.

Romans 1:18-20 tells us:

> *For the wrath of God is revealed from heaven against all ungodliness and unrighteousness of men, who hold the truth in unrighteousness; Because that which may be known of God is manifest in them; for God hath shewed it unto them. For the invisible things of him from the creation of the world are clearly seen, being understood by the things that are made, even his eternal power and Godhead; so that they are without excuse.*

This is a powerful passage of Scripture that basically says that the invisible things of God are revealed in us—not just to us, but in us. According to Psalm 19, creation is shouting out that there is a God! For anyone who pays attention, this is obvious. But even beyond creation, we have an inner witness. God has put a homing device on the inside of every person. If we could **"Be still and know that** [He is] **God"** (Ps. 46:10, brackets mine), the Holy Spirit would reveal these things to us.

I'm sure there are people who disagree with everything I'm saying, and they just dismiss it. They won't even think about it. But why not? If what they believe is true, wouldn't it stand examination? If evolution is proven, as they believe, wouldn't all of the facts confirm it? Why would they be afraid to hear about facts that are contrary? The truth is that people refuse to acknowledge that which is contrary to their belief system. They won't confront it. I'm just being bold and telling you that you need to take time to evaluate the facts you've been presented with. Know that God has already revealed these truths to you on the inside.

Get still, get quiet, and open your heart and say, "God, show me if You created the heavens and the earth in six days and if evolution is wrong." Read the scriptures that I've presented here. Evaluate the information given by Dr. Carl Baugh and Dr. Grady McMurtry. If you give this viewpoint a chance, I believe that God will reveal Himself in you and to you. Those who are living an unrighteous lifestyle have a motivation for disbelieving biblical creationism, and many have absolutely no conviction about any of this. The Bible says you can harden your heart (Heb. 3:8). You can have your conscience so seared that you can get to a place to where you don't believe anything and you have no conviction from God (1 Tim. 4:2).

That doesn't change the fact that everyone, at one time, had an intuitive knowledge of God on the inside. I don't ever argue with atheists. I go past all their arguments and just say, "You know the truth. You know that there's a God. If somebody were to put a gun to your head and tell you they're going to kill you, you'd call out to the God that you say you don't believe in." I go past their minds and arguments and straight to their hearts.

Some of you have embraced evolution and have never challenged it. You haven't closely examined it. You've just accepted the lies you've been told. But I believe that deep down, you know that it isn't possible! If you will allow Him, the Holy Spirit will reveal to you that you were created and designed by God. You aren't a mistake. Whether your parents knew that you were coming or not, God created you.

Lesson 10   Creation vs. Evolution

For thou hast possessed my reins: thou hast covered me in my mother's womb. I will praise thee; for I am fearfully and wonderfully made: marvellous are thy works; and that my soul knoweth right well. My substance was not hid from thee, when I was made in secret, and curiously wrought in the lowest parts of the earth. Thine eyes did see my substance, yet being unperfect; and in thy book all my members were written, which in continuance were fashioned, when as yet there was none of them.

PSALM 139:13-16

Before I formed thee in the belly I knew thee; and before thou camest forth out of the womb I sanctified thee, and I ordained thee a prophet unto the nations.

JEREMIAH 1:5

You didn't just randomly evolve. It's not up to you to pick and choose what you want to do. You were created, designed by God with a purpose. You are not an evolved animal; you are a created being. You are going to stand before God some day and give an account for what you did with your life. And you know this at a heart level. Whether your head agrees with it or not, your heart knows it. I encourage you to submit your heart to the Lord today and carefully and prayerfully examine what's just been presented to you.

For more information on Dr. Carl Baugh's ministry and museum, go to **www.creationevidence.org**.

To learn more about Dr. Grady McMurtry's ministry and research, visit his website: **www.creationworldview.org**.

You may also watch the interviews with Dr. Baugh and Dr. McMurtry by ordering my *Christian Philosophy* DVD series. To order, go to the Andrew Wommack Ministries website: **www.awmi.net**.

Lesson 10 — Creation vs. Evolution

SCRIPTURES

JOHN 1:1-5
In the beginning was the Word, and the Word was with God, and the Word was God. **[2]** *The same was in the beginning with God.* **[3]** *All things were made by him; and without him was not any thing made that was made.* **[4]** *In him was life; and the life was the light of men.* **[5]** *And the light shineth in darkness; and the darkness comprehended it not.*

REVELATION 14:6-7
And I saw another angel fly in the midst of heaven, having the everlasting gospel to preach unto them that dwell on the earth, and to every nation, and kindred, and tongue, and people, **[7]** *Saying with a loud voice, Fear God, and give glory to him; for the hour of his judgment is come: and worship him that made heaven, and earth, and the sea, and the fountains of waters.*

PSALM 19:1-4
The heavens declare the glory of God; and the firmament sheweth his handywork. **[2]** *Day unto day uttereth speech, and night unto night sheweth knowledge.* **[3]** *There is no speech nor language, where their voice is not heard.* **[4]** *Their line is gone out through all the earth, and their words to the end of the world. In them hath he set a tabernacle for the sun.*

GENESIS 1:1-3
In the beginning God created the heaven and the earth. **[2]** *And the earth was without form, and void; and darkness was upon the face of the deep. And the Spirit of God moved upon the face of the waters.* **[3]** *And God said, Let there be light: and there was light.*

GENESIS 1:28
And God blessed them, and God said unto them, Be fruitful, and multiply, and replenish the earth, and subdue it: and have dominion over the fish of the sea, and over the fowl of the air, and over every living thing that moveth upon the earth.

GENESIS 1:14-16
And God said, Let there be lights in the firmament of the heaven to divide the day from the night; and let them be for signs, and for seasons, and for days, and years: **[15]** *And let them be for lights in the firmament of the heaven to give light upon the earth: and it was so.* **[16]** *And God made two great lights; the greater light to rule the day, and the lesser light to rule the night: he made the stars also.*

ROMANS 4:17
(As it is written, I have made thee a father of many nations,) before him whom he believed, even God, who quickeneth the dead, and calleth those things which be not as though they were.

GENESIS 1:11
And God said, Let the earth bring forth grass, the herb yielding seed, and the fruit tree yielding fruit after his kind, whose seed is in itself, upon the earth: and it was so.

GENESIS 1:21
And God created great whales, and every living creature that moveth, which the waters brought forth abundantly, after their kind, and every winged fowl after his kind: and God saw that it was good.

GENESIS 1:24-25
And God said, Let the earth bring forth the living creature after his kind, cattle, and creeping thing, and beast of the earth after his kind: and it was so. **[25]** *And God made the beast of the earth after his kind, and cattle after their kind, and every thing that creepeth upon the earth after his kind: and God saw that it was good.*

GENESIS 5:24
And Enoch walked with God: and he was not; for God took him.

LESSON 10 — CREATION VS. EVOLUTION

SCRIPTURES

GENESIS 4:9-16
And the LORD said unto Cain, Where is Abel thy brother? And he said, I know not: Am I my brother's keeper? [10] And he said, What hast thou done? the voice of thy brother's blood crieth unto me from the ground. [11] And now art thou cursed from the earth, which hath opened her mouth to receive thy brother's blood from thy hand; [12] When thou tillest the ground, it shall not henceforth yield unto thee her strength; a fugitive and a vagabond shalt thou be in the earth. [13] And Cain said unto the LORD, My punishment is greater than I can bear. [14] Behold, thou hast driven me out this day from the face of the earth; and from thy face shall I be hid; and I shall be a fugitive and a vagabond in the earth; and it shall come to pass, that every one that findeth me shall slay me. [15] And the LORD said unto him, Therefore whosoever slayeth Cain, vengeance shall be taken on him sevenfold. And the LORD set a mark upon Cain, lest any finding him should kill him. [16] And Cain went out from the presence of the LORD, and dwelt in the land of Nod, on the east of Eden.

ROMANS 1:18-20
For the wrath of God is revealed from heaven against all ungodliness and unrighteousness of men, who hold the truth in unrighteousness; [19] Because that which may be known of God is manifest in them; for God hath shewed it unto them. [20] For the invisible things of him from the creation of the world are clearly seen, being understood by the things that are made, even his eternal power and Godhead; so that they are without excuse.

PSALM 14:1-3
The fool hath said in his heart, There is no God. They are corrupt, they have done abominable works, there is none that doeth good. [2] The LORD looked down from heaven upon the children of men, to see if there were any that did understand, and seek God. [3] They are all gone aside, they are all together become filthy: there is none that doeth good, no, not one.

EXODUS 20:8-11
Remember the sabbath day, to keep it holy. [9] Six days shalt thou labour, and do all thy work: [10] But the seventh day is the sabbath of the LORD thy God: in it thou shalt not do any work, thou, nor thy son, nor thy daughter, thy manservant, nor thy maidservant, nor thy cattle, nor thy stranger that is within thy gates: [11] For in six days the LORD made heaven and earth, the sea, and all that in them is, and rested the seventh day: wherefore the LORD blessed the sabbath day, and hallowed it.

MARK 10:6
But from the beginning of the creation God made them male and female.

GENESIS 7:11
In the six hundredth year of Noah's life, in the second month, the seventeenth day of the month, the same day were all the fountains of the great deep broken up, and the windows of heaven were opened.

PSALM 46:10
Be still, and know that I am God: I will be exalted among the heathen, I will be exalted in the earth.

HEBREWS 3:8
Harden not your hearts, as in the provocation, in the day of temptation in the wilderness.

1 TIMOTHY 4:2
Speaking lies in hypocrisy; having their conscience seared with a hot iron.

PSALM 139:13-16
For thou hast possessed my reins: thou hast covered me in my mother's womb. [14] I will praise thee; for I am fearfully and wonderfully made: marvellous are thy works; and that my soul knoweth right well. [15] My substance was not hid from thee, when I was made in secret, and curiously wrought in the lowest parts of the earth. [16] Thine eyes did see my substance, yet being unperfect; and in thy book all my members were written, which in continuance were fashioned, when as yet there was none of them.

JEREMIAH 1:5
Before I formed thee in the belly I knew thee; and before thou camest forth out of the womb I sanctified thee, and I ordained thee a prophet unto the nations.

A Godly Perspective on Homosexuality

God is not a respecter of persons, and He doesn't grade us on a curve or sliding scale. All sin is evil, and Scripture says that if we have fallen short on one point, then we are guilty of the whole Law (James 2:10). So, it would be wrong for a Christian to feel superior to homosexuals or to look at them and say, "Thank God, at least I'm not caught up in *that* kind of sin." Jesus warned against that attitude in His parable about the Pharisee and the publican:

> *Two men went up into the temple to pray; the one a Pharisee, and the other a publican. The Pharisee stood and prayed thus with himself, God, I thank thee, that I am not as other men are, extortioners, unjust, adulterers, or even as this publican. I fast twice in the week, I give tithes of all that I possess. And the publican, standing afar off, would not lift up so much as his eyes unto heaven, but smote upon his breast, saying, God be merciful to me a sinner. I tell you, this man went down to his house justified rather than the other: for every one that exalteth himself shall be abased; and he that humbleth himself shall be exalted.*
>
> LUKE 18:10-14

Notice how Jesus said that the man merely living a holy life was not justified in the eyes of God. The sinner who repented was justified. We need to be careful in discussing moral issues, that we don't fall into the trap of comparing ourselves among ourselves and measuring our performance against the performance of others (2 Cor. 10:12).

My purpose in discussing homosexuality is not to scold homosexuals or to prove what an ungodly act it is. The Bible is clear that homosexuality is wrong—just like adultery, lying, drunkenness, gluttony, and idolatry are sins—but in today's media, homosexuality is presented as an acceptable alternative lifestyle. I want to counter the misinformation floating around and show that homosexuality is a destructive way of life—by any standard.

In 2009, President Obama held a lesbian, gay, bisexual, and transgender (known as LGBT) pride month reception at the White House in which he said,

> There are unjust laws to overturn and unfair practices to stop. And though we've made progress, there are still fellow citizens, perhaps neighbors or even family members and loved ones, who still hold fast to worn arguments and old attitudes; who fail to see your families like their families; and who would deny you the rights that most Americans take for granted.... We must recognize that real progress depends not only on the laws we

Lesson 11 — A Godly Perspective on Homosexuality

change but, as I said before, on the hearts we open. For if we're honest with ourselves, we'll acknowledge that there are good and decent people in this country who don't yet fully embrace their gay brothers and sisters—not yet.[1]

The president's remarks accurately reflect the stance taken by the media and popular culture in America today. Homosexuality is seen as a way of life that is wrongfully discriminated against, and the LGBT community is pushing to gain legal protections. I agree that it is wrong to lash out against people practicing homosexuality or to persecute them unfairly, but it isn't persecution to point out wrong behavior. Society has been manipulated into believing that calling homosexuality immoral is somehow inappropriate or "close-minded."

The gay rights movement got its start after the Stonewall riots in Greenwich Village, New York City, in 1969. The protests began after police raided a bar for being a gay establishment, and the gay patrons fought back. Soon a march was staged to Central Park to bring awareness, and the gay rights movement was born. In the early 1990s, the movement really began to make headway with the claim that homosexuality was genetic. Suddenly, in the minds of many, homosexuality transformed from being an immoral choice to being an unavoidable and irreversible condition of birth.

Some Christians are hesitant to accept that homosexuality is immoral when so many sources are claiming it is a condition of birth. They say, "How can God punish someone for something that they can't control? If God made them that way, then they have no choice." It's a good question. We know God wouldn't condemn anyone to eternal punishment for factors beyond their control, so the first thing we need to do is examine the claim that homosexual behavior is genetic.

One of the studies that is used to promote the idea that homosexuality is genetic is a study of identical twins published by Bailey and Pillard in 1991. The investigation found that when one identical twin is gay, then the other twin is more likely to be gay also, meaning the other twin was more likely to be gay than another random person would be. The researchers noted that the findings were not proof that homosexuality is genetic, but the media ran with it anyway as sure evidence of the genetic link to being gay. They ignored other portions of the study, which showed that the rate of homosexuality among families with one gay twin was 200 to 300 percent higher than average—this included adopted siblings.[2] Adopted siblings obviously don't share a genetic link to the family with higher rates of homosexuality, so environmental factors were clearly the cause. In truth, this study makes a strong argument that homosexuality is *not* genetic.

Still, some continue to claim that homosexual behavior has hormonal or other biological causes. The first attempts to attribute biological causes to homosexuality arose in the late nineteenth century and were built upon the scientific principles of the Enlightenment.[3] Here again, we see the influence that philosophy has upon how we interpret life. To a scientific naturalist, everything must be reduced to a physical cause, so they try to attribute a physical explanation for *all* behavior, including homosexuality. But naturalism is a flawed philosophy—not all behavior is reducible to a physical cause.

---

[1] Barack Obama, "Remarks by the President at LGBT Pride Month Reception" (speech, The White House, Washington, DC, June 29, 2009). http://www.whitehouse.gov/the_press_office/Remarks-by-the-President-at-LGBT-Pride-Month-Reception/

[2] "Is Sexual Orientation genetic or is it a choice?" *Exodus Global Alliance*, Web, accessed August 31, 2012, http://www.exodusglobalalliance.org/causesc37.php

[3] Ranier Herrn PhD., "On the History of Biological Theories of Homosexuality," *Journal of Homosexuality*, Volume 28, Issue 1-2. Web, August 31, 2012, http://www.tandfonline.com/doi/abs/10.1300/J082v28n01_03#preview

Lesson 11 — A Godly Perspective on Homosexuality

Other studies have pointed to differences in brain structure or function between heterosexuals and homosexuals, but it is well known that behavior and experience cause the brain to reorganize itself. This ability is referred to as neuroplasticity, and it occurs throughout life. In other words, repeated homosexual experiences or emotions can cause a change in brain structure, as opposed to the behavior being caused by brain structure. Additionally, no hormonal differences have been discovered between heterosexuals and homosexuals, which is a serious blow against the argument that homosexuality has a biological cause.

In 1975, the American Psychological Association buckled to political pressure and removed homosexuality from its list of mental disorders. Although the APA still does not view homosexuality as a choice, they have been forced to admit that no conclusive evidence has been found to attribute homosexuality to biology. Their latest literature about homosexuality says, "Although much research has examined the possible genetic, hormonal, developmental, social, and cultural influences on sexual orientation, *no findings have emerged that permit scientists to conclude that sexual orientation is determined by any particular factor or factors*" (emphasis mine).[4]

Despite how badly some want to attribute biological causes to homosexual behavior, no biological causes have ever been found. The media has overstated the implications of research and misinterpreted other data, but—as the American Psychological Association openly states—homosexuality cannot be defined as genetic or a condition of birth.

Many factors influence the shaping of our identities, but the bottom line is that homosexuality is a choice. Some people might be more tempted by homosexuality than others, but that doesn't make the choice of engaging in homosexual behavior any less immoral. In the same way, adultery is always wrong—no matter how great the temptation or how significant the environmental influences.

The Apostle Paul wrote that no one engaging in a homosexual lifestyle will inherit the kingdom of God (1 Cor. 6:9). Therefore, we know that homosexuality is a choice—not an innate condition. So, it is important for Christians to speak the truth in love, rather than keep quiet and let people be deceived into believing that homosexuals aren't responsible for their choices. To keep quiet about the immorality of homosexuality would be contrary to God's command:

> *Thou shalt not hate thy brother in thine heart: thou shalt in any wise rebuke thy neighbour, and not suffer sin upon him.... But thou shalt love thy neighbour as thyself: I am the LORD.*
> LEVITICUS 19:17-18

I don't think I would need to spend much time convincing you that murder is immoral; we all intuitively know it is wrong. But the gay lobby has been so successful in promoting homosexuality as normal behavior that many Christians no longer view it as immoral.

The National Gay and Lesbian Task Force (NGLTF) has intentionally sought the endorsement of faith communities to increase the public perception that homosexuality is normal, and they have gained credibility by associating their agenda with established Christian denominations. Some denominations have even appointed homosexual men and women to leadership roles. This is in direct opposition to ministers who are being vocal about the immorality of homosexuality. The NGLTF says, "It is [imperative] that the

---

[4] American Psychological Association, "Sexual Orientation & Homosexuality: Answers to Your Questions For a Better Understanding," *APA.org*, 4. http://www.apa.org/topics/sexuality/orientation.aspx

Lesson 11 A Godly Perspective on Homosexuality

LGBT rights advocates work with and within communities of faith to reclaim from the right wing the true meaning of moral values,"[5] which shows they are intentionally infiltrating the church to undermine biblical values and promote the acceptance of homosexuality.

The gay lobby has been so successful at distorting the biblical perspective, we now have churches promoting the gay agenda—even though Scripture unambiguously denounces homosexuality. I understand having compassion toward people who are caught up in destructive behaviors and wanting to reach out to help them, but to endorse and promote homosexuality, you have to oppose the Word of God. This shocks me, but I have learned that there are many religious people who don't let the Word of God affect what they believe.

The story of Sodom very clearly reveals God's view of homosexuality. God sent two angels down to Sodom, and when Lot saw them, he invited them into his house to have a meal and spend the night. Scripture says that many of us have entertained angels unaware (Heb. 13:2), which means they don't always appear with wings and halos above their heads. So, the angels who visited Lot apparently looked like human beings, and every man in Sodom wanted to have sex with them.

> *But before they lay down, the men of the city, even the men of Sodom, compassed the house round, both old and young, all the people from every quarter: And they called unto Lot, and said unto him, Where are the men which came in to thee this night? bring them out unto us, that we may know them.*
>
> GENESIS 19:4-5

The King James uses the verb **"know"** to refer to sexual relations, but some other translations render the passage more explicitly: **"Where are the men who came to you tonight? Bring them out to us so that we can have sex with them"** (verse 5, *New International Version*). Lot was repulsed by their demands and tried to stop the citizens of Sodom from accosting the angels. The angels struck everyone blind (Gen. 19:11) and led Lot and his family out of Sodom. Once they were safe, God rained brimstone and fire from heaven as judgment to destroy the entire city (Gen. 19:24). You simply cannot read the account of Sodom and think that God approves of homosexuality.

But God isn't striking homosexuals or adulterers dead anymore. Under the New Covenant, there is a cure for sin. Our born-again spirits make it possible for God to relate to us with mercy and grace. In the same way, we are called to deal with all sinners by grace, no matter what kind of sin they are caught up in—but that doesn't mean we ignore wrong behavior.

Christians can commit the sin of homosexuality in the same way that they can get addicted to pornography or commit adultery, but there is no such thing as a church that promotes adultery, pornography, or lying and stealing. Christians might do some of those immoral things, but we don't build churches around embracing and promoting destructive behaviors. So, why are people forming church groups that promote homosexuality?

I have a few friends who have committed homosexual acts. They are still my friends, and I love them. I have helped them through those difficulties. God paid for the sin of homosexuality through Jesus, so He is not going to send people to hell just for the sin of homosexuality. The sin of rejecting Jesus is what sends people to hell (John 16:9). The sin of homosexuality is forgiven because of Jesus' sacrifice, but God's Word is clear that homosexuality is wrong.

---

[5] National Gay and Lesbian Task Force statement on faith, accessed August 31, 2012, http://www.thetaskforce.org/issues/faith

Lesson 11   A Godly Perspective on Homosexuality

If a man also lie with mankind, as he lieth with a woman, both of them have committed an abomination: they shall surely be put to death; their blood shall be upon them.

LEVITICUS 20:13

Again, under the Old Covenant, there was no cure for the sin of rebellion, whether it was homosexuality, adultery, or children rebelling against their parents. In the Old Testament, death was often the punishment for such rebellion. It was a way of getting the destructive behavior out of society in the same manner that a doctor cuts a cancerous tumor out of the body. It was done to prevent further spread throughout society and total separation from God. But we live under the New Covenant now, and faith in Jesus is the cure for all sin. We can be forgiven for things that Old Covenant believers did not receive forgiveness for.

Be it known unto you therefore, men and brethren, that through this man is preached unto you the forgiveness of sins: And by him all that believe are justified from all things, from which ye could not be justified by the law of Moses.

ACTS 13:38-39

God isn't striking people down for sin anymore, but sin is still wrong. Sin is deadly, you shouldn't indulge in it, and homosexuality is a sin. Scripture actually calls it the act of a dog (Deut. 23:17-18).

As I said, I am not against people who are caught up in homosexuality, but I am against the sin. Scripture says it is ungodly, and Christians don't need to make apologies for having the same opinion as God. People engaged in homosexuality are perverting God's creation, and He hates it. He doesn't hate the individuals. He loves them so much that He died in their place and took the punishment for homosexuality. Gay people are forgiven, but God still hates the sin because He knows how damaging it is.

The reason homosexuals are pushing so hard to be accepted by society is because, in their hearts, they know homosexuality is wrong (Rom. 1:18-21). They might say they don't feel any guilt, because they have always been gay, but it isn't true. I believe God's Word more than what they say (Rom. 3:4).

Every time you disobey your conscience, you put a little distance between you and God. By choosing sin, you push God away, and every time you step away from your intuitive knowledge of what is right, you put a layer of insensitivity between you and the Lord. Eventually, you can become so insensitive that it's like your conscience has been seared by a hot iron (1 Tim. 4:2). This is what the Bible calls being reprobate—no longer under conviction of sin. But homosexuality isn't the first step someone takes on the road to being completely insensitive to God; it's one of the last.

The hardening of your heart is a progressive process. It starts by not glorifying what God has done for you, then you move to not being thankful, and finally your thoughts and imagination begin to work against you (Rom. 1:21). At that point, you have begun a downward spiral through choices and actions that make you more and more insensitive to God. After which Scripture says,

Wherefore God also gave them up to uncleanness through the lusts of their own hearts, to dishonour their own bodies between themselves: Who changed the truth of God into a lie, and worshipped and served the creature more than the Creator, who is blessed for ever. Amen.

ROMANS 1:24-25

Lesson 11 — A Godly Perspective on Homosexuality

Idolatry isn't just falling down to worship a statue. You can worship money or any other number of things. Covetousness is idolatry (Col. 3:5), so physical possessions can become your god if you worship them. Everything in the media and pop culture is geared toward creating covetousness inside of you. It is the average condition of people today, and the Bible calls it idolatry.

> *For this cause God gave them up unto vile affections: for even their women did change the natural use into that which is against nature: And likewise also the men, leaving the natural use of the woman, burned in their lust one toward another; men with men working that which is unseemly, and receiving in themselves that recompence of their error which was meet.*
>
> ROMANS 1:26-27

I don't think it is inferring too much to say that the recompense spoken of here is the damaging effects of AIDS and other sexually transmitted diseases—not that God sent those diseases as punishment. God created laws to govern the earth, and ignoring those natural laws has consequences. If you jump off a bridge, you are going to fall. Likewise, sexually transmitted diseases are the natural result of sexual perversion. Then the Scripture says,

> *And even as they did not like to retain God in their knowledge, God gave them over to a reprobate mind, to do those things which are not convenient.*
>
> ROMANS 1:28

This is saying that God withdrew conviction from people who didn't want Him around. Jesus said that no one goes to the Father unless the Spirit draws them (John 6:44). It is not human nature to seek God—He has to draw us—and people can go so far in their rebellion against Him that God eventually stops trying to draw them to Himself. When that happens, those people become reprobate—they have no knowledge of the truth—and they don't care. (Don't worry—if you are afraid that you might be reprobate, then you aren't. Any desire to be right with God means that He is still drawing you into relationship with Him. So, if you desire relationship with God, you're not reprobate.)

I think we have a lot of reprobate people today who just don't care about God or what He thinks. Hitler bragged, "I have six divisions of SS men absolutely indifferent in matters of religion. It doesn't prevent them from going to death with serenity in their souls." But their serenity wasn't proof that they had nothing to fear; it was an indication that they were reprobate. Their consciences were seared as with a hot iron. As soon as they died, I guarantee they were wishing they hadn't been so indifferent. Unfortunately, we see those kinds of people rising to positions of leadership in businesses and politics all over the world today.

> *Being filled with all unrighteousness, fornication, wickedness, covetousness, maliciousness; full of envy, murder, debate, deceit, malignity; whisperers, Backbiters, haters of God, despiteful, proud, boasters, inventors of evil things, disobedient to parents, Without understanding, covenantbreakers, without natural affection, implacable, unmerciful: Who knowing the judgment of God, that they which commit such things are worthy of death, not only do the same, but have pleasure in them that do them.*
>
> ROMANS 1:29-32

Some of these things are not only allowed but encouraged in our society. Yet they are all listed as wrong behaviors that move a person toward becoming reprobate. This is the list in which homosexuality finds itself. It is a sin, and it's one of the very last sins in a progression of things that move us away from

Lesson 11 — A Godly Perspective on Homosexuality

God toward becoming reprobate. We don't want to go there, and anyone who is practicing homosexuality is flirting with pushing God away for good. The Apostle Paul wrote,

> *Know ye not that the unrighteous shall not inherit the kingdom of God? Be not deceived: neither fornicators, nor idolaters, nor adulterers, nor effeminate, nor abusers of themselves with mankind, Nor thieves, nor covetous, nor drunkards, nor revilers, nor extortioners, shall inherit the kingdom of God.*
> 1 CORINTHIANS 6:9-10

The phrase translated **"abusers of themselves with mankind"** is the Greek word *arsenokoites*, and it means a sodomite, a homosexual, or "one who lies with a male as with a female" (*Thayer's Greek-English Lexicon*). This passage specifically states that homosexuals will not inherit the kingdom of God. Other scriptures also clearly condemn homosexuality:

> *Knowing this, that the law is not made for a righteous man, but for the lawless and disobedient, for the ungodly and for sinners, for unholy and profane, for murderers of fathers and murderers of mothers, for manslayers, For whoremongers, for them that defile themselves with mankind, for menstealers, for liars, for perjured persons, and if there be any other thing that is contrary to sound doctrine.*
> 1 TIMOTHY 1:9-10

> *Even as Sodom and Gomorrha, and the cities about them in like manner, giving themselves over to fornication, and going after strange flesh, are set forth for an example, suffering the vengeance of eternal fire.*
> JUDE 7

> *And turning the cities of Sodom and Gomorrha into ashes condemned them with an overthrow, making them an ensample unto those that after should live ungodly.*
> 2 PETER 2:6

It simply is not possible to read the Bible and think that God approves of homosexuality. God forgives homosexuals because Jesus has already paid the debt, but the act of homosexuality is wrong. It's one thing for a person to know that homosexuality is wrong and to persist in it anyway, but it's something else to try to twist the Gospel into saying that homosexuality is normal behavior or that it can't be helped.

God would be unjust to command people not to do something they are genetically disposed toward doing. God doesn't make demands like that. When God tells you not to lie or steal, it's because you have the ability to avoid those behaviors. It would be unreasonable for God to say, "Stop being a man." You can't help the way you were created. But God never created anybody to be a homosexual. Even pro-gay organizations like the APA are admitting that homosexuality is not genetic. Being gay is a choice, just like lying or stealing.

God has never made anyone to be different than the gender they were at birth. If you are a man, then God intends for you to have sexual relations with a woman, and if you are a woman, then God intends for you to have sexual relations with a man. He doesn't make people any other way. The good news for anyone struggling with homosexuality is that you can be set free from the lies that have brought you to that place. You don't have to live under that burden anymore. God loves you, and He has already paid the price to deliver you from that lifestyle.

Lesson 11 — A Godly Perspective on Homosexuality

SCRIPTURES

JAMES 2:10
For whosoever shall keep the whole law, and yet offend in one point, he is guilty of all.

LUKE 18:10-14
Two men went up into the temple to pray; the one a Pharisee, and the other a publican. **[11]** The Pharisee stood and prayed thus with himself, God, I thank thee, that I am not as other men are, extortioners, unjust, adulterers, or even as this publican. **[12]** I fast twice in the week, I give tithes of all that I possess. **[13]** And the publican, standing afar off, would not lift up so much as his eyes unto heaven, but smote upon his breast, saying, God be merciful to me a sinner. **[14]** I tell you, this man went down to his house justified rather than the other: for every one that exalteth himself shall be abased; and he that humbleth himself shall be exalted.

2 CORINTHIANS 10:12
For we dare not make ourselves of the number, or compare ourselves with some that commend themselves: but they measuring themselves by themselves, and comparing themselves among themselves, are not wise.

1 CORINTHIANS 6:9-10
Know ye not that the unrighteous shall not inherit the kingdom of God? Be not deceived: neither fornicators, nor idolaters, nor adulterers, nor effeminate, nor abusers of themselves with mankind, **[10]** Nor thieves, nor covetous, nor drunkards, nor revilers, nor extortioners, shall inherit the kingdom of God.

LEVITICUS 19:17-18
Thou shalt not hate thy brother in thine heart: thou shalt in any wise rebuke thy neighbour, and not suffer sin upon him. **[18]** Thou shalt not avenge, nor bear any grudge against the children of thy people, but thou shalt love thy neighbour as thyself: I am the Lord.

HEBREWS 13:2
Be not forgetful to entertain strangers: for thereby some have entertained angels unawares.

GENESIS 19:4-5
But before they lay down, the men of the city, even the men of Sodom, compassed the house round, both old and young, all the people from every quarter: **[5]** And they called unto Lot, and said unto him, Where are the men which came in to thee this night? bring them out unto us, that we may know them.

GENESIS 19:5 (NEW INTERNATIONAL VERSION)
They called to Lot, "Where are the men who came to you tonight? Bring them out to us so that we can have sex with them."

GENESIS 19:11
And they smote the men that were at the door of the house with blindness, both small and great: so that they wearied themselves to find the door.

GENESIS 19:24
Then the Lord rained upon Sodom and upon Gomorrah brimstone and fire from the Lord out of heaven.

JOHN 16:9
Of sin, because they believe not on me.

LEVITICUS 20:13
If a man also lie with mankind, as he lieth with a woman, both of them have committed an abomination: they shall surely be put to death; their blood shall be upon them.

Lesson 11 — A Godly Perspective on Homosexuality

SCRIPTURES

ACTS 13:38-39
Be it known unto you therefore, men and brethren, that through this man is preached unto you the forgiveness of sins: **[39]** *And by him all that believe are justified from all things, from which ye could not be justified by the law of Moses.*

DEUTERONOMY 23:17-18
There shall be no whore of the daughters of Israel, nor a sodomite of the sons of Israel. **[18]** *Thou shalt not bring the hire of a whore, or the price of a dog, into the house of the* L<small>ORD</small> *thy God for any vow: for even both these are abomination unto the* L<small>ORD</small> *thy God.*

ROMANS 1:18-21
For the wrath of God is revealed from heaven against all ungodliness and unrighteousness of men, who hold the truth in unrighteousness; **[19]** *Because that which may be known of God is manifest in them; for God hath shewed it unto them.* **[20]** *For the invisible things of him from the creation of the world are clearly seen, being understood by the things that are made, even his eternal power and Godhead; so that they are without excuse:* **[21]** *Because that, when they knew God, they glorified him not as God, neither were thankful; but became vain in their imaginations, and their foolish heart was darkened.*

ROMANS 3:4
God forbid: yea, let God be true, but every man a liar; as it is written, That thou mightest be justified in thy sayings, and mightest overcome when thou art judged.

1 TIMOTHY 4:2
Speaking lies in hypocrisy; having their conscience seared with a hot iron.

ROMANS 1:24-32
Wherefore God also gave them up to uncleanness through the lusts of their own hearts, to dishonour their own bodies between themselves: **[25]** *Who changed the truth of God into a lie, and worshipped and served the creature more than the Creator, who is blessed for ever. Amen.* **[26]** *For this cause God gave them up unto vile affections: for even their women did change the natural use into that which is against nature:* **[27]** *And likewise also the men, leaving the natural use of the woman, burned in their lust one toward another; men with men working that which is unseemly, and receiving in themselves that recompence of their error which was meet.* **[28]** *And even as they did not like to retain God in their knowledge, God gave them over to a reprobate mind, to do those things which are not convenient;* **[29]** *Being filled with all unrighteousness, fornication, wickedness, covetousness, maliciousness; full of envy, murder, debate, deceit, malignity; whisperers,* **[30]** *Backbiters, haters of God, despiteful, proud, boasters, inventors of evil things, disobedient to parents,* **[31]** *Without understanding, covenantbreakers, without natural affection, implacable, unmerciful:* **[32]** *Who knowing the judgment of God, that they which commit such things are worthy of death, not only do the same, but have pleasure in them that do them.*

COLOSSIANS 3:5
Mortify therefore your members which are upon the earth; fornication, uncleanness, inordinate affection, evil concupiscence, and covetousness, which is idolatry.

JOHN 6:44
No man can come to me, except the Father which hath sent me draw him: and I will raise him up at the last day.

1 TIMOTHY 1:9-10
Knowing this, that the law is not made for a righteous man, but for the lawless and disobedient, for the ungodly and for sinners, for unholy and profane, for murderers of fathers and murderers of mothers, for manslayers, **[10]** *For whoremongers, for them that defile themselves with mankind, for menstealers, for liars, for perjured persons, and if there be any other thing that is contrary to sound doctrine.*

Lesson 11 — A Godly Perspective on Homosexuality

SCRIPTURES

JUDE 7
Even as Sodom and Gomorrha, and the cities about them in like manner, giving themselves over to fornication, and going after strange flesh, are set forth for an example, suffering the vengeance of eternal fire.

2 PETER 2:6
And turning the cities of Sodom and Gomorrha into ashes condemned them with an overthrow, making them an ensample unto those that after should live ungodly.

Facts and Statistics Regarding Homosexuality

The gay lobby tries to present homosexuality as a completely normal lifestyle. They want you to believe that homosexuals are just like everybody else, aside from their choice in sexual partners. But homosexuality is not normal.

One of the tactics the gay lobby has used to promote the normalcy of homosexuality is to claim a greater occurrence of homosexuality in the population than is true. The gay lobby used to claim that 10 percent of the population was homosexual. Those faulty figures were taken from a study published in 1948 by a zoologist named Alfred Kinsey, and his study has since been widely criticized for using an unbalanced number of college students and convicted sex offenders. More accurate studies have shown that only 1 to 2 percent of Americans claim to be gay, and according to the 2000 U.S. Census Bureau, less than 1 percent of American households are homosexual—a far lower rate of occurrence than the gay lobby wants the public to believe.

Homosexuality isn't just unusual and immoral—it's harmful. Consider the following facts:[1]

- 43% of white male homosexuals have sex with 500 or more partners in their lifetime.
- 28% of white male homosexuals have over 1,000 sex partners in their lifetime.

It is not normal to have sex with 500 to 1,000 different people, yet that is the case for almost half of the homosexuals in this study. This is a perversion by anyone's standards. That kind of rampant promiscuity explains why homosexual males report far less sexual fidelity than do heterosexuals.[2]

---

1 A.P. Bell and M.S. Weinberg, *Homosexualities: A Study of Diversity Among Men and Women* (New York: Simon and Schuster, 1978), 308-309.
2 Edward Laumann, John H. Gagnon, Robert T. Michael, and Stuart Michaels, *The Social Organization of Sexuality* (Chicago: The University of Chicago Press, 1994), 216.
   David P. McWhirter and Andrew W. Mattison, *The Male Couple: How Relationships Develop* (Saddle River: Prentice Hall, 1984), 252-253.
   Michael W. Wiederman, "Extramarital Sex: Prevalence and Correlates in a National Survey," *Journal of Sex Research*, Vol. 34, no. 2 (1997): 170.

Lesson 12 — Facts and Statistics Regarding Homosexuality

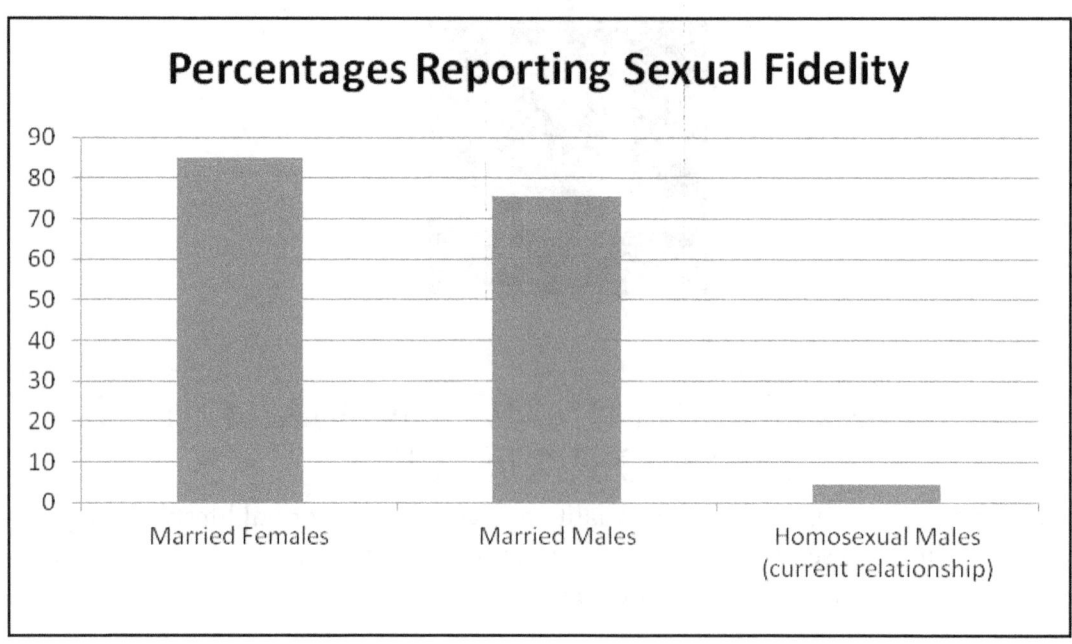

These statistics reveal that homosexuality is a sexual perversion; it's a lifestyle that is directly linked to promiscuity and unfaithfulness. Gay couples aren't just like heterosexual couples; the differences are vast. A study in the Netherlands, where gay marriage has been legal since 2001, revealed that "committed" male homosexual couples had eight sexual partners outside of their relationship every year.[3] Nobody would consider a heterosexual couple normal if they were sleeping with a new person every six weeks in addition to their spouse.

Somebody will object that they know a homosexual couple who has been faithfully committed for over twenty years, but that is far and away the rare exception, as these studies show.

On May 8, 2012, North Carolina passed a constitutional amendment that defined marriage solely as the union between a man and a woman. North Carolina's amendment passed 61 percent to 39 percent, making them the thirtieth state to adopt that position. In spite of the majority of states and Americans showing their opposition to gay marriage, President Barack Obama came out the very next day in full support of gay marriage. He cited friends and members of his own staff "who are in incredibly committed monogamous relationships, same-sex relationships, who are raising kids together."[4]

It might be possible that the individuals the president was talking about were in monogamous homosexual relationships, but if that is true, it would certainly be the exception rather than the rule. This is comparable to endorsing drunk driving because someone you know did it and got home safely without hurting anyone. That does happen, but we justly have laws against driving while under the influence, because it's dangerous.

The average homosexual relationship lasts one-and-a-half years, and 95 percent of the couples in a relationship lasting longer than five years have an open agreement to engage in outside sexual relationships.[3] By comparison, almost 50 percent of heterosexual marriages last more than 20 years.

---

[3] "Study finds gay unions brief," *The Washington Times*, July 11, 2003. http://www.washingtontimes.com/news/2003/jul/11/20030711-121254-3711r/?page=all (accessed August 31, 2012).

[4] Sam Stein, "Obama Backs Gay Marriage," *The Huffington Post*, May 9, 2012. http://www.huffingtonpost.com/2012/05/09/obama-gay-marriage_n_1503245.html (accessed August 31, 2012).

Lesson 12   Facts and Statistics Regarding Homosexuality

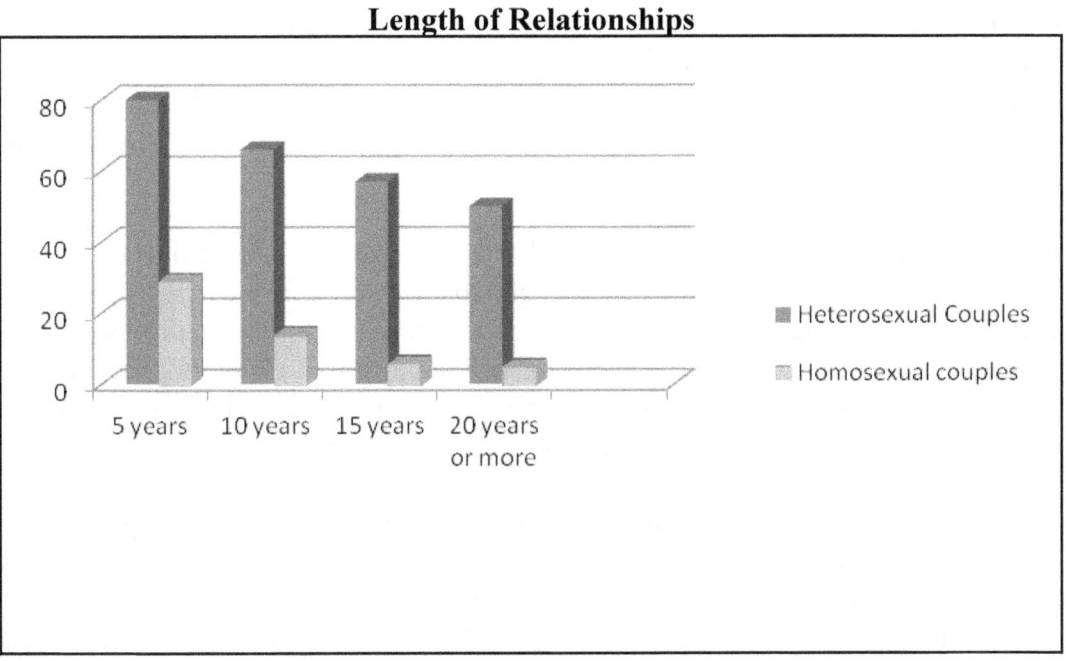

Source: National Center for Health Statistics Center for Disease Control and Prevention 2001 and the 2003-2004 Gay/Lesbian Consumer Online Census

Partner violence is also much higher in homosexual relationships. Among lesbians, the partner abuse rate is 44 times greater than in heterosexual relationships. Among gay men, the rate at which males are abused by their partners is 300 times greater. Those rates of violence are extremely abnormal. It simply isn't true that homosexual relationships are just like heterosexual marriages with the exception of being same-sex unions. Homosexuality is a vastly different lifestyle.

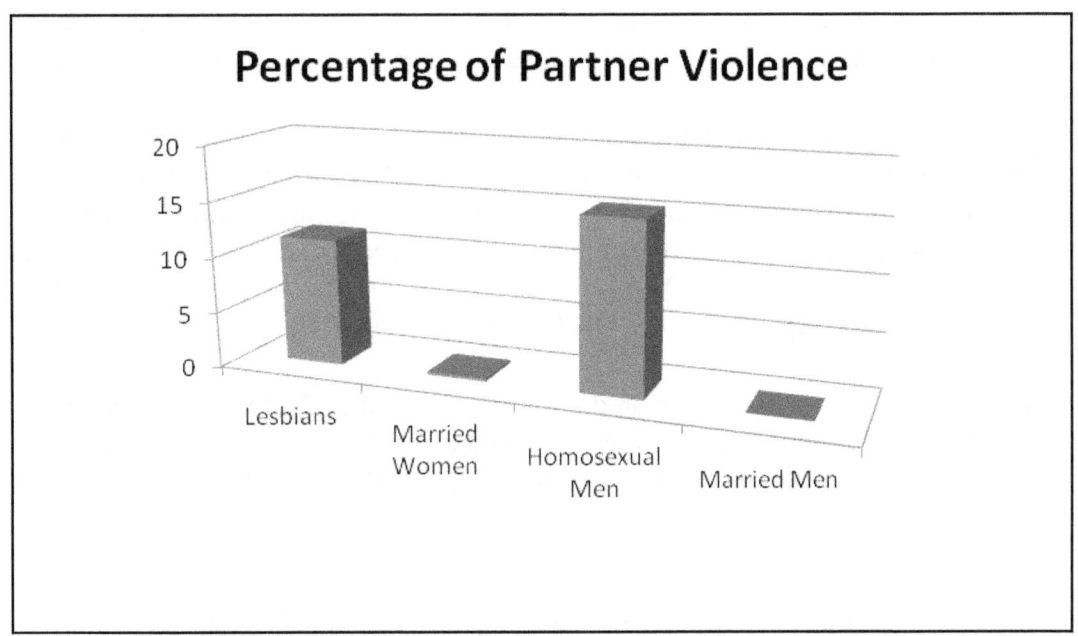

Sources: "Extent, Nature, and Consequences of Intimate Partner Violence," U.S. Department of Justice: Office of Justice Programs, July 2000, 30. https://www.ncjrs.gov/pdffiles1/nij/181867.pdf

Lesson 12   Facts and Statistics Regarding Homosexuality

In addition to being sexually and physically harmful, a study performed in England found that homosexuals are at least 50 percent more likely to suffer from depression, anxiety, and substance abuse.[5] If it were anything else causing that kind of increased risk, the government would be trying to regulate or ban the behavior. I just don't see how the dangers associated with homosexuality can be ignored. It is a destructive lifestyle.

A separate study published in the medical journal *BMC Psychiatry* noted that the risk of suicide jumped over 200 percent for individuals who had engaged in a homosexual lifestyle.[6] Again, the logical thing to do when you identify a behavior that causes such a dramatic jump in suicides is to warn people not to engage in the behavior. But because the behavior we're talking about is homosexuality, no one wants to say anything. It's not politically correct. In fact, our schools are actually encouraging the behavior by teaching that homosexuality is an acceptable lifestyle alternative to traditional marriage.

In Massachusetts, the father of a kindergartner was arrested and taken to jail during a scheduled meeting with the elementary school principal and a member of the school board over objections to the homosexual curriculum being presented in his son's *kindergarten* class.[5] Even though Massachusetts has a law that allows parents to opt their children out of curriculum they don't approve of, the education authorities in Lexington refused to allow parents to opt their kids out of the homosexual classes. In that school, the gay lobby interpreted the passage of the same-sex marriage law in Massachusetts as a go-ahead to indoctrinate vulnerable kids into their destructive worldview—regardless of whether or not the parents approved. Such propaganda has no place in the classroom of five and six year olds. It's a case of the world calling evil good, and good (the father trying to protect his son) evil (Is. 5:20).

The homosexual community is pressing for recognition of their civil unions, claiming that not doing so is discrimination. But what about the religious rights of Christians like this father? If civil unions are legalized and granted protected status, then churches will be forced by law to violate their religious convictions and perform marriages between homosexuals, or be forced to hire homosexuals and grant spousal rights to their partners.

Someone might be yelling, "That's not what would happen," but it has already happened, as with this father in Massachusetts. Churches have already been sued for refusing to allow homosexual marriages in their facilities in states where homosexuals have been granted protected status.[6] Religious organizations have been forced to close rather than violate their moral convictions and treat homosexuality as normal behavior.[7]

Health Risks of Homosexuality

Many increased health risks are also associated with homosexuality. Males who adopt a homosexual lifestyle have a 30 percent greater chance of dying or contracting HIV by age thirty,[8] and the overall life expectancy of gay men is twenty years less than heterosexual men.[9] Data as of 1989 showed the rates of

---

5   "Lexington, Mass., father of 6-year-old arrested, spends night in jail over objections to homosexual curriculum in son's kindergarten class," *Mass Resistance*, October 20, 2005. http://www.massresistanceorg/docs/parker/main.html (accessed August 31, 2012).
6   Ben Johnson, "Judge Rules Christian facility cannot ban same-sex civil union ceremony on its own premises," *LifeSiteNews.com*, January 13, 2012. http://www.lifesitenews.com/news/judge-rules-christian-facility-cannot-ban-same-sex-civil-union-ceremony-on/ (accessed August 31, 2012).
7   "Catholic Adoption Agency Forced to Close," *The Church of St. Catherine of Siena*, July 24, 2012. http://stcatherinenyc.org/2012/07/24/catholic-adoption-agency-forced-close/ (accessed August 31, 2012).
8   Tom McFeely, "What About the Children? American College of Pediatricians Warns Against Same-Sex Families," *National Catholic Register*, June 3, 2008. http://www.ncregister.com/site/article/15089 (accessed August 31, 2012).
9   John R. Diggs Jr. MD, "The Health Risks of Gay Sex," *Catholic Education Resource Center*, 2002. http://www.catholiceducation.org/articles/homosexuality/ho0075.html (accessed August 31, 2012).

LESSON 12   FACTS AND STATISTICS REGARDING HOMOSEXUALITY

anal cancer in male homosexual practitioners to be ten times that of heterosexual males, and growing.[10] For those with AIDS, the rates are doubled.[11]

Lesbians are at higher risk for certain gynecologic cancers, and they are more than twice as likely as straight women to be obese—which is associated with higher rates of cancer and heart disease. Gay men are twice as likely to have been diagnosed with, and then survived, cancer, and they are at higher risk for anal, lung, testicular and immune-system cancers. Experts also believe that lesbians are more likely to get breast cancer than heterosexual women.[14] The list of health risks seems never-ending. Here is a summary of what we've mentioned so far:

- Partner violence is 44 times greater among lesbians and 300 times greater among homosexual men.
- Homosexuals are at least 50 percent more likely to suffer from depression, anxiety, and substance abuse.
- The risk of suicide is 200 percent greater for homosexuals.
- Homosexuals are twice as likely to contract AIDS.
- Life expectancy is reduced by twenty years among homosexuals.
- Homosexual men are twice as likely to have been diagnosed with cancer.
- Lesbians are at a higher risk for breast cancer.
- Lesbians are twice as likely to be obese.

The Surgeon General puts warnings on cigarettes because they have been shown to reduce life expectancy by over ten years. Homosexuality is twice as deadly as cigarettes, by those standards. It is not the normal, healthy lifestyle that the gay lobby wants everyone to believe it is. If people were not "politically-correct phobic," they would put warnings out about the dangers of homosexuality.

As these statistics show, homosexuality isn't just morally wrong—it is a hugely destructive behavior. God doesn't want people getting hurt or destroying their lives by getting caught up in this. It is important to talk about the dangers because homosexuality is a choice, and you can avoid the consequences by avoiding the behavior. I'm not being hateful to point out the dangers of the homosexual lifestyle any more than the Surgeon General is being mean by putting warning labels on cigarettes. I'm trying to save people from being deceived and from getting hurt. The good news is that anyone practicing homosexuality can get out of that lifestyle. No one is destined to be gay.

I have had people working in my ministry and attending my Bible college who have been delivered from the homosexual lifestyle. By their own testimony, they had serious problems at one time, but now they are completely free. They are happier than they have ever been, and they are totally liberated from homosexual tendencies. Contrary to what many people have been told, homosexuality is not genetic. It is not the way God made you. No matter how trapped you might feel, Jesus can save you out of that lifestyle.

It is not only okay for Christians to speak out against homosexuality; it is imperative that we do, because the truth is what sets people free (John 8:32). Scripture is clear that no one engaging in a homosexual lifestyle will inherit the kingdom of God, and homosexuals won't know that God has a better, healthier, and more fulfilling plan for their lives unless someone tells them. You shouldn't be mean

---

10   Mads Melbye, Charles Rabkin, et al., "Changing patterns of anal cancer incidence in the United States, 1940-1989," *American Journal of Epidemiology* (New York: Oxford University Press, 1994), 139:772-780, p. 779, Table 2.
11   James Goedert, et al., for the AIDS-Cancer Match Study Group, "Spectrum of AIDS-associated malignant disorders," *The Lancet* (New York: Elsevier, 1998), 351: 1833-1839, p. 1836.
[14] Randy Dotinga, "Gay men face a higher risk of anal, lung, testicular and immune-system cancers," *U.S. News & World Report,* May 9, 2011. http://health.usnews.com/health-news/family-health/cancer/articles/2011/05/09/gay-men-more-likely-to-have-had-cancer (accessed August 31, 2012).

about it; truth shouldn't be used like a club to beat people into submission. But as long as your motivation is love, I encourage you to speak the truth and not be afraid of being criticized.

Lesson 12 — Facts and Statistics Regarding Homosexuality

SCRIPTURES

ISAIAH 5:20
Woe unto them that call evil good, and good evil; that put darkness for light, and light for darkness; that put bitter for sweet, and sweet for bitter!

JOHN 8:32
And ye shall know the truth, and the truth shall make you free.

Abortion

On a Monday morning in July, when the Colorado House of Representatives was celebrating the ninetieth anniversary of Planned Parenthood, a young woman took the floor to sing the national anthem. As an advocate for people with cerebral palsy, the House was honored to have her sing for them. The woman's emotionally engaging performance had the entire chamber singing along with her at one point. After a stirring round of applause, one of the representatives stood to tell the young woman's story—and the mood in the chamber suddenly changed.

The young woman was Gianna Jessen, a survivor of a saline abortion performed at a Planned Parenthood clinic in California, and her cerebral palsy was caused by the saline injected into her mother's womb. She was invited, the representative said, to put a face on the celebration of Planned Parenthood. The majority leader behind the celebration felt manipulated, and was later quoted as saying, "I think it was amazingly rude to use a human being as an example of…personal politics."[1] Yet abortion is precisely about human beings, not politics. It's about all the people who never get a chance to live and to sing.

The medical professionals who perform the abortions have billions of dollars' worth of incentives to harden their hearts against the human crisis that plays out before them every day. But if those choosing abortion could see the human pain, suffering, and death they are causing, any rational person would realize this is wrong.

Many who support abortion try to dehumanize babies living in their mothers' wombs by pretending that babies are just a mass of tissue until the moment of birth, but we know that isn't true. Everything needed for life is already present in our reproductive cells, and human development begins immediately after the male and female reproductive cells meet. In other words, babies are living human beings from the moment of conception. In the Psalms, it says,

> *For thou hast possessed my reins: thou hast covered me in my mother's womb. I will praise thee; for I am fearfully and wonderfully made: marvellous are thy works; and that my soul knoweth right well. My substance was not hid from thee, when I was made in secret, and curiously wrought in the lowest parts of the earth. Thine eyes did see my substance, yet being unperfect; and in thy book all my members were written, which in continuance were fashioned, when as yet there was none of them.*
> PSALM 139:13-16

---

[1] Ted Harvey, "Planned Parenthood Celebration Jolted by Abortion Survivor," *Catholic Education Resource Center*, 2006. http://catholiceducation.org/articles/abortion/ab0107.htm (accessed August 24, 2012).

The *New International Version* translates these verses as,

> For you created my inmost being; you knit me together in my mother's womb. I praise you because I am fearfully and wonderfully made; your works are wonderful, I know that full well. My frame was not hidden from you when I was made in the secret place. When I was woven together in the depths of the earth, your eyes saw my unformed body. All the days ordained for me were written in your book before one of them came to be.

The *Amplified Bible* says,

> For You did form my inward parts; You did knit me together in my mother's womb. I will confess and praise You for You are fearful and wonderful and for the awful wonder of my birth! Wonderful are Your works, and that my inner self knows right well. My frame was not hidden from You when I was being formed in secret [and] intricately and curiously wrought [as if embroidered with various colors] in the depths of the earth [a region of darkness and mystery]. Your eyes saw my unformed substance, and in Your book all the days [of my life] were written before ever they took shape, when as yet there was none of them.

God knows unborn children while they are still in their mothers' wombs. He knows you long before you are completely developed, while you are still a developing cell being **"made in secret."** God knows everything about how you will look when you are just an embryo. He knows your hair color, your eye color, how tall you will be. He knows absolutely everything, and He has already recorded everything about you in His book.

When someone has an abortion, they aren't just destroying a hunk of tissue. Abortion kills a living person known by God—a person whose features and characteristics have already been written down by God. Abortion destroys human beings into whom God has breathed life.

Abortion isn't a matter of "*choice*," as pro-abortionists want to spin it. No one has the right to kill an infant. Abortion is murder, and it's wrong. I'm not saying this to hurt anyone, but a problem can't be fixed until it is identified, so we need to be clear about the abortion crisis in our society. God has already provided forgiveness for anyone who has had an abortion, so I'm not reproaching anyone. I'm condemning the practice of abortion. No one should be given the freedom to kill a child. It's not right, and we need to stand against it.

The story behind Roe v. Wade, the famous Supreme Court case that legalized abortion in 1973, is an interesting one. The real name of the woman called "Jane Roe" in the case is Norma McCorvey. In 1969, she had already had two children and was pregnant with her third when she was chosen to be the plaintiff in the suit. She says she was worried about being able to take care of the child and wanted to get a legal abortion, but Norma never actually had an abortion. In fact, today, she is a pro-life activist who says her involvement in Roe v. Wade was the worst mistake of her life.

Roe v. Wade was based on a woman's personal right to privacy and to choice. The justices rationalized their decision by saying that an unborn child is not a living person, and so the child doesn't have legal rights that are protected by the state (like the right to life). This is not true—it's just the only logic they could come up with to legally justify abortion. We all know that an unborn child is a living human being, and science has since proven it.

Lesson 13 — Abortion

In 1973, there wasn't definite scientific proof that an embryo was a child. People hadn't questioned whether that was so. It was just commonly accepted that an unborn child was human. But in the absence of "scientific" research on this matter, the Supreme Court ruled that an unborn child was not a separate human, and therefore, the woman had a right to choose what to do with her own body. Although science has since proven that argument wrong, the practice continues.

Abortion shouldn't be about a woman's privacy or her right to control her future. It's about the life of an unborn child—life that should be protected. No one has the right to take the life of another, especially the innocent life of a child.

Scripture clearly shows that unborn babies are living human beings. After the angel Gabriel announced to Mary that she would conceive a child by the power of the Holy Spirit, Mary went to visit her older cousin Elisabeth, who was also pregnant at the time. Elisabeth was pregnant with John the Baptist, and Scripture says he leapt for joy in Elisabeth's womb when Mary entered the room—which means that he was experiencing emotion as an unborn six-month-old baby.

> *When Elisabeth heard the salutation of Mary, the babe leaped in her womb; and Elisabeth was filled with the Holy Ghost: And she spake out with a loud voice, and said, Blessed art thou among women, and blessed is the fruit of thy womb. And whence is this to me, that the mother of my Lord should come to me? For, lo, as soon as the voice of thy salutation sounded in mine ears, the babe leaped in my womb for joy.*
> LUKE 1:41-44

Under the New Covenant, the Holy Spirit comes upon us and He never leaves us, but it was exceptional to be filled with the Holy Spirit before Jesus ascended into heaven and the Father sent the Holy Spirit to abide with us forever. The Holy Spirit would come upon people to help them perform a specific task, but He didn't dwell in them continuously.

However, it was prophesied that John the Baptist would be filled with the Holy Spirit from his mother's womb (Luke 1:15), and this passage in Luke records the moment it happened—when he was still an unborn baby. The key point here is that the Holy Spirit doesn't fill inanimate tissue. He only fills living human beings. For John the Baptist to be filled with the Holy Spirit in his mother's womb proves that unborn babies are distinct human beings in God's eyes.

The relative maturity of babies doesn't determine whether or not they are living human beings. Babies don't have to be ready to care for themselves outside of the womb in order to be considered "alive." God designed babies to grow and mature in the womb. Even after babies are born, they still have to be fed and cared for. You have to protect babies, feed them, and provide them with the right environment and temperature. Infants can't survive outside the womb on their own because it takes several years for children to mature enough to be able to take care of themselves.

Developmental stages are just measurements of maturity—they don't indicate the beginning of life—whether the person is one day, fourteen months, or thirty years old. A baby's life doesn't begin at some arbitrary stage of development—babies are living people from the very moment of conception.

Jeremiah was ordained to be a prophet from his mother's womb, as was Isaiah. This truth was only highlighted in Scripture for a few individuals, but God is not a respecter of persons (Acts 10:34). He treats everyone all the same, which means that God knows everyone from the earliest stages of development. Even when you were being formed in the womb, God knew you and had already fashioned a purpose for you.

> *Then the word of the Lord came unto me, saying, Before I formed thee in the belly I knew thee; and before thou camest forth out of the womb I sanctified thee, and I ordained thee a prophet unto the nations.*
> JEREMIAH 1:4-5

Here again, this scripture says that God **"knew"** Jeremiah when he was still in the womb, which shows that God views a fetus as a person—not mere tissue. (I hate to use the term "fetus" to refer to an unborn human being, but I want to make sure those who do use that term get the point that what they call a "fetus" is a living human being.) The Apostle Paul also said that he was separated to preach the Gospel of Jesus Christ when he was still in his mother's womb (Gal. 1:15). These examples demonstrate how the Lord knows each of us from the earliest stages of development, and He puts gifts and life-purpose in us long before we are born.

Even though unborn babies are dependent upon their mothers while they are developing in the womb during pregnancy, God views babies as unique persons from the moment of conception. In God's eyes, a fetus is a living human being, and taking the life of an unborn baby is no different than taking the life of any other human being. The majority of society may not view it that way, and the United States Supreme Court may not agree, but Scripture says, **"Let God be true, but every man a liar"** (Rom. 3:4). In other words, it really doesn't matter what everyone else is saying. God says babies are living human beings from the moment of conception, and His Word is true.

This is what the whole debate on abortion comes down to: Is the baby a human being from the moment of conception or not? The answer is yes; an unborn baby is a living human being, and once life is conceived, you don't have the right to end it by abortion. It's not a matter of choice, or convenience.

Pro-abortion supporters are trying to say that abortion is about a woman's right to choose whether or not she wants be a mother and raise a child—totally ignoring the fact that abortion ends a life no one has the right to take. A woman who becomes pregnant is already a mother, so anyone who wants to exercise their right to "choose" should choose not to have sexual intercourse until they are ready to have a child.

As a society, we have been lied to. We've been told that abortion is only about a woman's right to choose, but that isn't true. Even if you don't consider the Scriptural evidence, medical science has shown that an unborn baby has a beating heart within the first month of pregnancy. This means that within two to three weeks of conception—before the mother even realizes she is pregnant—the baby is already a separate human being.[2] It isn't accurate to claim that abortion is about a woman's right to choose what happens to her own body, because unborn babies are not part of their mothers' bodies—they are separate individuals.

I'm certain people would feel a lot differently about abortion if they could see the fingernails, eyes, feet, hands, and delicate details of the aborted babies. Seeing those pictures, you know instinctively that unborn babies are not just hunks of flesh; they are viable human beings who should be given the chance to develop and become the people God wants them to be.

---

[2] American Congress of Obstetricians and Gynecologists, "How Your Baby Grows During Pregnancy," Last modified August 2011. http://www.acog.org/For_Patients
Linda Hinkle, "When Does An Unborn Baby Have A Heartbeat?" *LiveSTRONG.com*, June 14, 2011. http://www.livestrong.com/article/242600-when-does-an-unborn-baby-have-a-heartbeat/#ixzz1cZPN5lx0 (accessed August 24, 2012).

LESSON 13 — ABORTION

I don't think most people realize how quickly unborn babies take on mature characteristics. Scripture says that **"the life of the flesh is in the blood,"** so just the fact that a baby's heart begins to pump the baby's own blood within weeks of conception is a revealing truth (Lev. 17:11). Here are some other developmental milestones:[3]

- Day 22: The baby's heart begins to beat with the child's own blood, often a different type than the mother's.
- Week 3: The child's backbone, spinal column, and nervous system are forming. The liver, kidneys, and intestines begin to take shape.
- Week 4: The child is 10,000 times larger than the original fertilized egg.
- Week 6: Brain waves are detectable. Mouth and lips are present. Fingernails are forming.
- Week 7: Eyelids, toes, and a distinct nose form. The baby is kicking and swimming.
- Week 8: Every organ is in place, bones begin to replace cartilage, and fingerprints begin to form. The baby also begins to hear.
- Weeks 9 and 10: Teeth begin to form; fingernails develop. The baby can turn his or her head, can frown, and can hiccup.
- Week 10: The baby can "breathe" amniotic fluid and urinate.
- Week 11: The baby can grasp objects places in his or her hand; all organ systems are functioning. The baby has a skeletal structure, nerves, and circulation.
- Week 12: The baby has all of the parts necessary to experience pain, including nerves, spinal cord, and thalamus. Vocal cords are complete. The baby can suck his or her thumb.
- Week 14: At this age, the heart pumps several quarts of blood through the body every day.
- Week 15: The baby has an adult's taste buds.
- Month 4: Bone marrow is now beginning to form. The heart is pumping twenty-five quarts of blood a day. By the end of month 4, the baby will be eight to ten inches in length and will weigh up to a half a pound.
- Week 17: The baby can have dream (REM) sleep.
- Week 20: The baby recognizes his or her mother's voice. (This is also the earliest stage at which partial birth abortions are performed.)

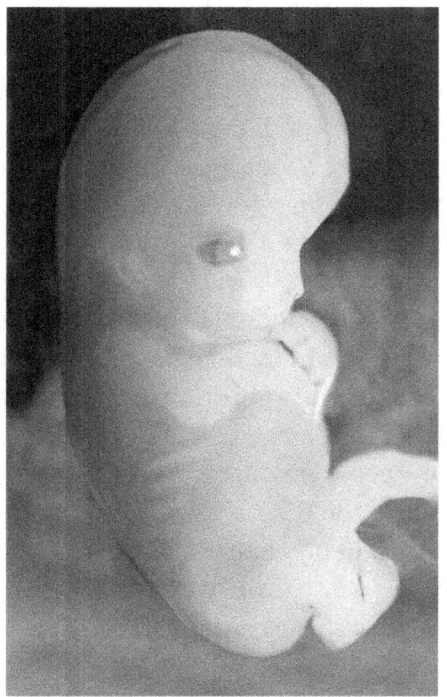

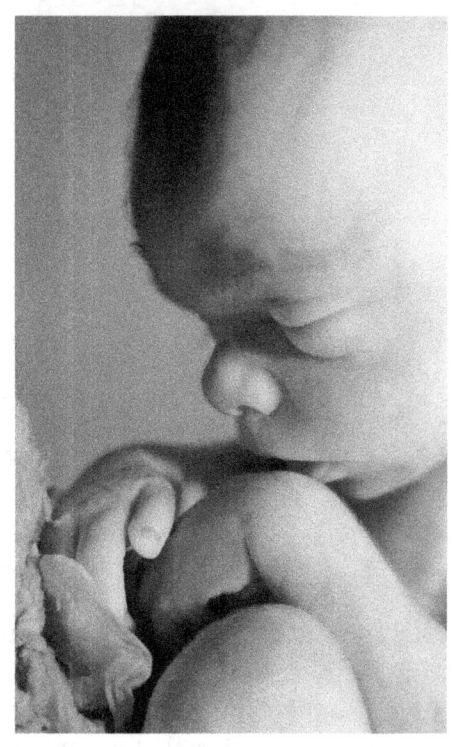

---

[3] National Right to Life, "Fetal Development from conception to birth," Last modified January 7, 2003. http://www.nrlc.org/abortion/facts/fetaldevelopment.html

I don't see how anyone can look at these scientifically documented developmental stages and still try to claim that unborn babies are merely a part of the mother's body—and it's her choice whether or not the baby should live. No, unborn babies are separate, living human beings who have as much a right to life as any other living person. It can't be argued that the baby is a part of the mother's body—unborn babies have their own blood type, fingerprints, feelings, brain waves, dreams, and all sorts of things we know are unique to individuals.

The women who go to abortion clinics aren't told any of this, but I think they would feel differently about abortion if they were. I think more people would see that abortion is not a matter of a woman's choice—it's about the right of an unborn child to live and fulfill God's creative purposes. There is not a civilized country on the face of the earth that gives any woman the freedom of choice to kill another person. Unborn babies are human beings, and nobody has the right to take those children's lives.

The abortion rate in the United States is alarming: 3,600 abortions are performed every day, which amounts to more than 1.3 million abortions every year—or one every twenty-four seconds. Since Roe v. Wade legalized abortion in the United States in 1973, nearly fifty million babies have been aborted.[4] (This is the total at the end of 2011, but with 3,600 babies being killed by abortion every day, the total continues to grow at a frightening pace. These staggering numbers do not take into account the fact that not all abortions done in the U.S. are required to be reported. Therefore, the number is actually much higher.) Right now, 22 percent of pregnancies in the U.S. end by abortion, and at current rates, one in four women will have had an abortion by age thirty. Consider this: 42 percent of all yearly deaths *in the world* are from abortion.[5] Those are some staggering statistics.

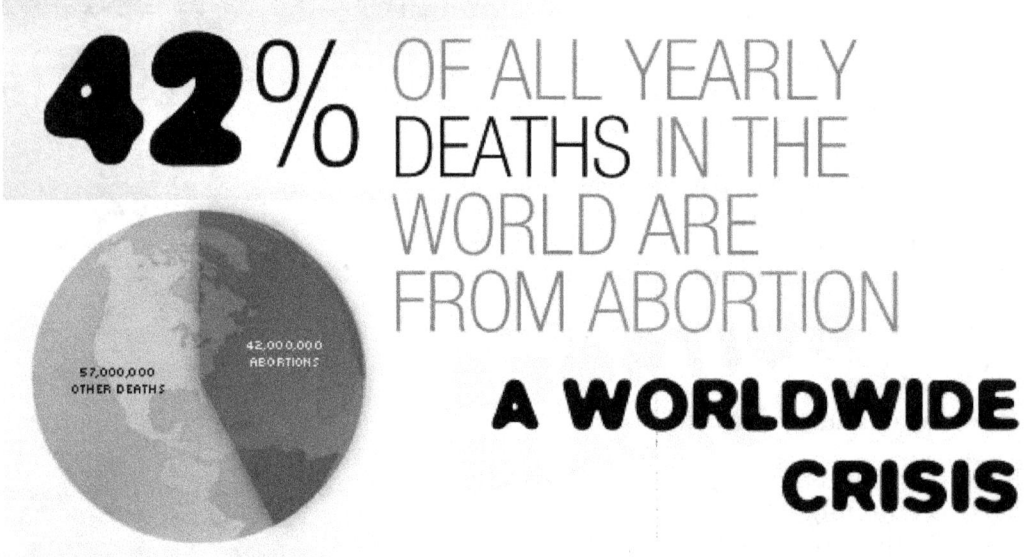

Despite all of the evidence proving that an unborn baby is a living human being, a lot of people aren't letting facts get in the way of what they believe. Abortion is accepted in our society, and some people are going to support it, no matter what evidence they're shown. In many ways, our society has become numb to the truth—which is that no matter what the circumstances are or how inconvenient the birth of a child might be, there is no justification for abortion.

---

4 "Facts on Induced Abortion in the United States," *The Guttmacher Institute*, web, http://www.guttmacher.org/pubs/fb_induced_abortion.html
5 "Abortion Facts," *Abortion Blackout*, web, http://www.abortionblackout.com/abortion-facts?page=3

We often hear abortion supporters defending the practice of abortion as a necessary option in so-called "hard cases" involving rape, incest, or medical issues. I'll get to those issues in just a moment, but first I think we should keep in mind that rape, incest, and medical issues only account for 6 percent of all abortions—that's a very small percentage. Recent research shows women give the following reasons for getting an abortion:[6]

- 74% said having a baby would interfere with their career, education, or ability to care for other family members
- 73% say they couldn't afford a baby
- 48% don't want to be single mothers, or are having relationship problems
- 25% don't want anyone else to know they have had sex or are pregnant
- 1% were the victims of rape
- Less than 0.5% became pregnant as the result of incest

The women involved in this study obviously gave multiple reasons for having an abortion, which is why the percentages don't add up to 100. But when all of the responses were examined, the study revealed that 92 percent of women have abortions for "social" or "other" reasons. Not only that, but of the less than 6 percent who cited medical reasons, researchers thought many of those women seemed to be giving their own opinion, such as morning sickness, rather than indicating a life-threatening condition or diagnosis by a medical doctor.[7] In any case, the vast majority of women admit to having abortions for the sake of convenience.

"Hard case" abortions raise some difficult issues, but they are still not a justification for abortion. To say that abortion is justified in cases where the child might be born with physical or mental disabilities is just wrong. It gives the impression that the value of human life depends on the health or condition of the person, as if our value is judged by what we can contribute to society—which is nonsense. Young people aren't more valuable than old people, and healthy people aren't more valuable than sick people. And nobody has the right to kill another person because they somehow judge the other person's quality of life to be insufficient.

All human life is equally valuable because we are made in the image of God. It isn't our place to decide who should live or die—even if we learn that an unborn child may have physical or mental handicaps that will make life challenging. The relative health of an unborn baby has no bearing on the fact that he or she is a living human being, and all human beings have the right to live.

History has shown the devastating effects of societies that start deciding who should live and who should die. It is not often discussed, but there is a direct link between the philosophy of evolution and the horrors of Nazism that erupted in Germany. In short, once people began to believe that humans were the result of evolution, they started to wonder which humans were the most evolved and what could be done to breed a better race—and which people should be removed from the gene pool.

Nazism was a philosophical blend of Social Darwinism and eugenics. Social Darwinism was the theory that humans were subject to the same forces of evolution that Darwin proposed for plants and

---

[6] Lawrence B. Finer, et al, "Reasons U.S. Women Have Abortions: Quantitative and Qualitative Perspectives," *The Guttmacher Institute*, web, http://www.guttmacher.org/pubs/journals/3711005.pdf
[7] Randall K. O'Bannon, Ph.D., "New Study Examines Reasons Women Have Abortions," *National Right to Life Center*, web, http://www.nrlc.org/news/2005/NRL10/NewStudy.html

animals. Eugenics is "the study of hereditary improvement of the human race by controlled selective breeding" (*American Heritage Dictionary*). Eugenicists thought that humans should take the same approach to reproduction that cattle ranchers take to breeding livestock—only breed the strongest and healthiest. Supporters of eugenics believed that Darwin's proposed force of natural selection was moving too slowly and steps needed to be taken toward favoring the best and eliminating the worst. This was the same philosophy behind Hitler's "master race" idea.

It's worth noting that Nazi Germany's first program of systematic murder targeted mentally and physically disabled children living in institutions within Germany or its controlled territories.[8] The sole purpose of the euthanasia program was to kill people the eugenicists believed were not worthy of life. Notably, the Nazi's first victims were infants and toddlers. The fact that they started killing the handicapped two years before they targeted Jews demonstrates that the evil of the Holocaust didn't descend upon Germany overnight; it was a slow, steady process. After society turned a blind eye to the killing of the handicapped, the Nazi government was emboldened to begin a more aggressive program of murder: the Holocaust, which killed six million Jews.

The eugenics movement in Germany spawned Nazism and resulted in the mass murder of millions of innocent lives, but the eugenics movement in the United States took a different form. The chief proponent of eugenics in the United States was a woman named Margaret Sanger. You may recognize her name: she founded the American Birth Control League in 1928, which later became known as Planned Parenthood. Sanger coined the term "birth control," and she promoted abortion as a way to kill unwanted babies—it was her idea for purifying the gene pool. Quotes from Sanger's writings leave no doubt about her motivations for promoting abortion:

- "We desire to stop at its source the disease, poverty and feeble-mindedness and insanity which exist today, for these lower the standards of civilization and make for race deterioration."[9]
- "We would make it a law that children should be brought into the world only when they were welcome, invited, and wanted; that they would arrive with a clean bill of health and heritage; that they would possess healthy, happy, well-mated, and mature parents."[10]
- "Every single case of inherited defect, every malformed child, every congenitally tainted human being brought into this world is of infinite importance to that poor individual; but it is of scarcely less importance to the rest of us and to all of our children who must pay in one way or another for these biological and racial mistakes."[11]
- "The campaign for Birth Control is not merely of eugenic value, but is practically identical in ideal, with the final aims of Eugenics." Sanger concludes, "Birth Control propaganda is thus the entering wedge for the Eugenic educator."[12]

Notice that Sanger believed only "well-mated" parents with a clean bill of health and *heritage* should be allowed to have children. Her ideals were blatantly racist. Among the people whom Sanger thought should

---

[8] "Euthanasia Program," *The United States Holocaust Memorial Museum*, web, http://www.ushmm.org/wlc/ en/article.php?ModuleId=10005200
[9] Margaret Sanger, "The Morality of Birth Control," (speech, delivered Nov 18, 1921), web, http://www.americanrhetoric.com/speeches/PDFFiles/Margaret Sanger - The Morality of Birth Control.pdf
[10] Margaret Sanger, "The Children's Era," (speech, delivered March 1925), web, http://www.womenspeecharchive.org/women/profile/speech/index.cfm?ProfileID=113&SpeechID=478
[11] Margaret Sanger, *The Pivot of Civilization*, (New York: Brentano's, 1922). Chapter 12, web, http://www.gutenberg.org/dirs/1/6/8/1689/1689.txt
[12] Margaret Sanger, "The Eugenic Value of Birth Control Propaganda," *Birth Control Review*, October 1921. http://www.nyu.edu/projects/sanger/webedition/app/documents/show.php?sangerDoc=238946.xml

Lesson 13 — Abortion

not be allowed to procreate were the "diseased, feeble-minded, and…the pauper element dependent entirely upon the normal and fit members of society for their support. There is no doubt in the minds of all thinking people that the procreation of this group should be stopped."[9]

For Margaret Sanger and Planned Parenthood, birth control and abortion were all about purifying the human race through controlled and selective breeding. She thought of abortion as a propaganda tool to "weed out" the members of society she deemed unworthy of life.

I know abortion is not a fun topic to discuss, but it would be wrong for us to quietly go about our lives, pretending that the horrors of abortion aren't happening. We have a duty to speak out for the unborn children who cannot speak for themselves. All you have to do is look at the procedure for partial-birth abortions, or the criminal conditions that have been found in some late-term abortion clinics, to see that abortion devalues human life and desensitizes society to the violence of murder.

If you don't already know, I'll describe partial-birth abortion in the least disturbing terms possible: It's a surgical procedure in which the baby is partially removed from the mother's womb, and then a doctor punctures the baby's skull and suctions out his or her brain tissue. This is performed on babies twenty weeks old or older.

I don't care how you look at it, partial-birth abortion is murder. Even the thin legal separation between what constitutes a partial-birth abortion and what meets the criteria for murder reveals the fallacy of the argument that abortion is about choice. Babies don't become living human beings after exiting their mother's wombs—they are living people from conception—and the value of human life isn't determined by age.

In fact, a doctor who performed late-term abortions at a clinic in Philadelphia is on trial for seven counts of murder because he performed abortions by inducing labor and killing the babies after they were completely out of the womb. See, it's a legal abortion to kill the baby as long as the baby's head is the only body part out of the womb, but if you deliver the rest of the baby's body before performing the procedure, then it's murder. What kind of twisted logic says it's okay to kill a baby in the womb, but it's first degree murder to kill the same baby two seconds later if he or she is completely out of the mother's womb?

We all recognize that it's just as wrong to kill a ten year old as it is to kill a two year old, but abortion supporters try to say that it's okay to kill a baby depending on how old he or she is, or whether the baby is in or out of the womb. It's a totally illogical argument. The stage of development has nothing to do with the value of human life. It's just as wrong to kill a one-day-old baby as it is to perform a partial-birth abortion on a baby while he or she is in the womb, or to kill the baby after he or she comes out of the womb. Murder is murder, no matter how old the victim is.

It saddens me that 70 percent of women who have an abortion claim to be Christian at the time of the procedure. As a church, we have failed those women. The only reason I can imagine a Christian supporting abortion is that they don't know the facts. They have bought into the lie that an unborn child isn't truly alive.

Scripture and science both prove that unborn babies *are* living human beings. When Roe v. Wade legalized abortion in 1973, the medical community hadn't completed all of the studies we know about today that prove unborn babies are viable human beings, so the Supreme Court decided to rule that a child in the womb had no rights. But we know better: Unborn babies are human beings, and they do have rights.

LESSON 13 — ABORTION

With current statistics showing that 33 percent of all women will have had an abortion by age 45, I suspect that most people know someone who has had an abortion. God loves every single one of those women, and He has provided forgiveness for anyone who will accept it, so I'm not trying to condemn anyone who has had an abortion. I'm not mad at anyone, and I'm not trying to hurt or slander anyone. I'm just trying to save lives and show people the importance of having a Christian perspective on abortion. In order to do that, we have to speak openly and honestly about it.

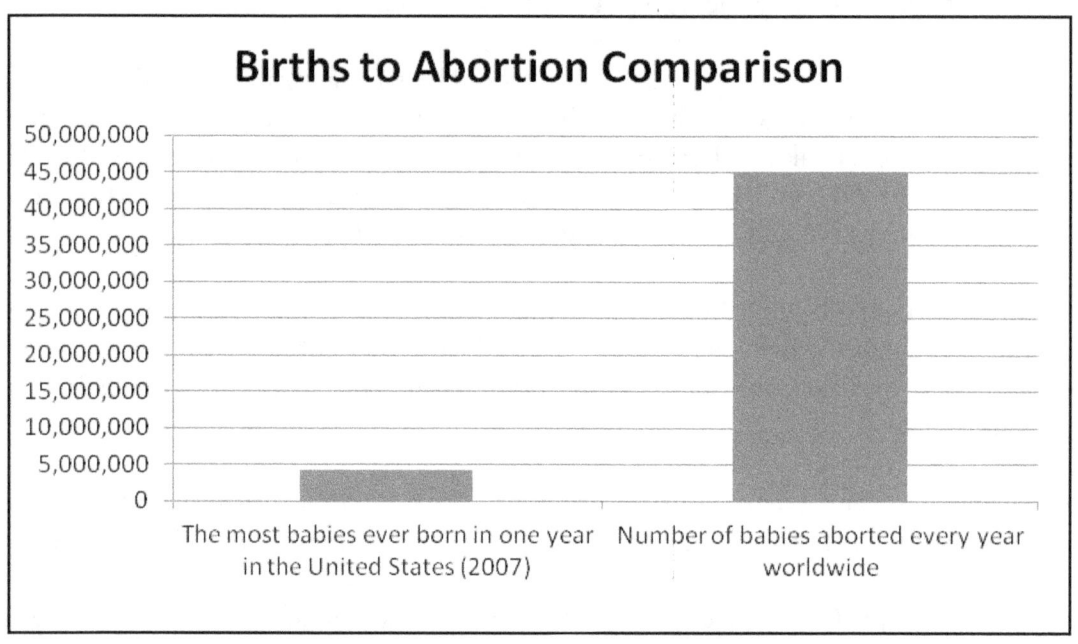

Socially, abortion causes a tremendous loss of human potential in our societies. Worldwide, approximately 125,000 abortions are performed every day—that's more than 42 million abortions every year.[13] To put that number in perspective, the most babies that have ever been born in the United States in one year is 4.3 million,[14] which would mean that for every infant born in the U.S., at least another ten babies around the world are killed by abortion. Imagine how much potential has been eliminated from our midst. We'll never know how many innovators and leaders have been killed by abortion, how many Martin Luther King Jrs. or Billy Grahams were never given the chance to make our world a better place. Additionally, the effect of abortion on women's health has been awful. Look at these facts:

- Having an abortion can triple a woman's risk of developing breast cancer later in life.[15]
- A study in England found an 80 percent increase in the rate of breast cancer since 1971, when the number of abortions rose from 18,000 to nearly 200,000 a year.[15]
- Women who have abortions are 30 percent more likely to develop a mental illness.[16]
- Women who have an abortion are three times as likely to develop drug or alcohol addiction.[16]
- Women with a history of induced abortion are at a significantly higher risk for psychiatric problems, adjustment disorders, bipolar disorder, depressive psychosis, neurotic depression, schizophrenia, parenting difficulties, and death from various violent and natural causes.[17]

---

[13] "Abortions in the world," *Worldometers: real time world statistics*, web, http://www.worldometers.info/abortions/
[14] Dan Glaister, "Number of babies born in the US reaches record levels," *The Guardian*, March 18, 2009. Web. http://www.guardian.co.uk/world/2009/mar/18/birth-rate-us-baby-boomers
[15] Simon Caldwell, "Abortion 'triples breast cancer risk': Fourth study finds terminations linked to disease," *Daily Mail*, June 23, 2010. Web. http://www.dailymail.co.uk/health/article-1288955/Abortion-triple-risk-breast-cancer.html#ixzz1dhsHHeJu
[16] David M. Fergusson, L. John Horwood, and Joseph M. Boden, "Abortion and Mental Health Disorders: Evidence from a 30-year Longitudinal Study," *British Journal of Psychiatry*, December 2008. http://www.physiciansforlife.org/content/view/1681/26/
[17] Priscilla Coleman, Ph.D., "Abortion Mental Health Research: Update and Quality of Evidence," Association for Interdisciplinary Research in Values and Social Change Research Bulletin, Spring 2008, Vol. 20, no. 2. http://www.abortionresearch.us/images/Vol20No2.pdf

Lesson 13 — Abortion

The health risks associated with abortion are astonishing. There are more risks than I have listed here, but I think this list is long enough to show the wide range of dangers associated with abortion. The point is that abortion isn't only wrong from a religious or moral standpoint—it's wrong from every way you can look at it.

LESSON 13 — ABORTION

SCRIPTURES

PSALM 139:13-16
For thou hast possessed my reins: thou hast covered me in my mother's womb. **[14]** *I will praise thee; for I am fearfully and wonderfully made: marvellous are thy works; and that my soul knoweth right well.* **[15]** *My substance was not hid from thee, when I was made in secret, and curiously wrought in the lowest parts of the earth.* **[16]** *Thine eyes did see my substance, yet being unperfect; and in thy book all my members were written, which in continuance were fashioned, when as yet there was none of them.*

PSALM 139:13-16 (NEW INTERNATIONAL VERSION)
For you created my inmost being; you knit me together in my mother's womb. **[14]** *I praise you because I am fearfully and wonderfully made; your works are wonderful, I know that full well.* **[15]** *My frame was not hidden from you when I was made in the secret place. When I was woven together in the depths of the earth* **[16]** *your eyes saw my unformed body. All the days ordained for me were written in your book before one of them came to be.*

PSALM 139:13-16 (AMPLIFIED BIBLE)
For You did form my inward parts; You did knit me together in my mother's womb. **[14]** *I will confess and praise You for You are fearful and wonderful and for the awful wonder of my birth! Wonderful are Your works, and that my inner self knows right well.* **[15]** *My frame was not hidden from You when I was being formed in secret [and] intricately and curiously wrought [as if embroidered with various colors] in the depths of the earth [a region of darkness and mystery].* **[16]** *Your eyes saw my unformed substance, and in Your book all the days [of my life] were written before ever they took shape, when as yet there was none of them.*

LUKE 1:41-44
And it came to pass, that, when Elisabeth heard the salutation of Mary, the babe leaped in her womb; and Elisabeth was filled with the Holy Ghost: **[42]** *And she spake out with a loud voice, and said, Blessed art thou among women, and blessed is the fruit of thy womb.* **[43]** *And whence is this to me, that the mother of my Lord should come to me?* **[44]** *For, lo, as soon as the voice of thy salutation sounded in mine ears, the babe leaped in my womb for joy.*

LUKE 1:15
For he shall be great in the sight of the Lord, and shall drink neither wine nor strong drink; and he shall be filled with the Holy Ghost, even from his mother's womb.

ACTS 10:34
Then Peter opened his mouth, and said, Of a truth I perceive that God is no respecter of persons.

JEREMIAH 1:4-5
Then the word of the Lord came unto me, saying, **[5]** *Before I formed thee in the belly I knew thee; and before thou camest forth out of the womb I sanctified thee, and I ordained thee a prophet unto the nations.*

GALATIANS 1:15
But when it pleased God, who separated me from my mother's womb, and called me by his grace.

ROMANS 3:4
God forbid: yea, let God be true, but every man a liar; as it is written, That thou mightest be justified in thy sayings, and mightest overcome when thou art judged.

LEVITICUS 17:11
For the life of the flesh is in the blood: and I have given it to you upon the altar to make an attonement for your souls: for it is the blood that maketh an atonement for the soul.

In the World, but Not of It

The secular world has basically beaten the body of Christ back into the four walls of the church. We can have religious opinions—as long as we keep them to ourselves. They don't want Christians saying anything publicly about God or morality, but we Christians have as much a right to free speech as anybody. It's okay for us Christians to have a philosophy that guides our opinions on current issues, and it's okay for us to express those opinions.

We looked at homosexuality, abortion, and creation versus evolution from a Christian perspective. We could keep going and discuss a Christian philosophy for marriage, raising children, work ethic, managing money, and every other topic we can think of. Although Scripture has guidance for every situation imaginable, it isn't practical for me to try to present a Christian philosophy for all of them in this study guide. Instead, I have tried to help establish a way of thinking that will allow you to form a Christian philosophy on your own—regardless of what situation you may be facing.

The world is heading in a different direction than God, so we can't just adopt the popular opinions and beliefs of society. As Christians, we are separate from the world. Our born-again spirits set us apart, and there should be a noticeable difference in the lives and opinions of people who have the life of God in them versus people who have only physical life.

People who have a relationship with God should be different from the world—which represents people who are separated from God. Scripture says that we are in the world, but we are not *of* the world (John 15:19). The Word of God shows us that we live in a hostile environment, and it warns us not to get too comfortable with the world's way of doing things. For example, it tells us,

> *Be ye not unequally yoked together with unbelievers: for what fellowship hath righteousness with unrighteousness? and what communion hath light with darkness?*
>
> 2 CORINTHIANS 6:14

This scripture is almost always applied toward marriage and the idea that Christians shouldn't marry unbelievers, which is true, but it isn't limited to that. It also applies to business dealings, friends, and other important relationships in our lives. I'm not suggesting Christians should avoid all dealings with unbelievers, but we do need to be careful not to allow the world to influence us.

The world is not embracing Christianity. Jesus plainly told believers that they would be rejected by the world just as He was. Another scripture says that all who live godly in Christ Jesus will be persecuted

(2 Tim. 3:12), so the only way to escape persecution from the world is to go with the flow of society. Once you start following God, then you are going to be living contrary to the tendencies of the world, and you will experience opposition at times. Being a Christian is more like swimming upstream than floating along with all of the trends and opinions of society. Even a dead fish can float downstream. It takes backbone to swim against the current.

If you are watching the same television shows and movies as unbelievers, or reading the same books and magazines, then you are going to experience some of the same results in your life. When you put garbage in, you're going to get garbage out. Yet the average Christian is fully identified with the world. They pipe the same junk into their lives, and they are living the way the world lives. Scripture says that you will be the way you think in your heart (Prov. 23:7), which means that thinking like the world will make you look like the world. You may be born again in your spirit, but your life is going to go the way of your dominant thoughts. Scripture says,

> *For to be carnally minded is death; but to be spiritually minded is life and peace.*
> ROMANS 8:6

It doesn't say that being carnally minded tends toward death or will lead to death for certain types of people. No, it says to be carnally minded is death—they are the same thing. To be spiritually minded, on the other hand, is to be focused on the Word of God. Spiritually minded people are not pressed into the mold of this world; they don't take in all of the same junk through the media, and they don't think like the world.

The world system that surrounds us is hostile to Christians. In fact, we need to have the same attitude that scuba divers have when they are underwater. I've only been scuba diving once, and even though I enjoyed it, it was a hostile environment. I couldn't just take off my mask and breathe underwater the same way I breathe on land. I had to take a special approach toward surviving in that environment.

Similarly, this world is not really our home. Christians have been born from above, and although we live and breathe on earth, this is still a hostile environment. If we don't understand that fact and just go about our lives nonchalantly, then the world is going to have greater influence on us. We can't watch television and sitcoms and think that sitcoms present a normal model for living. If we do, then we're going to get caught up in the same casual sex, fighting, and nastiness portrayed in those shows. As Christians, we should be different.

We live in a hostile environment, and if we are just taking it all in the way the rest of society is, then we are being corrupted by the world's way of thinking. We are different from past generations of Christians in that the world's philosophy is being piped into our homes via internet, television, and radio, twenty-four hours a day. To keep those negative influences from destroying us, we need to have a philosophy that we are in the world but not a part of it, which is exactly what Scripture says:

> *And what concord hath Christ with Belial? or what part hath he that believeth with an infidel? And what agreement hath the temple of God with idols? for ye are the temple of the living God; as God hath said, I will dwell in them, and walk in them; and I will be their God, and they shall be my people. Wherefore come out from among them, and be ye separate, saith the Lord, and touch not the unclean thing; and I will receive you.*
> 2 CORINTHIANS 6:15-17

This isn't saying that we should hate unbelievers, but we are supposed to treat them differently. For instance, I don't value the opinion of lost people as much as I value what the Word of God says. I don't believe everything an unbeliever tells me, no matter what their credentials are. You can have thirty-two degrees and still be frozen. I interact with unbelievers, and I don't think being around them defiles me in some way; that's not what I mean. I just don't embrace or accept everything they say.

This passage in 2 Corinthians is a command from God to come out from among unbelievers. Practically, I don't think this means we are supposed to withdraw into the walls of our churches and completely cut ourselves off from the world. No, we are the salt of the earth, and unless we live in society, we can't season the world. Christians should be in the public arena—running for political office, speaking on television, and publishing newspapers. The separation doesn't need to be physical, but everyone should be able to tell the difference between Christians and unbelievers. One of the very first scriptures that God spoke to me says,

> *And be not conformed to this world: but be ye transformed by the renewing of your mind, that ye may prove what is that good, and acceptable, and perfect, will of God.*
>
> ROMANS 12:2

The Greek word translated **"conformed"** in this scripture means to be poured into the mold of. As you go through life, it has a way of heating up and melting you. You don't reach old age with the same opinions and perspective you had when you were young. Things happen, and you lose the naiveté of youth. Yet, in a sense, you get to pick the mold that you are conformed to—but it takes effort, and you need to focus on the truth in God's Word. Otherwise, you'll be poured into the mold of the world, and you will end up being conformed to the world's way of thinking.

People with a worldly philosophy don't like it when Christians disagree with them, so speaking the truth inevitably brings persecution. Jesus spoke the truth, and the world killed Him for it. Just like the world persecuted Jesus, it will use criticism to try to squeeze you into its mold, but don't be intimidated. When you stand for the truth, God stands with you. You need to have opinions based on a godly philosophy, and you can't be afraid to speak what you believe.

Also notice that the Scripture goes a step beyond advising us to resist being conformed to this world; it tells us to be **"transformed"** by the renewing of our minds. The Greek word for **"transformed"** is *metamorphoo*, and it is the same root word for "metamorphosis"—the process by which a caterpillar morphs into a butterfly. In other words, we get total personal transformation by changing the way we think—which is why Christians need to have a godly philosophy that attempts to follow God's way of thinking. The Apostle John said,

> *Love not the world, neither the things that are in the world. If any man love the world, the love of the Father is not in him. For all that is in the world, the lust of the flesh, and the lust of the eyes, and the pride of life, is not of the Father, but is of the world. And the world passeth away, and the lust thereof: but he that doeth the will of God abideth for ever.*
>
> 1 JOHN 2:15-17

When you are filled with love for this world and all that it offers, then there is no room left for loving God. **"The lust of the flesh"** is talking about all of the cravings people have for emotional and physical satisfaction: fame, adoration, sensual gratification, and the rest. God created you with a need to meet physical and emotional needs, but the world makes an idol of those drives—which forces out love of God.

Lesson 14 — In the World, but Not of It

Christian values are vastly different. The Apostle Paul said that he counted all of his worldly accomplishments as dung compared to knowing Christ (Phil. 3:8)—and Paul was one of the most accomplished Pharisees of his day. He didn't mean there is no value in natural achievements, just not in comparison with relationship to Christ.

A lot of Christians think it is over the top to say we are in a battle against the world system. They don't think the world is a bad place, and they don't think lost people are bad people. I agree that lost people aren't bad in the sense of being malicious, but many of them are promoting a moral system that is completely contrary to the Word of God—which is obviously detrimental to Christians.

I believe one of the worst mistakes being made by the body of Christ is trying to relate to the world too much. Christians are adopting the ways of the world in an attempt to relate to lost people. Now we have seeker-friendly churches that have reduced their sermons down to ten-minute pep talks and have filled their services with entertainment. It's fine to try to relate to lost people, but not so much that the distinction between the world and Christianity is blurred. Unfortunately, I think the church has been negatively influenced by the world to a greater extent than it has been a positive influence on the world.

As Christians, we should be skeptical of the attitudes and opinions that prevail in the world. We should be different. Scripture refers to believers as "the church"—which, in the Greek, literally means called-out ones. Being separate isn't about being physically isolated. It's about being detached in our philosophy and opinions, so just because people in the world have credentials, that doesn't mean we should adopt their way of thinking. We shouldn't exalt the opinions of secular scientists, journalists, politicians, or other leaders above the Word of God—no matter what qualifications they have.

In 1999, many experts were predicting widespread computer problems when the date turned over to the year 2000. They were all claiming that the internal clocks in computers had not been programmed to count to 2000 after 1999, and that major computer malfunctions were going to result. The experts were predicting a major crisis that could lead to food, water, and power shortages, and they nicknamed the impending disaster Y2K.

Some Christians were saying that Y2K would be the beginning of the Tribulation period. They thought the world was going to descend into total anarchy. People were stockpiling food and weapons—so they could kill their neighbors if they tried to steal their food. Preachers were actually teaching on self-defense and killing others "in the name of the Lord," in order to protect their families.

I didn't agree with what was being taught about Y2K for a number of reasons. First, the Lord had told me to go on television, and my program wasn't scheduled to start until January 3, 2000. If everything that was predicted to happen actually occurred, then I wouldn't be on television, so I just felt in my heart that Y2K wouldn't result in disaster. Second, I have a philosophy that God doesn't want me hoarding food while my neighbors starve, and He sure doesn't want me to kill them. Third, Christian philosophy says **"give, and it shall be given unto you"** (Luke 6:38)—it doesn't say withhold to save yourself.

I didn't have a word from God that Y2K was a hoax, but my Christian philosophy showed me that what was being said by the experts and taught in some churches was not consistent with Scripture. People were being motivated by fear, not faith. The Bible says,

Lesson 14 — In the World, but Not of It

But the wisdom that is from above is first pure, then peaceable, gentle, and easy to be intreated, full of mercy and good fruits, without partiality, and without hypocrisy.

JAMES 3:17

There was no joy in any of the so-called wisdom that people were sharing about Y2K. All of those teachings on hoarding food and weapons were extremism based on terror. It violated everything I knew from Scripture, so I rejected those teachings publicly way before Y2K was near.

Of course, the world didn't end, and nobody ran out of food or water. It was just like the craze in the late '80s when former NASA engineer Edgar Whisenant wrote the book *88 Reasons Why the Rapture Will Be in 1988*. The book sold four and a half million copies, and generated a message that was preached throughout the world. When the Rapture didn't happen, Whisenant wrote three more books predicting why the Rapture would occur in 1989, 1993, and 1994.

It amazes me how gullible Christians can be, but it's because they don't have an established philosophy. They don't believe in the infallibility or inspiration of God's Word. They view the Bible as a book of wisdom containing vague suggestions that aren't necessarily relevant to their lives. But trusting in the accuracy and inspiration of Scripture will keep you from falling for all of the misinformation and fear that is being promoted by the world; having a Christian philosophy will protect you from all of that.

The world's wisdom is not working. People are taking pills to go to sleep, pills to wake up, and pills to get them through the day. Christians need something stronger to hold on to than "expert" opinions. God's Word has been proven true over thousands of years; it is reliable, and it needs to be the foundation of our lives.

You need to get to a place where you trust the Word of God more than the opinions of men. If experts say something that contradicts God's Word, then you shouldn't exalt their opinion—no matter how many credentials they have. There's an old saying that if you don't stand for something, you'll fall for anything. Most people are living their lives in a state of flux; they bend with the wind and follow whatever opinions are dominating society. Trusting in the Word of God, on the other hand, will give you firmly established truths by which to anchor your life. You won't be tossed to and fro, carried about by every wind of doctrine, or by the cunning of men who lie in wait to deceive (Eph. 4:14).

Everything in this world is going to pass away, but the Word of God will never fail. It is forever settled. Scripture says that God spoke the heavens and the earth into existence, and He holds all things together by His word. When you build your life on the Word of God, you are building on a foundation that will never fail.

I challenge you to begin reading the Bible with the openness to believe it is accurate and inspired. Read the New Testament, and ask God, "Are these things true?" Ask God to reveal Himself to you. I believe that when you do, you will reach the same conclusions I have: The Word of God is true, it is accurate, and it is relevant to your life. Once you start basing your philosophy on God's Word, it will completely change how you see and experience life.

Lesson 14 — In the World, but Not of It

SCRIPTURES

JOHN 15:19
If ye were of the world, the world would love his own: but because ye are not of the world, but I have chosen you out of the world, therefore the world hateth you.

2 CORINTHIANS 6:14-17
Be ye not unequally yoked together with unbelievers: for what fellowship hath righteousness with unrighteousness? and what communion hath light with darkness? **[15]** *And what concord hath Christ with Belial? or what part hath he that believeth with an infidel?* **[16]** *And what agreement hath the temple of God with idols? for ye are the temple of the living God; as God hath said, I will dwell in them, and walk in them; and I will be their God, and they shall be my people.* **[17]** *Wherefore come out from among them, and be ye separate, saith the Lord, and touch not the unclean thing; and I will receive you.*

2 TIMOTHY 3:12
Yea, and all that will live godly in Christ Jesus shall suffer persecution.

PROVERBS 23:7
For as he thinketh in his heart, so is he: Eat and drink, saith he to thee; but his heart is not with thee.

ROMANS 8:6
For to be carnally minded is death; but to be spiritually minded is life and peace.

ROMANS 12:2
And be not conformed to this world: but be ye transformed by the renewing of your mind, that ye may prove what is that good, and acceptable, and perfect, will of God.

1 JOHN 2:15-17
Love not the world, neither the things that are in the world. If any man love the world, the love of the Father is not in him. **[16]** *For all that is in the world, the lust of the flesh, and the lust of the eyes, and the pride of life, is not of the Father, but is of the world.* **[17]** *And the world passeth away, and the lust thereof: but he that doeth the will of God abideth for ever.*

PHILIPPIANS 3:8
Yea doubtless, and I count all things but loss for the excellency of the knowledge of Christ Jesus my Lord: for whom I have suffered the loss of all things, and do count them but dung, that I may win Christ.

LUKE 6:38
Give, and it shall be given unto you; good measure, pressed down, and shaken together, and running over, shall men give into your bosom. For with the same measure that ye mete withal it shall be measured to you again.

JAMES 3:17
But the wisdom that is from above is first pure, then peaceable, gentle, and easy to be intreated, full of mercy and good fruits, without partiality, and without hypocrisy.

EPHESIANS 4:14
That we henceforth be no more children, tossed to and fro, and carried about with every wind of doctrine, by the sleight of men, and cunning craftiness, whereby they lie in wait to deceive.

ABOUT THE AUTHOR

For over four decades, Andrew Wommack has traveled America and the world teaching the truth of the Gospel. His profound revelation of the Word of God is taught with clarity and simplicity, emphasizing God's unconditional love and the balance between grace and faith. He reaches millions of people through the daily *Gospel Truth* radio and television programs, broadcast both domestically and internationally. He founded Charis Bible College in 1994 and has since established Charis Bible College extension schools in other major cities of America and around the world. Andrew has produced a library of teaching materials, available in print, audio, and visual formats. And, as it has been from the beginning, his ministry continues to distribute free audio materials to those who cannot afford them.

www.ingramcontent.com/pod-product-compliance
Lightning Source LLC
Chambersburg PA
CBHW080934300426
44115CB00017B/2809